Cultural Archives of Atrocity

Critical studies on the aesthetic representations of atrocity the world over have taken different discursive dimensions from history, sociology, political to human rights. These perspectives are usually geared towards understanding the manifestations, extent, political, and economic implications of atrocities. In all these cases, representation has been the singular concern. *Cultural Archives of Atrocity: Essays on the Protest Tradition in Kenyan Literature, Culture, and Society* brings together generic ways of interrogating artistic representations of atrocity in Kenya. Couched in interdisciplinary, multidisciplinary, and cross-disciplinary approaches, essays in this volume investigate representations of atrocity in Kenyan literature, film, popular music, and other mediated cultural art forms. Contributors to this volume not only bring on board multiple and competing perspectives on studying atrocity and how they are archived, but also provide refreshing and valuable insights in examining the artistic and cultural interpellations of atrocity within the sociopolitical imaginaries of the Kenyan nation. This volume forms part of the growing critical resources for scholars undertaking studies on atrocity within the fields of ethnic studies, cultural studies, postcolonial studies, peace and conflict, criminology, psychology, political economy, and history in Kenya.

Charles Kebaya holds a PhD in television drama criticism from Kenyatta University and currently teaches Literature at Machakos University, Kenya.

Colomba Kaburi Muriungi is an associate professor of African literature in the Department of Humanities and also the Dean, Faculty of Humanities and Social Sciences at Chuka University, Kenya.

J. K. S. Makokha is a Kenyan poet, critic, translator, and academic. He is based at Kenyatta University in the Department of Languages, Linguistics and Literature.

Cultural Archives of Atrocity

Essays on the Protest Tradition in
Kenyan Literature, Culture and Society

Edited by
Charles Kebaya,
Colomba Kaburi Muriungi and
J. K. S. Makokha

Routledge
Taylor & Francis Group

NEW YORK AND LONDON

First published 2019
by Routledge
52 Vanderbilt Avenue, New York, NY 10017

and by Routledge
2 Park Square, Milton Park, Abingdon, Oxon, OX14 4RN

Routledge is an imprint of the Taylor & Francis Group, an informa business

Library of Congress Cataloging-in-Publication Data
Names: Kebaya, Charles, editor. | Muriungi, Colomba Kaburi, editor. | Makokha, J. K. S., editor.
Title: Cultural archives of atrocity : essays on the protest tradition in Kenyan literature, culture and society / edited by Charles Kebaya, Colomba Kaburi Muriungi and J.K.S Makokha.
Description: New York, NY : Routledge, 2019. | Includes bibliographical references and index.
Identifiers: LCCN 2019008152 | ISBN 9780367205454 (hardback) | ISBN 9780429262166 (e-book)
Subjects: LCSH: Kenyan literature—20th century—History and criticism. | Kenyan literature—21st century—History and criticism. | Motion pictures—Kenya—History. | Atrocities in literature. | Political violence in literature. | Political violence in motion pictures.
Classification: LCC PL8014.K4 C85 2019 |
DDC 809.896762—dc23
LC record available at https://lccn.loc.gov/2019008152

ISBN: 978-0-367-20545-4 (hbk)
ISBN: 978-0-429-26216-6 (ebk)

Typeset in Sabon
by codeMantra

Contents

Acknowledgements

The editors are thankful to all the contributors to this volume for finding time to respond to the call for papers and generously giving their contributions to the understanding of cultural archives of atrocity in Kenya.

The editors are indebted to Prof C. J Odhiambo, Prof. Wangari Mwai, Dr. Esther Mbithi, and Dr. Miriam Maranga Musonye who reviewed the initial proposal for this project and recommended that this monograph will not only be an important contribution to emerging studies on atrocity but also will be very useful in creating an understanding of the representation of atrocity in the creative arts in Kenya.

We are thankful to many of our colleagues and friends for their unwavering support in producing this volume. We would like to particularly thank Dr. Anne Ajulu-Okungu, Dr. Kamau wa Goro, Dr. Oscar Maina, Dr. Macharia Mwangi, Dr. Mugo Muhia, Dr. Oyoo Weche (now the late), Dr. Ezekiel Kaigai, Dr. Solomon Onchoke, Dr. Edwin Mosoti, Dr. Rachael Diang'a, Dr. Fred Mbogo, Dr. Felix Orina, and Mr. Eric Maritim, for finding time from their busy work schedules to review articles that form the chapters of this volume. Their incisive and insightful comments went a long way in improving the chapters herein; since you were not obliged to do so, we, the editors, are most grateful.

Finally, the editors would also like to thank Dr. Jennifer Abbott, Routledge, for having faith in this project and her dynamic editorial assistant for Literature, Veronica Rodriguez, for their assistance in preparing the manuscript for this publication.

List of Contributors

Macharia Gatundu is completing his M.A. thesis at Kenyatta University, Kenya. In his thesis, he adopted a post-colonial approach to the novels of Chika Unigwe, Lola Shoneyin, and Alain Mabanckou, and focuses on gender and power transformations and the reconfigurations of African masculinities in the face of rapid globalization. His research and academic interests are contemporary African literatures, and questions of nationalism, power, gender, and identity.

Mikhail D. Gromov is an assistant professor of literature at the United States International University in Nairobi since 2005, teaching African, European, and world literature. Gromov holds a Master's degree in African literature and Swahili language from Moscow Lomonosov State University (1989); PhD (1993) and D. Litt. (2005) in African literature from the Gorky Institute of World Literature (Moscow). He has served as an Assistant Professor at Moscow University, 1992–2002 and as a researcher and temporary lecturer at the University of Nairobi (Department of Literature) in 2003–2004. He has published a number of works on modern Swahili literature and is one of the co-authors in the recently published *Outline of Swahili Literature* (Brill 2009). He actively participates in international conferences on African literature in Europe and Africa. His areas of interest are: literatures of Eastern and Southern Africa in English and indigenous languages, Swahili literature, and comparative literature.

Charles Kebaya holds a PhD in television drama criticism from Kenyatta University, Kenya. He has authored a number articles in refereed journals such as "Popular Art and the Reconfiguration of Police Atrocities in Kenya" (2018), "The Criminalization of Youth in Popular Art in Kenya"(2018), "Inventing Women: Female Voice in Kenyan Television Drama"(2017), "Historicizing Kenyan Comedy" (2015); he has co-authored a number of articles such as "Popular Music and Identity formation among Kenyan Youth (2016) and "Community Theatre and Development Practices in the Nyanza region of Kenya" (2015), co-edited a number of books such as *Language and Translation: Theory, Pedagogy and Practice* (2016) and *African Drama and Theatre: A Criticism* (2012). His book, *Federico Garcia Lorca's*

Subversive Theatre: A Case of Blood Wedding and Yerma was published in 2011. He is also the executive producer of a documentary film, *Drugnets* (2015). His research interests are in the areas of Television Drama, Dramatic Criticism, Popular Culture and Cultural studies.

Simiyu Kisurulia is currently serving as a lecturer at the University of Kabianga, Kericho. For many years, he taught in various high schools, served as an education officer, children's officer, and social development officer in different parts of Kenya. He has published several articles in refereed journals.

Titus Karuri Macharia is a masters student in the Department of Languages, Karatina University in. He is currently a teacher of English and literature at Kerugoya Girls' High School where he also doubles up as the Head of Languages. He has made research presentations in national and international conferences. His research interests include discourse analysis, semantics, phonology, cognitive linguistics, pragmatics, and sociolinguistics.

J. K. S. Makokha is a Kenyan poet, critic, translator, and academic. He is based at Kenyatta University in the Department of Literature. He has written and edited several volumes of literary criticism. He serves on the advisory boards of the Journal of Somali Studies and the Institute of African Studies, Kenyatta University. His research interests lie in nexus of gender, cultural, and post-colonial studies.

Colomba Kaburi Muriungi is an associate professor of African literature in the Department of Humanities and the Dean, Faculty of Humanities and Social Sciences at Chuka University, Kenya. Her research interests include African children's literature, gender and cultural studies, and postcolonial studies. Colomba has vast experience in research and has published 28 research articles, attended learned conferences and presented papers. Colomba has also supervised many students at PhD and masters Level to graduation, reviewed papers for publication, and also participated in community empowerment programmes. Additionally, Colomba competitively qualified and attended the International Deans´ Course Africa 2017/2018, which is organized by the German Academic Exchange Service, the German Rectors' Conference, and the Osnabrück University of Applied Sciences, in cooperation with the Alexander von Humboldt Foundation. Colomba holds a doctorate in African children's literature (2006) and master of arts degree in Literature (2003), both from the University of the Witwatersrand, Johannesburg, and a bachelor's degree in education (Arts) degree from Kenyatta University, Nairobi.

Grace A. Musila is an associate professor in the Department of African Literature at the University of the Witwatersrand, Johannesburg.

She is the author *A Death Retold in Truth and Rumour: Kenya, Britain and the Julie Ward Murder* (James Currey/Boydell and Brewer 2015); which explores Kenyan and British interpretations of the 1988 murder of British tourist Julie Ann Ward in Maasai Mara Game Reserve, Kenya. She also co-edited *Rethinking Eastern African Intellectual Landscapes* (Africa World Press 2012) with James Ogude and Dina Ligaga. She has written articles and chapters on Eastern and Southern African literatures and popular cultures.

Eva Nabulya is an assistant lecturer in the Department of Literature at Makerere University, Uganda. She completed her PhD in English from Stellenbosch University, South Africa in 2017. Her PhD research is on the interface between rhetoric theory and ecocriticism, focused on environmental-activist literature in East African. Her other research interests are African literature, and drama.

Edgar Fred Nabutanyi holds a PhD from the English Department, Stellenbosch University. He is currently a lecturer in the Department of Literature, Makerere University. While his teaching interests are in children's literature, critical theory, practical criticism, and media studies, his research interest converges around issues of public discourses in the public sphere regarding how these channels — fiction and media — are subverted and assimilated by vulnerable and minority subjectivities for self-enunciation. The central thesis of his research is that vulnerable minorities like children, women, ethnic, and sexual minorities stealthily reconfigure the public sphere with such illocutionary force to make their issues matter and transform their lives from mere statistical footnotes to critical societal issues. He is also interested in how the new media is disrupting literature in interesting ways — not only providing new avenues of consuming literature, but also subverting the literary canon.

Gĩchingiri Ndĩgĩrĩgĩ is an associate professor of English at The University of Tennessee, Knoxville. He has published widely on Ngũgĩ wa Thiong'o's fiction and drama. His most recent work has been published in *Journal of African Cultural Studies* (2017), *A Companion to Chimamanda Adichie* (2017), *Research in African Literatures* (2016), *Popular Music and Society* (2016), *Ufahamu* (2015), *Unmasking the African Dictator: Essays on Postcolonial African Literature* (University of Tennessee Press 2014), *African Theatre Journal* (2014), and the Modern Language Association's *Approaches to Teaching the Works of Ngũgĩ wa Thiong'o* (2012).

Waiganjo Ndirangu was ranked sixth in a national short-story call-out in 2010 and his creative work has appeared in *Kwani? 06- Fiction Omnibus* and *Itch* magazine. He wrote for Storymoja's Stories-for-Chela charity campaign in 2015 and was the Literature Master for Jungle Quiz, a mobile and PC app by Chong Lip Phang (2017). He has a poetry collection pending publication and runs uprisingwriting.blogspot.com. He holds a bachelor's degree in Education and a master's degree in literature, both from Kenyatta University and has taught in Kenyatta High School in Taita Taveta and Kinango Secondary School in Kwale.

Larry Ndivo holds a PhD from the University of Nairobi and is currently a lecturer in the Department of Linguistics and Languages at Machakos University. He has in the past conducted research as a postdoctoral research fellow in trauma, forgiveness, and reconciliation at the University of Free State in South Africa. Besides teaching, his research interests include prison and narratives of crime, autobiographical works, gender perspectives, and writings on perpetrators of crime. He has been involved in research in indigenous languages and cultures and their archival through grants by *National Geographic* and Foundation for Endangered Languages under the auspices of the Indigenous Peoples Foundation. His recent research work has been published in *Eastern African Literary and Cultural Studies* (2016) and *Agenda: Empowering Women for Gender Equity* (2015).

Bwocha Nyangemi is a fiction writer and a literary critic. He has written both short stories and poetry while at the same time critiquing prose fiction and poetry. Bwocha has published *The Inevitable Burden and Other Stories* (2013), and two poetry anthologies. His research interests lie in contemporary human condition.

Nahashon O. Nyangeri is a Lecturer in the Department of Linguistics, Languages and Literature, Jaramogi Oginga Odinga University of Science and Technology. He is the co-author of *"Ulinganishi katika Tafsiri: Suluhisho kutoka kwa Isimu Tendaji"* (Daud Publishing Co. Ltd). He has written several Kiswahili short stories and Children's books. His research mainly centres on pragmatic aspects of literary communication and translation. He has been involved in coordinating and participating in language and literature conferences in East Africa. He is a doctoral student studying translation at the University of Nairobi.

George Ouma Ogal is a graduate student at Karatina University in the Department of Languages. He has presented research papers in national and international conferences in various Linguistic fields. His major research interests include Cognitive Linguistics, Discourse Analysis, Sociolinguistics, English Semantics and Pragmatics, Phonetics and Phonology. He is currently compiling his final thesis entitled "A Cognitive Blending Analysis of English Idioms in Kenyan Newspapers".

Jacqueline Ojiambo is a PhD candidate in the English Department of Stellenbosch University. She holds a master's degree in literature from The University of Nairobi and Bachelor of Arts in Literature and Communication from the same university. Her research interests are African cinema, specifically, Kenyan cinema. Her dissertation is titled "Films by Kenyan Women Directors as National Allegories". Through reading Kenyan films directed by women as national allegories, her study examines how the films address present concerns and realities while at the same time connecting the past, present, and the future.

Miriam Pahl is a PhD student in the Department of African Studies at the School of Oriental and African Studies in London. Her PhD research entitled "Precarious Lives in the Postcolony" concentrates on the concept of the human, humanity, and personhood in contemporary African genre fiction. Beyond this, she is interested in political philosophy, human rights, decolonial thought, and postcolonial and transnational literary studies. She currently lives in Nairobi and works for the German Academic Exchange Service. Miriam studied English-speaking cultures and cultural studies (BA) and transnational literary studies (MA) at the University of Bremen, Germany. She also holds a bachelor's degree in cell biology from the University of Osnabrück, Germany.

Alina N. Rinkanya is an associate professor in the Department of Literature, University of Nairobi, where she has been working since 1986; she teaches European, Eastern African, American literatures, as well as courses in literary theory. She completed her master's in literature from the Leningrad State University in 1980 and PhD in African literature (dissertation on Kenyan novel in the 1980s and 1990s) from Gorky Institute of World Literature (Moscow) in 2001. She has published a number of articles and book chapters on East African writing and has participated in international conferences on African literature in Europe and Africa. Her areas of interest include literatures of Eastern Africa, women's literature, comparative literary studies.

Charles Kipngeno Rono is a graduate student at Moi University. He completed a diploma course in media technology in 2007 at Kenya Institute of Mass Communication. Rono developed an interest in literary studies while in high school, and on graduating with a diploma, he enrolled for a bachelor's degree first at the University of Nairobi and later in Moi University where he graduated in 2015. His area of interest lies in medical humanities.

Kiprotich E. Sang holds a Master of Arts in Literature from Moi University and a Bachelor of Education Arts Degree in English and Literature from Kenyatta University. Currently, Sang pursues a PhD in Literature from Moi University.

Robin Steadman is an Arts and Humanities Research Council (AHRC) Creative Economy Engagement Fellow at the University of Sheffield where she studies data, diversity, and inequality in the creative industries. She recently completed her doctorate in African languages and cultures at School of Oriental and African Studies (SOAS) University of London. Her doctoral research explores how and why Nairobi-based female filmmakers can be considered to constitute a film movement and hers is the first major work on these filmmakers and their unique female-led industry. Her research is forthcoming in *The Companion to African Cinema* and she is also currently working on a project examining African documentary film production funds.

Benon Tugume is a lecturer in the Department of Literature, Kyambogo University. He has carried out extensive research on the African novel in the areas of human rights, violence, and gender. He has recently published in the *Journal of Literature, Languages and Linguistics* (2017) *How the Centre Cannot Hold In Chinua Achebe's Things Fall Apart: Objectification and Alienation of Children (2017)*, Imbizo: International Journal of African Literary and Comparative Studies (2016) *Female Chauvinists and Male Patriarchs: A Critical Analysis of Gender Relations in Ama Ata Aidoo's Changes: A Love Story* (University of South Africa Press). He is currently working on *Interrogating the Male-Female Gender Dichotomy in Nawal El Sadaawi's Woman At Point Zero* and *Reading Gender Inequality, Callousness and Rebellion in Tsitsi Dangarembga's Nervous Conditions.*

Robert Wesonga holds a PhD in film studies and theatre arts from Kenyatta University, Kenya. He teaches literature at the University of Kabianga in Kericho (Kenya). His research interests include literature, theatre arts, and film studies. He is also a creative writer with a number of unpublished projects, but notably has published a short story, "Holy Mission", in the anthology, *The Warm Heart of Africa*, Nairobi: Longhorn Publishers, 2017. ISBN. 996631574-8/ 9789966315748. Wesonga has published one book and several articles in refereed journals, both local and international. He runs a creative writing blog: *My Creative World*: http://wesongarobert. blogspot.co.ke)

Wafula Yenjela teaches literature at South Eastern Kenya University. He is also an adjunct lecturer at Africa Nazarene University. He holds a bachelor's degree (literature and linguistics) and master's degree (literature) from the University of Nairobi, Kenya, and a PhD in literature from Stellenbosch University, Cape Town, South Africa.

Foreword

Grace A. Musila

Perhaps the best-known quote from African American sociologist and human rights activist WEB Du Bois' *The Souls of Black Folk* (1903) is his prophetic diagnosis: "the problem of the twentieth century is the problem of the color line — the relation of the darker to the lighter races of men in Asia and Africa, in America and the islands of the sea" (14). In the course of his graduate studies at Harvard University — where he would become the first African American to attain a doctorate from the institution, after being made to take his Bachelors studies again because they wouldn't recognize his first degree from the historically Black Fisk University — Du Bois received a fellowship that enabled him to spend a year at the University of Berlin, Germany in 1892. It is while in Germany that Du Bois's pan-African sensibility was further sharpened, as he witnessed the onward march of the imperial project in Africa, soon after the Berlin conference of 1884–1885 had formalized the official partitioning of Africa amongst the imperial powers.

A century later, in 2003, with Europe having confirmed Du Bois' prophesy, unleashing untold horrors and violence across the globe, another prominent Black intellectual, the Jamaican philosopher, novelist, and dramatist Sylvia Wynter would update Du Bois' prophesy, and write:

> the struggle of our new millennium will be one between the ongoing imperative of securing the well-being of our present ethnoclass (i.e., Western bourgeois) conception of the human, Man, which overrepresents itself as if it were the human itself, and that of securing the well-being, and therefore the full cognitive and behavioural autonomy of the human species itself/ourselves. (Wynter 260)

Wynter's thought nuances Du Bois' spotlight on race in ways that track Europe's redefinition of the human from the medieval theocratic emphasis on the True Christian self as contrasted with the Unchristian others, to racialized renaissance redefinition of the human as the rational self in contrast with the peoples of the New World territories and Africa mapped as subrational and therefore subhuman. With this self-assignment of the human as exclusively synonymous with the Western bourgeois ethnoclass, renaissance Europe was incapable of conceiving of competing definitions of the human; in fact, "all other modes of being human would instead have to be seen not as the alternative modes of being human that they are 'out there', but adaptively, as the lack of the West's ontologically absolute self-description" (Wynter 282).

Wynter's mapping of the exclusionary definition of the human as synonymous to the Western bourgeois ethnoclass and its self-prioritization to the exclusion of the rest of the humanity is important to our understanding of the intermeshing histories and structures behind the multiple forms of hurt and precarity that preoccupy the essays collected in this volume. In fact, she explicitly draws this connection by observing that "all our present struggles with respect to race, class, gender, sexual orientation, ethnicity, struggles over the environment, global warming, severe climate change, the sharply unequal distribution of the earth's resources — these are all differing facets of the central ethnoclass Man vs. Human struggle" (261). Thinking about postcolonial societies' struggles for freedom with this contestation over definitions of the human in mind, we begin to understand those struggles as not only struggles for self-determination, but, as briefly successful attempts to challenge the racist definition of the human; before these victories were co-opted (Wynter 262).

Du Bois' and Wynter's reflections resonate with Kenya's historical trajectory and the patterns of production of Black precarity from British colonial violence and the Mau Mau anticolonial resistance to the forms of state-engineered brutality that have marked successive post-independence regimes in Kenya. Overarching each of these manifestations of violence and harm — colonial and postcolonial prison violence; urban precarity; state-choreographed inter-ethnic conflicts; patriarchal predation on vulnerable women; dysfunctional public infrastructure — are contestations over definitions of the human and the resources that sustain it.

Elsewhere, in *Omens of Adversity: Tragedy, Time, Memory, Justice* (2014), David Scott revisits the Grenada Revolution of 1979 and its collapse in 1983. While Scott is interested in the usefulness of the categories time and tragedy in understanding the collapse of the revolution, he makes a pertinent observation about memory and trauma in his introductory remarks:

> It is precisely when the future has ceased to be a source of longing and anticipation that the past has become a densely animated object of enchantment. After all, not so long ago, in comparative terms, the past was largely conceived as a storehouse of disenchantment; it existed to be overcome, not to be excavated and memorialized. Then, the past had temporal significance only insofar as it was tethered to the engine of history driving inexorably toward the future. Now,

by contrast, the past has loosed itself from the future and acquired a certain quasi-autonomy... in such a context of seeming temporal reversal, ... the concern with the generative effects of psychic trauma becomes entirely intelligible, even unavoidable. In a sense, psychological trauma is nothing but a past that will not go away, a past that returns, unbidden, involuntarily, to haunt or unsettle or somehow mangle the present. (Scott 13)

While concerned with the collapse of the Grenada revolution, and its decisive postponement of the promise of socialist revolution, not only in the Caribbean, but in the world at large, Scott's meditation on haunted time and a future that "has ceased to be a source of longing and anticipation", offers equally resonant insights for thinking about postcolonial Kenya's temporal arc; mapped as it is in typical Fanonian terms, from the palpable anticipation of freedom from British rule to the collapse of the nationalist project into "an empty shell, a crude travesty of what it might have been" (Fanon 119). Equally crucial is Scott's emphasis on the psychological traumas of "a past that will not go away, a past that returns" (Scott 13).

Similar to many postcolonial artists, the traumas of Scott's "past that returns" continue to exercise its influence on Kenyan writers, artists, filmmakers, musicians, and cultural artists, in whose work the figure of the artist remains the main pathfinder offering what Chinua Achebe terms "a second handle on existence" (Achebe 139). Across these artforms, these cultural workers theorize, archive, witness, interrogate, register, and contest the different atrocities that have scarred the nation's psyche at different points in Kenya's post-independent history. Beyond this archival and interrogative role, these artists insist on imagining different futures, breathing new life into the dream of freedom. They refuse the surrender demanded by the repeated cycles of co-option, betrayal, and marketization of Kenyans' visions of the future at different points in the nation's history: the dream of freedom at the fall of British rule in 1963. The dream of multiparty democracy when President Moi finally caved in to local and international pressure to legalize multiparty politics. The euphoric promise of the second liberation when Kenyan opposition parties united to vote out the ruling party, Kenya African National Union and President Moi, in 2002. At each of these junctures, Kenyans soon woke up to futures that differed radically from what they had envisioned. And while the terrible taste of betrayal is repeatedly burnt into the national psyche with each disappointment and its attendant violence that produced a complex triad of victim-witness-perpetrators, art continues to provide succour to imaginings of freedom and the urgency of articulating a different defining statement of the human, to riff off Wynter.

Cultural productions provide what Fred Moten calls "poetic knowledge" in reference to poetry's — and broadly, art's — capacity to "transport us to another place, compel us to relive horrors and, more importantly, enable us to imagine a new society" (9). In some respects then, Kenyan artistic mediations on the atrocities and traumas of history across the genres of poetry, fiction, music, visual art, film, and satire, not only respond to the widely acknowledged difficulties of articulating trauma, but they also resonate what Christina Sharpe terms "wake work" in her exploration of the precarity of Black Being across global history from the vantage point of what Saidiya Hartman terms the afterlives of slavery in which "black lives are still imperiled and devalued by a racial calculus and a political arithmetic that were entrenched centuries ago [creating] skewed life chances, limited access to health and education, premature death, incarceration and impoverishment" (6). The essays in this collection grapple with ways of responding to Sharpe's invitation to

> defend the dead, to live in the wake, to do wake work; the hard emotional, physical, and intellectual work that demands vigilant attendance to the needs of the dying, to ease their way, and also to the needs of the living [and] rupture the structural silences produced and facilitated by, and that produce and facilitate Black social and physical death. (10, 22)

Expectedly, art becomes an important practice in the emotional and intellectual labour demanded by wake work.

In view of the possibilities signalled by art, it a nonetheless noteworthy coincidence that two of Kenya's most celebrated thinkers, Nobel laureate and environmentalist, Wangari Maathai, and prolific novelist and thinker, Ngugi wa Thiong'o, both close their best-regarded books with the metaphor of a traditional three-legged stool. In *Unbowed: A Memoir* (2007), Maathai considers the three-legged stool an eloquent metaphor for the importance of a healthy interface between democratic governance, resource management, and peace for the well-being of society:

> The three legs represent critical pillars of just and stable societies. The first leg stands for democratic space, where rights are respected, whether they are human rights, women's rights, children's rights or environmental rights. The second represents sustainable and equitable management of resources. And the third stands for cultures of peace that are deliberately cultivated within communities and nations. The basin, or seat, represents society and its prospects for development. Unless all three legs are in place, supporting the seat, no society can thrive. Neither can its citizens develop their skills and creativity. When one leg is missing, the seat is unstable; when two legs are missing, it is impossible to keep any state alive; and when no legs are available, the state is as good as a failed state. (Maathai 294)

In addition to one of the essays in the present collection examining what Rob Nixon (2) terms the unspectacular, incremental, and accretive slow violence of environmental attrition, the rest of the essays variously engage with forms of harm inflicted on Kenyan society by the instability of one or more of the legs in Maathai's stool. And while it may be absent from the stool, Maathai obliquely nods to the role of neoliberalism in Kenya with the fall of the Cold War, as freeing the once complicit donors to speak up against the Moi regime's human rights abuses, even though these interventions remained partial to the extent that they were more interested in the strengthening of the neoliberal project in Kenya than in the well-being of Kenyans as Stephen Brown (2007) has shown elsewhere. In this environment, the gains of withheld aid forcing the Moi regime to comply with multiparty democracy were cancelled out by the structural adjustment policies of the International Monetary Fund which included major cuts in social spending as conditions for loans. Cedric Johnson underlines that neoliberal reforms "spawned a global nouveau riche and created a wider availability of consumer goods [but] these massive transfers of public wealth into private hands have simultaneously created unprecedented inequality, mass immiseration and vulnerability for the multitude around the world" (xxiii). In Kenya, this multitude wears the face of the urban precariat, memorably depicted by Meja Mwangi in his classic *Going Down River Road*, which is examined in one of the essays here.

While Maathai's stool offers a diagnostic reading of the conditions necessary for a healthy society, Ngugi's earlier stool in *A Grain of Wheat* – also examined in one of the essays here — offers an equally fitting synopsis of the questions grappled with and futures imagined by the writers, artists, and film-makers in this volume. That this stool is to be created by Gikonyo as a gift to his estranged wife, Mumbi, nods to the Gikuyu myth of creation, which traces the nation's roots back to the first couple, Gikuyu and Mumbi. Unlike the original couple though, this nuclear unit is haunted by betrayal as Gikonyo gets arrested on suspicion of being sympathetic to the Mau Mau movement, succumbs to British torture, and betrays the movement by confessing to the Mau Mau oath of loyalty, thus buying himself early release. In a cruel irony, Mumbi's joy over the news of Gikonyo's release compromises her judgement; in the euphoria, she has sexual relations with Karanja, a hitherto much-resented collaborator. That Gikonyo starts thinking about the stool en route home through the rehabilitative pipeline of colonial British correctional institutions seems to portend the fragility of the nation to come after independence. The novel closes with Gikonyo fine-tuning his design of the stool while in hospital, and simultaneously facing up to his own betrayal:

> He would carve the stool now, after the hospital, before he resumed his business, or in-between business hours. He worked the motif in detail. He changed the figures. He would now carve a thin man,

with hard lines on the face, shoulders and head bent, supporting the weight. His right hand would stretch to link with that of a woman, also with hard lines on the face. The third figure would be that of a child on whose head or shoulders the other two hands of the man and woman would meet. Into what image he would work the beads on the seat? A field needing clearance and cultivation? A jembe? A bean flower? He would settle this when the time came. (203)

Like most of the other core characters in the novel, Gikonyo occupies the entangled victim-witness-perpetrator role, which disrupts simplistic moral dualisms of victims and perpetrators. Instead, Ngugi underlines the ambiguity and complexity that marks the story of Kenya, not only at independence, but right across the nation's history; even as he retains a sense of moral clarity on the justness and unjustness of some actions, agents, and institutions. Confronted by the impossibility of purity in a colonial context that contaminates everyone, Gikonyo is forced to let go of his anger and sense of betrayal against Mumbi and the child she bore with Karanja. In place of this anger, he turns to art to sculpt an alternative handle on the reality that is open to human frailty without losing faith in the human capacity for beauty. And while Mumbi's cool response to his sudden change of heart cautions against excessive optimism, the novel ends with a candid acknowledgement of the impossibility of innocence in a world framed by limiting contestations over a limited vision of being human, but nonetheless invites hope and optimism about the possibility of living in its wake, and tending to the future.

Works cited

Achebe, Chinua. *Hope and Impediments: Selected Essays*. New York: Double-Day, 1989.

Brown, Stephen. "From Demiurge to Midwife: Changing Donor Roles in Kenya's Democratisation Process". *Kenya: The Struggle for Democracy*. Ed. Godwin Murunga and Shadrack Nasong'o. Dakar and London: CODESRIA and Zed Books, 2007. 301–330.

Du Bois, WEB. *The Souls of Black Folk*. Penguin Books: New York, 2018 [1903].

Fanon, Frantz. *The Wretched of the Earth*. London: Penguin, 2001 [1967].

Hartman, Saidiya. *Lose Your Mother: A Journey Along the Atlantic Slave Route*. New York: Farrar, Straus and Giroux, 2008.

Johnson, Cedric. "Introduction". *The Neoliberal Deluge: Hurricane Katrina, Late Capitalism and the Remaking of New Orleans*. Ed. Cedric Johnson. Minneapolis: University of Minnesota Press, 2011. xvii–l.

Maathai, Wangari. *Unbowed: One Woman's Story*. London: Arrow Books, 2006.

Moten, Fred. *Freedom Dreams: The Black Radical Imagination*. Boston, MA: Beacon Press, 2002.

Nixon, Rob. *Slow Violence and the Environmentalism of the Poor*. Cambridge, MA: Harvard University Press, 2011.

Scott, David. *Omens of Adversity: Tragedy, Time, Memory, Justice*. Durham, NC: Duke University Press, 2014.

Sharpe, Christina. *In the Wake: On Blackness and Being*. Durham, NC: Duke University Press, 2016.

Wa Thiong'o, Ngugi. *A Grain of Wheat*. London: Penguin Books, 2012 [1967].

Wynter, Sylvia. "Unsettling the Coloniality of Being/Power/Truth/Freedom: Towards the Human, After Man, Its Overrepresentation – an Argument". *CR: The New Centennial Review* 3.3 (2003): 257–337.

Introduction

Conceptualizing Representations of Atrocity in Art

Charles Kebaya

Lawrence Langer while writing about Holocaust Literature posits, "How should art – how *can* art – represent the inexpressibly inhuman suffering of the victims, without doing injustice to that suffering?" (1). This question casts aspersions on the ability of art to accurately offer deep multilayered insights into the intense and seemingly impenetrable realms of violence and horror on two fronts. The first aspersion is grounded on what should be considered an atrocity. This is because the label "atrocity" refers not to the intrinsic properties of an act, but our responses to it. That is to say, to call something an "atrocity" expresses not only moral objection but the innumerable excesses of moral indignation as well. In other words, the concept of "atrocity" expresses a traumatized response. In a similar context, Robert MacDonald in his introduction to Jerzy Kosinski's *The Painted Bird* writes:

> The position of the artist in dealing with material of this nature is particularly difficult. As the one man whose imagination should be capable of mastering such material, he is necessarily compelled to try to do so. Yet it is the nature of artistic experience that, if it cannot be directly absorbed as being immediately relevant to its audience, it will inevitably degenerate more or less into a purely aesthetic stimulus, exciting or depressing...because the enormities that are taking place below it are no longer possible to grasp. (ix)

Thus, in evaluating any work of art in reference to atrocity, one must acknowledge the inherent dilemma between experiences to be expressed and choices of the artistic media used for their expression. Hence, if art functions as the definitive articulation of human values, acts of atrocity, as the antithesis of humanity, would seem to defeat any attempts to be expressed through art.

The second aspersion relates to a number of risks involved in any artistic representation of atrocity. Artists, in their attempts to creatively capture atrocious experiences or events, might perilously trivialize human suffering in the name of art. There is the risk of stimulating an abhorrent fascination with, or a chilling indifference to, bodily suffering. In

Regarding the Pain of Others, Susan Sontag avers that artists risk depicting atrocity in a "terrible distinctness" in their artistic portrayal of such
"unnecessary, indecent information" (56). There is also a danger of opting for a plausible happily-ever-after ending in works of art, which is at
odds with violence and horror. Based on these risks, therefore, it is possible to side with Langer's thought-provoking supposition that there is
something peculiar about the representation of atrocity in art. Inspired
by Langer's question, however, essays in this volume explore multifaceted ways in which various atrocities are framed and represented in art
within the Kenyan context.

   In their book, *Violence Performed: Local Roots and Global Routes
of Conflict*, Patrick Anderson and Jisha Menon suggest that "violence
acquires its immense significance in a delicate pivot between the spectacular and the embodied" (5). The subtle axis here is what brings the
public to convene around scenes of mass atrocity, as Mark Seltzer observed in his classic study of trauma and wound culture. According to
Seltzer, the pathological public sphere functions as a form of "convening
of the public around scenes of violence", with a "fascination with torn
and opened bodies and torn and opened persons, the collective gathering
around shock, trauma and the wound" (3). Fascinated as we are by torn
bodies, we continue to grapple with their representation in art. There is,
however, a contradictory process at play in representing atrocities: the
compulsion to speak and make the trauma visible and the pressure to
remain silent in the face of one's inability to articulate a truthful representation of the experience.

   Art is viewed as a site of possibility for this problematic representation
between the experience, the understanding, the re-enactment, and the
recollection of atrocity. This is predicated on the fact that arts propose
different perspectives on the question of representation of atrocity. For
instance, by showing and enacting the atrocity, performing arts such as
theatre and music offer ontological approaches to the epistemological
tension between telling and showing. In other words, while texts narrate
the horror, sometimes metaphorically, performance art brings us face-
to-face with the suffering body and the difficult embodiment of otherness as "a people" not just "people in a film or theatre performance".
In a film, for instance, the audience is forced to watch in revulsion the
dying moments of their favourite character or the painful experiences
of a character being tortured by authorities, allowing us to assume that
there is a general cultural context in which this shared knowledge is
recognizable. Thus, essays in this volume view spaces of performance
not as sites of construction of truth or a mirror to atrocity, but as spaces
of resistance where being present, listening, and reflecting becomes an
ethical responsibility. It is important to point out that we have a responsibility as cultural critics and artists to reflect on the historical, material,
and existential conditions of various atrocities in society.

In terms of aesthetics with regard to the art of atrocity, representations entail social, cultural, and political considerations, extending far beyond the limits of any singular artistic creation but primarily with an eye to understanding how atrocities happen and their implications, thereby aiming to bring us closer to understanding the experience of atrocity. In this way, the dual potential of art this volume explores is foregrounded as it meets the historical and moral responsibilities. In reflecting on violence and human suffering, as Theodor Adorno in *Minima Moralia: Reflections from Damaged Life* insists, art keeps with its role of portraying concrete suffering before our eyes as a way to counter the abstractions that distance one person from the material reality of another's pain.

In Kenya, studies on atrocity have taken different discursive dimensions from history, politics, and human rights perspectives. These perspectives are usually geared towards understanding the manifestations, extent, political, and economic implications of atrocities. In all these cases, the question of representation is of central importance. For instance, the 2007/08 post-election violence witnessed in Kenya provoked a two-month period of violence which has been described as the country's most severe human rights crisis. For many, it was the worst of all atrocities, and it equals what William Schabas calls the "crime of crimes". In order to lay bare multiple narratives that speak of the 2007/08 post-election violence, there has been a remarkable output of creative productions in varied media such as film, fine art, fashion, dance, theatre, and photography. In all these productions, Kenyan Creatives have sought to show how ordinary voices can contribute to the construction of a new "post-conflict" nation, while adding to ongoing processes of reconciliation and national healing. However, existing academic and normative scholarship on 2007/08 post-election violence converge on explaining its baffling causes and effects, the moral good of electoral contestations, and political legitimacy among other concerns (Murunga 2011 and Gona 2013). This gives us clear indications that the 2007/08 post-election violence and extra-judicial atrocities in Kenya have been widely documented, but less well known are their artistic representations. Essays in this volume, therefore, present a systematic examination of creative arts such as films, theatrical productions, exhibitions, and film screenings refiguring 2007/08 post-election violence, peace, and reconciliation processes.

It is important to note that a number of creative works such as Ngugi's *A Grain of Wheat*, Meja Mwangi's *Carcase for Hounds*, Muthoni Likimani's *Passbook Number F. 47927*, Wanyiri Kihoro's *Never Say Die*, Wahome Mutahi's *Three Days on the Cross*, Katama Mkangi's *Mafuta*, Kinyanjui Kombani's *Last Villains of Molo*, David Mulwa's *Clean Hands*, Sitawa Namwalie's *Cut off My Tongue*, and Stephen Derwent Partington's *How to Euthanise a Cactus* as well as recent films, such as

4 *Charles Kebaya*

Phillippe Bresson's *For the Love of My Son*, Tosh Gitonga's *Nairobi Half-Life*, and other art forms such as popular music have sought to engage with post-colonial atrocities in Kenya. As essays in this volume show, these creative works reflect the memories, creative geniuses, and social identities of the artists whilst offering a mirror to their audiences coming to terms with a collective memory that is often traumatic in itself. The seeming paradox between creative representation and the reality of horrifying events such as ethnic violence presents challenges in the relationship between ethics, poetics (art), and politics.

The breadth of the contributions to this volume reflects this remarkable evolution in our thinking about atrocity within the Kenyan context, while also affirming its status as an essentially "contested concept". Deliberately broad in scope and intellectual ambition, the volume considers questions such as, why are atrocities carried out with such viciousness and cruelty? How, if at all, does the demonization of perpetrators of atrocity prevent us from confronting the complicity of others, or of ourselves? In what ways are past and current atrocities in Kenya represented in cultural studies such as literature, film, music, and the popular arts? What are the challenges we face in teaching and learning about violence and horror? And how does the language we use contribute to or impair what can be taught and learned about atrocity? In an attempt to answer these questions, this volume considers historical, fictional, contextual, sociological, environmental, and cultural perspectives in representations of atrocity thereby bringing together multiple generic ways of interrogating artistic interpellations of atrocity in Kenya. In this regard, the volume explores how art forms question perceptions and interpretations of atrocity, tackle such controversial and painful subjects, and how, by representing the unrepresentable or speaking the unspeakable, the artists incessantly inspect and develop broadening insights into understanding the cultural archives of atrocity in the Kenyan context.

Although the method is fundamentally literary-critical, the book spans across a wide array of disciplines, living up to the multidisciplinary, interdisciplinary, and cross-disciplinary stance envisioned by the editors while conceptualizing this project. Yet it bears clarifying that the book adopted an eclectic approach, letting individual authors themselves determine the appropriate theoretical and/or conceptual framework suitable for their chapters. The net effect of this approach is to present our esteemed readers with multifaceted and valuable competing perspectives of looking at atrocity as represented in literary imaginaries and other forms of artistic cultural representations in Kenya.

This volume comprises 21 chapters grouped in four distinct parts. Part 1, which focuses on representations of atrocity in the contemporary Kenyan novel, features 11 chapters dealing with how the Kenyan novelist grapples with atrocity in the contemporary novel written either in English or Kiswahili. This part comes first on account of the pre-eminence of the novel as the most prominent and studied genre in Kenya, receiving the highest number of submissions to this volume. Edgar Nabutanyi opens this section with an incisive exegesis of how Yvonne Owuor in her novel *Dust* narrates trauma that various characters undergo as a result of atrocity. Set during the 2007/2008 post-election violence, the novel explores various atrocities that have happened in Kenya since independence, and the prevalence and persistence of historical amnesia and silence, in various ways, arising from these atrocities. In chapter 2, Eva Nabulya explores the textual framings of environmental atrocity in Okiya Omtata Okoiti's *Voice of the People* and Nganga Mbugua's *Different Colours*. While focusing on stylo-rhetoric strategies used to frame environmental atrocity, the chapter presents untold sufferings of people as a result of environmental degradation and locates them within contemporary eco-critical debates.

Chapters 3 and 4 explore the innumerable atrocities which characterize prison life. While reading Wahome Mutahi's *Jail Bugs* and *Three Days on the Cross*, Macharia Gatundu explores how the novelist decries and resists violence in prison through the restoration of voices of incarcerated bodies in chapter 3. In his analysis, Gatundu acknowledges the fact that narrative texture is sombre and highlights the pain of innocent individuals caught in the grinding gears of a despotic regime which is committed to stamping out any form of rebellion, real or imagined. In chapter 4, Larry Ndivo explores the pain that innocent individuals undergo at the hands of prison wardens. Ndivo examines Benjamin Garth Bundeh's *Birds of Kamiti*, and avers that the police torture suspects to deride and coerce them to confess and then prosecute them. The convicted victims suffer unprecedented psychological pain that leaves them with traumatic memories of the legal process. In chapter 5, Robert Wesonga looks at socio-economic atrocities in Meja Mwangi's *Going Down River Road* and Kinyanjui Kombani's *The Last Villains of Molo*. Wesonga analyses how language provides the means by which individuals living in atrocious socio-economic circumstances vent out their unenviable experiences in life.

Chapters 6, 7, and 8 focus on violence and horror as a result of political activities in Kenya. While examining Kinyanjui Kombani's *The Last Villains of Molo*, Muroki Ndung'u's *A friend of the Court* and Ogova Ondego's *From Terror to Hope,* Waiganjo Ndirangu considers the symbolism of human relations in the light of the ethnic violence that plagues the nation. Waiganjo shows how peace efforts remain elusive due to recurrent ethnic conflicts. Turning to Ngugi wa Thiong'o's *Wizard of the Crow,* David Wafula in chapter 7 interrogates how Kenya's turbulent political history provides a rich archive of sycophants' annihilation of their souls and, by extension, the soul of the nation that they desecrate in their quest for tokens, for power embodied in autocrats, and for their survival. Chapter 8 analyzes the vicious cycle of political atrocities in

Ngugi wa Thiongo's *Wizard of the Crow*. Charles Rono reads Ngugi's *Wizard of the Crow* as a serious indictment on the dangers of absolute power in society as demonstrated by the Ruler's and sycophants' bizarre bodily metamorphosis in order to continue to mete out violence on innocent citizens. Alina Rikanya in chapter 9 examines how gender-based atrocity spreads far beyond the domestic sphere in the Kenyan urban women's novel after 2000. Rikanya shows how gender-based atrocities restrain women's agency and fundamental rights in all spheres of life. Thus, the modern urban environment and women's urban mentality are read as twin enablers of the modern women's struggle for self-emancipation from gender-based atrocities.

Chapter 10 and 11 end Part 1 with a focus on atrocity in Kenyan novels written in Kiswahili. Simiyu Kisurulia, in chapter 10, interrogates the politics of violence and impunity in *Pango* and *Kufa Kuzikana*. Simiyu shows how politicians use ethnic violence to gain and clutch on to power. In chapter 11, Mikhail Gromov looks at political atrocity in Kenyan Swahili novel written after the year 2000. By reflecting on the political situation in the society critically, Gromov shows how political atrocities disrupt the social well-being of a people and argues that by documenting various horrors of political violence, the Swahili novelist wants future generations to learn the futility of political ambitions.

Part 2, narrating Mau Mau violence and trauma in the Kenyan novel, comprises three chapters that bring to the fore insights on how the Mau Mau movement can be viewed as an injustice and historical atrocity. Colomba Muriungi, in chapter 12, examines how Mau Mau atrocities are not only portrayed but also subverted in settler writing in Kenya. While analysing how Robert Ruark represents the Mau Mau movement in *Something of Value,* Muriungi shows possibilities of reading other discourses on the text in addition to the main ideology that the author projects. In chapter 13, Benon Tugume analyses grotesque images of colonial and Mau Mau violence in Ngugi's *Weep Not Child* and *A Grain of Wheat*. Tugume shows traumatizing images of colonial and Mau Mau violence, and the consequences the two forms of violence have on individual characters and personal relations in the two texts. Gĩchingiri Ndĩgĩrĩgĩ, in chapter 14, focuses on emergency-era trauma in Ngũgĩ's *A Grain of Wheat*. Paying attention to Mugo's struggles as a frame of reference in the traumatic experiences, Ndĩgĩrĩgĩ explores a social turn in trauma witnessing by connecting to a community of fellow victims, that is, characters in the text.

Part 3 is concerned with representations of atrocity in popular arts, and it comprises four chapters that focus on how popular arts such as film and music depict atrocity. Anchored on selected stories from *Kwani?05'*, Miriam Pahl in chapter 15 analyses how the Kenyan social imaginary is shaped and negotiated with respect to the global imaginary of Kenya and "Africa" on the one hand, and local perceptions of the Kenyan nation and ethnicity on the other. Contesting the notion that "post-election violence" is limited to atrocities committed the 2007/08 atrocities perpetrated purely as a result of the disputed elections, Pahl analyses narratives that contest this ahistoricism and shows the complex injustices of the past and present that led to the violence in 2007/08. Using Judy Kibinge's feature film *Something Necessary*, Jackie Ojiambo in chapter 16 examines how the collective pain and suffering of a nation is portrayed in film. Ojiambo shows how perpetrator-victim relationship is foregrounded in film in the light of the 2007/08 post-election violence and how film narrative changes our sensibilities when we view the perpetrator as a victim as well.

Investigating the production and circulation of films about 2007/08 post-election violence in Kenya, Robin Steadman in chapter 17 shows how film can be used as a tool for reconciliation. Steadman also presents a discussion of the 'public lives' of film in order to understand their tangible role in post-conflict reconciliation and nation-building. From a conceptual metaphor perspective, George Ouma Ogal and Titus Karuri Macharia in chapter 18 explore bestial zoosemic labelling in Kenyan political songs. Ogal and Macharia show that language often propagates and sustains varied ideologies in Kenya's political landscape disadvantaging the general citizenry. In chapter 19, Kiprotich Sang interrogates the possible role of Kalenjin popular music in the construction, performance, and dissemination of violence. Sang demonstrates how supposed transgressions against the Kalenjin nation are structured by popular musicians to arouse and direct primitive violent energies towards perceived aggressors, whom they see as the 'other'.

Representations of atrocity in Kenyan poetry forms the focus of Part 4. The final section of this volume comprises two chapters which explore how Kenyan poets writing both in English and Kiswahili depict various atrocities in the Kenyan society. Focusing on selected poems from Jared Angira's two anthologies of poetry, *Tides of Time: Selected Poems* and *Lament of the Silence & Other Poems*, Bwocha Nyangemi explores how the poems mirror Kenya's history of repression from the 1960s to the present in chapter 20. Nyangemi shows how the silenced voices of the 'workers' of the nation help unveil atrocities meted out to the silent masses. The final chapter of this volume (chapter 21), focuses on the analysis of atrocity in Kiswahili poetry. Nahashon Nyangeri examines the unspeakable and horrific gross violations of human rights characterized by ethnic conflicts in three Swahili anthologies of poetry: *Chembe cha Moyo* (Mazrui 1988), *Bara Jingine* (Mberia 2001), and *Sauti ya Dhiki* (Abdalla 1973). Nyangeri asserts that Swahili poetry is seen as a tool that reflects various social and political violations and as a means of expressing personal reactions to violence, and thus, reads it as an avenue to revolt against oppressive situations and regimes, convey the "unconveyable" and provide an alternative voice for articulating issues bedevilling society.

In sum, the 21 chapters in this volume, *Cultural Archives of Atrocity: Essays on the Protest Tradition in Kenyan Culture and Society,* centre around the representation of atrocity within the Kenyan context from various perspectives irrespective of the artistic medium of expression. Authors herein provide refreshing insights and perspectives to the study of artistic representations and interpellations of the unspeakable within the imaginaries of the Kenya nation. The volume, therefore, sheds more light on how we remember and represent, reflect upon what thoughts we might be excluding, what conceptions we might be considering only in a restricted or limited form, and how our thinking might, even in small ways, echo the very thinking of the social imaginaries of atrocity in Kenya. Researchers, academicians, graduate students, and the general public will find this volume a useful resource. The volume will serve as a critical resource for scholars undertaking inter- and cross-disciplinary studies of atrocity within the fields of ethnic studies, literature, film, cultural studies, postcolonial studies, sociology, peace and conflict studies, criminology, psychology, political economy, and history in Kenya. It is hoped that this volume contributes in more than one way to the understanding of atrocity in Kenya.

Works Cited

Adorno, Theodor W. *Minima Moralia: Reflections from Damaged Life.* Radical Thinkers Classics. Trans. E. F. N. Jeffcott. London: Verso, 2005.

Anderson, Patrick, and Menon, Jisha, eds. *Violence Performed: Local Roots and Global Routes of Conflict.* New York: Palgrave, 2008. 5.

Gona, George. "Dealing with the Aftermath of the Election Violence of 2007/2008: Kenya's Dilemmas." *(Re)-membering Kenya vol. 2: Interrogating Marginalization and Governance.* Ed. George Gona and Mbugua wa Mungai. Nairobi: Twaweza Communications, 2013.

Kosinski, Jerzy. *The Painted Bird.* New York: Modern Library/Random House, 1970.

Langer, Lawrence. *The Holocaust and the Literary Imagination.* New Hauen and London: Yale University Press, 1975.

Murunga, Godwin R. *Spontaneous or Premeditated? Post-Election Violence in Kenya.* Uppsala: Nordic Africa Institute Discussion Paper No. 57; 2011.

Schabas, William. *Genocide in International Law: The Crime of Crimes.* Cambridge: Cambridge University Press, 2009.

Seltzer, Mark. "Wound Culture: Trauma in the Pathological Public Sphere", 80 (October, 1997): 3–26. doi:10.2307/778805.

Sontag, Susan. *Regarding the Pain of Others.* London: Penguin, 2003.

Part 1

Representations of Atrocity in the Contemporary Kenyan Novel

1 Narrating Trauma in Yvonne Owuor's *Dust*

Edgar Nabutanyi

Introduction

Yvonne Adhiambo Owuor's latest novel *Dust* – set during the 2007/2008 post-election violence – has justifiably attracted considerable critical attention. This is probably because of its candid and poignant exploration of the Kenyan post-colonial polity and its related violent experiences. By foreshadowing and/or establishing a link between the 2007/2008 post-election violence and the earlier bouts of horror, many literary commentators read Owuor's *Dust* as a literary illustration of Kenya's history of violence. While reading *Dust* as an allegory of Kenyan political and historical regimes of violence is persuasive, this chapter argues that the text offers itself to alternative readings. For example, it can be justified that the text is a tale that deploys innovative focalization to allow abused and violated victims of the Kenyan state to testify to their pain. The chapter argues that Owuor's *Dust* crafts a register for characters like Akai Lokorijom and Aggrey Nyipir Oganda to disclose their impossibly suppressed traumatic experiences. While the chapter reads Akai's loss of her twins after being abandoned by her family and lover – Hugh Bolton – as an example of a tragically traumatic Kenyan colonial experience, it focuses on Nyipir's torture after his refusal to take the oath in 1969 as a case of state-inspired violation that defies articulation in normal diction. Therefore, when Akai and Nyipir finally reveal their past pain to Ajany after the death of Odidi, the chapter posits that they do so because Ajany assumes the position of an empathetic listener as argued by Felman and Laub. She becomes that someone who not only empowers the victim to talk about his/her traumatic past, but also one, who as a surrogate narrator, constructs for them an appropriate register to do so.

Kali Tal provides one of the most succinct definitions of the literature of trauma when she posits that someone who has lived through a traumatic experience or one who chooses to write about horror from a witness's perspective can both author this type of literature (Tal 17). This seems to be a perfect description of Yvonne Owuor's novel *Dust*, because Owuor creates "an aesthetic experience [...] a product of a literary decision" (Tal 116) to disclose some of the silenced atrocities in Kenyan society. If the "literature of trauma holds at its centre the reconstruction and recuperation of the traumatic experience, but it also actively engages in ongoing dialogue with the writing and representation of non-traumatised authors" (Tal 17), then, it can be argued that this intention has resonance with Owuor's writing in *Dust*.[1] This is because the chapter finds Tal's argument that literature of trauma not only reconstructs, but also recuperates the traumatic experience convincingly reflected in *Dust*. The two nouns in Tal's argument above – "reconstruction" and "recuperation" – are significant because of their implicit suggestion that fiction is a necessary therapeutic vehicle for the deconstruction and comprehension of individual or collective horror. This chapter concurs with Tal's argument that writing about trauma whether by a victim of and/or a witness to trauma is akin to a therapeutic dialogue.

This therapeutic dialogue is of utmost importance when one is reminded of Ruth Leys' postulation in *Trauma: a Genealogy* that "the central paradox of trauma: the traumatic event is etched in all its literality in the brain, but it is disassociated from the ordinary integration and thus unobtainable for conscious recollection" (239). The essence of Leys' argument is that trauma defies normal forms of articulation. Here, Leys is perhaps in agreement with Elaine Scarry, Cathy Caruth, and Anne Whitehead, who variously argue that because trauma destroys the linguistic resources of both the victim and witness and is incapable of transmission in normal registers, it is only in literary language that it finds seamless expression. In the words of Anne Whitehead, "trauma can be presented in a narrative, but only in a literary form which departs from conventional linear sequence of discourse" (6). If one were to agree with Caruth, Leys, and Whitehead that it is in literary texts that traumatic experiences find perfect forms of expression, then, Yvonne Adhiambo Owuor's novel *Dust* qualifies as an example of Kenyan literature of trauma. It is prudent to label *Dust* as an example of Kenyan literature of trauma because it neatly fits into the key parameters of trauma fiction as outlined by Caruth, Leys, Tal, and Whitehead. This is because its subject matter constitutes traumatic content and it is rendered in a manner that mimics articulation of trauma. This point is particularly underlined by *Dust's* disjointed, repetitive, fragmented, nonlinearity narrative posture, disruptive chronology, textual erasures, and silences.

Set in post-colonial Kenya, *Dust* is simultaneously a political and personal tale. While the text's reference of particularly violent episodes in Kenyan (colonial and post-independence) history characterized by assassinations, corruption, and disillusionment is central to its political/historical theme, its domestic story focuses on the suffering of a peripherally fictionalized Oganda family of four that include: Nyipir, Akai, Odidi, and Ajany. It is noteworthy to mention that the political and familial stories are intractably intertwined with the secrets of other characters like Hugh Bolton, Petrus Keah, and Ali Dida Hada. Using the wastelands of North Western Kenya as a backdrop to her novel, Owuor brilliantly deploys setting, the omniscient narrator, stream of consciousness, and a disjointed, repetitive, fragmented, nonlinearity and disruptive chronological plot to disclose the repressed experiences of various characters.

The novel opens with the brutal murder of Odidi Oganda on the eve of the Kenyan post-election violence of 2007/2008. Odidi's death acts as a catalyst that involuntarily opens the crevices of anguish and horror that the Ogandas have bottled up in their isolation from the rest of Kenya. It also brings the Ogandas and other characters whose lives are intertwined with their reality such as Isaiah Bolton, Ali Dida Hada, and Petrus Keah together. This does not only provide key information about the respective characters and their trauma, but also provides an insight into how widespread state-sponsored atrocities are in modern Kenya. Against the backdrop of the crumbling edifice of Wuoth Ogik – aptly named by Nyipir as 'where the journey ends' – Owuor's novel shines a light into the crumbling and tattered lives of its occupants. It also empowers and crafts a register for the inhabitants of Wouth Ogik to disclose their painful pasts despite their reluctance to do so. Their reluctance is perhaps brilliantly exhibited by Akai's fit of anguish and rage that is indexed by her threat to shoot Ajany and fleeing from home. Although different characters are haunted by experiences they are unwilling to disclose, this chapter explores how Akai and Nyipir are reluctantly persuaded by Ajany to unburden to her their violent past that plays out against the tapestries of Kenya's present-past. The revelation is painfully prised out of them thanks to Owuor's innovative narrative technique.

Although *Dust* discloses the traumatic experiences of characters like Akai and Nyipir, many Owuor scholars take the intersection between public tales of trauma and personal stories of suffering to read the text as a metaphor of political violence. For example, in his 2015 MA dissertation, Amos Boiyo Burkeywo argues that "*Dust* attempts to dig up the repressed memories through Nyipir and other characters by reflecting on Kenyan history. Memories of torture, violence, loss and hidden secrets haunt Nyipir" (16). He goes on to draw parallels between a traumatized nation and a suffering family. In many ways, Burkeywo's reading of *Dust* is persuasively illuminating. This is because Akai's and Nyipir's tales of horror are interwoven with horrific events in Kenyan history. This perhaps explains why Burkeywo seems to impute that Owuor allegorizes Nyipir's agency for the violent nation. While it is true that Nyipir's life intersects with important historical events in Kenyan public life – right from colonialism to post-independence – the construction of Nyipir as a metaphor of the Kenyan nation debuses him of his agency. Rather than read Nyipir metonymically, this chapter argues that his experiences of suffering can be focused upon to argue that Owuor uses fiction to empower peripheral subjects to articulate their suffering.

Burkeywo's allegorical reading of *Dust* dovetails neatly into Taiye Selasi's observations that *Dust* is novel about Kenya because it interrogates what Kenya is. Selasi goes on to argue that "Owuor tells her country's stories – and they are plural: urban, rural, Indian, English, Luo and Kikuyu – with bitter honesty" (np). For Selasi, *Dust* is a novel that documents the various types of Kenyan history. It is noteworthy that Selasi underscores the plurality of Kenyan histories. Indeed, many passages in the novel bear out the truth of this statement. That different Kenyas are brought to the fore in Owuor's novel is undisputed. This is because while the text offers glimpses into mainstream Kenyan characters such as Odidi's partner Musali, it also focuses on Kenyan periphery subjects such as Nyipir and his family. The multiple Kenyas and Kenyans are separated by geography: for example, the northern drylands separate the Ogandas from the rest of Kenya. However, the most obvious gulf between the different Kenyas is the indifferent and violent treatment of the citizens by the Kenyan state. This recalls Nyipir's warning to Odidi "the only [...] war you fight [...] is for what belongs to you. You can't live the songs of people who don't know your name" (Dust 10). Nyipir's evocation of fighting for what belongs to one scripts the binary of "us" and "them" at the core of the Kenyan histories that Selasi underscores.

The reading of *Dust* as a narrative of violence perpetrated by "them" against "us" is also signalled in the work of Sibi-Okumu, Tom Odhiambo, and Nelson Mlambo. Sibi-Okumu notes the recurrent trend in Kenyan writing that attempts to make sense of the unsettling Kenyan present by interrogating its past. He goes on to argue that *Dust* is an example of Kenyan writing that attempts to enlighten Kenyans about their traumatic past "through methodological and unbiased research and prepare[s] not only to tell [them] what happened but also to speculate on why it happened" (44). Although Sibi-Okumu's argument is anchored on the political assassinations that have dogged Kenyan public life since independence – and Owuor variously focuses on this topic in *Dust* – Sibi-Okumu's argument is applicable to all aspects of Kenyan history that the novel traces. Nyipir's witness of the murder of Aloys Kamau, or his participation in the disposal of corpses of freedom fighters as well as the massive poaching after independence are incidents that *Dust* documents. Therefore, Sibi-Okumu is persuasive in arguing that Owuor uses fiction to excavate the violent history of the Kenyan state.

The reading of *Dust* as a fictional excavation of Kenyan history is a theme taken by Tom Odhiambo in his reading of the text. Odhiambo argues that *Dust* brings to the surface the truth that Kenya is a divided country contrary to the mass-mediated campaigns that normalized violence on its own people for political expediency. He notes that *Dust* jolts Kenyans "back into reality; away from the songs of hope retailed on Kenyan TV, radio, newspapers, in churches, at rallies by politicians, in lecture halls and even by NGOs that are supposed to be auditing the delivery of goods and services by the government" (56). The essence of Odhiambo's argument in the above quotation is that Kenya operates under a dichotomous framework. On the surface, there exists the cosmetic 'beloved' country where the political and civil societies are variously engaged in civic duty. Underneath the gloss of public 'do good and feel good' is the real Kenya. It is this Kenya, Odhiambo argues, that Owuor brings to the surface in *Dust*. Odhiambo's premise is plausibly convincing when read with lens that magnify the different underhand state-sponsored shenanigans that are disclosed in the novel.

The centrality of the exposition of state-sponsored shenanigans is a trope taken up by Parselelo Kantai in his reading of *Dust*. For Kantai, the resonance of *Dust* lies in its exposition of familiar Kenyan tropes such as political assassination, and the silences and cover-ups that follow the respective untold tragic stories that have characterized the nation since the colonial period. He notes that the story of *Dust* is the "story of loss [...] of national silences in the face of secret violence. However, it is much more than that. It is a tragic story of a nation as experienced by a family that rejects and embraces its central myth" (np). In this regard, Kantai's reading of *Dust* echoes Odhiambo's analysis insofar as both scholars underscore the fact that *Dust* deconstructs the myth of Kenyan publicized histories as a beloved and peaceful country. Here, one is reminded of two events in *Dust* – the discovery of Hugh Bolton's skeleton in the red cave at Wouth Ogik and Ajany's reconstruction of the same Hugh Bolton's face from her memory of the portrait and skeleton in the guest house room in Nairobi for Isaiah Bolton. If one were to read these events of the plot as simultaneously unearthing and/or disclosing a past that many – Nyipir and Akai – would wish to remain buried, then, it can be argued that *Dust* is a novelistic exposure of a dark Kenyan history that many political and state actors in Kenya desire to keep buried.

The discussion above underlines the fact that a substantial number of Owuor scholars concentrate on the political theme of the novel, specifically on how *Dust* exhumes the tragic and violent history of the Kenyan nation. In many ways, this reading of *Dust* is comparable to the popular reading of Moses Isegawa's 2000 novel, *Abyssinian Chronicles*. This hypothesis is anchored on the similarity between Parselelo Kantai's, Tom Odhiambo's, Taiye Selasi's, and Sibi-Okumu's reading of *Dust*, on the one hand, and Andrew H. Armstrong's and Jacqui Jones' interpretation of *Abyssinian Chronicles*, on the other hand. Both Armstrong and Jones variously argue that Isegawa's juxtaposition of the national dictatorship under President Idi Amin with the household tyranny of Serenity and Padlock makes domestic abuse refract national annals of brutality. Uncannily, the same argument can be made for Owuor's text and its reading by Parselelo Kantai, Tom Odhiambo, Taiye Selasi, and Sibi-Okumu. The above-mentioned and similarly oriented critics demonstrate how the traumatic experiences of the Oganda household mirror or mimic the tragic and silenced bouts of national violence of the colonial and post-colonial Kenyan state.

However, it is important to note that *Dust* has not only elicited a political/historical reading. Scholars like Simon Lewis, Jalinda Schuerman-Chianda, and Nelson Mlambo and to a certain extent Taiye Selasi have paid attention to the craftsmanship of the novel. For example, Simon Lewis does not read the complex and complicated narrative stance in the novel as an allegorical political thriller that reconfigures a family saga to provide insights into the historical quest of the Kenyan nation. On the contrary, he argues that the merger of personal narrative, political thriller, historical documentary, and quest motifs transforms *Dust* into a seminal Kenyan text because of Owuor's use of language and style in a manner that ensures that every page "exudes the harsh sounds and powerful smells of Kenya [...] the dazzle of the desert sky makes you almost squint as you read" (np). It can be argued that the above passage underlines sensory and poetic aspects of Owuor's writing in *Dust*. Therefore, it is plausible to agree with Lewis that the pulsating and sensuous language that moves readers to hear, see, and feel the temporal and spatial corporeality of the characters is what makes the text resonate with many of its readers.

The life-evoking character of Owuor's diction is an aspect that Jalida Scheuerman-Chianda gestures to as well. Although her reading acknowledges the centrality of the political theme that is an attractive trajectory in scholarly engagement with *Dust*, she also highlights the charms of the novel because of Owuor's narrative technique. This is particularly an accurate description of how Owuor's craftsmanship transported Scheuerman-Chianda into a nostalgic past:

> in an instant, Yvonne had transported me back to that day when I arrived for the first time in Kalolol at the age of 6. The dust in every nook and cranny of my body, the searing heat, the sudden burst of wind, the naked yet ancient and majestic landscape. (np)

Although Scheurman-Chianda's nostalgia in the above passage is temporal and spatial in character, it can be argued that it also symbolizes an insertion into Kenya's troubled history. The chapter agrees with Scheuerman-Chianda insofar as Owuor's narrative technique captures the essence of the setting of the novel. Owuor's ability to capture the naked visceral and pulsating majesty of the setting of the novel is perhaps one of the many things that make her novel resonate with many readers.

It can be argued that the historical lessons and testimonies of violent public affairs that *Dust* brilliantly explores and exposes can only make sense in the quintessentially Kenyan context. Owuor manages this feat by ensuring that the streets of Nairobi or the drylands of Turkana are quintessentially Kenyan in character for the novel to unravel what

Scheuerman-Chianda calls a tale of "death, love, despair, hope, discovery, betrayal, forgiveness, stolen lives and histories, identities and new beginnings" (np). It is perhaps the brilliance of Owuor's eclectic style that prompts Taiye Selasi to argue that *Dust* is a novel for "only readers who truly love books – books full to brimming with imagery – will appreciate the magic Owuor has made of the classic nation-at-war novel" (np) She goes on to note that "with splintered lyricism, she [Owuor] tells the story of the Oganda family" (np). An example of what Taiye calls the lyricism and profound imagery of Owuor's novel is the two-word refrain of the prologue "Odidi runs" (*Dust* 3). The afterthought-like quality of the narrative – highlighted by the oscillation between the past and the present – cohere brilliantly with the flashback and disjointed narrative texture of the novel to mirror the novel's subject matter.

Other readers of the novel also pick on the brilliance of the narrative style that Selasi underscores in her review. Critics such as Tanzanian novelist, Adbulrazak Gurnah, Ron Charles, and the Ugandan poet Juliane Okot Bitek, similarly highlight the significance of an appropriate narrative technique to unravel the subject matter that Owuor deals with in *Dust*. For example, Gurnah focuses on the importance of the metaphor of dust to Owuor's narrative intention in the novel. He argues that "dust and intermittent floods are made into a metaphor: water turns dust into mud, which can then be shaped and sculpted, just as dispersed histories are brought together by memory and stories" (np). The chapter agrees with Gurnah's analysis of how a metaphorical understanding of the title of the novel greatly contributes to the explication of its major theme. If one were to agree with Gurnah's idea of the circularity of the dust metaphor – dust begets mud that transforms memory into stories – then, Ajany's literal bringing to life through sculpturing her grandfather, uncle, and Hugh Bolton is a good example of how fiction can be deployed to excavate traumatic tales.

The preceding discussion highlights two recurrent motifs in the scholarly work on Owuor's *Dust*. One trajectory, pushed by scholars such as by Parselelo Kantai, Tom Odhiambo, Taiye Selasi, and Sibi-Okumu argue that Owuor uses the tragic tale of a family's experiences to symbolize the Kenyan history of violence and violation. Another school of thought, composed of critics such as Simon Lewis, Jalinda Schuerman-Chianda, Nelson Mlambo, and to a certain extent Taiye Selasi, acknowledge the significance of *Dust*'s political/historical theme, but go further to unveil the beauty of its narrative texture. The meeting point of both camps is the fact that the subject matter of *Dust* precludes the narrative style that Owuor deploys. Here, one is reminded of Taiye Selasi's statement that "this is form as content, a text in the shape of its subject matter" (np). The chapter returns to this characterization of *Dust* later. However, it argues that the resonance of *Dust* perhaps arises in its seamless connection between content and form. In other words, while the subject matter of *Dust* demands the narrative posture that Owuor employs, it is also true to argue that it is perhaps this kind of narrative structure that is well-suited for the story narrated in *Dust*. Granted that these and similarly oriented scholars sampled above provide insightful and plausible readings of *Dust*. The chapter argues that, like all great texts, *Dust* is open to a variety of readings. While some critics can approach the text from a political/historical perspective, others can read the text from an aesthetic point of view. This chapter demonstrates that it can also be productively read as a trauma narrative.

Of Mothers' Love and Pain: Writing Akai's Trauma in *Dust*

Granted that a political/historical and aesthetic reading of *Dust* is persuasive and convincing, chapter argues that the text opens itself to alternative readings. A critic can anchor his/her analysis on the novel's fragmentary structure and multiple narrative angles to read it as an example of trauma fiction. This is because its style mimics that of exposé of traumatic content. This thesis is in part supported by Taiye Selasi's characterization of *Dust* as a text whose form replicates its content. To put it differently, *Dust* is an example of a text, which is shaped by its content. As an example of Kenyan literature of trauma, this chapter argues that *Dust's* narrative technique – the use of flashback, disjointed and fragmented plot, stream of consciousness, elision, omniscient focalization, repetition, and silence – is a register that Owuor crafts for her traumatized characters to unravel their repressed pain. In the words of Juliane Okot Bitek, *Dust* works only for those who can decipher its silence since it is "inaccessible to those who cannot read the coded language that erupts in the political arena" (np). The code or special language of *Dust* that Bitek signals above is comparable to the special register required to disclose traumatic memory. It is important to note that the revelation is triggered by the sudden and violent death of Odidi.

Although Odidi's death triggers the disclosure of the repressed memories of different characters, it is that of his parents that stands out. The family secrets and festering wounds that Nyipir and Akai had successful sealed are ripped open. It is important to note that although Akai and Nyipir need to disclose their horror to heal, they do this reluctantly. For example, when Ajany and Nyipir arrive in Wuoth Ogik with Odidi's body the omniscient narrator observes that:

> Akai recoils, tears herself away. Her eyes are thin slits, her nostrils flare, and when Ajany looks again, her mother is still, steady point with a finger on a trigger and a smile on her face. Click-clack. Selector set to burst. Clear gaze. Gun pointed at heart, a glint from the barrel like light on a pathologist's scalpel. Certainty. Akai will pull the trigger if Ajany moves in her direction again. (Dust 37)

This passage raises several questions in the readers' mind. Does Odidi's death drive his mother mad? Is this a bizarre manifestation of parental favouritism? Is it a demonstration of Akai's profound hatred for Ajany, given that she had previously thrown the sickly Ajany to the vultures? Is Akai's temporary insanity a consequence of her violent past? Does the current loss trigger the memory of previously traumatic loss? The above questions suggest that Akai's escape into the desert gestures either to her unwillingness to accept the death of her son or her aversion, call it phobia, to a previous loss that she believes is being re-enacted in Odidi's death.

Akai's strange and violent reaction to loss – especially, if the loss in question triggers recall of an equally devastating loss in the past as the death of Odidi inevitably does, reminds us, as Jeremiah A. Schumm, Ana-Maria Vranceanu, and Stevan E. Hobfall argue in *Ties that Bind: Resources Caravans and Losses Among Traumatised families*, that "loss initiated in childhood can snowball into resource loss spirals later in life, leaving individuals ill-equipped to handle [new] challenges" (42). If the essence of the above quotation is that concealed past trauma can re-emerge with catastrophic consequences later in life, then, it can be argued that the previous loss triggers Akai's manic actions. The chapter suggests that Akai's catastrophic loss that she has repressed for long is the tragic loss of her twins in the desert.

Owuor uses flashback, ellipsis, fragmented structure, omniscient narrator, and stream of consciousness techniques to bring to light this repressed episode in Akai's life. The eight-page passage (Dust 344–351) in which Akai narrates to Ajany this painful episode in her past reminds us of Taiye Selasi's argument that the non-linear and fragmented plot of *Dust* resembles the movements of a human mind.[2] It is significant that this disclosure comes towards the end of the narrative. It can be read as a disclosure of a painful past that Akai has been reluctant to share, but which she is forced to confront at the end of the narratives to get closure. The confession starts with the passage: "Akai tells Ajany that Hugh had pushed her onto a boat with an El Molo guardsman who tied a sheep to the prow and gave Akai fifty shillings. 'You come?' she [had begged Hugh who had shouted back] after baby" (Dust 346). Two issues stand out about this passage.

First, is the cross-purpose technique at the core of the exchange between Akai and Hugh Bolton. While Bolton is getting rid of his pregnant Kenyan lover, Akai naively reads it as a brief separation from her lover before the grand reunion after the delivery of the pregnancy. Second, the centrality of the omniscient narrator signals how painful the recollection is to Akai. This passage is painful for Akai because she cannot believe her naivety and/or wishful thinking to the effect that "the child's father is a senior officer who was preparing his army to come for her" (Dust 346). What is remarkable about these passages is the dominance of the short curt sentences and matter-of-fact tone. They give the impression of the speaker spitting them out impatiently, as if speaking is a burden s/he must bear with or a load she must dispense with as fast as possible. It can be argued that Akai's tone and the quality of her sentences in this and later passages are determined by the painful content she is forced to unravel. She is relating the bitterly painful facts of her life, which she naturally would like to repress.

When Akai's wishful bubble burst – Hugh Bolton does not come to claim her after the delivery of the twins – she and her family become the laughing stock of the group. To save face, her stepfather painfully discards the Akai part of the family: "Akai's beloved stepfather become a laughingstock among the elders [...] this man who had fought almost to death anyone who had tried to do so before [...] he moves Akai and her mother out, to save face. He did so in tears" (Dust 347). This passage underscores Akai's pain because she perceives herself as the cause of her own and familial shame. In a world where patriarchy and masculinity coalesce around a rejection of any form of weakness and emotionality among men, it is not only devastating to see one's beloved father and elder reduced to tears, but also heart-wrenching to know you are the cause of this pain. It can be argued that the duality of painful realization accentuates Akai's pain.

Akai's pain is compounded by the loss of her twins under circumstance she is helpless in averting. It is important to note that when Akai gives birth to "Ewoi, the boy. Etir, the girl", (Dust 347) the midwife declares that it is a "terrible portent" (Dust 347). If one understands the import of the midwife's statement as a euphemism for killing the twins because twins are taboo in this community, then, one can understand Akai's threat "'touch them, I'll break your neck" (Dust 347). Why does Akai disregard the midwife's warning that the twins were a "terrible portent?" Why is she ready to protect them at whatever cost? It can be argued that Akai's defiance in the above passages is the manifestation of a loving mother ready to do anything to protect her children. It might also be argued that this is a case of deluded and wishful thinking – she hopes that Hugh Bolton would reclaim her and the children so that they can live happily thereafter. Given the anguish that she and her family have endured, she sees the twins as the price she should pay for a happy future. It can be argued that the twins are also a prized compensation for her suffering.

Whatever her motivation, the twins do not bring bliss to Akai's life. Because of an argument over the twins, Akai and her mother part on bitter terms. When her mother sends her off to die (Dust 348) across the desert amid a debilitating drought, Akai lives her worst nightmare. *Dust's* depiction of Akai's attempt to save her twins in the desert reminds us of Anne Whitehead's argument that "trauma emerges as that which, at the very moment of its reception, registers as a non-experience, causing conventional epistemologies to falter" (5). Akai's suffering in the desert is comparable to Whitehead's argument that trauma manifests as an incommunicable "non-experience". It is unsurprising that Owuor deploys an innovative register to render the depicted trauma interpretable and legible. Owuor's register – characterized by Akai's one-word sentences, ellipsis, stream of consciousness, matter-of-fact tone, omniscient narration, and prolonged silences – is a grammar suitable for the traumatized subject to sidestep the overwhelming effect of her pain that makes it not only difficult to articulate, but also impossible to express by means of conventional discursive methods what she has lived through.

The oscillation between the omniscient narrator and first-person narrator illustrates the thesis above. This is because the narrative style mimics the narration of the horror and suffering that this lonely woman with two children undergoes in the harsh environment of the Northern Kenyan desert. While the omniscient narrator fills in the gory details of the suffering, Akai in testimonial-like, one-worded sentences and poignant silences highlights the pain.

> After that, she strapped her crying children, one to her back, and the other to her front. Unthinking, she hunted for liquid, pursuing mirages, trusting that at least one would yield water.
> Water
> She scrambled into dried-up water holes. Her breast milk dried up. The sun seared Ewoi's and Etir's skin red. They were dry-mouthed, thirsty.
> 'One morning they stopped crying'
> Akai's voice is cracking.
> Ajany's eyes are extra wide. (Dust 348)

This passage reminds us of the fact that writers "[bear] witness" to and allow readers to "[face the] horror" (Douglas 149) of the awful subject matter portrayed in the texts. Why does Owuor use the omniscient narrator, first-person focalization, painful vocabulary, short sentences, and poignant silences to depict Akai's suffering? An attempt to answer this question recalls Shoshan Felman and Dori Laub's argument that "the victim's narrative – the very process of bearing witness to massive trauma – does indeed begin with someone who testifies to an absence, to an event that has not yet come into existence, despite the overwhelming nature of the reality, of its occurrence" (57). If as Felman and Laub argue, listening to the victim's testimony is the starting point of understanding their trauma, then, this passage is significant in understanding the pain that Akai has gone through. It can be further argued that until that moment when Akai with the aid of the omniscient narrator puts into words her hitherto suppressed experience, that we understand what she has suffered.

The passage reveals that Akai suffered both physical and emotional anguish. While her thirst, hunger, and fatigue constitute her physical pain, her emotional pain arises from her impotence and helplessness to save her twins. Although she does everything in her power, including searching for water everywhere in the desert, preserving the camel meat and even attempting to bite through her skin to draw blood for the twins, she loses them. It is not only the horror of losing one's children, but watching them die and/or leaving them to die because you are helplessness that underlines her horror. The inordinate nature of Akai's trauma is accentuated by the involuntary reactions of Ajany to her mother's tale. The "extra wide" (Dust 348) eyes, the chattering teeth, the "Pinpricks of darkness [...] Revulsion. Fear. Terror" (Dust 350–351) are adjectives that emphasize Akai's trauma. If the listeners to a half-a-century-old story are powerfully affected and/or react with revulsion, fear and terror, then, it can be plausibly argued that Akai's experiences were profoundly traumatic.

In conclusion, if Ajany is a surrogate for the reader, her reaction to her mother's tale recalls Shoshan Felman and Dori Laub's fear of voyeuristic exploitation of the pain of others (Felman and Laub 4) or LaCapra's warning that a reader may "become a surrogate victim who appropriates the victim's voice or suffering" (135). The chapter argues that Akai's story evokes the suggested emotional responses. As readers, we feel we cannot empathize enough and are therefore in danger of a voyeuristic consumption of her pain. The tale of a mother who leaves one of her twins (Ewoi) for hyenas and another (Etir) at the base of the hill only to be saved by nature – "rain had fallen in the northern hills. The desert used to be a lake. A flash flood raced through a *laga* and dragged Akai downstream" is truly traumatic (Dust 349). Despite her miraculous survival and assumed fearlessness when she tells Hugh Bolton "My father wants his bride price" (Dust 349), it is obvious to readers that her experience has deeply scarred her.

The chapter argues that in unveiling Akai's suffering, Owuor is guided by Kelly Oliver's postulation that witnessing works of trauma help to "ameliorate the trauma particular to othered subjectivity" (Oliver 7). This is true of *Dust* because of Owuor's textual and linguistic resources that she deploys to articulate Akai's trauma. These are techniques that mimic the "forms and symptoms" of trauma in their disjointedness, "repetition and indirection" (Whitehead 3). Here, the chapter concurs with Ron Charles's argument that not only does "Owuor's style evince a rare and brave choice: to feel and to make her readers feel, to strand us from our intelligence", (np) but it does also help us understand what it means to be a mother and a woman like Akai to watch your children die. It can be argued that readers are moved to empathize with Akai – a woman who loves and suffers for and/or because of Hugh Bolton. Owuor ensures that the lives of Kenyan women, like Akai, who are exploited variously and later discarded by colonialists become important topics of debate in the Kenyan public sphere.

"Do It for the Father of the Nation": Scripting Torture in *Dust*

Stating that Nyipir is "a good man", his colleagues ask him to take the oath, if not for his own sake, at least for the sake of the father of the nation, but most definitely to not put them in the position where they should have to torture him into compliance. I find this passage a convoluted manifestation of a diabolic justification of atrocities committed on behalf of the state. This is because of the diabolic logic that places the responsibility of the victim's pain on his conscience. My exploration of how Owuor discloses Nyipir's trauma is anchored by her spotlighting the terrible criminalization of individual morality, especially if it is deemed to endanger the state. While Akai is a victim of colonial, racialized, and patriarchal privilege, her husband Nyipir is a victim of a scared and paranoid post-colonial state. Nyipir, whom Abdulrazak Gurnah describes as an "old-world dapper in slightly shabby 1970s coat and 1950s brown leather fedora-never [whose apparel] speaks of his early incarnation of a thief, gun runner, rebel and patriot", (np) is a taciturn patriarch who has witnessed, suffered, and repressed various atrocities perpetrated by and on him during both the colonial and postcolonial times. The quest to reunite with his brother and father, who had never returned from Burma, sets him on a tragic trajectory with the Kenyan colonial and post-colonial state. The nostalgia and longing for the lost father and brother turn into a nightmare that Nyipir has successfully repressed in his mind.

This is poignantly captured in a stream of consciousness passage in which Nyipir cogitates on whether his "dying had started long ago. Long before the murder of the prophets named Pio, Tom, Argwings, Ronald, Kungu, Josiah, Ouko, Mbae" (Dust 23). Although the above list of political assassinations lends credence to a political/historical reading of the novel, I suggest that the verb "dying" – by connoting cessation, despair, and disillusionment – perfectly captures Nyipir's melancholy that symbolizes his traumatic experiences. This thesis is supported by Nyipir's confession that he was "Kenyan once" (Dust 123). The melancholic renunciation of his nationality signals a disillusioned and disenchanted character. Nyipir's disenchantment is perhaps because of the inordinate suffering he has endured and the realization that as a victim, he will forever be silenced by the impunity of the state. Resigned to not talk about the macabre work of burying the victims of state violence in gunnysacks, witness to the murder of Aloys Kamau (Dust 166–168), and a host of other atrocities perpetrated on behalf of the state, Nyipir transforms from the state's poster boy to its villain when he refuses to take the oath after the assassination of Tom Mboya in 1969.

This chapter refers to the torture he is subjected to, at the hands of the state he had dedicated his life to serve, as an example of an impossibly traumatic experience to disclose. This inordinate pain blocked out of Nyipir's psyche until the closing pages of the novel whereupon the prompting of Ajany reminds us of Peter Tirop Sematei's argument that traumatized characters in Kenyan fiction choose either "therapeutic amnesia [or] traumatic memory" (92). Simatei's dichotomous choices undergird the matrix that Owuor deploys in *Dust*. The alteration between repression and final disclosure is cognizant of the idea that "memory [is] a burden to the extent that the state-enforced amnesia criminalises remembrance" (Sematei 92). Like all traumatized Kenyan fictional characters, Nyipir has two options, namely, to feign "therapeutic amnesia or traumatic memory". Aware of the pain that the state can inflict and its omnipresence, it can be argued that Nyipir prefers to block out his experiences from revealing. This is because he knows that attracting the attention of the Kenyan state comes with dire and painful consequences. It can also be argued that his silence is a way of protecting his family from the pain he is aware the state can inflict on them if it feels threatened by the disclosure of its secrets. This perhaps explains why he gives AK-47s to both his children and he is mortified when one holiday, Odidi returns his AK-47 claiming he does not need its protection. Nyipir's cryptic response that his son cannot sing songs of people who do not know his name, in one way underlines the dichotomy of 'them' against 'us' that is perhaps informed by the injustice that Nyipir suffers at the hands of the state.

The deep-seated and ingrained fear to relive the horror he had once been subjected to by the Kenyan state is painfully prised out of Nyipir's memory when Owuor deploys a cocktail of narrative techniques to bring to light what happened to Nyipir in those police cells in 1969. The narrative structure of the exposé recalls Nelson Mlambo's description of *Dust's* style as "enriched by the fragmentary manner of writing which captures the hallucinatory sequences of a memory haunted by history's wounds, hopes, thirstiness and aspiration" (2). This is an apt description of the plot of *Dust*, especially when the passages where Owuor discloses Nyipir's torture are taken into consideration. Mlambo's description of *Dust's* plot as fragmented and hallucinatory is given credence in the selected passages partly because of the oscillation between four narrative points of view – Nyipir's and Keah's recollection of what happened to the former in 1969, omniscient narration, stream of consciousness explanations, as well as Nyipir's first-person occasional interruptions that mimic a painful exposé of traumatizing content. This reminds us of Geoffrey Hartman's postulation that on the poetic or figurative level, trauma fiction "may correspond to two types of cognition" – the event (content) and the symptoms of the event (form) (536). This is an apt description of the content of Nyipir's tale because of techniques used in its unveiling mimic disclosure of traumatic content.

The various points of focalization help accentuate or put into perspective Nyipir's traumatic tragedy. The disclosure of Nyipir's torture is crafted as a classic Aristotelian reversal, namely his transformation from a poster child of the new Kenyan nation to its enemy. This reversal is underscored by the passage: "in that arena of spectacle, Nyipir Og'anda had led the cavalcade, lugging a smaller red, black, green and white flag while riding on a high-stepping black horse" (Dust 24). This passage depicts him as an insider of the new Kenyan state. This is because he is entrusted with the symbol of the new state, namely the flag that he un-furls on independence night. Conversely, one can read this passage as Nyipir's vote of confidence or belief in the ideals that the birth of the Kenyan nation symbolizes. Therefore, it is understandable that he feels anger and impotent despair when the national project starts to unravel. It is not so much the assassination of nationalists like Tom Mboya that triggers the despondency, but rather the sense of betrayal at the hands of the regime that he finds unbearable.

Nyipir's metamorphosis – from optimism to despondence, poster child to enemy of the Kenyan state – is enunciated in *Dust* by omnisciently nar-rated commentaries, stream of consciousness explanatory passages, and direct first-person cryptic interjections. I read his repeatedly interjected refrain "Nineteen sixty-nine was a very hard year" (Dust 300) in two ways. First, it is a deceptively curt remark that seeks to dismiss or draw the reader's attention away from or forfeit any elaboration of the trauma it acknowledges. Second, it is an apt factual description of his inordi-nate suffering, especially given its matter-of-fact tone and construction. Therefore, the question that this declaration seeks is, what made 1969 a hard year? To get a possible answer to this question, one needs to con-sider the passage: "my turn came. Nineteen sixty-nine. When Tom died. They wanted me to drink their oath. Couldn't" (Dust 299). The matter-of-fact tone of the passage – underlined by the short factual sentences – not only carries a sense of finality and closure, but it also seems to suggest that Nyipir suffers because of principle. It may be true that Nyipir re-fused to take the oath on principle – the assassination of Tom Mboya by the Kenyan state was something he would neither forgive nor forget. However, it is plausible to argue that he refuses to take the oath because the vow evokes past horrors associated with another atrocity linked to oath-taking: the death of Aloys Kamau to which he was complicit.

This puny and ineffective stand to mourn and recognize people like Aloys Kamau as more than mere statistical footnotes in Kenyan regimes of violence places Nyipir's life in jeopardy. The case in point is the pas-sage: "should he speak of nights soaked in water-urine-blood, darkness and nothing? Could he give voice to the terror of nonexistence, dark-ness's invasion, how it penetrated the soul and never left" (Dust 299). Nyipir's traumatic experiences are scripted by the rhetorical questions, hesitant verbs, and bloodcurdling imagery. While the auxiliary verbs "could" and "should" signal his reluctance to recall the past, the maca-bre imagery offers a glimpse into the horror he is reluctant to disclose.

It can also be argued that the auxiliary verbs are contemplative – they mimic Nyipir's struggle to either disclose his experience or get an appropriate register to do so. This reminds us of Anne Whitehead's argument that trauma narrative adopts an experimental literary form that "does not succumb to closure and coherence, but retains within itself the traces of traumatic disruption and discontinuity" (142). If Whitehead's central thesis is that the best narrative structure of disclosing trauma is one that mimics its symptoms, then, Owuor effectively succeeds in unravelling Nyipir's traumatic past by her brilliant use of contemplative digression and ellipsis. These techniques cohere with punctuated silences, stream of consciousness, and omniscient narration to mimic the victim hinting at, apprehensive of, but ultimately failing to muster the courage and a language to disclose his experiences of horror.

This thesis is given credence by the passage where both stream of consciousness and omniscient focalization cohere to disclose the inordinate torture Nyipir is subjected.

> 'Akai?' said his peer, an officer who had trained with him in Kiganjo, who beat his body and toyed with his testicles. Creeping, crawling shame. He cannot tell Ajany that he had wailed, '*Unisamehe!*' Mercy! Can't describe the ways of losing faith. Can't speak of dread when he knew he had lost control of his death. Violence had pierced his skin, broken teeth and bones, until he could tell who a person was simply by the intensity of rage in a touch. They had pointed a gun at his head. *Click, click, click, click, click, click.* He fell, slithered on his belly like a snake, a trail of bowel-loosened muck stained his trousers, the floor. Shit, urine, sweat, blood, tears, and shame. '*Af-f-ande, n-n-naomba un-ni-nisamehe.*' I beg you, forgive me. '*Nihurumie.*' Have mercy. (Dust 300 emphasis in the original)

The oscillation between the omniscient narrator and the stream of consciousness is instructive in demonstrating the difficulty of testimonial narratives. While the stream of consciousness informs us of what Nyipir cannot disclose to his daughter, the omniscient narrator provides the gory details of the torture that had been inflicted on Nyipri for refusing to take the oath. The kind of torture that Nyipir is subjected to explains why he cannot tell his daughter at this point in the narrative, but also why it has taken him over 50 years since the act to even think of or contemplate what had happened to him. To comprehend the intensity of the torture, it is instructive to pay attention to the diction of the omniscient narrator. The casualness of the torture is captured in the nonchalant diction of his peer who 'beats' his body and 'toys' with his testicles. The diction reduces and makes acceptable, if not mundane, a painful and embarrassing act. By reducing torture to child-like play, devoid of any emotion despite the excruciating pain the victim feels, Owuor accentuates the suffering that Nyipir has endured at the hands of the state. Furthermore, by underlining the fact that his colleague performs the torture, Owuor stresses how commonplace torture has become. Its familiarity that verges on the mendacity belies its viciousness.

Equally significant are the adjectives that Owuor deploys to depict Nyipir's reaction to the torture. The fear-provoking expressions like "creeping, crawling", the stuttering and italicized Swahili expressions such as *"unisamehe, af-f-fande, n-n-naomba, un-nu-nisamehe"*, nouns like 'mercy' and pain-inducing verbs like "pierced, broken, slithered" and grimy adjectives like a "trail of bowel-loosened muck" usefully depict the horror of Nyipir's torture. These and related phrases and words work to underscore the ghoulish intensity of the pain to which he is subjected. For example, the Swahili expressions, which translate as 'forgive me, boss/sir and I am begging', coming from an obviously proud patriarch, like Nyipir signal shame induced by pain. Perhaps it is the shame and not the anticipated pain of reliving a horrific past that explains Nyipir's reluctance to disclose to Ajany his suffering. For how can a man burden a daughter with such horrific knowledge? The intensity of the beating that drives Nyipir to cry out reminds us of Elaine Scarry's description of torture as the totality of pain (qtd in Harpham 206). To survive this kind of excessive pain, Nyipir must either cry out as he does or construct an inviolable space in his mind that the pain cannot penetrate. This is perhaps a reasonable explanation of why he fails to tell Ajany what had happened to him in 1969. Silence, it can be argued becomes that inviolable space that Nyipir can go to protect himself and his loved ones from the memory of torture.

It can also be argued that the stuttering and/or stammering quality of Nyipir's expressions in this passage mimic not only the intense pain he is forced to recall, but also the absence of a register to articulate it. Owuor's diction aims to imitate the debilitating impact of pain on language or the inadequacy of language to describe pain. This reminds us of Elaine Scarry's seminal argument that trauma destroys language and to speak about trauma is to use a primordial language – the cry, which in the case of Nyipir is a stutter. Relatedly, the adjectives of sloth and/ or filth show how torture dehumanizes the victim. The dehumanization, which in the above passage is handwritten in filth and sloth, becomes a licence to torture and to maim. If the victim is othered by his broken body that is covered in human excretion, then, the tormentor does not only have complete power to do whatever he wants, but he is also absolved from any moral obligation to the victim. This is because the victim has ceased to be a human being who can evoke empathy and restraint. Therefore, the omniscient narrator's disclosure becomes a struggle and commitment to speak in "a voice that is paradoxically released through the wound" (Caruth 2).

In conclusion, it can be argued that Owuor allows us to imagine the depravity that drives tormentors like Petrus Keah to jokingly refer to themselves as – "mentors of delinquent citizens" (Dust 300). It is obvious that the delinquent in Keah's remark in the above passage refers to his victims like Nyipir, the people he drives into depressing conditions. This nonchalant impersonality and brutality allow Owuor to juxtapose physical and psychological torture in this section of her narrative to provide a comprehensive exploration of the atrocities perpetrated by the modern Kenyan state. The comprehensive depiction of Nyipir's torture and depravation resonates with Scarry's concept of "the totality of pain" which (she argues) is "world-destroying" (qtd in Harpham 206). While Nyipir's pleas gesture to the desire to stop the pain as a way of regaining the world he has lost to pain, the unconcerned, jolly torturers and the animal-like status that Nyipir is reduced to reminds one of Scarry's truism that there has "never been an intelligent argument on behalf of torture" (qtd in Harpham 206). This not only evokes our empathy, but also makes us see the monstrosity of the Kenyan state.

This reminds us of Achille Mbembe's argument in "Necropolitics" (2003) that the state has the power to decide who lives and who dies. Mbembe's argument is demonstrated in *Dust* because Nyipir is clearly marked as one who must die. In the eyes of Petrus Keah and the other torturers at the police station, Nyipir is less than a human being who must be crushed without any consequences. It is perhaps because he has been marked as someone who must die that when he survives, Nyipir does not have a vocabulary to describe what had happened to him. Therefore, his cryptic understatement "Nineteen sixty-nine was a very hard year" is an oblique acknowledgement of the pain to which he has been subjected. It can be argued that this simple sentence allows Owuor to fashion an appropriate register for her traumatized victim to disclose his experiences. This profundity relies on her dexterity and subtlety in the reconstruction of the Kenyan state in a manner that accords with Foucault's concept of the murderous function of the state: "the condition for the acceptability of putting to death" (228) as eloquently scripted in Nyipir's experiences. The actions of the state signal a sense of apprehension for the lives directly under its control – the lives we are forced to fear for and concern ourselves with in this powerful story. It is perhaps Nyipir's resilience to survive or the impersonally diabolic capacity of the state to destroy its real or imaginary enemies that turn his torturer – Petrus Keah – into his saviour.

Conclusion

On the surface, *Dust* closes with a semblance of normality, namely, that both Akai and Nyipir have survived their respective ordeals and have consequently raised a respectable family of an engineer-turned-gangster and an incredible artist. Underneath the feel-good Kenyan story lies the struggles of the respective characters to come to terms with their horrific experiences. In writing *Dust*, it can be argued that Owuor not only gives her characters a register and a platform to disclose their past, but also her writing acts as a testimonial outlet for Kenyan victims of atrocities to reveal their suffering. This makes *Dust* a memorial or a form of public mourning of the victims of the Kenyan state. Owuor's writing recovers such victims from mere statistical footnotes to beings whose experiences matter in the public sphere; Akai might have solicited a willing Nyipir to kill and dispose of the body of her tormentor and Nyipir may have been aided to escape by Petrus Keah (Dust 301). However, the novel underscores the fact that their lives are irrevocably damaged by what they have gone through. This is because they cannot unsee or unlive their experience. The case in point is Nyipir's impotence because of the torture. Keah's pieces of advice that *"amnesia is also medicine"* (Dust 301 emphasis in the original) and that Nyipir must run and think of "forgetfulness, and how to create it" (Dust 301) are not a panacea for post-traumatic recovery. By writing *Dust* and crafting a voice and register for Akai and Nyipir to reveal their traumatic experiences, Owuor underlines the veracity of Judith Lewis Herman's argument that "remembering and telling about a terrible event are the prerequisites both for the restoration of the social order, and for the healing of the victims" (1). I agree with Herman's argument because Owuor's narration of Akai's and Nyipir's suffering is therapeutic both to society and the individual characters. This is because Ajany and Isaiah Bolton, to whom the stories are narrated here, represent a society that must come to terms with its violent past to heal. Ajany's and Isaiah Bolton's comprehension and empathy for Akai and Nyipir is an acknowledgement of their unmerited suffering. This is possible because *Dust* "separately or simultaneously [helps us to] see, hear, smell, taste and touch the world of the [traumatized] characters" (Ferguson 1). However, Nyipir's question as to how one survives what a person like him has gone through defies easy answers. Whereas Keah proposes amnesia as a tested therapy, Nyipir's and Akai's cases demonstrate that the physical wounds can heal, but the scarred psyche cannot. However, as much as opening about the past is terribly painful, *Dust* underlines the paradox of trauma, namely, that while it defies conventional forms of disclosure, it desires articulation for its victims to survive.

Notes

1 I find Tal's main argument of the dual construction of trauma narrative, namely the intersection between authorship – autobiographical and fictional rendition of such tales – and the utility of literature of trauma convincing. While it could be argued that the utility of literature of trauma plays a pivotally and significantly liberatory function in the public sphere, its authorship is equally important because it acts as bedrock of collective memory.

2 Selasi argues that *"Dust* moves as the human mind moves, forward and backward, incoherent, indulgent, lingering on the light on a tree, sliding into mucky reverie".

Works Cited

Armstrong, H. Andrew. "Narrative and the Re-ci[r]ding of Cultural Memory in Moses Isegawa's *Abyssinian Chronicles* and *Snakepit.*" *Journal of African Cultural Studies* 21.2 (2009): 127–143.

Burkeywo, Boiyo Amos. *Narrating Kenyan History Through Fiction in Yvonne Owuor's Dust.* M.A. Dissertation. University of Nairobi.

Caruth, Cathy. *Unclaimed Experience: Trauma, Narrative, and History.* Baltimore: John Hopkins University Press, 1996.

Charles Ron. "Review: Dust by Yvonne Adhiambo Owuor." *The Washington Post* 4 February 2014. www.thewashington post.com.

Douglas, Kate. "Translating Trauma: Witnessing Bom Bali." *ARIEL: A Review of International English Literature* 39.1–2 (2008): 147–165.

Felman, Shoshana, and Laub, Dori. *Testimony: Crises of Witnessing in Literature, Psychoanalysis, and History.* London: Routledge, 2002.

Ferguson, Christine. "Sensational Dependence: Prosthesis and Affect in Dickens and Braddon." *Literature Interpretation Theory* 19 (2008): 1–25.

Foucault, Michel. *The Birth of Biopolitics: Lectures at the College de France (1978–1979).* Ed. Michel Sinellart. Trans. Graham Burchell. Basingstoke: Palgrave Macmillan, 2008.

Gurnah, Abdulrazak. "Dust by Yvonne Adhiambo Owuor Review – A Complex Vision of Kenya." *The Guardian* 19 March 2015. www.theguardian.com.

Harpham, Geoffrey. "Elaine Scarry and the Dream of Pain." *Salmagundi* 130/131 (2001): 202–234.

Jones, Jacqui. "Traversing the Abyss: Moses Isegawa: An Interview and Commentary." *English in Africa* 27.2 (2000): 85–102.

Hartman, Geoffrey. "On Traumatic Knowledge and Literary Studies." *New Literary History* 26.3 (1995): 537–563.

Kantai, Parselelo. "Beyond Oppression-Liberation-Mandeleo." *Chimurenga Chronic* 16 December 2014. www.chimurengachronic.co.za.

LaCapra, Dominick. *Writing History, Writing Trauma.* Baltimore: Johns Hopkins University Press, 2001.

Lewis, Simon. "Review: Debut Novel, Dust, a Complex and Intense Vision of Kenya." *Post Courier* 11 February 2015. www.postcourier.com.

Leys, Ruth. *Trauma: A Genealogy.* Chicago: The University of Chicago Press, 2000.

Mbembe, Achille. "Necropolitics." *Public Culture* 15.1 (2003): 11–40.

Mlambo, Nelson. "Dust: A Review." *Nawa: Journal of Language and Communication* 8.1 (2014). www.questia.com.

Odhiambo Tom. "Dust." *Nairobi Law Monthly* (2014): 56–57.

Okot Bitek, Juliane. "The Powdering of History: Yvonne Adhiambo Owuor's *Dust.*" *Warscapes* 26 October 2015. www.warscapes.com.

Oliver, Kelly. *Witnessing: Beyond Recognition.* London: University of Minnesota Press, 2001.

Owuor, Yvonne Adhiambo. *Dust.* New York: Alfred A Knopf, 2013.

Scarry, Elaine. *The Body in Pain: The Making and Unmaking of the World.* New York: Oxford University Press, 1985.

Scheuerman-Chianda Jalinda. "Dust by Yvonne Adhiambo Owuor – Review." *African in Words* 30 January 2014. www.africainwords.com.

Schumm, Jeremiah, and Ana Maria Vranceanu. "The Ties that Bind: Resource Caravans and Losses among Traumatised Families." *Handbook of Stress, Trauma and the Family.* Ed. Don Catheral. New York: Brunner-Routledge, 2004. 33–51.

Selasi, Taiye. "The Unvanquished: Dust by Yvonne Adhiambo." *The New York Times* 28 February 2014. www.nytimes.com.

Sibi-Okumu, John. "Dust." *Awaaz Voice* 11.2 (2014): 43–44.

Simetai, Torip Peter. "Colonial Violence, Postcolonial Violations: Violence, Landscape and Memory in Kenyan Fiction." *Research in African Literatures* 36.2 (2005): 85–94.

Tal, Kali. *Worlds of Hurt: Reading the Literatures of Trauma.* Cambridge: Cambridge University Press, 1996.

Whitehead, Anne. *Trauma Fiction.* Edinburgh: Edinburgh University Press. 2004.

2   An Eco-critical Reading of *Voice of the People* and *Different Colours*

Eva Nabulya

Introduction

Environmental degradation hardly strikes us as a form of atrocity yet its slow incremental repercussions (Nixon, 2011) certainly translate(s) into horrendous irreversible distortions to livelihoods. This chapter explores textual framings of destructive environmental acts as atrocity in Okiya Omtata Okoiti's *Voice of the People* and Nganga Mbugua's *Different Colours*. While focusing on stylo-rhetoric strategies used to frame these environmental atrocities, the chapter interrogates emerging ideas and locates them within contemporary eco-critical debates. Drawing on Kenneth Burke's notion of persuasion to attitude, the chapter argues that these texts do not just articulate environmental atrocity, they should also be read as acts of protest against environmental devastation. Discussions in this chapter proceed with the full awareness of the Kenyan socio-environmental history and its affinity to the situation in other African countries, and therefore recognize its allegorical associations. Though they solidify artistic commitment to matters of environment in East African literature, their closeness to sociopolitical history enhances the stance of these texts as protest literature.

Different Colours is set in an imaginary region of Kenya called Banana County, but the actual setting seems to bear the characteristics of the Kisii region and Kianyaga (Obebo 2015). Its setting is further confirmed because the main character Miguel is said to have trained in an "Artists' sanctuary near Lake Iposha", the Masaai name for Lake Naivasha in the Kenyan Rift Valley. Similarly, the events which spark off action in *Voice of the People* seem to echo the 2006 attempt by the Uganda government to sell off part of Mabira Forest land to a foreign investor to grow sugarcane (Akaki 2011). Besides, the imaginary background against which human environmentally destructive activities are pitted, the two stories accentuate their atrocious nature. *Different Colours*, for instance, extensively represents the diversity and beauty of nature and its replication in human nature, while *Voice of the People*, illuminates the interface between environmental abuse and political depravity. Thus, grappling with the challenges of representing the unspectacular but incrementally devastating effects of environmental degradation, the works underscore related pitfalls of capitalist development, a concern raised by Ngugi wa Thiong'o in *Petals of Blood* and enunciated by the Kenyan environmental activist and 2004 Nobel Peace Prize winner, Wangari Maathai. In the same light, both works offer insight not only into the inextricable intertwinement of human and nonhuman welfare, but also on the dynamics of representing environmental degradation and the related conflicts, and the ways in which Literature can position itself as a tool of protest.

Environmental issues have been one of the major concerns in East Africa in the last two decades. The East African Community, for instance, is cognizant of the reality of climate change and has conscripted member states to put adaptation measures in place (Mallya, 2010). In Kenya alone, there is enough evidence of the enormity of the effects of deforestation. Every year, the economy loses an estimate of KSH 3,650 as a result of deforestation (UNEP report, 2012). Reduced water flow in rivers adversely affects irrigation agriculture and hydroelectricity production, which in turn increases production cost across different sectors in addition to raising prices of goods. This means that the slow "incremental and accretive" (Nixon 2) nature of environmental calamities due to climate change like desertification or drought does not at all make them any less severe than the effects of war. Yet ecologically devastating activities like deforestation, wetland encroachment, and pollution are still rampant in the region. Sadly, environmental issues are less conspicuous of all other forms of atrocities, not only in the media but also in literature.

Environmental degradation as atrocity, although first articulated by Rob Nixon (2011), has been alive in contemporary African literature. Ogaga Okuyade's *Eco-critical Literature: Regreening African Landscapes* brings together a collection of essays on representations of environmental devastation and related protest mostly from Western and Southern Africa. For the present work, apart from gesturing towards the silence on ecological issues in East African literature, Okuyade provides useful insight on representation. He notes that African artists contribute to the environmental debate by "deploy(ing) cultural art forms to arrest the reader/audience with different rhetorical devices" (xii). This partly resonates with Nixon's assertion that literary representations need to render environmental issues "apprehensible to the senses" (14). While Nixon emphasizes facilitating perception, emotional response, and evoking action as the effect of literary environmental representations, Okuyade goes further to suggest how such effects can be achieved. In these terms, these two scholars point to the importance of style in environmental literature.

Notably though, there are structural challenges involved in the representation of environmental issues. In the first place, all schemes which draw literature into the sociopolitical arena with claims to practical relevance face stern criticism from poetic purists. But a greater challenge lies in rendering the not so easily perceivable impact of environmental brutality perceptible. The texts in focus *Voice of the People* and *Different Colours* approach the question of representation differently. While *Different Colours* seeks to "arrest" (Okuyade above) the audience through allegorical constructions and affective description of natural features, which potentially heightens emotive responses towards destructive activity, *Voice of the People* focuses on describing protest action against environmental destruction and in so doing emphasizes the severity of the issues raised. Hence these two works complement each other in revealing environmental atrocity and related representation challenges. This chapter concerns itself with ways in which literary style facilitates the articulation of environmental atrocity. The next section attends to stylistic innovations through which environmental atrocity and related issues are framed in *Different Colours*.

Facilitating Perception through Allegory in *Different Colours*

Different Colours features the story of how a landscape artist Miguel saves a magnificent waterfall on Orange River in Banana County. Miguel comes to Banana County with the sole purpose of painting the waterfall on canvas, but in the course of his exploration discovers that Dick Teita, a local businessman, has hired people to excavate rocks which support the waterfall. Miguel enlists the support of Angela, his landlady, and the latter mobilizes the village community, market women, a few men, and youth against the destructive project. The selfish Dick Teita is arrested and prosecuted, hence the danger facing the waterfall is temporarily averted. Meanwhile, in their efforts to save the waterfall, Miguel and his journalist friend Derek attract the attention of an international tourist company, which offers to develop the area around the waterfall by constructing a modern tourist hotel. This project is expected to cause changes or injury to the physical landscape. The village community is thus faced with a dilemma: whether to give in to the lure of development and risk to lose a whole way of life revolving around the waterfall, or, to maintain the old order and miss out on jobs and amenities the tourist project promises. As such, Mbugua invites the audience to reflect on the negative impact of capital development on the physical environment.

Notably, *Different Colours* as a novel is an act of communication, of raising awareness, of influencing attitude and of activism, which enables allegorical readings. The writer, Ng'ang'a Mbugua, is quoted by the press saying, "I wanted it to pass as a message to the youth, that they can take care of the environment, mobilize change, and seek justice" (Mureithi, 2012). To this end, the narrator embarks on a detailed description of the general landscape, the waterfall, and of the efforts through which the waterfall is saved from destruction. The plot is driven by a call to protect the waterfall as a symbol of the harmony, peace and, compelling beauty of nature under threat from capitalistic advances. Through allegory and description, Mbugua generates a wealth of meanings on issues of ecotourism, environmental justice, and activism which in turn enhance an emotive response towards the destruction of the waterfall. The next few paragraphs explore the way allegory facilitates the framing of the destructive designs on the waterfall as atrocities.

The term allegory is used in a broad sense to refer to both a way of reading and of writing in which artistic representations are open to more than one level of meaning, drawing from Northrop Frye (90). Although many studies associate allegory with metaphor (Jeremy Tambling 2010, Joel Fineman 1981, Angus Fletcher 1964), this chapter does not subscribe to the view. It acknowledges that allegorical interpretation involves transference of meaning, but contests the view that an allegory is necessarily a form of extended metaphor (Fineman and Greenblatt 45). Rather, allegory differs from metaphor because it does not indicate a direct text-based relationship between the image or situation in the story and the assumed target meaning. This chapter contends that allegory is an expression in "dualistic or pluralistic" terms (Benjamin and Tiedemann 211; Fletcher 221), creating two or more levels of meaning without explicitly saying so. It is 'expression', because allegorical meanings are not always derived from defined images or figures, but can emanate from situations in which the surface level of meaning is presented as complete and conclusive.

Allegory in *Different Colours* corresponds to at least three modes, all of which enable enormity of destruction to emerge: to begin with, there is the basic mode where one element is read as representative of another – the kind Tambling identifies in the work of Dante Alighieri (Tambling 3); in another mode, the particular in the text does not have to represent a particular in the physical world, rather, the writing may communicate a sense of a second level which is unlimited in meaning possibilities and relations. Tambling seems to be referring to this category when he notes that "allegory can never reach the 'totality' proposed in the symbol" (168). In other words, the allegorical at this level is not attributed to a specific referent, and neither is it believed to ever arrive at a definite meaning. It simply opens up avenues for the reader to consider the phenomena in focus in broader ways. The third mode, identified in this chapter stems from the understanding that the ordinary and the particular often represent the universal as in the reflections of Fredric Jameson (1986). This mode can be premised on the geo-historical setting of texts, as is the case with the works in focus. Mbugua's narrative, as shall be illustrated, facilitates these three modes through detailed descriptions of the waterfall and the rest of the landscape.

The waterfall, to begin with, is depicted in two versions: the actual and the painting. As emerges from detailed descriptions, the character of the waterfall points to a meaning beyond the entity. In the first place, its magnificent beauty and grandeur potentially appeal to several senses. The narrator notes that from a distance, its vapoury mist "spewed(s)" into the air creates "a permanent rainbow" (72). When Miguel draws near, he sees a mighty river with lots of water, about eight meters wide, falling over a cliff about 40 meters deep in large waves topped by "little feathery bubbles" (73). For him the water appears like "a huge spray of thick white foam held together by thousands of intertwined rivulets" (73). To Miguel, the sight and the sounds are breathtaking and the narrator remarks that Miguel "could have listened to its divine music for all the days of his life". This description in a way elevates the waterfall beyond the normal and invites allegorical associations.

Moreover, the waterfall is constructed as a significant presence in Banana County, deeply entrenched in the life stories of the people. The narrator remarks that "many had an emotional attachment to the river because it had played a part in their romantic lives" (192–193). For the older men, it is a place of their circumcision, while for some people like Angela's son Tom Tenge, whose father's body had been discovered on the river banks, the river raises bitter memories. In sum, each of the characters in the novel has their own unique connection with the waterfall, and it is thus part and parcel of their lives. Through this motif, Mbugua points to the entanglement of human lives and the landscape, and thereon to the fact that destroying the landscape is tantamount to partially destroying human lives.

From another angle, the waterfall, as described in the novel, draws attention to the great power and vitality of nature. The huge amounts of water falling, the speed at which the water runs, and the deafening roar it produces leave Miguel so shaken that he is initially unable to translate the sight into a drawing; "All his drawings came out like tempests. It was as though he were painting a violent scene" (93). This violence, which reveals itself in Miguel's sensual perception, contrasts conventional ideas of nature. Yet it represents an unkempt force underlying natural systems, which are often brushed off in preference for more endearing imagery. Although Miguel struggles to suppress his natural impulse to communicate this trait in the painting, it still manifests in the harsh colours of strong brown, green, and red that he uses (225). Mbugua further highlights this force by juxtaposing human eco-aggressive activities at the stone quarry on one side of the waterfall, and the chilling fury of the falling waves on the other. As such, Mbugua gestures towards the insurmountable power of nature, and nature's potential to retaliate with even more violence, upon human violation.

Miguel's artistic rendition, on the other hand, communicates attributes of the waterfall inaccessible to the senses at any single encounter.

For instance, the painting captures some of the stories and beliefs around it as narrated to Miguel by Tobby, the herdsman. Outstanding among these is the sad story of a young woman known as Sister Gloria, the village beauty, who having been abandoned by her lover and her family throws her child and herself into the waves. The villagers believe that her spirit haunts the vicinity of the waterfall in the form of a strange bird. There are also stories of crime committed along the river, such as concerning the murder of Angela's husband. Skilfully, Miguel weaves these stories into the colours of his painting. The final piece has simulations of a screaming woman falling down with the waves, a strange bird flying over the waterfall, and blood flowing into the river at the foot of the waterfall. This strategy, apart from underpinning the entanglement of human and natural history, calls into view the special status of natural features in many African societies. It is also notable that in the past, such beliefs and superstitions have enhanced environmental protection. But just like in the novel, the advance of capitalism and new belief systems have supplanted culturally cultivated awe of nature, necessitating new models of environmental ethics.

The painted version of the waterfall, laying emphasis on the multiple colours playing upon the waters when Miguel first sees the waterfall, is an encapsulation of Mbugua's message on diversity, not only of nature but also of culture. In the painting, Miguel uses "strong brown and deep green colours" (225). The narrator reports that "the trees stood out sharply with the colours of the flowers shining a brilliant red, orange and yellow. The plants gave the waterfalls a surreal appearance" (169). In relation to this style, Tom Tenge, Angela's son, summarizes Mbugua's message in his comment on the painting. The boy suggests that Miguel's painting should be named "different colours" because "all these different colours are coming together to form one big and beautiful painting. It is just like our country and our nation. We have people who are so different from each other but they are part of one nation" (258). Despite the authorial intrusion, this is an important statement especially in the context of Kenya with its history of ethnic violence. But the message can also apply to a broader context of racial and cultural subjugation. The assertion also invokes the Jamesonian conception of national allegory. According to Jameson, literature of the developing world can be read as representing the "embattled situations" emanating from the colonial experience (Jameson 67). In the context of ethnic politics in Mbugua's country Kenya and their rootedness in the colonial experience, the allegorical status of the novel becomes confirmable.

As noted above, the major message emerging from Mbugua's description of the waterfall in the two renditions is the need to appreciate diversity. Throughout the novel, diversity is portrayed as good and beautiful. For instance, various creatures which cross Miguel's path as he walks for the first time on the dusty road to Banana County (1), "birds of different

colours and sizes playing their own music" and the forest which is alive
with "sounds of all shades" (69), all leave Miguel dazzled. This endorse-
ment of diversity also refutes views which advocate the protection of
the physical environment based on its instrumental value (anthropocen-
trism). Actually, Mbugua criticizes this human-centred attitude towards
the environment through his castigation of Dick Teita, who, seeing no
immediate monetary value in the waterfall, decides to excavate the rocks
that support it.

Mbugua's description of the landscape is also in harmony with the
message above. From the very opening of the novel, Mbugua explicitly
encourages the reader to meditate on peace and harmony found in nature's diversity. The narrator asserts that:

> One of the reasons why he (Miguel) had chosen to paint landscapes
> was because he wanted to create an ideal world in which beauty and
> harmony mattered above all else. In the same way that the various
> shades of colour blended into each other, creating unity and tran-
> quillity that held the eye captive, so too did Miguel hope that people
> of different colours and cultures would embrace to create a society
> at ease with itself. (Mbugua 125)

The commitment to diversity in this quotation rings through the description of the landscape which dazzles Miguel on his first trip to Banana
County, on the village path to Angela's house and on his way to the
waterfall. These sceneries, in turn, resonate with the description of
peace, order, beauty, and majesty of the waterfall elaborated above. In
addition, Miguel's life story too demonstrates the need to embrace diversity. Miguel is rejected by his father because he does not pursue common
career choices like his brothers, but it is through his artistic career that
he becomes a hero of environmental protection in his country. In the
same way, he and Derek, though initially excluded as foreigners, save
the biggest communal, natural treasure of Banana County. This unity of
meaning, in itself, becomes an image which reinforces unity in diversity
in the novel.

Finally, Mbugua indicates that Banana County's landscape is representative of the natural landscape elsewhere, through various links. In
introducing Miguel, for instance, the narrator asserts: "wealth, beauty
and secrecy. Those were the very qualities of nature that he had always
strived to capture in his paintings" (7). The generalized expression,
"qualities of nature" opens the claim to include nature elsewhere. In addition, the landscape seems too ideal to be real. It is presented as compel-
lingly beautiful and possessing extraordinary warmth and harmony that
seems to seep into the lives of those who live in proximity to it. The very
first paragraph of the novel, for example, describes a scene with a flock
of birds in the sky, trees lining up the dusty road, creatures of different

kinds visible here and there in the bush, and a green covering in the horizon about which the narrator concludes, "a visual feast fit for the eyes of kings" (1). Elsewhere in the novel, the narrator continues to pay special attention to the landscape. For instance, on the way to Angela's cottage Miguel thinks the tea plantation is "like a green carpet spread out on the earth" (37). Beside the cottage is a large tree with outstretched branches, and Miguel feels the 'illusion' of a big hug from the tree (Mbugua 43). Such allegorical construction sets a good ground for the depiction of the danger facing the waterfall, and the landscape in general. It is also against that background that the landscape acquires such significance that a threat to it becomes a threat to the survival of the community.

Choreographing Protest: Irony and Point of View in *Different Colours*

Mbugua's story suggests a correlation between environmental destruction and ignorance. The devastating action on the waterfall in Banana County is not the work of a foreigner. Ironically, a member of the community Dick Teita, has hired several youths in the area to run the dangerous project. It is obvious, however, that these youths, as well as the rest of the villagers, have no idea what the consequences of digging away at the rocks beneath the waterfall can be. Mbugua seems to suggest that protest against environmental destruction must begin with sensitizing the community. This is confirmed through the strategies Miguel, Angela, and Derek employ in saving the waterfall. Notably, the role of women in the protest is quite prominent, and it is not clear why the husbands of the market women are not involved. Mbugua here runs the risk of being accused of projecting the familiar unfounded association of women with nature, which Ngugi has also been accused of (Wright 31). But this may be a way of emphasizing the significance of the community network and ethics, which the environmental protection campaign needs to draw on.

Through Derek's efforts at publicity, an international organization, The Flora and Fauna Fund, takes interest in the waterfall matter. This organization proposes to patron a partnership with "a company that runs environmentally-friendly tourist hotels" (237) for the construction of a tourist hotel in Banana County. But Mbugua describes the proceedings of this plan with both scepticism and hope, inviting the audience to investigate the validity of such a solution. At a community meeting, Gottfried explains that the tourist Hotel project would be run with input from the community. Gottfried then gives a brief explanation of what he wants the community to know about the sharing of the proceeds, the decision-making structure, and the possible challenges of opening Banana County to the outside world. When he gets no opposition, the narrator comments, Gottfried accompanies his final remark "with a wicked smile" (241). Gottfried is depicted as withholding some information from the community, making it hard for them to make an informed decision. Mbugua's ironic stance, which distances him from the decisions in the story, unveils the imperialistic motives of Gottfried and enables the audience to question the exploitative scheme peddled as a means of protecting the waterfall.

In addition, the narration gestures towards the looming danger of social and economic exploitation in the tourist hotel venture. Although Gottfried explains that, the company intends to "keep 70 per cent of the earnings while the village keeps 30 per cent" (237), the village committee composed of illiterate people is not well equipped to enforce this agreement. Besides, the relationship referred to as a "partnership" between company officials and the team of half-literate members of the community is not feasible. This puts the community at a great disadvantage. The promise of employment may also not materialize because none of the people in this community, including youths like Tobby, have academic qualifications to take up meaningful positions with the hotel. Besides, there is the danger of sexual exploitation which is known to be part of the tourist industry (Carrigan xi). It is also implied in Gottfried's statement: "the jobs created can keep young people here busy and stop them from quarrying near the waterfall" (237), that the waterfall might be gazetted off. This means that the people of Banana County might lose their freedom to visit the waterfall, anytime as has been the case. With these overtones Mbugua calls attention to the dilemma surrounding environmental protection, modernization, and development.

Drawing on the allegorical dimension of the novel revealed, the story of environmental management in Banana County can be said to be representative of the scenario in many developing countries. Just like in the story, many communities in Africa, Asia, and the Pacific Islands, as Anthony Carrigan (2011) indicates, have magnificent natural endowments which are endangered due to population and economic pressures. Unfortunately, these resources are often hijacked and exploited in the name of development, by foreign agencies. By raising these issues Mbugua's novel potentially influences the attitude of readers positively or at least raises awareness as a means of protest.

Representing the Threat of Deforestation: Sociopolitical Dimensions of Environmental Degradation in *Voice of the People*

Voice of the People is a satirical comedy set in an imaginary African country. It features a people's protest against a government decision to endorse the destruction of a forest to create space for a tourist resort project. The author, Okiya Omtatah Okoiti, is an active politician and leader of the Justice and Development Party, who protested fervently against human rights abuse in the post-election violence in Kenya in

2008. It is also noteworthy that Okoiti acknowledges his indebtedness to Wangari Maathai, the Kenyan environmentalist and winner of the 2004 Nobel Peace Prize (Okoiti 2013), in the writing of this drama. Actually, Nasirumbi the lady protagonist in the drama seems to be a symbolic representation of Maathai in terms of what she stands for and her approach to environmental activism.

The plot of the play is driven by a conflict between Boss, the head of state, and Sibour his henchman on one side, and Nasirumbi and Indondo, the journalist, on the other. When the play opens, Nasirumbi has got information about Boss' intention to destroy Simbi Forest. She confronts Boss, and learns that the latter is bent on implementing his plan. Nasirumbi and her group of grass-root women, The Mother's Front, carry out demonstrations around the city and publicize the issue. Meanwhile, Boss plans to protect his decision to destroy the forest by organizing a referendum. Both Indondo and Nasirumbi, knowing that Boss manipulates all elections to his end, plot to divert Boss and defeat him before a referendum can be held. But Boss dispatches Sibour to find ways of silencing Nasirumbi. The latter's residence is robbed and the government threatens to ban Voice of the People, the newspaper Indondo works for, if it does not stop publishing about the activities of the Mothers Front. The interesting scheme Nasirumbi and Indondo devise forms the rest of the story.

Although Boss, with the support of Sibour, is prepared to fight Nasirumbi and the values she stands for at all costs, he is no match for journalist Indondo. The latter in collaboration with Nasirumbi traps Boss and causes him to organize a national gathering in which Boss expects an official from the World Bank to crown him champion of the environmental cause, but which marks Boss' own downfall. The drama ends on an ironical note: Boss is seen kneeling before the masses holding a corpse of a child, an embodiment of the many children dying around the country due to lack of medical care, instead of a Golden Shield of Honour. Thus, the plot which begins as an environmental activist story ends up with the toppling of the corrupt head of state and his henchmen. As such, *Voice of the People*, unlike *Different Colours* which focuses more on the challenges of representing environmental violence, offers insights into the representation of protest, not only against environmental degradation but also against one of its major causes, political corruption. The stylistic devices Okoiti employs also configures the play as protest literature.

In the plot, Okoiti stages arguments between the two opposing parties, describes the nefarious actions of Boss and Sibour in detail, and employs reversals. This representation strategy draws the audience into the drama and constitutes persuasion. In particular, Okoiti's mode of representation exhibits a desire to influence the audience concerning issues of deforestation and resource management in general *vis-a-vis* economic advancement. If one is to adopt Simon Estok's view that activism happens when "something is shared with other people that may evoke change" (Estok 267), then textually implicit motives to influence the audience to take action or at least into changing their attitudes towards particular phenomena constitutes activism. But the controversial question of whether a literary text can claim to cause change cannot be accommodated here. Noteworthy is the fact that Okoiti employs various persuasive devices to render the conflict around the destruction of Simbi Forest emotionally apprehensible, and in this move, registers the drama as environmental activist literature. The next section engages with the literary devices facilitating this textual activism.

Irony of Character and Persuasive Personality in *Voice of the People*

Persuasion as a mode of communication, also known as rhetoric, is an ancient area of study that has gone through major transitions since the reflections of Aristotle (tr Buckley 1851) and Quintilian (Watson 1902). However, its core principles remain the same. A recent work by Robert Cockcroft and Susan Cockcroft (2005) re-emphasizes the factors determining persuasive power of a text as being the personality of the communicator, the logical appeal of the message, and its emotive power, in line with Aristotle's three "means" of persuasion *ethos*, *pathos*, and *logos*. In seeming resonance with this thought, Okoiti employs irony to structure persuasive personality, and to appeal to the emotions and reason of the audience. Irony is often used as a blanket term for inconsistencies, incongruences, and absurdities in attitudes, situations, events, character, and language. This section employs it in its broad sense to accommodate verbal, situational, dramatic, irony of character, and what G.G. Sedgewick identifies as "rhetorical irony" (26), which he considers synonymous with allegory.

Although this chapter does not subscribe to the view that all irony is allegorical, there is an allegorical dimension of irony detectable in Okoiti's play. As already noted, the situation around which the plot is woven echoes an actual historical happening in Uganda. Besides, the corrupt schemes depicted in the play are not estranged from the sagas which appear often in East African newspapers. Against such a backdrop, Okoiti's representations are likely to generate meaning as well as emotional response beyond the imaginary world of the drama. This mode of irony underlying the whole plot lends much vitality to the drama and fortifies its claims to textual activism. It is also on the same grounds that the insight on representing protest and protesting through textual means, which the play offers, becomes more pronounced. Besides, the rest of the facets of irony mentioned above anchor on this mode to produce the target emotive effects in the audience.

There is a direct relationship between Aristotle's concept of *ethos* or persuasive personality, as rendered by subsequent scholars, and character irony. It is ironic when a character behaves contrary to expectation in terms of social status, position, relationship, or role, and pretends to believe that it is normal. Since a character is persuasive if they exhibit virtue and a desirable attitude towards the issue in focus, inappropriate action and speech destroys trust between the audience and the communicator and disenables persuasion. While textual persuasion can be realized through the relationship between the writer and the audience, Okoiti employs a kind of internal persuasion mode where the characters persuade the audience directly. To facilitate this, he makes characters reveal themselves, virtuous or otherwise, to the audience and to present their arguments without author moderation. At some points the author persona adopts an ironic stance towards some characters, manifesting as pretence behind the narrative voice. A good example can be derived from the stage directions in the first sequence where the two conflicting parties meet. The narrator notes: "Boss is in his early sixties", goes ahead to objectively describe his dress and surroundings, and concludes: "an aura of cowboy toughness hangs about him". Later, he notes that Boss "helps" Nasirumbi sit down (Okoiti 8, 19), indicating Boss' gentlemanly demeanour, much in contrast to Boss' own speech and action. In the next few paragraphs I point out the ways in which this mode of irony has been used for environmental persuasion.

Boss, in *Voice of the People,* is presented with incongruous action and speech, which draws the audience away from him in negative persuasion. When the drama opens, he is talking to an international property agent, and the conversation reveals that he is planning to buy a villa for ten million US dollars as a birthday gift to the First Lady, using proceeds from the national annual tea exports (2). The audience also gets to know that Boss owns other extortionate property abroad. Worse still, a murderous side of his is also revealed when he discovers that Indondo has a copy of the official Blue Print on the tourist resort project and says, "heads must roll" (41). He is also ready to kill the purported World Bank envoy if she gets in the way of the project.

The absurdity and irony in Boss' character are further emphasized by his hypocrisy. He professes to be "a tree hugger at heart" (10) but is plotting to destroy a forest. He refers to himself as "an intellectual and a democrat" and emphasizes that "in a democracy there are no masters" so "the people will be cheated if (they) don't hold a referendum" (14–15), yet he intends to rig the votes. This is confirmed by himself. He brags to Sibour, "By synthetically enhancing the democratic process, Boss will get the results he wants in any vote" (20). As the play progresses, Boss becomes more and repugnant to the audience and elicits negative feelings.

Sibour is not any better. He tells Indondo that "nothing will come between me and the riches of Simbi" (34). In addition, he is a bloodthirsty person who would kill even where Boss would spare. He threatens Indondo with a gun, and literally begs Boss to let him kill Indondo (42–43) and Nasirumbi (44–45) because they are obstacles to the tourist resort project. Unlike Boss who seems to attach some value to nature, judging from his botanical garden, Sibour exhibits utter disregard for nature. For instance, he refers to forest land as "idle" land (28), revealing his extreme ignorance and greed. The audience's repugnance towards Sibour is also fanned by his lack of a solid personality. He is a sycophant who worships Boss and addresses him by praise epithets such as: "Son of war God" (3), "son of Plague" (5) and "son of Thunder" (8), and also a greedy schemer. Indondo challenges him saying, "you are a mere speculator, dependent on patronage and graft" (35), and Nasirumbi ridicules him by her action of burning the two million shillings he gives her as a bribe. Thus presented, Sibour has no chance to persuade the audience to support the tourist resort project, but instead arouses anger and indignation against himself and similarly corrupt leaders.

Through negative representation, Okoiti makes both Boss and Sibour so detestable that they are left with no chance to be trusted, but instead are despised. The audience may easily conspire with the narrator to enjoy their humiliation. So, on the background of anger at Boss' selfish schemes and Sibour's murderous nature, Okoit builds scorn and ridicule. Boss is greatly demeaned through Indondo's trickery. Indondo capitalizes on Boss's greed for money and power, coupled with his stinking corruption to conjure up a hoax of a secret agent from The World Bank. Boss, anxious to do anything to obtain a favourable Environmental Assessment Report from the purported official, dresses up in women clothes for a meeting with the agent (61). The audience is entertained by the sight of a manipulator now being manipulated. Boss's ridicule reaches a climax at the end of the play where Boss, fully under Indondo's control, kneels down to receive what he does not realize is a corpse of a child, and the ultimate symbol of the murder of his people, their environment, and their future. Through this symbolic irony, Okoiti achieves negative persuasion.

Nasirumbi stands in direct contrast to Boss and the two conjure up an image of a monster against an angel. The audience, at the bidding of the author, can easily be inclined to support the cause Nasirumbi represents. Sibour reports to Boss that she is a secondary school teacher who has "won top awards" in the subjects she teaches (6). She "survives on her small salary", but has the passion to serve her community's needs. The Mothers Front she leads "volunteer(s) to clean streets", runs "a lunch programme for street families", and "organize(s) rural women to plant trees in the country side" (6). The audience first becomes aware of her moral uprightness when she insists on issuing a receipt to Boss for the donation he makes to The Mothers Front, even though Boss insists he does not need the receipt (22). Since Nasirumbi takes the favourable "stance" (Cockcroft 31), her witty statements are likely to influence the audience positively. By Aristotle's standards she is virtuous, which in itself is a means of persuasion. In a way Okoiti predetermines the effects of the internal persuasion simply by creating deplorable characters to represent one side of the issue.

Towards Appeal to Reason and Situational Irony in *Voice of the People*

In rhetoric terms, a good argument is structured in a special way and draws from known facts. Okoiti portrays the cutting down of Simbi natural forest as atrocious partly by shaping the argument around natural history. Nasirumbi asserts that the forest is the "only water source" for the surrounding communities (12), and a cultural site believed to be sacred, whose destruction means the disruption of the sociocultural life of the people. This is true of many communities around forests in East Africa. She also adds that the forest forms a connective corridor for wildlife between two game reserves, and so cutting it would result in "inbreeding" for the animals and probably cause deaths (17). In addition, Indondo also cautions that the forest embeds "valuable biodiversity" (35) which is irreplaceable. These points strengthen Nasirumbi's argument and invite the audience to meditate on human-nonhuman relations. On the other hand, Boss and Sibour argue that what is crucial for the state is poverty alleviation and since the tourist resort would create hundreds of jobs (27), and "kick-start and grow the economy" (13), Simbi forest can be sacrificed. By presenting these two sides to the issue, Okoiti attempts to offer a balanced case. However, the volume of coverage allowed for Nasirumbi's argument betrays authorial mediation and greatly threatens artistic objectivity.

The argument above invites the audience to consider complications surrounding economic growth and natural resource management. Indondo rightly argues that "one cannot eradicate poverty simply by increasing economic growth, trade, consumption and exploitation of resources" because poverty is "a well-funded project in the modern world" (27). This statement highlights the fact that poverty in a developing country, like in the world of the drama, is sometimes caused by factors unrelated to low capital growth, such as corruption, or foreign exploitative schemes. He also asserts that poor resource ownership policies make "development" "an alibi for theft" (26), as crafty politicians conjure up fake projects to steal national resources. Boss, for instance, has private interests in the tourist project but pretends to be interested in economic growth. It is also ironic that Boss who should be the embodiment of patriotism and the custodian of state resources confesses, "I will pay for the villa from this year's tea export earnings" referring to the ten-million-US-dollars villa he wants to purchase abroad.

Indondo also explains that often foreign investors end up taking capital back to their mother countries by importing skilled labour and some raw materials (29). So ironically, the projection of employment opportunities and poverty alleviation is never realized. For Nasirumbi, it makes no sense to destroy the environment to meet current needs. She argues, "Destroying our environment to cater for our needs today is like eating our offspring. Where do we get the justification to saddle posterity with our needs?" (13). These arguments not only speak against the lure of investment for poverty alleviation, *vis-a-vis* the preservation of the environment in the imaginary worlds alone, but they challenge the audience to reflect on the matter in contemporary contexts.

Nasirumbi/Indondo's argument is supported by situational irony. In the first place, while Boss is bent on destroying Simbi forest under the pretext that it does not meet the immediate needs of his country, he brags about his garden, "I have beautiful trees and flowers from around the world. You won't believe the diversity" (Okoiti 23), thereby acknowledging the undeniable value of the physical environment in human life. In addition, Boss wants to be recognized as a champion of environmental protection so much that he falls prey to Indondo's scheme. The audience's anger and indignation against him is soothed when he organizes a national occasion on which he is utterly humiliated and defeated.

Conclusion

The centrality of political sanity in the battle against environmental devastation cannot be underestimated. Both Mbugua and Okoiti connect environmental atrocity with Political depravity. In *Different Colours* Dick Teita works for an anonymous person highly placed in government, who has even declared that he will buy a lot of property in Banana County "for my political bosses to clean their money" (214). When inspector Yusuf trails and comes across the evil team, Dick Teita is on gunpoint being forced to sign off some documents (217). The plot does not give more details about these people but the reader can tell that they are working for corrupt officials in power, destroying landscapes with little or no regard for the livelihoods that depend on it, for private gains. In *Voice of the People*, Boss' greed for power and property are what motivates his grabbing of Simbi Forest land. Okoiti invites the audience to reflect on the role of democracy, especially in the hands of crafty leaders, in upholding environmental welfare. The situation Okoiti uses to generate this message in the play indicates two enduring challenges: ignorance of the electorate and corruption of the political leaders. Poorly developed political systems and the absence of a transparency culture in governance are also aggravating factors.

Despite the fact that the two texts exhibit very little sympathy for development projects, the realities of the dilemma cannot be denied. Social

Development Goals are centred on capital growth. But both Okoiti and Mbugua question the logic of pursuing capital growth with its associated lure of job creation *vis-à-vis* environmental sustainability. In that light, the works generate meaning beyond the text in line with the Jamesonian idea of national allegory. Jameson's thought may continue to provoke criticism because of its *othering* of the literature of developing countries as non-canonical (65), but the chapter values his recognition of the uniqueness of African literature in regard to its focus on the political rather than the personal (69). In resonance with this view, the African theorist Chidi Amuta asserts that any criticism of African literature should consider its rootedness "in the process which constitute African History" (80). Indeed, the social and political conditions attending corruption in the imaginary worlds of the texts cannot be divorced entirely from colonial history.

Effective allegorical representation of social, political, or environmental issues seems to demand special structural and stylistic innovations. This is more so because of the implicit motive to influence change. The two works, discussed here, highlight the contribution of irony in (environmental) textual protest as well as narration of protest. Notably, irony has great potential in exciting emotions like anger and indignation, especially because of its capacity to communicate a meaning accompanied by an implicit "evaluative attitude" (Hutcheon 13). But it is worth noting that while a detailed description is essential in enhancing perception, objectivity is of paramount importance. Audience involvement and persuasion is not achieved by suggesting solutions but by letting the solutions emerge from situations presented.

Works Cited

Akaki, Tony. *Mabira Forest Giveaway: A Path to Degenerative Development.* iUniverse, 2011. Print.

Amuta, Chidi. *The Theory of African Literature: Implications for Practical Criticism.* Zed Books [with] Institute for African Alternatives, 1989. Print.

Benjamin, Walter, and Rolf Tiedemann. *The Arcades Project.* Harvard University Press, 1999. Print.

Buckley, Theodore Alois. *Aristotle's Treatise on Rhetoric.* HG Bohn, 1851. Print.

Carrigan, Anthony. Postcolonial Tourism: Literature, Culture, and Environment. Routledge, 2011. Print.

Cockcroft, Robert, and Susan Cockcroft. *Persuading People: An Introduction to Rhetoric.* 2nd ed. Palgrave Macmillan, 2005. Print.

Estok, Simon. 'Activist Ecocriticism: An Introduction'. *Forum for World Literatures* 1.6 (2014): 261–271. Print.

Fineman, Joel, and Stephen Greenblatt. Allegory and Representation. Baltimore: Johns Hopkins University Press, c1981. Print.

Huggan, Graham, and Helen Tiffin. Postcolonial Ecocriticism: Literature, Animals, Environment. Routledge, 2010. espace.library.uq.edu.au. Web. 19 Aug. 2014.

Hutcheon, Linda. *Irony's Edge: The Theory and Politics of Irony*. Psychology Press, 1994. Print.

Jameson, Fredric. 'Third-World Literature in the Era of Multinational Capitalism'. *Social Text* 15 (1986): 65–88. Print.

Magati Obebo. 'Banana County That Draws Its Beauty from Stone Carvings'. *Daily Nation*. n.p., 26 May 2015. Web. 30 July 2016.

Mallya. *EAC Position on Climate Change Negotiations*. East African Community, 2010. Print.

Mbugua, Ng 'ang'a. *Different Colours*. Nairobi: Big Books, 2012. Print.

———. *Terrorists of the Aberdare: A Novella*. Nairobi: Big Books, 2009. Print.

Mureithi, Carlos. 'Book Rejected by Publishers Wins Top Award'. *Daily Nation* 10 May 2012. Web. 22 July 2016.

Musambi, Evelyn. 'Nation Journalists Nominated for Literary Prize'. *Daily Nation*. n.p., 15 August 2014. Web. 28 July 2016.

Ngugi wa Thiong'o. *Petals of Blood*. Nairobi: Dutton Books, 1977. Print.

Nixon, Rob. *Slow Violence and the Environmentalism of the Poor*. Cambridge, MA: Harvard University Press, 2011. Print.

Northrop Frye. *Anatomy of Criticism: Four Essays*. Vol. 3. Princeton, NJ: Princeton University Press, 1957. Print.

Okoiti, Okiya Omtatah. 'Omtatah: Why I Quit Seminary'. *Daily Nation*. n.p., 27 December. 2013. Web. 12 Apr. 2016.

Okuyade, Ogaga. *Eco-Critical Literature: Regreening African Landscapes*. New York: African Heritage Press, 2013. Print.

Omtatah, Okoiti. *Voice of the People: A Play*. Vol. 25. East African Educational Publishers, 2007. Print.

Sedgewick, Garnett Gladwin. *Of Irony: Especially in Drama*. University of Toronto Press, 1967. Print.

Tambling, Jeremy. *Allegory*. Routledge, 2009. Print.

UNEP. 'Deforestation Costing Kenyan Economy Millions of Dollars Each Year and Increasing Water Shortage Risk – UNEP'. *UNEP NEWS CENTRE*. n.p., 11 May 2012. Web. 11 Nov. 2016.

Watson, John Selby. *Quintilian's Institutes of Oratory: Or, Education of an Orator*. In Twelve Books. Vol. 2. G. Bell, 1902. Print.

Wright, Laura. *'Wilderness into Civilized Shapes': Reading the Postcolonial Environment*. University of Georgia Press, 2010. Print.

3   Locating Bodies, Embodying Resistance in Wahome Mutahi's *Jail Bugs* and *Three Days on the Cross*

Macharia Gatundu

Introduction

Narratives of prison life are rife with innumerable atrocities. The prison system takes an even darker hue when abetted by despotic regimes. In Kenya, the prison is viewed as a depository of alleged dissidents of former president Moi's regime. This chapter attempts a Foucauldian reading of Wahome Mutahi's *Jail Bugs* and *Three Days on the Cross*. It interrogates the representation and exercise of power within the confines of prison. Focussing on Mutahi's depictions of prison life, the chapter demonstrates how bodies, which according to Foucault are the direct locus of power, are deployed and affected in the exercise of power and resistance and, as a consequence, how characters acquire important understandings of power. A Foucauldian reading aligns Mutahi's fiction with protest narratives which decry violence through restoration of the voices of the incarcerated bodies. Undeniably, depictions of violence in prison narratives is an ambivalent enterprise. One, there is the question of availability of a language capable of representing violence and trauma as close to reality as possible. Two, there is the essential fact that whoever attempts to represent this violence through witness accounts must always be wary of essentialism – s/he must acknowledge the fact that there are those who did not survive the violence – that is, there are *other* voices, voices of those who cannot and will never speak or are eternally silenced. Unlike testimonies and autobiographies, works of fiction are able to bridge this gap as they are capable of artistically pushing beyond the limits of reality.

Wahome Mutahi's carceral narratives effectively employ satire and humour to tackle the otherwise serious social and political issues that make him Kenya's leading humourist (Mutonya 35–37; Ogola, "Writing 'Conflict'" 208). Mutahi, risking his career and life, 'tells the truth laughingly' (to borrow the phrase from John Ruganda), as is best captured in *Jail Bugs*. He is able to satirize corruption, inefficiency, and violence in the prison system and the state. Using the prison image, he ridicules the culpability of the state and its subjects through the first-person narrative voice of a prison journal kept by Albert Kweyu, a man convicted for hit-and-run. In *Three Days on the Cross*, Mutahi narrates, not without a tinge of pain, the violence meted out to innocent civilians illegally detained by police. The narrative texture is sombre and highlights the pain of innocent individuals caught in the grinding gears of a despotic regime which is committed to stamping out any form of rebellion, real or imagined.

Mutahi's concern with everyday power relations and the oppression of people at the periphery is underscored in the two texts. In prison, justice is depicted as non-existent. The prison is the law – the warders are the adjudicators and administrators of its power. The wardens can violently appropriate and affect the body, the mind, and the soul of a prisoner. As depicted in *Three Days on the Cross*, in detention the enormity of the crime is irrelevant as long as the prisoner confesses to a pre-determined set of crimes. The *norm* is, eventually, the prisoner *must* confess with the sincerest compunction. This confession is, however, usually extracted through violence and must always tally with the police officer's checklist of a set of crimes. A classic impasse: *damned if you do, damned if you don't*. Herein, then, lies the question of whether what exists in prison is a power relationship or a relationship of violence.

Analytics of Power

Deviating from a top-down conceptualization of power (*a la* Hobbes), Foucault proposes an interrogation of power at the capillary, at the point where "multiple bodies, forces, energies, matters, desires, thoughts, and so on are gradually, progressively, actually and materially constituted as subject or as the subject" (*Society* 28). A Foucauldian reading of Mutahi's selected fiction is apt because his works are concerned with mundane power relations of people at the capillary; they are centred on the lives of the *ordinary* citizens, *ordinary* relationships – the home, the church, the drinking shebeens among others (see Ogola, "Writing 'Conflict'" 211–215; "Confronting and Performing Power" 75–76). Foucault perceives this approach of interrogating power as an "analytics of power" (*The History* 82) as opposed to a 'theory of power'. For him, any claim to knowledge (discourses) is tyrannical and, as such, should be treated with scepticism and placed under continued criticism and politicization (*Society* 26; *Essential Works* 457). Mutahi is wary of power, be it at home, in the church, or that which is exercised by the state.

In his analysis of power, Foucault makes an important elucidation, he argues that power is never localized here or there, it is never in the hands of some, and it is never appropriated in the way that wealth or a commodity can be appropriated. Power functions. Power is exercised through networks, and individuals do not simply circulate in those networks; they are in a position to both submit to and exercise this power;

they are always its relays. In other words, power passes through individuals. It is not applied to them (*Society* 29). Therefore, the most germane question in an 'analytics of power' is not who possesses power, but rather, the "how of power" (*Society* 24) – how power operates and is exercised. This points to "the rules of right that formally delineate power" and the truth-effects that power produces (*Society* 26). Of interest in this chapter is, one, how power is exercised and how it operates, in the prison/detention, and two, how bodies experience power/violence and how they take part in these relationships, and how this, as a consequence, allows or denies latitude for resistance.

Foucault postulates that the evolution of power occurred in two, mutually inclusive, ways. The first of these is the "*disciplines: an anatomo-politics of the human body*" and "*regulatory controls: a biopolitics of the population*". The former "centered on the body as a machine: its disciplining, the optimization of its capabilities, the extortion of its forces, the parallel increase of its usefulness and its docility, its integration into systems of efficient and economic controls", while the latter "focused on the species body, the body imbued with the mechanics of life and serving as the basis of the biological processes: propagation, births and mortality, the level of health, life expectancy and longevity, with all the conditions that can cause these to vary" (*The History* 139). Thus, according to Foucault, power seeks to discipline bodies in society making them docile while at the same time optimizing their economic output. However, as Achille Mbembe notes in "The Banality of Power and the Aesthetics of Vulgarity in the Postcolony", it is misleading to reduce power in the postcolony to mere economics. Power in the postcolony does not necessarily seek to 'discipline' and "create useful individuals or to increase their productive efficiency" (19). Instead, it seeks to dramatize its own significance and appetite by requisitioning the bodies of its objects and ending these lives whenever they are considered a peril to the public well-being (20–22). In *Three Days on the Cross*, Momodu's and Chipota's bodies are not appropriated by the state for any disciplinary goal. They are, rather, taken as sites on which the power of the police can inscribe itself and 'truths' revealed so that the force can prove its thoroughness. The climax of this power is its nefarious ability to make the detained/incarcerated bodies disappear. It is important, therefore, to note that, whereas for Foucault power "is tolerable only on condition that it mask a substantial part of itself...[and] [i]ts success is proportional to its ability to hide its own mechanisms" (*The History* 86), in the postcolony the contrary proves to be true.

Since the focus of 'disciplines' is the body, "one of the first effects of power is that it allows bodies, gestures, discourses and desires to be identified and constituted as something individual" (*Society* 29–30). This is the *productivity* of power. The *disciplines* and *regulatory controls* simultaneously individualize and totalize; the former *works on* the individual's body, its biological processes, while the latter aspires for the well-being and productivity of the population. Foucault states that:

> 'Discipline' may be identified neither with an institution nor with an apparatus; it is a type of power, a modality for its exercise, comprising a whole set of instruments, techniques, procedures, levels of application, targets; it is a 'physics' or an 'anatomy' of power, a technology. And it may be taken over either by 'specialized' institutions. (*Discipline and Punish* 215)

Discipline is, for that reason, but a possible procedure of power and it "create[s] apparatuses of knowledge, knowledges, and multiple fields of expertise" (*Society* 38). In its tendency to classify, enumerate, and name, power creates a field of expertise. It is this 'field of knowledge/ expertise' which Foucault refers to by 'discourses' when he hypothesizes the power-knowledge nexus. The formation and application of these disciplines/discourses (power-knowledge) do not define/adhere to any code of law but rather to a *norm*. As an institution, therefore, the function of the prison is to identify, compartmentalize, label, and punish all those whom the society has rejected or cannot easily identify, label, and categorize as 'normal'. The prison does this according to its own knowledge of a *norm*. What this implies is that the exercise of power in the prison is, as a norm, not 'normal' since those who exercise it and those on whom it is exercised do not exist within the societal's realm of the *normal*. The paradox of this *abnormality* is highlighted by the fact that both the warders and prisoners share the same dis-eased space in the periphery. Elsewhere, Ngugi observes:

> Night warders are themselves prisoners guarding other prisoners. Only they are paid for it and their captivity is self-inflicted or else imposed by lack of alternative means of life (*Detained* 5)

The precariousness of the warders' position is revealed in the above excerpt. The fissures in the power they exercise is magnified. For example, Sergeant Pilipili makes sexual advances towards a prisoner's wife. The woman is incensed not so much because she has been deceived that her husband would be released, but because she has been touched by a prison warden. She laments, "What will the village people say when they learn that a prison warden has touched my body? What will they say when they learn that I have been touched by this rubbish in uniform?" (*Jail Bugs* 110–111). What is apparent here is that under a regime which exploits and oppresses its citizenry, often its prisoners will be perceived as victims. The wardens and policemen are representatives of the oppressive power and, thus, are only worthy of disdain if not pity.

"Virtually every instance of personal domination is intimately connected with a process of appropriation" (Scott 188). The exercise of power-knowledge in the prison relies on the appropriation of the body, of "extracting symbolic taxes in the form of deference, demeanor, posture, verbal formulas, and acts of humility" (Scott 188), his/her space, and the division of time. The first procedure of power in the prison, it appears, is to appropriate the prisoner's body and, as a consequence, his identity. In the prison, the prisoner is no longer identified by his name but by a number assigned him (*Jail Bugs* 2; see Ngugi 3). Albert Kweyu tells it this way:

> I was introducing myself. I am number P/F/1270. Only yesterday, I was Albert Kweyu; *Mister* Albert Kweyu to my juniors at the post office; A.K. to the boys at my regular drinking joint and Alb to my wife on those occasions when she wants to touch my soft spot. (original italics, *Jail Bugs* 2)

The numerous power relations severed by the prison system can be seen here. This number is a label of excision from other *normal* power relations that the narrator was a part of: his juniors at work, his drinking buddies, and his wife. It denies the subject his individuality and subjectivity and gives him a slot, a space to be identified with and in the general prison population. The biopolitics of prison power uproot individuals and create technical routes involving disembodied documentation in the interest of facilitating effective surveillance and control of the prison population. This power in the prison seeks to discipline and normalize the individual *body* for the collective well-being of many and that of its own *self* (*Philosophy* 235–242). The prisoner's body is bound by routine, into certain postures, within given spaces and time. Time is divided into units and schedules which are constantly scrutinized. This desire to scrutinize and regularize absolutely is epitomized by the high watchtowers – the Panopticon – the most productive and most efficient technology of power (*Discipline and Punish* 195–228).

Through body seizure, power engages its skills in inscribing truth upon the object's soul as is purportedly achieved through confessions. However, a confession in prison is not usually voluntary as prison warders have to often rely on torture, "confession's 'dark twin'" (*Deacon* 101). Torture creates its own body of knowledge and expertise. There are individuals/experts (the likes of Ode and Ummure) who 'know' and have the techniques which are most *productive* in extracting 'truthful' confessions. They (the experts) can discern what pain is not enough and when the confession is untruthful. However, torture as a procedure of power inscribes itself on both the bodies and souls of the tortured and the torturer. Corporal Chris Wandie has had enough of the violence he has taken part in as "the blindfolds man". After serving diligently,

"Wandie finally made up his mind that he had done enough of savagery and needed to do something human to salvage his soul" (*Jail Bugs* 140). His propitiation is leaking the information, of how the police torture innocent people so as to extract false confessions of involvement with the July 10 Movement, to Peter P'Njuru, the editor of the *Daily Horn* (155–156). It is Wandie's change of heart that gives Chipota a second chance to life.

Power here is a double-edged sword, cutting both ways. According to Foucault, power is relational, pervasive, and productive (*The History* 92–97; *Essential Work* 298–325). No one can escape power. Thus, power constitutes individuals in two ways: one, they are inescapably subjected to power and, two, through these relations of subjection they become subjects. The question, then, is 'what is power?' For Heller, "power is *transformative capacity* to influence and modify the actions of other individuals in order to realize certain tactical goals" (italics in original, Heller 83). Both the wardens and the prisoners have certain 'tactical goals' which guide their choices of behaviours and repertoire for actions. For the prisoner, the immediate goal is to survive each day and minimize as much as possible any injury to his *self*. Though administrators of state power, the warders' goals do not necessarily go hand in hand with the national ideologies, as embodied by the sovereign – the 'Illustrious One'. Most of the wardens are poor citizens. The gun and baton they wield, and the 'right' to (il)*legally* violate the body and space of the prisoners in their custody is the only power they can exercise. A good number are illiterate and they make up for it through the butt of the gun (*Three Days*119; *Jail Bugs* 189). Wardens take kilos of meat from the prison kitchen as it is unlikely they can afford to buy it for their own homes (*Jail Bugs* 47, 58–59). In *Three Days on the Cross*, Corporal Wandie takes the meals of the prisoners under his watch. He is not intent on torturing them, but it is because he, too, cannot afford a decent meal. He does this job, not because he likes it but because he wants to change his lot. Here, power acts independently of the prison system and the state. It can be argued that power springs from an individual's desire and will to change his life. At this point, power can be defined as "[t]he ability of individuals to create change – no matter how insignificant" (Heller 83). This change may be individual or collective.

Understood this way, then it is possible to see power as exercised by the power*less* – those who on the surface appear to 'have' no power. Power, therefore, exists and is exercised by both the oppressed and the oppressor. This is because either would like to change and "to influence and modify the actions of [the] other" (Heller 82) in spite of "whether that change limits human freedom or promotes it" (84). A question may be rightfully asked, what if this power is bent on more than just influencing or modifying the action of the other? What if it seeks to destroy the *other* completely?

Power Relations or Relations of Violence

In a repressive regime, what exists is a relationship not of power but of violence. Foucault observes that:

> [a] relationship of violence acts upon a body or upon things; it forces, it bends, it breaks on the wheel, it destroys, or it closes the door on all possibilities. Its opposite pole can only be passivity, and if it comes up against any resistance it has no other option but to try to minimize it. ("The Subject and Power" 220)

Violence is not power, although power may rely on it. Violence is when power does not look for consent but rather seeks to invade, to penetrate forcefully, the body and space of an*other* – to modify his/her behaviour. Thus, in spite of the overt prison intention – rehabilitation - the system relies on violence for its efficiency. It has its own peculiar techniques of violence and discourses which it employs. These techniques even have their own jargon: 'welcome/reception committee' (*Jail Bugs* 3–4; *Three Days* 45), 'arithmetic' (*Jail Bugs* 52), and 'telephone exchange action' (*Jail Bugs* 63) among others. All these are directed onto the body and space of the prisoner. These techniques are not random in their emergence(y) and administration. They are ritualized. The prison ensures that these rituals of violence (or ritualized violences) are always visible in application and border the spectacular: the walls, the armed wardens, the batons, and the boots (which are used generously), the guns (reservedly used, but always on the ready) and the high watchtowers, the peepholes on the dormitory doors. The door-less toilets which ensure that the prisoners do not escape scrutiny even in those minute and intimate moments of bodily processes. Power's productivity here is manifold. The prisoners themselves are constantly and forcefully scrutinizing each other's bodies (*Jail Bugs* 18). This determined will to enclose, to monitor severely, and to control the body, the space, and the time of the *other* is telling of the anxieties of the prison and the state and their tendencies to be violent.

Violence bares its fangs and becomes apparent when Chipota asks his torturers to instead kill him rather than torture him, Ode says:

> We would kill you if we wanted to and that would be the end of the matter. But we are not ready for that yet. We are ready for other things like making you talk. *We know how to make people talk.* (emphasis added, *Three Days* 56)

The state's pernicious technologies of power over life are here portrayed by Ode's assertion that they can extend life to the point of convenience and then end it. This is a relationship of violence and it makes its objects wish for death, yet will hold it far from their reach for as long as it deems productive. It is able to extend the object's life to the point of death or to the point where the object's body is no longer productive – no more confessions can be 'squeezed' from it. Violence here invokes more the wickedness of the criminal, than the crime itself. Getting hold of the *real* criminal is unimportant as long as another *body* can be made to confess to that crime. It, therefore, focuses/relies on isolation, the need to protect the society from the fictitious bad influence. This power "continuously refers and appeals to exception, emergency and a fictionalized notion of the enemy. It also labours to produce the same exception, and fictionalized enemy" (Mbembe, "Necropolitics" 16).

Beyond this point, the body and the soul of the prisoner are of no value to the technologies of power and can be terminated or condemned into solitary confinement for an indeterminate period. For Haki and Albert Kweyu, in *Jail Bugs*, it is confinement in the madhouse. Unluckily for Momodu it is death (*Three Days* 1–5; 180–182). All these are done in the name of protecting the many or the state under "the Illustrious One". This is a contradiction of power since the state cannot destroy the life it claims to protect – its claims to protect the life of the many by neutering the one is paradoxical. As a consequence, to exercise and to maintain its sense of power, if it must commit homicide, the state must do so far from public witnesses and spectacle. The police officers surreptitiously kidnap their targets, move them from one police station into another, and shuffle them around the city until they make their bodies disappear altogether.

In *Three Days on the Cross*, after the shuffling and the blindfolding, Chipota and Momodu are finally driven out into the countryside to be clandestinely executed. This is after enduring three days of torture by a police force bent on getting a confession of their involvement in the banned anti-government movement. The detainment of the two is illegal and the power exercised by the policemen relies on the ambiguity and loopholes created by the corrupt state and its agents. To assure itself of its own supremacy, the regime has to rely on confessions. Confessions assuage the fears and anxieties of the office holders in the system, and those of the "Illustrious One". The officers to carry out this are the most trusted and discreet individuals – those who will carry out the murder astutely and precisely, within the shortest time and with minimal repercussions. This is violence-power at its most destructive.

The apogee of violence is death. Yet this is the very limit of power. That is, while power can be exercised to modify/influence the life (the *live* body) and actions of the *other*, violence is keen on obliterating him/her completely – to the death. Beyond death power cannot exist only violence and it is manifest by the tendency to disfigure or dismember, to conceal or to bury in unmarked graves the bodies of those who have been violently destroyed. This, however, should not be interpreted to imply that use of violence means total domination. Whereas violence seeks to reduce resistance, to annihilate even into nothingness, *domination* is here understood as paralyzing the other completely, to incapacitate and make incapable of desire, of decision, or choice – to lobotomize– more than just *zombifying*, for even the popular classic zombie reacts to the basic desire to consume brain matter.

In *Three Days on the Cross*, Superintendent Isaac Ode, in his 28th-floor office (a Panopticon), is quite proud of the work he and his team are doing:

> After all, few of the suspects who had been picked up by his men had gone free. Most of them had either been jailed or detained. He smiled when he remembered that those who had ended up in court all pleaded guilty to the charges before them, thanks to certain persuasive methods that he and his men used. (46)

Superintendent Ode and the 'reception committee' have the stage ready for the exercise of their "persuasive methods". Since "the principal locus of both the self-narration of power and the places in which it imagines itself is the body" (Mbembe, "The Banality" 9), the detainees are first stripped naked (*Three Days* 52–53) marking the prodigality of the skewed power relations as the gaze is turned onto the helpless captive. This subjection is meant to emasculate and to neutralize his individuality. Chipota is thus symbolically and literally emasculated as he is given the "cigarette treatment" (*Three Days* 153) – his penis is burnt with a cigarette. However, this subjectivization also affects the policemen as they have to model and remodel themselves according to their uniform, their rank, and cadre, especially since they do not want to incur the wrath of the sovereign, the "Illustrious One" (161–165). In *Jail Bugs*, the body of the prisoner is appropriated by the powers of the prison and it is then divided into useful and non-essential organs. The narrator notes that the mouth of the prisoner should be mum and the ears always alert (2).

In his analysis of the "arts of resistance", James Scott observes that the open interaction between subordinates and those who dominate is characterized by a wide range of *acting* and wearing of masks – he calls these acts "public transcripts" (*Domination* 2). Scott argues that both the hegemonic and the subordinates have to adhere to their respective *public transcripts*. He observes that "[i]f the weak have obvious and compelling reasons to seek refuge behind a mask when in the presence of power, the powerful have their own compelling reasons for adopting a mask in the presence of subordinates" (10). Therefore both parties are prisoners of each other's expectations. The prison commandant, in *Jail Bugs,* thus, has to transform his body so that it *speaks* of power: his voice is like a "concrete mixer" (3) and his face is contorted. The narrator observes:

> If the man had a normal face once, he had now transformed it into a grimace, not out of pain but out of obvious disdain for what he was looking at, meaning the new arrivals in prison. (3)

Elsewhere, the narrator quips, "...it seems that part of the warden's training is on how to screw the face when looking at the prisoners" (161). What we notice therefore is that in the prison space there is untamed relation of violence which results in intimidation, torture, and sometimes, the eventual death of the victim's body.

The Paradox of Violence or Opportunity for Resistance

Foucault's analysis of resistance is often discounted (Death 236) or read as incoherent (Taylor 152–154) and incapable of facilitating/supporting resistance (Widder 413–414). This, however, should not be construed as an omission but, rather, emerges from his aversion for a 'theory of power' as pointed out above. Therefore, conceptualizing a 'theory of resistance' is, for Foucault, ambiguous since it would only lead to the displacement of one tyrant and the enthronement of another. If the oppressed were to come together and oust the oppressors, they (the oppressed) would establish a system of oppressing their former masters, it is for this reason that Foucault is wary of revolutions. As such, power would be situated as an eternal binary antagonism between those who do (not) 'possess' it at a particular time in history – something which Foucault strives to critique. Following Foucault's counsel for an 'analytics of power' rather than a 'theory of power', our reading of Mutahi's narratives inverts Foucault's concept and thus locates resistance at the capillary and as something that cannot be possessed by individuals. Foucault observes that "where there is power, there is resistance" (*The History* 95), herein, then, an 'analytics of resistance' is, consequently, possible through a reversal of his conception of power and the "heterogeneous process(es) of subjectification" (Death; Heller 79).

Acknowledging, that power relations can be inverted into relations of resistance shifts the focus from the actors to the "practices and rationalities" of resistance and, in so doing, shows how power and resistance are mutually constitutive (Death 236). Whereas it is easy to quickly disregard and condemn the wardens and the policemen as inhuman agents of the prison and the state, Mutahi humanizes them by giving us a look into their private worlds, into the different dimensions of their lives. This strategy is important since it places them in multifarious institutions and their varied power relations – the home, the church, the local community, etc. This implies that whereas the wardens are exercising prison's power over the bodies of the prisoners, they may be doing so as to make up for their subordination elsewhere or for *their own* profit and not necessarily that of the prison or the state. This is in spite of their techniques and routes of exercising power being, nevertheless, grounded within the prison/state discourses. The *personal* drive often results in drag and friction to the larger system and therefore opening spaces for resistance. On the other hand, disciplinary power will seek to reduce as much as possible this wastage. Therefore, the form/dimension/shape in which resistance takes place is closely linked to the regimes and technologies of power and these are, in turn, shaped by the manner/form/dimension in which they are resisted.

Prisoners do not have open fora in which to create new routes of exercising resistance, they have to invert and reconfigure the same routes which prison employs to exercise power. The prisoners quickly strip in obeisance, as soon as the directive is issued. Nevertheless, this exercise which is meant to penetrate and scrutinize their bodies is, for the prisoners, an opportunity to get better clothes or to steal and wear an extra pair of pants – which are later traded for a cigarette or a piece of meat. In spite of these constant strippings, the prisoners still manage to reappropriate their bodies and transform them into objects of concealing and transporting contraband in and out of the prison. On the other hand, those prisoners who are sent to work in the wardens' quarters become privy to the private, and mostly miserable, lives of the wardens, which adds to the prisoners' repertoire for resistance.

As a consequence, resistance becomes feasible because the hegemony does not and cannot control all the mechanisms of power and all those that it employs are always potentially reversible. This possibility is due to: one, the *"mechanisms of power that individuals use to exercise power...do not depend on the existence of those individuals for their own existence"* (original italics, Heller 85); and two, because of "the inevitable disjunction between an action's *intention* and its actual *effect"* (original emphasis, Heller 87). This is what Foucault means when he avers that "[p]ower relations are both intentional and non-subjective" (*The History* 94–95; Heller 79–80). Noting the existing disjunction between power's *intention* and *effect*, Heller makes a noteworthy elucidation. He distinguishes between the oft-quoted and misunderstood terms; *tactics* and *strategies* (*The History* 99–100; Heller 87–88). Heller summarizes *tactics* as "the *intentional* actions carried out in determinate political contexts by individuals and groups" (original emphasis, Heller 87) and *strategies* as "the *unintentional* but institutionally and socially regularized–effects produced by the non-subjective articulation of different individual and group tactics" (original emphasis, 87–88). This distinction is important since it facilitates our reading to demonstrate how the disjunction between the prison's *intention* (tactics) and *effect* (strategies) in the exercise of power and its non-subjective nature offer occasion for the constitution of resisting subjects. Thus, offering an opportunity/space for resistance.

In the two texts, the policemen and the wardens, serving as adjuncts of the juridical, do not uphold the ethos of 'innocent till proven guilty'. They seem to operate on their own rather powerful ethics whose vagueness is their source of power. These are a "God-given" set of laws which are unstated yet should be known to every prisoner/detainee. In prison, the Prison Commandant is the creator of these laws and the wardens its enforcers. This ambiguous power conceals the violence it orchestrates by holding the prisoner accountable for what it does not prescribe or proscribe. Thus, the prisoners are always wary of breaking laws whose existence cannot be proven or disapproved. The prisoner has to be always horrified "for a real or imagined crime in this place where the prisoner is assumed guilty even before he has broken any law" (*Jail Bugs* 36). Since this prison exists within a diseased state, such laws do not exist only in the prison. Outside its walls, Pancho is arrested and prosecuted for "something that they cannot prove: loitering with intent" (78). Here 'intent' rings true of power "continuously refer[ing] and appeal[ing] to...a fictionalized notion of the enemy" (Mbembe, "Necropolitics" 16).

In *Jail Bugs*, the wardens believe that the purpose of the prison is rehabilitation (126), yet violence and inhumane treatments are the order of the day. This is possible because the prison is an institution which "presents a paradox of intentionality" (Heller 88). That is, the face function of the institution is 'rehabilitation' but, on actual sense, its goal is to be "the best means, one of the most efficient and most rational, to punish infractions in a society" (Foucault, "What Calls for Punishment?" 280; Heller 88). The narrator, Albert Kweyu (A.K), is initiated into the prison's rituals of violence by stripping (*Jail Bugs* 5–6). This is a *tactic* meant to violate a person's individual space. It is meant to display power's ability to scrutinize even the darkest recesses of the object's anatomy. This is then followed by a painful headcount in which the baton "taps" the head of the prisoner. Here power inscribes itself onto the object's body as closest to his bone and, consequently, to his soul as possible. The Prison Commandant claims:

> Our duty is not to punish but to correct and that is why I always insist to my officers that they *must never* beat up a prisoner since there are other *more civilised ways of punishing* crime. (emphasis added, 126)

The contradiction between the prison's *tactics* and *strategies* is apparent here. While the prison's *tactics* claim to rehabilitate, the system fails to ready the prisoners for a normal life back in *human* society. The absurdity of the prison system is thus laid bare. The prison's *tactics* claim to rehabilitate the prisoners, however, it does this through uprooting them and denying them any shred of humane treatment. Thus, beyond the prison walls the prisoner is incapable of being integrated back into the society from which he was netted. There is, among the prisoners, the constant anxiety that one has nothing to go home to. The likes of Pepeto and Fixer are more at home in the prison – at least, here they know and understand what entails the *norm* and can operate well within it. The prison's *strategies*, in the end show that this is the place where "[a] criminal [i]s not going to be reborn. He is about to be re-made with harder metal" (*Jail Bugs* 82). It is in the borstal institution that Pancho graduates into another level of violence:

> I was there long enough to learn how to bear the pain of having my head knocked and how to make other people feel pain by knocking their heads. I was no longer to be the one to be hit without hitting back. They were two years of what I would call the 'university of life'...My life was already made. (97)

The lesson which the prison appears to have taught Pancho is how to reappropriate his body and transform it into an object of meting out violence on other people. This disjunction is a productive interstice because herein individuals *make* themselves – their choices constitute their identities.

The prison system borrows heavily from the political ethics of the state. Herein too, bodies eat and stomachs have to be filled – the warden's and the prisoner's alike. The kitchen staff can easily strike deals with the wardens by ensuring that the wardens get a kilo or two of meat and beans from the kitchen. This transaction is smoothly carried out because, after all, it is not their meat (*Jail Bugs* 47). The prison's clinical officer is an indefatigable man whose motivation to work is only commensurate with his appetite (38). Since medicine as a discourse has its own claim to truth, it is, thus, possible that through him the prisoners are *capable* of "falling sick" and contracting diseases (of course, at a fee) that not only make them "entitled" to a well-cooked balanced diet (45) but also help them escape being "profitably engaged" in hard labour (35) – a contradiction between power's tactics and its strategies. The clinical officer is able to exercise power *intentionally* to displace the prison law without replacing it. He offers an alternative route for the exercise and experience of power, for resistance. He is able to touch and affect the power mechanisms of the prison creating a disjuncture. The dangers of this disjuncture are that it works for a brief period/duration before tactics and strategies converge. At the point of convergence, the power relation is replaced by *violence*. Here the clinical officer must prescribe (at a fee, *again*) the drugs for the prisoners confined in the madhouse (185–186). The madhouse is another prison within the prison – the prisoner is already separated from the social body as a deviant – sentenced to prison – and in here he has to be medicated so as to separate him from his *self*. Here power's productivity, minimum supervision and surveillance results in the highest discipline effect, morphs into violence: the prisoner willingly takes the drugs so as to escape reality.

Locating Bodies, Displacing Power

In *Jail Bugs*, Charge in Block G sleeps on elevated ground (24). High up
on this pedestal, he is able to exercise power on those beneath him. He
commands some measure of admiration and can ask/demand for favours
from up here. He asks Pepeto to make sleeping room for the newcomer,
A.K (25). He has a special meal, in the ward and even has his own mug
while the rest of the prisoners share one (58). Pancho tells A.K., "Wait
until you become a man" (58). 'Men' enjoy better meals as Charge does.
Meals which even the wardens can barely afford in their own homes
(59). This high sleeping place is meant to be for surveillance, as the
prison power trickles down. However, instead of being a space for rever-
ence of the prison laws and power, it becomes a space for the subversion
of the all-pervasive Prison Act. On this ground, Charge makes sexual
advances to a newcomer and homosexuality finds a place here. Pancho
comments: "I guess now that he is a cock and not a cockroach, Charge
will feel like a man. He has been a laughingstock for being a cockroach
at his age" (132). The ambivalence is, thus, revealed. There is the 'cock'
and the 'cockroach'. Being the latter is better than the former especially
when coupled with age. This, however, does not deter the other prisoners from admiring Charge and his new catch (130–131; 150). For the
narrator, however, the idea of homosexual desires is more palatable and
pervasive in the madhouse – the prison within a prison. There, in finer
detail, he describes the scene as two men fondle each other's breasts
(159). Thus, the madhouse, the prison's most productive and efficient
space for discipline and surveillance becomes a space for the subversion
of sexual desires.

The prison authority views the prisoners as a homogenous body:
'thieves, conmen and rapists' (*Jail Bugs* 3). This is in spite of the differences in the nature of the crimes allegedly [not] committed. This homogeneity is meant for effective administration. However, while the system
readily seeks to reduce their individuality, for the prisoners themselves it
is as important as the peculiarity of the crime that landed them in there.
The nature of the crime is quite important for survival in prison. A.K
"learned the lesson that the crime that lands one in this place determines
what kind of friends and enemies you will make moments after the frisk-
ing exercise with Walrus". (19)

Faced by the banal violence of the prison, the most urgent need and
desire, for the prisoners, is to survive the present. Survival requires living
with the *hope* that the outside world cares for the prisoner. The prisoner
has to live with the hope that his wife is still as faithful, and his mother
still alive, or perhaps his loot is still safe awaiting his release. However,
few prisoners have any of these to look forward to and therefore have to
result to imagined and imaginary narratives of *criminal* heroism which
subvert the prison ethos and help them survive the quotidian violent

reality. Petty crimes are also shunned: "None of the inmates want to be associated with small crimes" (91). A.K feels somewhat as an outsider because his crime is insignificant, if not a sorry incident. Hitting and running over an innocent child is not worth narration unless one was driving a getaway vehicle, with the police hot in pursuit, after a successful bank heist. Prisoners have to reimagine their life histories – to reimagine themselves as heroes, or as victims of the system. Since the prison, as pointed above, operates and borrows from the ethics of the state: to eat or be eaten, a crime committed in the line of feeding and clothing oneself and his/her family is, for the prisoner, the epitome of 'goodness'. Under a corrupt and inept regime, where power is exercised and paraded by one's ability to eat and eat well without being caught, the prisoner celebrates his achievement through narratives as one of the many. This is not a parody of the national ethics but rather is a way of taking part in a system that cannot be resisted otherwise – the ethos of the "'goat that grazes where it is tethered'" (Mbembe; "The Banality" 9–10).

It is through such narratives that prisoners invent and establish new solidarities through which they are able to escape vulnerability and survive violence. The crime which led to the prisoner's exclusion becomes the criterion of admission into new communities. These communities are fluid. Newcomers are accordingly admitted with respect to their crimes, a characteristic important for individual and collective survival. Irrespective of the prison one lands into, whether Sura Ngumu or Wakora Wengi, one is bound to find a community into which his crime will have him admitted. These imagined and imaginary self-narratives are, however, not limited to 'admirable' crimes, they also include snippets of the triumph of the prisoner's brains over the warden's brute brawn. For instance, Fixer has his epic narrative of how he was able to convince Kivunja, a warden, to escort him out of prison for a piece of his stashed loot of precious stones. Instead, Fixer goes on a sexual tryst with Amina (84–90). The tale, like many others, is ludicrous and unbelievable. Whether true or fictitious is irrelevant. What is most important for the prisoners is that these narratives help them escape and survive the prison's everyday violence through humour. These tales are cathartic. They symbolically enable the prisoners to enact power, or a semblance of it. There is nothing as captivating as a narrative of the stupidity and inefficiency of the system as in Sergeant ('Major') Pilipili's case (108–110). These narratives, then, are the prisoner's triumph over prison atrocities; over the system, its inefficiency and the culpability of its representatives – the wardens. These narratives are employed in explaining the violence of the system as a projection of the wardens' own miserable lives.

In spite of the power exercised by the wardens, the prisoners have an advantage over them in that they get opportunities to get a glimpse of the *hidden transcripts* of the wardens, as mentioned earlier. Those prisoners who work in the warders' quarters and offices see the warders without their masks. These instances of witnessing the forbidden are important in the prisoners' attempt at displacing and inverting power. These moments offer rich material for the prisoners' narratives of self-creation. With these, they are able to ridicule the prison's power and authority and alleviate their own suffering, however fleetingly. The warders, on the other hand, cannot and do not get such an opportunity. Constant surveillance and violence have *disciplined* the prisoners to always be wary, if not wily. This is because "the more menacing the power, the thicker the mask" (Scott 3). In the dormitories, the prisoners reimagine and narrate tales of triumph and those which ridicule authority. These tales are narrated openly and quickly stop whenever the sound of approaching boots are heard. The prisoners feign sleep only to resume their jocular tales to the sound of receding boots. Violence appears to be the only tool available in the warders' route for exercising power in the prison space, and in the process of exercising this power, the prisoner learns concealed subversive survival tactics – almost displacing this power.

Conclusion

Narrating violence is a strategy of protest and a way of coming to terms with violence. The most important facet of this self-narration is that it is not only a way of keeping one's sanity, but also of giving voice to the fears, pain, and anxieties of other imprisoned bodies. This is reminiscent of the advice Wasonga Sijeyo gives to Ngugi, "[...] just watch your mind... don't let them break you and you'll be all right even if they keep you for life...but you must try...you have to, for us, for the ones you left behind" (*Detained* 8). Chipota, while lying in his cell in the basement of a city's high-rise, contemplates his fate – the cell he is in was surely built with torture in mind (*Three Days* 134), how many other people have undergone the same fate, he wonders. He wishes that he too has the strength and the means of scratching a message on the cell's walls. A memento – a narrative of being one, of being united, in pain. Whether he lives to tell his tale is beyond him. What is important is that someone else preceding him resisted no matter how brief their resistance might have been.

Mutahi's fiction, therefore, is a protest narrative denouncing the insensible violence and corruption of the state and its unprecedented effects on people. For Mutahi, the prison is caught in an impasse of intentions, its claims to rehabilitate are not in tandem with the power regime it serves. This discrepancy has a violent effect on the bodies and subjectivities of the individuals netted in it. Mutahi shows that the prison system fails to rehabilitate individuals but dehumanizes and destroys them. These narratives give voice to the many prisoners and detainees who were silenced both literarily and literally. What Mutahi shows is that no matter how much violence a despotic regime oppresses its subjects/prisoners, they find escape and tools for resistance in operating within and borrowing from the vocabulary of the state. Thus, prison/state neither succeeds in disciplining the prisoners nor do the prisoners transform the prison/state – each is comprised and compromised by the other.

This chapter has argued that under a system which is bent on *forcefully* transforming the actions and bodies of its subjects, the emergent relation is a *relation of violence* not of power. A *relation of power* is only present wherein the individual's desire for change, no matter how small, is realized.

Works Cited

Deacon, Roger. "An Analytics of Power Relations: Foucault on the History of Discipline." *History of the Human Sciences* 15.1 (2002): 89–117.

Death, Carl. "Counter-conducts: A Foucauldian Analytics of Protest." *Social Movement Studies: Journal of Social, Cultural and Political Protest* 9.3 (2010): 235–251. Taylor and Francis. doi:10.1080/14742837.2010.493655.

Foucault, Michel. *Discipline and Punish: The Birth of The Prison*. Trans. Alan Sheridan. Vintage, 1977.

———. *The History of Sexuality: An Introduction*, vol. 1. Trans. Robert Hurley. Penguin, 1998.

———. *Society Must Be Defended: Lectures at the College de France 1975–1976*. Ed. Mauro Bertani and Alessandro Fontana. Trans. David Macey. Picador, 2003.

———. *Michel Foucault, Power: Essential Works of Foucault 1954–1984*, Vol. 3. Ed. J. D. Faubion, Trans. Robert Hurley. New Press, 2002.

———. "Foucault at the Collège de France I: A Course Summary." *Philosophy and Social Criticism* 8.2 (1981): 235–242.

———. "What calls for punishment?." In his *Foucault Live (Interviews, 1966–84)*. semiotext(e), 1989.

———. "The Subject and Power," *Michel Foucault: Beyond Structuralism and Hermeneutic*. Ed. Hubert Dreyfus and Paul Rabinow. University of Chicago Press, 1983. 208–228.

Fraser, Nancy. *Unruly Practices: Power, Discourse and Gender in Contemporary Social Theory*. Polity, 1989.

Heller, J. Kevin. "Power, Subjectification and Resistance in Foucault." *SubStance* 25.1.9 (1996): 78–110. JSTOR. doi:10.2307/3685230.

Mbembe, Achille. "Necropolitics." *Public Culture* 15.1 (2003): 11–40. Trans. Libby Meintjes.

———. "The Banality of Power and the Aesthetics of Vulgarity in the Postcolony." *Public Culture* 4.2 (1992): 1–30. doi:10.1215/08992363-4-2-1.

Mutahi, Wahome. *The Jail Bugs*. Nairobi: Longhorn, 1992.

———. *Three Days on the Cross*. Nairobi: East African Educational Publishers, 1991.

Mutonya, Maina. "Crying as we Laugh: Writing Human Rights in Wahome Mutahi's Prison Memoirs", *Journal of the African Literature Association* 7.1 (2012): 35–54. *Taylor and Francis*. doi:10.1080/21674736.2012.11690198.

Wa Thiong'o, Ngugi. *Detained: A Writer's Prison Diary*. Nairobi: Heinemann, 1981.

Ogola, George. "Confronting and Performing Power: Memory, Popular Imagination and a "Popular" Kenyan Newspaper Serial. *African Studies* 64.1 (2005): 73–85. *Taylor and Francis*. doi:10.1080/00020180500139064.

———. "Writing 'Conflict': Whispers as a 'Restorative' Narrative". *Social Dynamics* 30.2 (2005): 207–220. *Taylor and Francis*. doi:10.1080/02533950408628693.

Ruganda, John. *Telling the Truth Laughingly: The politics of Francis Imbuga's Drama*. Nairobi: East African Educational Publishers, 1992.

Scott, C. James. *Domination and the Arts of Resistance: Hidden Transcripts*. Yale University Press, 1990.

Taylor, Charles. "Foucault on Freedom and Truth." *Political Theory* 12.2 (1984): 152–184.

Widder, Nathan. "Foucault and Power Revisited." *European Journal of Political Theory* 3.4 (2004): 411–432.

4 Derision, Delirium, and Denied Justice in Benjamin Garth Bundeh's *Birds of Kamiti*

Larry Ndivo

Introduction

Crime and punishment is a subject that has continued to stimulate scholarly debates. Arguments abound on whether after committing a crime and being punished for it, one is reformed or not. There appears to be a paucity of scholarly engagement on matters concerning unfair arrests, detentions, or unwarranted torture, especially in the Kenyan context. This chapter argues that the police as presented in Benjamin Garth Bundeh's memoir use torture to deride and coerce suspects to confess; then, they prosecute them and when convicted, the victims suffer unprecedented psychological pain that leaves them with traumatic memories of the legal process. The study borrows from trauma theory and provides an alternate perspective of examining prison writing in Kenya. The chapter contributes to existing studies on prison literature by demonstrating the interplay between denied justice and psychological trauma in literature.

Literary studies on prison writing in Kenya have largely concentrated on government repression and, in rare cases, the crime autobiography. Kennedy Walibora has examined prison writers in Kenya, specifically those of the conscience. Walibora's "Prison, Poetry and Polyphony in Abdilatif Abdalla's *Sauti ya Dhiki*" discusses Abdilatif Abdalla's prison poetry while under incarceration for sedition against Jomo Kenyatta's regime in post-independence Kenya. Walibora reckons that "the terribly unpleasant prison conditions that the poet experienced, enabled, and enhanced the occurrence in his poetry of a psychic or philosophical journey..." (129). The reference to the psyche illustrates the psychological dimension of imprisonment and hints at how Kenyan prison writers have endeavoured to narrativize their mental turmoil.

Evan Mwangi makes a case for the need to study less examined Kenyan texts by noting that the mention of John Kiriamiti's *My Life in Crime* in Kenyan popular fiction serves "to repudiate the dominant canon" (102) which is usually examined at the expense of popular texts that are considered less serious. Indeed, there have been studies on popular Kenyan novels such as Roger Kurtz's *Urban Obsessions Urban Fears: Postcolonial Kenyan Novels*, Tom Odhiambo's *The '(un)Popularity' of Popular Fiction in Kenya: The Case of David Gian Maillu*, Mathew

Christensen's *African Popular Crime Genres and the Genres of Neoliberalism*, and Nici Nelson's *Representations of Men & Women, City & Town in Kenyan Novels of the 1970's & 1980s* amongst others. However, apart from Walibora's research, these studies remain silent on the traumatizing aspects of imprisonment which is examined in this chapter.

George Ogola argues for the study of popular texts since they "are products of an era, providing insights into an emerging urban culture" (9). Prison literature, like the text under study, is part of popular texts that help us understand society, making it an important strand for analysis. Prison acts as an important space for creative and critical material providing a rich source of literary discourse. For instance, in the colonial period "the prison and detention camp was the location for physical punishment, in the form of exposure to extremely unhealthy conditions, poor diet and corporal punishment" (Branch 241). It appears that even in post-colonial Kenya, little if nothing, has changed regarding the conditions in prison. Consequently, this chapter posits that by the time Bundeh writes his memoir, the prison was still a locus for torture and a symbol of injustice. Bundeh's *Birds of Kamiti* unravels how the persona resists prison discourse and identity to reclaim his personality as a father, a son, and a loving husband. To this end, the chapter examines derision, delirium, and Denied Justice in Bundeh's *Birds of Kamiti* from the narrator's point of view. It is important to note that in this chapter the term narrator and the author are used to refer to the same personality.

Trauma theory focuses on the relationship of words and trauma and helping us to "read the wounds" through literature. The theory which derives from psychoanalytic sources holds that traumatic knowledge from the source consists of two contradictory elements. One is the traumatic event, registered rather than experienced. This goes beyond perception and the consciousness, and falls directly to the psyche. The other is on a kind of memory of the event. This often relies on the narrator's perpetual troping of the event without figuring it through the dissociated psyche. Literature relies on these two levels at as reads various traumatic experiences in works of art.

Brief Overview of *Birds of Kamiti*

Benjamin Garth Bundeh's *Birds of Kamiti* is a memoir in which the writer adopts a persona to remember the events connected with his arrest and subsequent conviction for the murder of Mr. Nigel Fawsset, an old white businessman and business associate. Narrated in retrospect, the story highlights the persona's struggle to repudiate the police evidence against him when he lodges an appeal in the hope that justice can be meted out to him. While serving his time on death row, the persona encounters the debilitating effects of capital punishment and the terror it unleashes on the human soul. The horrendous events that unfold at

Kamiti are despicable and they attest to the animalistic tendencies that human beings are reduced to when incarcerated. The writer, therefore, uses the memoir genre to memorialize the dark events connected to his years in prison. Although his experience is one that can be described as unspeakable and one which the writer would rather forget, he has to relive the trauma – to remember the painful details; hence, he has to confess (through the writing of his story) what happened to him so that he can begin his traumatic healing.

Bundeh's breakthrough happens when he conducts his appeal and gets acquitted of the murder of Fawssett. He regains a sense of self-worth although he harbours bitterness towards the government for unfair imprisonment. His pain and anguish are a major hindrance to his emotional and psychological healing. However, he finds a sense of closure about the death of some of his colleagues through the assurance that the birds of Kamiti keep vigil over their graves. His testimony is symbolic of the victims of unjust legal systems whose stories are cast into oblivion through capital punishment and subsequent death.

Derision: Torture and Coerced Confession

Benjamin Bundeh's memoir foregrounds stories of individuals incarcerated in Kenyan prisons for contested crimes. This is best exemplified by political memoirs by former detainees who claim that they were unjustly detained, especially during the reign of President Daniel Arap Moi. Such political memoirs include Wahome Mutahi's *Three Days on the Cross* and *Jail Bugs*, Koigi wa Wamwere's *I Refuse to Die: My Journey for Freedom*, Ngugi wa Thiong'o's *Detained: A Writer's Prison Diary*, Kenneth Matiba's *Aiming High: The Story of My Life,* and Wanyiri Kihoro's *Never Say Die: The Chronicle of a Political Detainee* among others. Wanyiri Kihoro's memoir, for instance, recounts his torture by police for alleged involvement in subversive politics demonstrates his psychological anguish resulting from police torture. By highlighting police atrocities, both Bundeh and Kihoro, convinces readers to take sides and empathize with their suffering thereby absolving them of the accusations levelled against them by the police.

Birds of Kamiti presents a discourse of hope and perseverance owing to the narrator's experiences while in prison. Like other Kenyan prison writers, Bundeh writes his memoir on toilet chapter in addition to scribbling in between the lines in the Bible. In this way, this chapter reckons that the prison space inspires creativity and a sense of imagination. This perception is affirmed by Walibora who posits "prison lends itself towards self-reflection and introspection" (130). Bundeh's incarceration provides fodder for his bitterness towards government percolating his imagination and hence his memoir serves as a fissure to let out the fury churning out of the depths of his mental recesses. Bundeh casts prison as a site of physical and psychological torture. Incarceration alienates him from his family and his belief in the Kenyan legal process. He narrates experiencing a growing sense of déjà vu and utter fear because of being kept in the dark about his hanging. When the judge reads out his sentence, the persona attests that the wheels of delirium gain momentum: "I began to feel as though I was caught in a ring of iron which was all the time contracting, with the aim of crushing me in the end" (67). The persona's psychological anguish is profound especially the minute the judge utters the word death in his ruling. He half-consciously conveys his emotions to the reader as events unfold in the courtroom:

> When my death was mentioned, I bolted upright, stark terror charging through me, pounding in my temples and racing through my heart. I was breaking down. But I didn't faint. I just stared at the vague shapes in the courtroom. Then I saw my wife shuddering and screaming. It was a sharp piercing scream of a trapped animal. I saw her struck by the death that had been imposed on me. She was in mortal agony, clinging to my sister who was also in acute state of panic. My mother was there too shuddering in an agony hard to describe. She then fell down: it was all sure-real (sic). (68)

This description starkly presents the unfolding court drama as if it were a surreal motion picture thereby showing the narrator's state of mind as delirious. It further comes across to him through bizarre and nebulous images exposing the fear gushing through his brain, which almost leads to a total nervous breakdown. He much later confesses that being on death row is equal to keeping "... the mind in balance on false hope" (108). He feels betrayed and abandoned by the judicial system; thus, justifying his virulent thoughts a few moments before the judge sentences him.

Bundeh's self-consciousness is characterized by the impending sense of death as he takes time to gaze at fellow prisoners whilst being led to his cell. His consciousness betrays the ambivalence of the narrative voice in the memoir: "My body followed the hangman without conscious direction from the brain" (72). In retrospect and conscious at the time of writing of the memoir, Bundeh can, recollect the events that characterized the few moments of his agonizing walk of death and the ensuing psychological trauma of trying to count the number of steps that human being takes in their lifetime before realizing that one of them is going to be the last one! He observes that in one cell there are four prisoners who "looked like figures out of a nightmare, like ghosts" (73). His perception – distinction of reality and imagination – is blurred by the shock of his death sentence but he is acutely aware of the fear and terror overpowering his cellmates.

While the narrator's solace is found in his confinement with other death row inmates, he often succumbs to self-pity as he observes, "Now I had become one of them. We were the worst among the wicked, the most wretched among the criminals. We were demons in hell-fire, emaciated and wasted" (73). The persona's perception of the plight of the death row convicts conveys loss of identity and extreme levels of dehumanization: "We looked worse than a crowd of beggars. We were phantoms: sexless, ghastly creatures" (73). In this light, capital remand becomes a trope for the Kenyan government's violation of human rights – a source of the individual's mental breakdown.

Through the narration, the reader gets to understand that there are birds in Kamiti prison, which form the image from which the text borrows its title. These birds are a trope that embodies the prisoners' longing for freedom as well as their problematic space into which the alleged crime has cast them. For the persona, it is a space that he can neither qualify nor quantify. The fact that he, through introspection, describes his time on death row through blurred images reveals his state of mind at the time as he confesses: "Throughout that period of my life, I felt as though I was suspended between Heaven and Hell" (73). The narrator's mortal fear of death draws the reader's empathy towards his humiliation as he disintegrates sobbing, whilst a cellmate assumes the responsibility to encourage him through emotional support and sharing of basic items including a toothbrush – that the narrator describes as "the highest rank of generosity in prison" (74). This serves to show the dehumanizing conditions that the convicts undergo in prison added to psychological pain that is later reflected through the emotional scars that those who survive incarceration carry into their freedom.

Delirium: The Fear of Death

Birds of Kamiti is a memoir that provides a scathing appraisal of the Kenyan penal system that traumatizes the narrator. We can then argue that Bundeh writes this narrative to help him cope with the traumatizing exigencies of being accused of the murder of Fawssett. Dialectically, the narrator's identity is recreated through the prison space. He adopts a journey motif that encapsulates different moments from his capture, torture, and forced confession to conviction and incarceration on death row at the Kamiti maximum security prison. It is through this journey that the reader experiences the bouts of delirium that he undergoes, first through torture in order to confess, and later through the smell of death as he witnesses the execution of his fellow inmates.

It is the hanging of Ogollah, one of the death row inmates, that leads to the narrator's capitulation into deep psychological pain as he struggles to understand how a human being can execute a fellow being. Perhaps this is what Cathy Caruth considers trauma when she observes that it is

> "much more than a pathology, or the simple illness of a wounded psyche: it is always the story of a wound that cries out, that addresses us in the attempt to tell us of a reality or truth that is not

otherwise available" (*Unclaimed*, 4). The death cries of Ogollah are so traumatising to the persona that he loses faith in God and religion: "I found it difficult to understand the comfort people get from religion, those people who believe in a just God". (112)

Whilst confessing to his sense of despair, the persona reveals to the reader how death row inflicts lasting traumatic experiences. These memories are dialectically linked to the convicts' emotions of pain and suffering as they wait for the hangman to summon them to their death. Bundeh writes to illustrate how he was a witness to what Felman and Laub refer to as "witness to a trauma, to a crime or to an illness whose effects explode any capacity for explanation or rationalization (*Testimony* 4). As a result, Bundeh opens up about the bouts of delirium that they suffered collectively: "We would sometimes experience hallucinations and terrible nightmares" (117). Perhaps these experiences of emotional breakdown are to blame for the death row convicts' deterioration into immoral behaviour whilst in incarceration. The persona says, "Prisoners did things which decency scarcely provides the words to tell" (98); thus, intimating that prison isolation is to be blamed for the convicts' unhinged personalities and indulgence in what the persona describes as indecent behaviour. It is for this reason that the writer surmises that "These men with strange tastes were sick men" (99) who should have been counselled as opposed to being punished.

Birds of Kamiti depicts Kenyan prison suffering and Bundeh's cry for justice emblematizes the sorry conditions of death row inmates convicted for crimes which are sometimes suspect. This perception is given impetus by Odemba's plea to Bundeh that he must go out and tell the world what is happening in Kamiti (114). The unsaid anguish of death row prisoners is also reflected in subtexts that are expressed through prison wall graffiti: "Please contribute coins here to buy God a pair of glasses so he can see the suffering of man and beast" (112). Such texts demonstrate that the convicts undergo untold suffering and pain to an extent that they start doubting whether God hears their cries. The narrator's confinement undermines his sense of identity and his ability to understand God and the nature of human beings. In a sense, Bundeh and his jailbirds have already undergone social death since they are denied access to sunshine; they are warned against engaging in any form of exercise or even holding conversations with one another. Social death has been defined by Lisa Guenther as "the effect of a (social) practice in which a person or group of people is excluded, dominated or humiliated to the point of becoming dead to the rest of society" (*Solitary Confinement* 5). It is for this reason that Bundeh's fellow inmates urge him to tell the world about their suffering and abandonment in death row.

Denied Justice: Death Row as a Traumatic Experience

Birds of Kamiti is characterized by multiple voices of bitterness, regret, contrition, despair, and optimism amongst others. The narrator, for instance, describes the voice of the police as one of derision. When Bundeh attempts to negotiate with the police after his arrest, he is categorically informed, "Murderers are not people! We can do whatever we like with them" (2). This statement demonstrates the scorn that the police exhibit towards suspects even before conclusive evidence is adduced in court to convict them. Perhaps, the police, perpetrators of lies against the persona, hinge their confidence in Herman's argument that "perpetrators will fight tenaciously to ensure that their abuses remain unseen, unacknowledged, and consigned to oblivion" (*Trauma* 246). Courtroom proceedings reproduced in this memoir are part of the persona's testimony to his truthfulness. In equal measure, the persona also derides the police for being dishonest and uses sarcastic language to describe their actions and their words. Bundeh describes the Investigation Officer's actions after his testimony against him with a sense of contempt:

> When the cross-examination was over, the witness was so pleased with himself that he even forgot to bow before he walked out of the witness box. Drunk with his historic role as the man who solved the murder case of a white man, the old superintendent left the courtroom. (64)

The biting tone and sense of betrayal are visible in Bundeh's words in this context when he describes the Investigation Officer as someone mentally intoxicated with lies. We can deduce that the persona appears to suggest that the police who incriminate suspects on trumped-up charges are themselves criminals who should be punished by law. The narrator declares that "The police are not angels, whatever they say is not Gospel truth" (145) and that the judge's ruling should be overturned since he had been passionate with his judgement. In Bundeh's argument, the responsibility to bear witness and to be empathetic falls on the judge. As a result, the failure by Justice Brar to see the persona as a victim of police injustice casts him as a defensive person thereby affirming the psychoanalytic views of "denial, distancing and disassociation" (Herman 244).

The sense of dehumanization in this memoir is captured through the hangman who is also the butt of Bundeh's derision. Bundeh describes him as a man who talks "rumbling cheerfully" (96). The incongruent juxtaposition of the two words is indicative of the narrator's distaste towards the hangman. The warder confesses his dehumanization by roaring in laughter when he says thus, "We don't know if capital punishment is a deterrent, but we know that the men we hang will not murder again" (116). From the warder's words, it would appear that the purpose of capital punishment is not to punish and reform the convicts; rather, it reflects the legal system's determination to deter people from crime even as it fails to prosecute fairly. The hangman's penchant for the convicts' suffering portrays his cruelty and lack of empathy for their emotions. It is for this reason that one of the convicts declares that he wishes to be executed quickly so that he can be in heaven before the devil knows about his death since "[a]t the moment the devil has plenty to track among the living" (114). While the prisoner's words, on the one hand, create a sense of humour when he jokes about the devil, on the other hand, it demonstrates the desperation that sinks into the minds of the prisoners waiting for death in the cells.

Birds of Kamiti is a story about Bundeh's incarceration, subsequent suffering on death row, and his eventual release after appealing against the judge's lopsided sentence. Through the eyes of the narrator, we perceive the testimonial representation of the other, prisoners who were hitherto voiceless owing to the silencing nature of Kenyan prisons at the time. His testimony comes across as a successful means through which he rediscovers the self – the innocent. According to Herman, "Remembering and telling the truth about terrible events are prerequisites both for the restoration of the social order and for the healing of individual victims" (*Trauma* 1). Thus, although it is not possible for Bundeh to regain his economic status after being released from prison, his ability to narrate about his victimization and psychological torture while incarcerated will definitely mark an important step in his journey towards the attainment of closure.

In this memoir, truth and lie converge and diverge depending on who is speaking. As a result, the text provides an interesting discourse for a discussion on 'truth claims'. For instance, the prosecuting officers provide unsubstantiated accusations against Bundeh. From the beginning of the memoir, the police are cast as liars who perpetuate a sense of injustice. In the preliminary hearing in court, the narrator confesses:

> As the policemen continued testifying, I suddenly realised that I could be tightly trapped in the thick, oozy webs of police lies. I watched myself being captured and turned into an outrageous carnival show. The policemen had woven such a web of lying adjectives that even my experienced lawyer found himself in a rather difficult situation when cross-examining them. (23)

In this quotation, the reader is persuaded to see the police officers as unreliable witnesses since the evidence they provide cannot be corroborated: "The confession statement allegedly made by the second accused had no corroboration whatsoever" (23). Thus, because Gallagher posits, "genuine confession works against the propagation of oppression" (*Truth* 179) then the reader can surmise that the police are dishonest in their quest to convict the persona for the murder of Fawssett as this results in his oppression.

Bundeh's incarceration is reminiscent of the psychological agony that he undergoes which culminates in a personal struggle to resist succumbing to resignation and eventual death in prison. Delegating to himself a sense of social responsibility, he says, "Though I was an innocent victim of the law in that crowded, stinking part of the world, I was also an observer" (78–79). The first person's point of view is believable because it renders first-hand testimony to the reader. The narrator is both an observer and a participant in the drama of life; that is, the social injustices unfolding in society.

The author's version of the court case gains credibility when he describes the confessions of other convicted criminals who pour out their hearts to him. This way his narrative echoes Mary Fulbrook's words that "memory does not take place in a vacuum but under specific historical circumstances" (*German* 147). In *Birds of Kamiti*, the narrator's memory is fed by his historical experience, interaction, and observation of fellow death row inmates. There seems to be an unspoken pact between him and the reader; that if the persona does not censure his inmates' stories, he would also not corrupt his own story. This is aptly captured in the opening lines of his memoir: "This story is about my personal experiences and recollections of the events of these two and half years. There is no creativity involved in my writing, just remembrance" (1).

The sense of injustice that pervades the narrative is illustrated through coercion and the manner in which the prisoners are transported. They are carried around as chattels, which is discerned in the vocabulary when the narrator uses the word "freighted" and eventually describes how their humanity is taken away, and they are reduced to mere numbers. This echoes Gallagher's words that forced confessions and subsequent incarceration "remould individual identity" (*Truth* 8). Being dehumanized and denied healthy living conditions, the prisoners are alienated and this exacerbates the sense of injustice. Bundeh confesses about his agonizing experience with injustice after being convicted for the murder of a white man even though the evidence adduced in court is questionable:

> My cry is the desperate cry of one who has been made to go through the most unbearable experience a human being can be asked to endure. It led to a total breakdown of confidence in myself, in other people, in the State, and even in the goodness of life itself. Nobody could be trusted. Nothing was worth doing. (1)

By juxtaposing his lack of faith in himself vis-à-vis that of others, the narrator is admitting that whatever breaks a person's will to the extent of losing faith in the self is worthy to be publicly shared and to be believed. He lets the reader know that the police torture him, deny him food and drink in order to coerce him to confess to the murder of Fawssett. This is the confession that is used against him in court and one that he has to fight against if he is to be freed from jail.

Prison warders' search of convicts for contraband is a form of injustice towards the prisoners' sense of dignity and identity. The persona describes it as "the most repugnant" (4) because it demeans both the victim and the warder conducting the search. The persona's experience with the stripping of clothes and indecent groping by warders is dialectically intertwined with his forced confession and denied justice. According to Gallagher, "In the act of confession, prisoners continue the shedding of their selves that is preliminarily indicated by the physical stripping that is incarceration's common initiation ritual" (*Truth* 8). The shedding of clothes is the first step towards the remaking of the prisoner's identity. It is a mark of dehumanization and a reflection of the prisoners' powerlessness in the hands of warders who wield power against them. The writing of the memoir thus serves a crucial role in helping the persona to reconstruct his identity and reclaim his humanity that was denied through incarceration.

Birds of Kamiti is a testimony to the fact that court cases can drag and at times justice is not just delayed but it can be denied altogether. This is witnessed in the case for Ogollah and Ndambuki who hang for cases that other convicts seem to believe the two had not committed. Probably, the birds are Ndambuki's alibi attesting to his harmless nature when they feed from his hands and later make his grave rendezvous for their singing and dancing. Ogollah's alibi is Otieno who confesses: "Let the absolving words be said over my comrade Ogollah, and your own body be his food and your blood his sprinkling; for unlike me, he is dying for a crime he never committed" (112). The fact that these are "voices" of others as opposed to that of the narrator, lends the memoir a sense of believability since the writer infuses objectivity by letting others speak for themselves.

It is the sense of injustice that leads the persona to inscribe on the wall of their cell: "Please contribute coins here to buy God a pair of glasses so he can see the suffering of man and beast" (112). Like Abdalla in his poem *Sauti ya Dhiki*, Bundeh "comes across as an inexorable purveyor and defender of the truth" (Walibora 138). The persona's belief in his innocence becomes his driving force when he chooses to represent himself during the appeal: "I became convinced that my survival would depend on my ability to speak for myself, to argue my own case, since I was the defendant" (119). This choice is largely informed by the lack of faith in the judicial system. Bundeh refuses a court-appointed lawyer for fear that there might be collusion to deny him freedom:

> I don't need anybody's help! This government has charged me with an offence I never committed, it has convicted and sentenced me to death, and now it wants to provide me with a lawyer to defend

my life? You'll not fool me any longer. If your government wants to help me, why then doesn't it just set me free? It certainly has all the powers. This is my life and your government has nothing to do with it. (118)

Although the persona's action appears absurd, it is the government's offer to provide a lawyer, which essentially comes across as pointless. We are thus inclined to agree with the persona that "it is irresponsible for a prisoner condemned by the government, to allow the same government to engage a lawyer to defend his life" (118).

It is thus prudent to note that Bundeh's claim to torture and mistreatment at the hands of the police appears to repudiate what the police refer to as his confession. Further, Gallagher's discussion of testimonies coerced from suspects lends the persona's appeal weight because "Reduced to a psychophysical technique, judicial confession becomes solely admission, leaving both testimony and truth behind" (*Truth* 7). Therefore, Bundeh painstakingly pokes holes into the police evidence and successfully manages to demonstrate that Ex 29 is a false confession that the police fabricated in order to convict him. As a result, in his appeal he pleads with the judges, "Now, if the police could give such false evidence against me why should the court believe any other evidence they gave in court?" (135). Bundeh also opines that it is possible that he was "a victim of racial and economic prejudices" (146). Considering that Fawssett was white and of economic means, the persona speculates that his own life may have been deemed inconsequential and thus the biased ruling against him. It is also of import to factor in the possibility that there could have been diplomatic influence from the British High Commission's office to see that the perpetrator of the murder of their citizen is imprisoned.

Conclusion

This chapter has attempted to argue that Bundeh's *Birds of Kamiti* is a confession of the writer's unfair arrest, subsequent conviction, and incarceration for the murder of Nigel Fawssett. The persona's forced confession is used against him in court and when he is sentenced to death, he undergoes immensurable psychological turmoil that leads him to experience bouts of delirium. Bundeh is traumatized by the mistreatment during incarceration and more so by the imminent death hanging in the air as he witnesses first-hand the execution of his death row inmates. Thus, the chapter has argued that Bundeh writes about his incarceration to bear witness to the horrifying deaths of convicts because of capital punishment. Like Ngugi's diary, Bundeh's memoir "is the reaction, the active gesture of rebellion and rejection, that enables him to resist the pressures of imprisonment and maintain his sanity" (*Prison Diary* 614).

The chapter has identified instances of derision through which the memoir illustrates the use of language to signify acts of dehumanization and the need for human rights to be respected. Lastly, it has concluded that the persona in this text can only experience justice if the reparative process is objective and not biased against him. Hence, the writing of this memoir serves as therapy for the writer to unburden his soul as he relives the traumatizing experience of being on death row for a crime he believes he had not committed.

Works Cited

Brooks, Peter. *Troubling Confessions: Speaking Guilt in Law and Literature.* Chicago: University of Chicago Press, 2000.

Bundeh, Benjamin Garth. *Birds of Kamiti.* Nairobi: Spear Books (EAEP), 2004.

Caruth, Cathy. ed. *Trauma: Explorations in Memory.* Baltimore: The Johns Hopkins University Press, 1995.

Coetzee, John M. *Truth in Autobiography.* Cape Town: University of Cape Town Publishers, 1984.

Felman, Shoshana, and Dori Laub. *Testimony: Crises of Witnessing in Literature, Psychoanalysis and History.* New York: Routledge, 1992.

Gallagher, Susan V. *Truth and Reconciliation: The Confessional Mode in South African Literature.* Portsmouth: Heinemann, 2002.

Guenther, Lisa. *Solitary Confinement: Social Death and its Afterlives.* Minneapolis: University of Minnesota Press, 2013.

Herman, Judith. *Trauma and Recovery: The Aftermath of Violence – from Domestic Abuse to Political Terror.* New York: Basic Books, 1997.

Kihoro, Wanyiri. *Never Say Die: The Chronicle of a Political Prisoner.* Nairobi: EAEP, 1998.

Kiriamiti, John. *My Life in Crime.* Nairobi: Spear Books (EAEP), 1984.

Koigi wa Wamwere. *I Refuse to Die: My Journey for Freedom.* New York: Seven Stories Press, 2002.

Matiba, Kenneth. *Aiming High: The Story of My Life.* Nairobi: The People, 2000.

Mutahi, Wahome. *Three Days on the Cross.* Nairobi: Heinemann, 1991.

———. *The Jail Bugs.* Nairobi: Longman, 1992.

Mwangi, Evan. "The Incomplete Rebellion: Mau Mau Movement in Twenty-First-Century Kenyan Popular Culture." *Africa Today* 57.2 (Winter 2010): 86–113.

Peters, Edward. *Torture.* New York: Basil Blackwell, 1985.

wa Thiong'o, Ngugi. *Detained: A Writer's Prison Diary.* Nairobi: EAEP, 1981.

Walibora, Kennedy. "Prison, Poetry, and Polyphony in Abdilatif Abdalla's 'Sauti ya Dhiki'". *Research in African Literatures* 40.3 (Fall 2009): 129–148.

Wilkinson, Jane. "A Writer's Prison Diary: Ngugi wa Thiong'o's Detained." *Africa: Rivsta Trimestrale di Studi e Documentazione dell'Istituto Italiano per l'Africa e L'Oriente,* 38.4 (Dicembre 1983): 613–623.

5 Socio-economic Atrocities in Meja Mwangi's *Going Down River Road* and Kinyanjui Kombani's *The Last Villains of Molo*

Robert Wesonga

Introduction

This chapter locates the concept of atrocity in Kenya's socio-economic context extending the meaning of atrocity beyond physical violence or outrage. It analyses how language provides the means by which individuals living in atrocious socio-economic circumstances vent out their unenviable experiences of life. Specifically, it examines how the framings of discourses in two novels correspond to characters' socio-economic conditions. The chapter investigates speech acts of characters in Meja Mwangi's *Going Down River Road* and Kinyanjui Kombani's *The Last Villains of Molo* showing how language is not only used to alienate, but also to galvanize the masses to protest against the "other", and by extension, against atrocious socio-economic realities. In this regard, language is seen as an agency of mediation between characters and their socio-economic environment. Although the two novels are separated by three decades, evidenced from their dates of publication, they demonstrate that language used to depict socio-economic atrocities is more or less stable – even disobeying the passage of time. The chapter uses content analysis to read both the fictive and street discourses of the lower-class characters in the two novels and in modern-day Nairobi. This chapter holds that society is complex, and therefore, there are complex realizations of atrocity. Significantly, the chapter shows that language sets itself apart as perhaps the most advanced expression of atrocity.

Besides being a medium of expression, language functions as an agency of power, protest, alienation, and identity. Ruth Wodak observes that people present themselves to others through their choice of language or varieties of language (847). This chapter studies how characters in the selected two urban novels express their being to others and to the world around them through their speech behaviour. In addition, it compares incidences of character discourse in the two novels to the language which has been sampled from speakers in the low-class estates in Nairobi. Clearly, the two novels (with regard to dates of publication) are separated by close to 30 years. The sample has been arrived at with the intention of demonstrating that instances of language use under investigation continue to hold stable, in spite of the passage of years.

The first section of this chapter interrogates language use in *Going Down River Road* showing how characters, through language, shape and express their identity, alienate themselves, and express power over others. As Foucault in *Discipline and Punish* opines, "Power is something exercised, put into action, in relationships – an active relation, rather than a possession or static state of affairs." (26). In this regard, power is exercised through speech as read in the discourses of various characters in the two texts. The second and final section focuses on *The Last Villains of Molo* with the intention of investigating how the speech acts of various characters reveal a double-pronged endeavour to respond to two situations: (a) sad history of ethnic violence and (b) desperate socio-economic conditions in the city of Nairobi.

The Language of the Hardened Low-class Nairobi in Urban Fiction

Anchored on the notion that the environment within which people live determines their language, this section examines correlations between human language and socio-economic realities as portrayed in Meja Mwangi's novel. In his fiction, Meja Mwangi depicts the hardened life-styles of most of his characters based on the socio-economic conditions that they are living. A case in point is the characterization of Dusman, Toto, and Magendo in *The Cockroach Dance*. They are living in the low-class estates of Nairobi that is characterized by violent speech and physical violence. The use of curse words, a key trait of speech behaviour of male characters in the novel, constitutes expressions of power, alienation, and identity. Quoting Michel Foucault, Timothy Jay opines:

> Curse words are words we are not supposed to say; hence, curse words themselves are powerful. The words contain and are produced by social practices. The articulation of a curse word thus has incorporated into it social rules about gender identity, race, power, formality, prohibition, etc. (18)

The neighbourhood where the main characters in *Going Down River Road* reside spurs a linguistic register as exhibited by the two main characters in Meja Mwangi's novel. Ben and Ochola live in overcrowded slums where the low-class population of the city lives. Here, the author uses language as an agency through which characters express their

frustrations with their lowly life. Mwangi describes Ben's neighbourhood on Grogan Road (Kirinyaga Road in today's Nairobi) as follows:

> There were all sorts of people in the neighbourhood. There was a
> childless old woman who lived on hawking green vegetable matter.
> There were two refuse collectors, a Grogan Road mechanic who
> swore he was not a thief, and three retired whores who only did the
> occasional special duty with the landlord or somebody else. [...] and
> the unlicensed roadside cobbler, two neighbours who spent the days
> racing one another round own in the course of their duties before
> coming home to be good neighbours at night. Then there were Max
> and his bugs in the room next door. The lot could only be described
> as professional trouble-makers. Ben hated them. But more than Max
> and his gang, Ben loathed their monstrous Grundig stereogram. It
> appeared someone had turned it full volume a long time ago, then
> lost the volume control dial. (Mwangi, 3)

In this excerpt, Mwangi gives readers a panoramic view of residences in
low-class Nairobi, which accommodate people who have been brought
together by harsh socio-economic realities. Ben's residence on Grogan
road is peopled with thieves, prostitutes, hawkers, peddlers of drugs and
other illicit substances, and labourers like Ben and Ochola. The description paints a picture of confusion, similar to the psychological turmoil
that most of the inhabitants of Ben's tenement show because, often times,
they come home to momentarily try and escape the harsh environment
on the streets. The dialogue between Ben and Wini reveals a lot:

> The boy screamed his heart out. The usual morning crust of hard bread
>   aroused no interest. And as though enough was not enough, he
>   kicked the offered cup of cold milk into the urine sodden bed.
> "The boy is ill," she said and picked up the empty cup.
> Ben clenched his teeth and struggled to stay calm. The screams tore at
>   his nerves, while Wini's relaxed pose frustrated him madly.
> "What should I do with him?" she asked.
> "*First shut him up*, he is worse than Max's records."
> "But how?"
> "*Put your foot in his mouth*," he shouted. She looked at
> him and even more aggravatingly calm said in a matter-of
> fact tone:
> "**Men are bastards**." (Mwangi 5) (Emphasis mine)

This dialogue shows how living conditions in which the characters
find themselves have made them callous and irritable. The dialogue is
sandwiched in-between descriptions that define the low-class band of
neighbours that Ben has and the squalor in which they live. The difficult

conditions have rendered Ben inhuman so that he now suggests that Wini should insert her foot in the baby's mouth to silence him. After a hard day's work on the previous day, Ben goes out on a drinking spree at the famous *Karara Centre* where cheap and illicit liquor is sold. As such, the slightest noise makes him irritable.

The difficult conditions in the city for lowly paid Wini have driven her into part-time prostitution. In this trade, she has encountered the callousness of men, thus justifying her assertion that "men are bastards" (5). The impact of the work environment on city dwellers is revealed through Ben's work-related escapades. The following conversation ensues between Ben and the register clerk one morning on reporting to work:

> The tiny register clerk peered at him through the tiny office window. When he spoke, his breath stank of *karara* and dirt. He was hung up and disheveled.
> "Name?" he croaked.
> "Ben."
> "Ground duties today, Ben."
> "Ground duties, my *arse*. Check again."
> The roster clerk did so, his dirty eyes squinting at the duty roster that shook in is unsteady hands.
> "Still reads ground to me," he drawled. Ben craned his neck.
> "Let me see." He read then cursed. "This is last week's arrangements!"
> "Sure," the other nodded.
> "*Bullshit…*" (Mwangi 11) (Emphasis mine)

It is evident that Ben detests his job and only does it for survival. He hates it because it is difficult and poorly remunerated. This chapter infers that life and work in Nairobi have turned the likes of Ben into the objects they curse. They are the scum of the earth, and thus their identity is not far removed from such low and gross objects as *arse* and *bullshit*. The language the author uses to describe Ben's situation as cited in the excerpt confirms this: he does not talk, he either *croaks* or *curses*. Such language is replicated by fellow-labourers at Development House and is enough proof that a difficult life is the origin of such linguistic coarseness. Ben, Ochola, and their workmates all represent the hardest working part of the city; the scum of the city – even the *arse* and *bullshit* of it. Having become all these base things, they have no qualms mentioning them.

It is not only the harsh working environment that spurs an unrestrained traumatized mindset that makes characters like Ben to use swear and taboo words in their everyday speech and in the home environment too. His abrasive speech also stems from the hardships that he undergoes at home. He and Ochola live in a slum along the filthy Nairobi River.

Time and again, the duo have to contend with the Nairobi City Council Askaris who are sent to evict them and burn down their settlements. Besides, Ben finds himself in a very precarious situation after his prostitute girlfriend, Wini, leaves her son, Baby, with him and gets married to a Whiteman. In addition to the already difficult life that he is leading, Ben has to figure out how to take care of Baby – something he has never done in his life. David Crystal has written on the relationship between language, conflict, and psychology:

> There are the many daily examples of taboo speech, usually profanities or obscenities that express such emotions as hatred, antagonism, frustration, and surprise. The most common utterances consist of single words or short phrases (though lengthy sequences may occur in accomplished 'swearers'), conveying different levels of intensity and attracting different degrees of social sanction. (61)

Thus, Crystal links the use of swear or taboo words to the emotional and psychological state of individuals. Timothy Jay further explains how personality factors that accrue out of socio-economic conditions motivate the use of curse words; that human beings are able to achieve, through use of swear words, such emotional states as "stress reduction" (Jay, 18). The need to achieve emotional and psychological stability, hence, becomes a personal necessity for those living in various forms and levels of social and economic hardships. This without doubt applies to the case of Meja Mwangi's characters.

The type of language used by Mwangi's characters shows how they are oppressed by their socio-economic environment. Their difficult working and living conditions have conditioned them to instinctively curse, rebuke, and verbally and physically assault. Ben and Ochola also use the obscene and swear language to alienate their seniors at Development House construction site. The profane language, therefore, should be read as a form of protest against oppressive home and work environments.

Ethnic Atrocity as Precursor to Atrocious Language in Urban Fiction

Drawing illustrations from *The Last Villains of Molo*, this section examines violence in speech as an incident arising from ethnic-based violence. In *The Last Villains of Molo*, ethnic animosities create socio-economic challenges faced by the main characters. Consequently, this section shows how such harsh socio-economic realities motivated by ethnic strains result in the use of atrocious language. Hence, character discourses and narrative descriptions are analysed in order to reveal the use of atrocious language in the text. The narrative description by the writer sets an appropriate mood for character dialogues and validates the disgust that characters feel, living in such undesirable conditions:

> The dance floor was full of young school children, some hardly fourteen. How they gained entry into the club despite the age restrictions in the club was a mystery. The *smell of cigarette smoke hung* in the air. The *booming* hip hop music *reverberated* everywhere. (2) (Emphasis mine)

With this description, the writer appeals to our sense of smell and hearing to create a feeling of repulsion and disgust at the despicable conditions of the characters, which make them talk the way they do. The expressions *"cigarette smoke hung"*, *"booming"* and *"reverberated"* in this quote are used to create the visual aura in the mind of the readers on the kind of environment that the characters are operating in. Like in *Going Down River Road*, in *The Last Villains of Molo* readers are thrust into a language which reveals the characters' frustrations accruing from their difficult socio-economic conditions. One of the drunken teenage boys at Los Angeles Club, for instance, uses swear words in a carefree manner, illustrating that such language use for him is the order of the day. While assaulting a girl in the club, he uses swear words *"Bloody....!"* and *"Bastard!"* to humiliate the girl and Bone. The boy's behaviour, though verbal, works the same way as Bone's physical behaviour. Like Bone's physical outrage against the boy, the boy's insults are meant to humiliate and to protest against anything or anyone that resists or irritates. Therefore, the verbal atrocity and physical violence are both attempts to express power over "the other" – the girl and Bone. Bone responds in his characteristic fashion – by kicking the boy – a physical expression of the violence. Through vivid description, the author reveals the social conditions of the boy which justifies that he is, like many other teenagers on this side of Nairobi, a victim of these conditions. The harsh social conditions drive the boy to use profane and swear speech. For this type of lowly teenagers, cheap liquor becomes the only way of escaping harsh realities and gives them temporary solace. The socio-economic condition of the teenager is captured thus:

> The drunken teenager was all over her, rumbling incoherently and spitting saliva into her face. He was suffering from a very bad dose of halitosis, the breath he emitted betraying a combination of the cheap spirits he had taken and complicating things further. (5)

In essence, atrocious speech and physical violence are seen as the means by which various characters hit back at their unenviable socio-economic situation. The author's comment combines with character dialogue to prove that the rough linguistic register borne in *Sheng* or English swear words is motivated more by the harsh socio-economic realities than by anything else. This case is illuminated in the exchange that follows:

> Irungu was immersed deep in thought when *Chokoraa* (street urchin) jolted him out of his memories. He screeched to a halt, the *mukokoteni* (handcart) an inch away from the boy. "Damn you!" he hissed, "can't you watch where you are going?"
> "Ah! *Ishia!*" Get lost, the street urchin shot back.
> Stung more by the frustration of work than the boy's contempt, Irungu slid under the long handle of the handcart and seized him by the collar, almost lifting him off his feet. (Kombani 127)

Sheng is prevalent in *The Last Villains of Molo*. Street urchins use "*Ishia!*" an equivalent of "*Go to hell!*" to dismiss Irungu. Characters use *Sheng* as they consciously strive to grapple with the frustrations of their immediate socio-economic environment. For instance, while the drunken boy uses language to resist Bone's intrusion into his affairs, the latter uses language and physical violence to display his power. This occurrence is in concurrence with Foucault's assertion of Power:

> Power relations include two elements: "that 'the other' (the one over whom power is exercised) be thoroughly recognized and maintained to the very end as a person who acts; and that, faced with a relationship of power, a whole field of responses, reactions, results, and possible inventions may open up. (220)

The need to show the psychology of "the tough guy" and his dominance over "the other" drive several *Sheng* utterances by youthful characters in the text. Expressions such as "*Iko nini?*" (What is it?), "*Kwani?*" (So what?) and "*Uta do?*" (What will you do about it?) serve as illustrations of the language of hardened youth and is often used to express their defiance against tough socio-economic conditions in which they live and to portray "the other" as weaker or lesser. It is instructive to note that these utterances only occur in an environment of quarrel and looming violence between urban teenagers in the novel.

In *The Last Villains of Molo*, language is used as an alienating tool and often, to express the "us versus them" dichotomy between the affluent and less affluent in society. The well-to-do boys in the secondary school that Irungu attends, before he escapes into the streets of Nairobi, use language to alienate him because he is poor and to identify themselves within a group of the privileged. One of the boys, aware of Irungu's poverty, refers to him as a son of a prostitute and son of a whore when it is clear to him that Irungu cannot afford some of the items that the rich boys can buy. They use the language of insults to demean him and elevate themselves socio-economically. The boy says of Irungu and other poor boys: "… these sons of whores never have any decency in them" (134). This is symptomatic of the language that those who are socio-economically well-endowed use to mete out discrimination and oppression to the less affluent in society. Besides, this kind of language roughs up Irungu in no less a manner than physical violence would. This reason makes him respond violently in equal measure by knocking the boy cold before running away from school. In effect, the language of the rich boys in school is responsible for sending Irungu farther down the social ladder by transforming him from a poor schoolboy to a street urchin. Kombani writes: "He did not go back to the dormitory. Neither did he go home again. He took the night bus to Nairobi, 'son of a prostitute' ringing in his mind" (135).

Names of the main characters in Kombani's novel – who are all victims of ethnic violence in Molo – have been altered and it depicts the history of ethnic violence which led to their harsh socio-economic environment. Importantly, these names are derivations from the traits of the characters and are fashioned in *Sheng*. They are in fact derivations from their delinquency which has been created by the very difficult socio-economic realities within which ethnic violence has placed them. *Sheng* is, therefore, used as an apt marker of the language of the disadvantaged that should be read both as a means of assigning an identity to characters and as a means of protest. Initially, the five characters have names which assign them to different ethnic entities: in Kenya Kimani, Irungu, Kibet, Kiprop, and Lihanda. The first two are Agikuyu names, the next two Kalenjin names, and the last a Luhya. The young boys are turned into perpetrators of ethnic violence by their respective ethnic communities but later become victims of it. Kombani, in his novel, narrates how the five schoolboys all turned against other, while living in Molo, as a result of their respective ethnicized narratives of their tribal extractions.

These same characters find themselves in Nairobi several years after the violence and immediately strike a close companionship in the city. Interestingly, they drop their ethnic-designating names and assume new identities: Bone, Bafu, Bomu, Rock, and Ngeta. These are, in fact, epithets that the characters begin to call each other because of their respective criminal leanings. From the author's comment and description, Bone means a hardened city felon; Bafu a city trickster and conman; Bomu, an addict and dealer in Marijuana; Rock a city ruffian of sorts, and Ngeta, a city mugger. The role of Sheng in uniting the youth as a people with a common identity cannot be gainsaid. As Leonard Muaka observes, this effect of *Sheng* is spreading well, even to rural establishments:

> Sheng is pervasive among Kenyan youths and they have adopted it as an identity marker. It is a variety that unifies them, creating in-group solidarity against outsiders. Rural youths also attempt to align with their urban counterparts because they view their way of speaking to

be trendy. Although these rural youths can hardly speak like their
urban counterparts due to their lack of knowledge of English and
exposure to a variety of mass media, their temporal identification
with them is something that most rural youths would like to project
in non-threatening situations. (220–221)

The assertion in this section of the chapter is that there is a clear matrix among language in literature, language in naturally occurring situations, and socio-economic factors. In this case, it is the specific matter
of language being used to protest, express power identity, and alienate.
These *Sheng* names are hence a protest against ethnic stereotypes and
constructs that have a role in causing violence (Waiganjo, 48). It is imperative to note that the Molo violence pitted the Agikuyu against the
Kalenjin. Therefore, by dropping their original names and giving them
Sheng names, the writer demonstrates the need to turn against cultural
constructs that lead to ethnic violence. He also projects the possibility
that it is the youth that must play the leading role in the creation of
a cohesive nation (Waiganjo, 45). The characters give themselves these
names as a form of protest against a society that has created their problems hence their endeavour to de-tribalize themselves and shed off entities that are responsible for turning them into young murderers. This
shows how language use in the Kenyan urban novel has held stable over
the years, and, indeed, how such language is also realized outside the
authors' fictive world – in the streets of modern-day Nairobi. In *The
Last Villains of Molo*, for instance, this is realized by expressions like
"*Uta do?*" (What will you do?) a language that is meant to assert one's
presence and agency within a rough socio-economic environment. It is
a display of psychological dispositions that resist the tough world and
express one's power over others or the harsh socio-economic realities.

Conclusion

This chapter has established a connection between language and atrocity. Specifically, the chapter has shown how character-speech acts in
the two selected novels are motivated by atrocious socio-economic
situations. Besides, the chapter has shown how physical violence that
is exhibited by the characters is concurrent with their violent speech
behaviour. The two novels studied in this chapter have been read as
exemplifications of how violence (both physical, socio-economic, or otherwise) begets violence. Just as the ethnic violence in *The Last Villains
of Molo* thrusts the five boys into a situation that forces them to become
criminals with an abrasive linguistic register, so does the difficult life
of low-class Nairobi turn Ben and Ochola into violent men characterized by profane discourses in *Going Down River Road*. At the level
of descriptive narration, the writers' choice of descriptive language and

Sheng as agencies of narrating socio-economic atrocities has been found to complement the speech behaviour of the main characters. Undeniably, the language used in the novels investigated in this chapter reflects the language of the less affluent in contemporary Nairobi since both are motivated by (and, consequently, are reactions to) similar social, economic, and political atrocities.

Works Cited

Crystal, David. *The Cambridge Encyclopedia of Language.* New York: Cambridge University Press, 1987. Print.

Erikson, Erik, H. "Reflections on the Dissent of Contemporary Youth." *International Journal of Psychoanalysis* 51 (1970): 11–22. Print.

Foucault, Michel. "Power." *The Essential Works of Michel Foucault.* Ed. James D. Faubion (Trans. Robert Hurley et al.). New York: The New Press, 2000. Web. 20 Oct. 2016.

Foucault, Michel. *Discipline and Punish: The Birth of the Prison.* Trans. A. M. Sheridan Smith. New York: Pantheon Books, 1975. Print.

Foucault, Michel. *The Archaeology of Knowledge and the Discourse of Language.* Trans. A. M. Sheridan Smith. New York: Pantheon Books, 1972. Print.

Githiora, Chege. "Sheng: The Expanding Domains of an Urban Youth Vernacular". *Journal of African Cultural Studies.* (2016). Web. 13 Nov. 2016. doi:10.1080/2015.111796.

Graham, Linda. J. "Discourse Analysis and the Critical Use of Foucault." *Australian Association for Research in Education Annual Conference* (2005): 2–15. Sydney: Queensland University of Technology. Web. 12 Nov. 2016.

Jay, Timothy. *Why We Curse: A Neuro-psycho-social Theory of Speech.* Philadelphia: John Benjamins Publishing Company, 2000. Web. 13 Nov. 2016.

Kombani, Kinyanjui. *The Last Villains of Molo.* Nairobi: Longhorn, 2004. Print.

Marcia, James E. (1980): "Identity in adolescence". *Handbook of Adolescent Psychology.* Ed J. Adelson. New York: Wiley. Web. 20 Sept. 2016.

Meade, Rose. R. "Foucault's Concept of Counter-Conduct and the Politics of Anti-Austerity Protest in Ireland." *Journal of Contemporary Community Education Practice Theory* 5.3 (2014): 1–13. Web. 28 Oct. 2016.

Muaka, Leonard. "Language Perceptions and Identity among Kenyan Speakers". *Selected Proceedings of the 40th Annual Conference on African Linguistics.* Eds. Eyamba G. Bokamba et al. (2011): 217–230. Somerville, MA: Cascadilla Proceedings Project. Web. 13 Nov. 2016.

Mwangi, Meja. *The Cockroach Dance.* Nairobi: Longman, 1979. Print.

———. *Going Down River Road.* Nairobi: Longman, 1976. Print.

Waiganjo, George, N. "Possibilities Projected in the Novels of Ethnic Violence: A Study of Kenyan Long Fiction." Nairobi: Kenyatta University, 2014. Print.

Wodak, Ruth. "Language, Power and Identity". *Language Teaching* 45.2 (2012): 215–233. Web. 15 Nov. 2016.

6 Symbolism of Human Relations in Kenyan Narratives of Ethnic Violence

Waiganjo Ndirangu

Introduction

This chapter analyses how the symbolism of human relations projects ethnic violence in Kenya as portrayed in Kinyanjui Kombani's *The Last Villains of Molo*, Muroki Ndung'u's *A Friend of the Court*, and Ogova Ondego's *From Terror to Hope*. The chapter posits that the positioning of character (s) within a given text can render them the status of symbol(s) and hypothesizes that the corroborated result of the characters' interactions (symbols interacting with symbols) point to certain symbolic outcomes whose authorial rendering deems favoured. Based on these suppositions, the chapter explores the portrayal of ethnic violence in selected novels showing how, through characters, a unique authorial rendering is provided towards the forms of ethnic violence depicted in the novels. Content analysis has been employed in interpreting symbolic roles of specific characters in the texts by following their entry, development, and exit as players in the narrative of ethnic violence.

This chapter starts by identifying possibilities arising from actions between and among characters and the symbolic import that these possibilities portend. Such outcomes are visible in the works of early literary writers. Israel Zangwill's two main characters in the play *The Melting Pot*, for instance, overcome the feudal histories of Russian Jews and Russian Christians and marry, projecting the playwright's resolution of choice as reconciliation and not revenge. This becomes evident when David meets Vera's father who is the Russian officer responsible for the annihilation of David's family in the 1903 Kishinev pogrom. Zangwill's intentions are therefore readable in the possibility he projects through the outcome of his play. In a different case, Bigger Thomas is projected as a representative of the black race in the 1930s America in Richard Wright's novel, *Native Son*. Discussing Bigger Thomas, Franz Fanon, in "The Fact of Blackness", refers to him as a symbol that represents all black men. In that same way that one character can represent an entire race (with its circumstance of fear and unjustified guilt), so does Bone represent the Kikuyu youth and Nancy, the Kalenjin youth, both caught up in a vortex of complex emotion, sense of duty, and feelings of guilt in

Kombani's *The Last Villains of Molo*. While the characters may not be depicted as conscious of their significance, the author expects his ideal reader to make sense of those symbols. However, before embarking on the discourses that characterize ethnic violence in the selected texts, the chapter provides a brief overview of each of the texts.

Brief Overview of the Texts under Study

Kinyanjui Kombani in *The Last Villains of Molo* presents a band of five slum-dwelling young men with slang nicknames: Bone, Rock, Bafu, Ngeta, and Bomu. From Ngando, the slum where they live in 2001 Nairobi, they hasten into the city at night, slipping in and out of criminal doings to achieve a semblance of fun. The reader experiences the boys in the ugliness of their violent life of want as they mug, pickpocket, and simply squeeze life out of a Nairobi that is unsympathetic to those without means. Enter Nancy, a beautiful rich girl with whom Bone becomes involved, and good fortune seems to have struck. But Nancy is here for blood. She is the generous benefactor who quietly lures the boys to their death in a larger scheme.

Within a year, Bomu and Bafu are dead, through police fire and at the hands of a mob in town, respectively. Nancy's motive is revealed through a series of flashbacks where we learn that these characters' pasts crossed nine years ago (1992) in the Kenyan North Rift at the height of the 1992 ethnic clashes. Apparently, during these ethnic clashes, attack and counter-attack turned young villagers into warriors, warriors into deserters, and strangers into friends. Bone (then Kimani) kills Nancy's father but spares her. Kiprop is a wounded enemy warrior rescued by the former two. Although virtual enemies, they find themselves caught up in a war that does not make sense. In their attempt to run off to Nairobi, Irungu, a fifth young man who aids the group's escape is presumed dead after a vicious ambush on the Molo-Sitoito road. But he survives and runs into the others in the streets of Nairobi. Ngando becomes home for the tight band of five. The nine years since Molo 1992 are characterized by saddening loss, grit, and friendship. In 2001, Nancy comes home from the US to befriend the Five and then kill them all to avenge her father's death. Her instructors, the masterminds of the project are her uncles and elders. The plan almost succeeds but, in the end, love, humanity, and youth win over the older generation of vengeful tribalists. Nancy switches sides and settles with Bone, living with Ngeta, Rock, and an adopted orphan together in Molo as friends once again.

From Terror to Hope is a story told in the first-person narrative by a boy who witnesses ethnic clashes at 12 years. He tells of his tribulations: the night of the raids that made him an orphan, life in an Internally Displaced Persons (IDP) camp and then with a foster family that put him through school. Finally, he tells of his excellence in an American university where he delivers the valedictorian address for his class at graduation.

A Friend of the Court is set in 1991–1992 in Kenya's Rift Valley. Young lawyers, Gareth Maitika and Rosaly Gakeni, start a joint practice in Nakuru. Among their first clients are residents threatened with eviction through leaflets calling for violence against the 'outsiders' if they (outsiders) do not vacate the area. Already, militia training is going on in a nearby forest, Rugitoini, but the police do not respond. What ensues is a twisted confrontation between the fledgling law firm on the one hand and the government elements behind the impending violence on the other. While the two lawyers strive to stall violence, politicians who stand to benefit from such violence thwart those efforts by compromising the Attorney Generals' office, the police, and the provincial administration. The same party leaders use every rule in the book to fix the coming elections. But they fail to reckon with the nondescript legal outfit, a determined chief magistrate, and a hired goon who switches sides. And so, the battle begins both in and out of court involving much legal push and shove, during which period chaos persists and many lives are lost. The battle ends with the remanding of three government ministers and violence stops. In the resolution to a secondary romantic strand in the story Gareth and Gakeni, both under 30, acknowledge that they have feelings for each other.

A Note on the Contexts of the Three Texts

It is worth noting that the fictional settings of the three texts keep relatively close to actual names of places, historical periods, and events that characterize Kenya's past. Kinyanjui's presentation carries a stronger stroke of realism while Muroki uses a medley of both actual and fictional place names. For instance, while Muroki has 'NKU party' representing 'KANU', the ruling party of the time, and Ogova uses 'El Molo' for 'Molo', the area where clashes take place, Kinyanjui retains all actual names in the North Rift and at least one character (President Moi) is historical. Ogova's work uses realism the least. It is set in several places without names although the descriptions of children's games played and the people's names allude to East Africa – initially rural and later urban settlements. The only explicitly mentioned area is the fictional area of 'Kunaru' where an IDP camp is located, which echoes 'Nakuru', a town in Kenya's Rift Valley and the epicentre of ethnic clashes from 1992 to 2007/8.

A Note on the Choice of Characters in the Three Texts

The three authors have clearly invested in youthful characters, a fact that this chapter taps into considerably in the subsequent analysis. Some of these characters are born into, face, or emerge out of the circumstance that is pervasive in a population. In pursuing the life-path of a single character, the authors bring out the centrality of his role to the entire fictional plot, and its representational value to the relational possibilities that this chapter hinges on. The result of one such symbolic character interacting with another equally symbolic character can itself be interpreted as being a symbolic outcome. In this regard, the youthful 'Slaughter House Five', and Nancy in Kombani's *The Last Villains of Molo*, Donald Maitika in Ndung'u's *A friend of the Court*, and 'the narrator' in Ondego's *From Terror to Hope* are examined either individually or as part of a larger entity when bringing out the symbolic human relations. As these symbolic characters interact during the course of the plot, their import is to be read as aligned to a specific individual resolution; a symbolic possibility revealed and defined by the author. Here, we hold that in the treatment of ethnic violence as subject matter, each author has prescribed an outcome or outcomes that are discernible from the author's entire ensemble of artistic expression. It is these outcomes that this chapter reveals together with the symbolic possibilities they project.

Symbolic Human Relations and Possibilities

This section delineates symbolic human relations and possibilities that the three authors have postulated in their portrayal of atrocity:

Optimism and the Birth of a Tenacious Nation

Optimism is birthed in the three texts, sustained through the stories, and emerges as a most palpable culmination. All through the affliction in the three stories, Kombani, Ndung'u, and Ondego reward their readers with a strong affirmation of humanity's undying hope – defiance against death and despair. It would appear that, while visiting the delicate matter of ethnic violence in fiction when a nation is still grappling with the adverse effects of a similar experience – both real and recent – these reasonably sensitive authors have not made short shrift of such violence. *The Last Villains of Molo* and *From Terror to Hope* begin with violence that weaves its way into all aspects of the characters, especially in the former text. In *A Friend of The Court*, ethnic-targeted violence is meticulously planned and eventually callously delivered. With so much hurt and death, how then is it possible to achieve both verisimilitude and optimism? In *The Last Villains of Molo*, Irungu's 'resurrection' after being assumed dead for four years is a good case of hope never lost. He survives a deadly attack on the Molo-Sitoito Road, one of many that characterize ethnic violence in Molo, Kenya in 1992. When their bus drives right into an ambush, he is shot with an arrow in the thigh but just before the Kalenjin warriors finish him off, their retreat signal is heard and Irungu is one of the few who lived (77). Like many other victims of ambushes and village raids who go missing in this period, Irungu is presumed dead. The assumed efficiency of his attackers at the time makes this conclusion easy. The news of his survival does not get to his best friend, Kimani till 1996. In the four years, Kimani has lost all family and friends. Living in the streets of Nairobi, he has nothing left to lose. But when the two childhood friends meet, the element of misery and squalor in the boys' lives is distinctly subdued by hope and abundance of life – a death-defying possibility. This possibility is also seen in the news of Ngeta's escape from death in Key West after six months of being presumed dead. By then, Bone and Rock are settling down in Molo with Nancy, a reformed member of the gang who had all but obliterated a 'family'. Effectively, the tragedies of yesterday are symbolically prevailed over by the enduring spirit of humanity and its undeterred grip on hope.

Nancy's sense of humanity too is redeemed from doom. From pre-adolescence, her uncles drill hatred and bitterness in her mind. They teach her that only revenge carried out by her own hand is fair payback for her father's killer. Nine years later, she plays her role as a diversion with chilling efficiency, keeping Bone away from his friends while her accomplices kill them off (131, 138). She is so smooth at it that Bone suspects nothing until, finally, she points a gun at him (160). While the loss of her own parents in the 1992 violence is part of her reason for revenge, it becomes clear that persistent indoctrination and blackmail form her immediate motivation. If she abandons family and tribe, they will withdraw their support to her and hunt her down like a traitor. This threat is spoken several times around the incidents of Bomu's and Bafu's deaths when she repeatedly appeals for a more humane punishment than death for the 'Slaughterhouse Five' (133, 140). Yet every time because of these threats she is forced to carry on with the original plan. Her deadly con job of pretending to love Bone while looping death closer around him, marks her out as the immutable antagonist but for one blemish – the revelation that she is herself internally agonized over which side she should be on. At the moment of reckoning between revenge and forgiveness – when she should take Bone's life – she makes the humane choice, a choice that redeems her from the shackles of her past.

It is also reassuring to see that when the tables are turned in favour of the hunted, they do not avenge their pain. In *The Last Villains of Molo*, two of the Slaughterhouse Five have been killed by the time Bone and Rock catch up with the killers; the 'family' has been badly hit. The Ngando and Key West informal settlements are worse enemies than before (151). The question at this juncture is whether the two men whose humanity has been tested to the limit, not once but twice, will pull through or succumb to the evil pursuing them. Will the vortex of evil swallow them and make them worse than those who torment them or shall the subdued flame of humanity at their core refuse to die? Ultimately, humanity holds out and nobly so. The test of their lives comes when they have Angeline Chebet and Senior Superintendent Rotich at their mercy. Instead of taking their lives, Bone, Rock, and Nancy choose to let them go free as long as they give up the revenge project. Considering the pain of the tragic loss of their two brothers, this is a generously humane offer from the two killers.

Donald Mwihoti in *A Friend of The Court* is in a position relatively similar to that of Nancy's in *The Last Villains of Molo*. Although generally aligned with the fundamentally evil characters, Mwihoti redeems himself by defecting, which greatly improves the protagonists' fortunes. While he tops the list of the most wanted criminals in the land as "carjacker, bank robber, assassin for hire, enforcer, international smuggler" (21), and is currently available on hire to cause chaos, he chooses to give this information to the two lawyers. He goes into great depths to expose the truth and sacrifices a chance to cross the border and run so that he can make sure the power-wielding masterminds of the violence are brought to justice. At the very end, Maitika thinks of him as "a man branded from the beginning with dishonour for whom at the end of it, could be found a measure of redemption" (382). In the same novel, a police officer positioned in El Molo at the height of the violence with orders to keep out anyone who might interfere with the ongoing onslaught, contravenes his orders and saves lives instead. He tells MP Wamarema,

> I am not supposed to be here. I wasn't ordered to be here. But I came. Think of those we have saved even as you cry for the dead! Ok! This affair brings me no joy. I just do as I am told, that's all. Sometimes I do what is right. (320)

It is the acts of such few sane men in the midst of such madness that effect hope and alleviate the bleakness of violence.

Chief Magistrate Jagjit Singh is part of that optimism. Although serving in a subordinate court in a corrupt and politically biased judiciary, he keeps his court clean of political manipulation and delivers justice. He has previously been intimidated by the government and 'punished' with transfers into 'sleeping' parts of the country for making rulings against the whims of political power brokers: "He had rubbed the authorities the wrong way during the early years of National Kenya Union (NKU)'s de jure stewardship" (49). But he keeps his ground under pressure from the Attorney General's office. This ensures that the private prosecution by a small and hitherto obscure law firm precedes, to the chagrin of political bigwigs, the serving Attorney General and by extension the government of the day.

The existence of heroes and heroines, who dare to change lives, even in small ways, is also represented by the residents of Ikiria Nyoni who refuse to be intimidated into silence by goons. After Gakeni and Maitika tour potential hotspots in El Molo and end up without finding willing witnesses, Mwihoti directs Maitika, "go to a place called Ikiria Nyoni, Twenty kilometres east. It is where I come from. The locals there have also been warned to leave. But they are not the kind to be so fearful as to be silent of all they know...They are *Matigari*" (150). The reference to Ikiria Nyoni residents as *Matigari* is explained to mean those who survived detention by and forest fights with the British colonialists in the 1950s and their descendants. This village of Ikiria Nyoni lives up to its name by providing such key witnesses to the trial as Njenga. Mwihoti's numerous escapes from security dragnets keep him alive to continue his help in the all-important suit. He is, after all, the 'friend of the court', his criminal record notwithstanding. Though his death is imminent and he is sought by the police right from the beginning, he has connections with certain government agencies and keeps slipping out of danger. Only until the case is nearly won is he cornered and killed (361). That he survives that long to help as much as he does gives the protagonist force much optimism.

From Terror to Hope presents a character who survives the violence to achieve academic success. He is able to get an adoptive family who sends him to school where he gets the highest marks in the country (29). While in high school, he wins an essay writing competition and its first prize, a scholarship to Columbia University (34). He emerges as a top student there too and therefore delivers the valediction (47).

Overall, for each set of characters in the three stories, the same violence and resultant challenges that threaten their existence seem to strengthen them. Probably because optimism is the combined sum of their individual attitudes towards life, they collectively render such a mark of optimism on each story that it is justifiable to say that the three stories are, by general character, 'optimistic'. Optimism therefore becomes both an outcome in the fictional nations of the texts under study and a projected possibility in the material nation in which the stories are set.

Flight from Ethnic Groupings as a Symbol of the Journey to Nationhood

One most noticeable feature in *The Last Villains of Molo* is the ease with which alliances develop between characters from different ethnic groups. By this we do not mean that alliances formed across tribal lines are impossible or impractical. It is, however, a more easily admissible argument that in a war fuelled by pitting one community against another, ethnic battle sides are easier to operate in. According to Paul Goldman, the ethnic alliance has certain advantages over any other alliance and:

> These strengths include compactness, the existence of primary loyalties and highly adaptive organisational capacity in the pursuit of 'common goals'. Tribe, which is the fabric in which the haughty

design of ethnocentrism is woven, is... the oldest and most successful organisational type ever devised. Its power and potential are
therefore beyond doubt and ...it strengthens the ability of the individual and the collective to survive. (75)

The question may arise therefore whether Kombani's readily disintegrat-
ing ethnic bonds do so credibly in the face of 'ethnic's' formidability as
a unit of the war. One of the cases in question is the meeting of four
of the five friends: Kimani, Kiprop, Lihanda, and Kibet in May 1992.
Kibet is in pursuit of Lihanda for many kilometres and finally tracks
and locates him with Kimani and Kiprop. Just when he ought to finish
this enemy off, he develops second thoughts about his role as a warrior,
with persuasion by Kimani. Before long he turns into a friend, violates
the warrior's oath, conceals the 'enemy' for days before deserting the
militia and his home for good. Of all four, he is the one who probably
needs the group least. Furthermore, he is evidently on drugs, having
pursued his quarry for a long time after fellow warriors had fallen back.
Unlike Kiprop who is injured, Kibet does not need Kimani for anything
and as far as he knows, Lihanda is part of the gang that raided their
homes. And therefore, the questions: what are his motivations? Where is
his credibility as a character? It does not help that the narrator does not
shed light on other psychological or historical forces that might have influenced Kibet to desert. It is a matter of conjecture therefore, that Kibet
had been an unwilling recruit and looking for redemption all along.
Perchance, like Lihanda, he was forcibly recruited. This assumption is
however soundly discounted by the over-enthusiasm he displays when he
pursues Lihanda.

    Human goodness is a tribute overwhelmingly displayed by the pro-
tagonists. Kimani has killed. But he also saved the life of a young girl.
While that might define him as erratic, closer scrutiny reveals that he is
better than that. The only reason he kills the man in the hut is to save
Lihanda, another young man he has met for the first time. Although he
has come with a gang of raiders, he does not go for blood unless he has
to. He deliberately avoids more death by lying to other raiders that he
and Lihanda have killed everyone inside. The seemingly simple cover-up
ensures that Nancy lives. By it, he risks being treated as a traitor for
showing leniency to the 'enemy'. Although unknown to him then, the
same simple act also ensures that the only witness and victim lives to
hunt him down. But on the whole, it is possible to say he takes one life
and saves two. When he later hides in a feeding trough and finds himself with a wounded Kalenjin boy, he could kill him too or run on. But
he stays and nurses him: "I could not leave him here to bleed to death,
Kalenjin or not, could I? (98)". Kibet too, makes conscious choices that
save lives of the other three, even risking his own life. He keeps their
presence in the burnt-out village secret. In time he provides an ingenious

passage out of dangerous territory by carting them away amid sacks of charcoal ostensibly for the market (102).

Lihanda has himself lived in many places with different people from different tribes. With his astounding ability to speak many languages, he naturally therefore accepts people of different tribes more readily than the average boy of his age or even adults who have not travelled as much. Fortunately for Lihanda, his mother had prepared him for the world with such teachings as: "...make a friend every day of your life... In life, friends will help you even more than your own relatives" (67). Of the four, he is the better-practised citizen of the new world. The two overriding attitudes that bind the four boys together, though born of different blood, are respect for human life and the non-conformity of youth.

Once the unwilling warriors have deserted and their loyalty has shifted from tribe to friendship, their lives are imperilled and they must run to save their newly found tribelessness. Their flight from Molo to Ngando is distantly allusive to the historical escape from Mecca to Medina by the Muslim prophet, Mohammed. The two scenarios mirror each other in that the escapee's ideological standpoint makes him a target for persecution and flight becomes the only way of preserving his life and salvaging his endangered beliefs. Kimani is in constant danger within the dominantly Kalenjin settlements as are Kibet and Kiprop, within Kikuyu settlements. Lihanda is safe in neither of these areas. But sticking together poses a greater danger to all. If they are found out they will all die, for the prevailing ethnocentric dogma is overly assertive. The young men are up against stubborn beliefs; beliefs such as those commented on by Francis Imbuga in the play *Aminata*, (1988) when he wrote, "The time-tested ways of our people are best..." (41). Like the older generation in Imbuga's play, Mzee Kipyegon and other extremists are without the wisdom to '[A]ccept change' (41). To openly embrace 'change' like Mzee Kipyegon's son, Mwalimu Kipruto, one has to expose himself to certain death either in the hands of fellow tribesmen as a 'traitor' or in the hands of 'enemy tribe' as a 'spy'. The four youths must therefore take flight to a place where their spiritual-social dispensations have a chance to thrive without posing danger to their persons. This particular outcome suggests that the future lies in a nation with less and less dependency on tribal affiliations.

Compromise as a Symbol of Victory for All

In the ethnic clashes as presented in *The Last Villains of Molo*, definitive victory that would have seen the absolute displacement of specific ethnic groups from certain areas in the Rift Valley does not happen. What happens is an in-between; areas like Kamwaura that had been earmarked for ethnic cleansing are still occupied by people of mixed ethnicities nine years later. When Bone finally goes back to settle, the old neighbours are still there, except for a few people still missing since the clashes. This being the resolution of choice, the author intimates that alternative resolutions are improper and that it is impractical to separate warring sects by designating separate settlements in a nation home to many ethnic groups. For Kombani, it appears clear that the larger nation remains superior to any ethnic grouping. This is discussed further in the subsequent section.

Compromises yield partnerships. Nancy gives up the only remaining family connection and partners up with Bone. She brings in money saved from the partially abortive revenge project and Bone brings in his inherited land. From these, a house is already being erected. From a different perspective, Nancy abandons her revenge mission, forgiving Bone for killing her father. Bone too overlooks her involvement in his brothers' deaths and together, former enemies erect a family. Their bond in the story stands as a monument that bears historical injuries yet is a compromise. That there is a child on the way is confirmation that the compromise is viable and a great promise for the future.

In the second war, there are no resources or control to be gained; revenge is the single intention. The war is its own benefit – appeasement for the depraved and the Slaughterhouse Five are marked for extermination. Bone is sought for killing Nancy's father; Bafu and Bomu for betraying their tribe when they deserted; Ngeta for being an enemy soldier and Rock for associating himself with the criminal gang of the Slaughterhouse Five. In the end, however, the killer squad disbands before the mission is accomplished. We would expect that, having been caught in the act by the would-be-victims, the culprits would be given a quick death; at the very least brought to lawful justice. But Angeline Chebet and Rotich will not be exposed to the authorities and they can begin to pick their lives from the shattered bits of nine years ago (178). On the whole, a compromise ensures that no party to the conflict loses everything but that they all gain something. It gives all a point from which to begin their post-conflict lives. Some of these gains can take the form of victory. For the unfinished revenge, Angelina Chebet must now figure out a way of making a living without revenge as her raison d'être. That is a psychological milestone for a victim of the 1992 tribal clashes. Senior Police Superintendent Rotich also has a chance of living beyond the death of his brother. He might probably begin to be a professional police officer instead of a corrupt goon. Both of these possibilities are important in his redemption.

Bone's victory lies in his affirmed humanity through his many trials. His winning attribute is one better than 'forgiving': he is 'giving'. In the end, he is once again free to revisit his past without fear that elements in it will kill him. By resettling in his inherited plot of land, his shaky subsistence in Ngando is replaced with an assured sustenance. As a consolation for the loss of his family, he has just begun a new family with Nancy. Nancy shares the most benefits with Bone, including a new family and a chance to move on beyond a near-crippling past. Being a beneficiary of Bone's exceeding generosity of heart, her own attitude to life begins to change. Eventually, she begins to believe in the inherent human good in Bone to which no measure of revenge is superior; not even revenge for her dead father. The bitter orphan-turned-con-lover is gone and replaced by a conscientious homemaker. Though she is perhaps the most traumatized – literally 'sleeping with the enemy' and living on as if all is well, she is also the most victorious of them all – she has been rescued from a vengeful and murderous company and welcomed straight into a warm loving family. Compromise is here projected as a possible outcome of ethnic violence.

Bone and Nancy are perhaps the richest symbols in *The Last Villains of Molo*. Firstly, they are symbolic of young spirit caught in the maelstrom of political and ethnic chaos, in which case they easily represent all youth caught up in the skirmishes as unwilling warriors like Kimani in 1992 and Nancy in 2001. Secondly, they symbolize their respective tribes by birth: Kikuyu and Kalenjin; two ethnic entities some of whose elements continually hurt each other yet both are only seeking survival and re-demption. As the two youngsters deal with murder, betrayal, revenge, reconciliation, and love, their personal struggles embody the struggles of their tribes and by extension any other set of ethnic groups similarly engaged in conflict. When Bone and Nancy settle in Kamwaura, theirs is the coming together of two worlds. It is as though they have hurt and bled on behalf of everyone they represent. By this union, no more blood-shed or hurting is needed; the gods have been appeased. Also, other than the example they set for other youths, this outcome is validated further by the resultant progeny – de-ethnicized children from whom tribal loy-alty can never again be exacted.

Returning Home: No Separate Settlements for Ethnic Groups

The attempt to remove non-Kalenjin residents from areas around Molo (or El Molo in *A Friend of the Court*) is central to the conflict in the texts and equally significant is the outcome the authors have offered for it. Yet in none of the three texts is the possibility of separate set-tlements a resolution. The sheer magnitude of resources committed to this ethnic cleansing as portrayed in *The Last Villains of Molo* bears the signature of a grand plan: to reconstitute pre-colonial boundaries. A section of radical residents of Kalenjin origin, like Mzee Kipyegon a diehard pastoralist, base their argument for not mixing with Kikuyus on the myth of how his ancestors came to earth. The Kalenjin are pas-toralists; the Kikuyu newcomers are cultivators – they cannot mix. They must not be allowed to settle and grab Rift Valley as they had allegedly grabbed other parts of Kenya. Two and a half months before actual violence begins, the old man is aware of the secret plans to solve the Kikuyu problem once and for all (38). There is much evidence in the novel that indicates that the extremists were completely committed to following the evictions through. In the course of the violence, the narrator consistently paints a picture of a well-organized militia. Its training is unmistakable in view of their coordinated attack and retreat actions. They seem to have very effective communication systems for instance in their ambush on a Kikuyu gang in Ndoinet Forest at the end of May 1992. On the evening of the same day, a military helicopter hovers above a burning village and apparently directs an overwhelming Kalenjin warrior force to surround their Kikuyu counterparts. Judging therefore by the investment and preparations, the initiators of the cleansing in such places as Kamwaura and other Molo South villages mean it to be total and permanent.

In *A Friend of the Court,* powerful government ministers fund, organize, and make nightly visits to training camps in Rugitoini Forest. That they make tremendous effort to smother the lawsuit by Gakeni and Company Advocates through their ministerial offices and political clout, is enough indication that evictions of select people from Rift Valley are a business they are taking seriously. Indeed, there is no doubt that the evictions will be permanent when one considers that far from preventing it, the police are used to ensure maximum damage. How then do victims go back to settle? After the murderous acts among neighbours, how are they to live together again?

There are several indications that encourage resettlement. One of these is the existence of moderate Kalenjins. At the same time that Mzee Kipyegon is most convinced that ethnic cleansing is unavoidable, his son, Mwalimu Kipruto, who teaches in Molo town, has a contradicting viewpoint and disagrees with his father's radicalism. He has better education and some travel experience. Others of a similar mind include Kibet, the warrior who deserts. Although Mwalimu Kipruto and Kibet are considered traitors and killed nine years later, they are representative of the moderate Kalenjin who does not mind living amongst other tribes. There is also a group of elders that seems to be working to resolve resettlement disputes emanating from the 1992 skirmishes. So far, they have made Bone's return quite comfortable and are making good progress towards the recovery of Nancy's family land, which a relative of hers had sold to a newcomer in the area. (180).

Another indicator is the incident of interethnic marriages as in the case of Bone and Nancy. In a scenario where both spouses hail from conflicting tribes, their household cannot be ruled in totality as either enemy or friend. At the very least, it would disrupt the homogeneity of organization by a tribe. The last indicator is deductive. The alternative to mixed-ethnic settlements are, for example, a settlement on mythical ancestral lands such as the Central province for the Kikuyu; migration to urban centres; resettlement in formerly unoccupied land by the government. Yet none of these is presented in the novel as practicable. Those victims who hike lifts to Central province end up in IDP camps like Kwa Mbira near Limuru. There is no semblance of settlement in such places:

> ...When we first arrived at Kwa Mbira in Limuru, getting food on the table was really difficult. My mother struggled for the two of us, working in lodgings and hotels twenty-four hours a day. We lived in a single room, with me spreading rags on the floor each night. It was pathetic. (114)

Having lost their means of livelihood, women like Irungu's mother work as commercial sex workers to raise their children. Irungu himself is taunted at school and the stigma of being a refugee finally causes him to drop out of school. His mother eventually gets infected with the HIV virus and is ailing alone at home. According to the novel, ancestral lands are not an option for resettling victims. Those who make their way into Nairobi do not fare any better, they find themselves in the streets where an entirely different war is happening daily – the fight for food and shelter. After causing a three-day street riot between council askaris and street children in February 1996, Bone and his four friends escape to Ngando – a filth-ridden slum. "The first house they resided in would have made a pig flinch. For one whole year of torrential rain, the five men braved the flooded room and the cold chilly nights..." (119). Later, when they moved to what should have been a better section of the slum:

> They walked between two rows of *mabati* houses whose doors faced each other. Nancy gasped. The space between the rows was less than a metre. A small ditch meandered the whole length of the narrow space. Above them, on the two lengths of hanging wire, wet bedding and not so clean clothes still dripping. At the door at the end of the row of houses, Bone unceremoniously stopped, produced a rusty key from somewhere at the rafters and opened the corroded padlock. (16)

Apart from having to put up with inadequate sanitation facilities and crowded rooms, they have to contend with occasional fights with residents of a nearby slum. Informal urban settlements therefore have nothing to offer victims evicted from their farms. Finally, there is no indication in the novel that the government intends to resettle the victims elsewhere. The fictional president Moi (who carries the same name and speech mannerisms as the president of the time) tells an impromptu audience that they should stay since no one will build houses for them wherever else they might run to (79). As we have seen, therefore, resettlement in the old farms is the only possibility that has been favourably presented in *The Last Villains of Molo*. Indeed, Bone's return to Kamwaura is given the prominence of a homecoming in the prologue. Resettlement in *A Friend of The Court* is a foregone conclusion since once the cause of conflict is resolved, people will live together as they had before.

Intervention or Interference? The Place of Politics, Judiciary, and Foreign Agencies in Ethnic Conflicts

The questions of who and how of foreign parties meaningfully participate in the resolution of ethnic conflicts are attended by quite a few intimations in the three texts. To begin with, politics and politicians do not only interfere in the harmonious coexistence of ethnically diverse populations, but are actually the masterminds of ethnic violence in *A Friend of The Court*. "[K]eep your anger for parliament, *mheshimiwa*, that's where the makers of this thing are" (320), are the words of a police officer to an El Molo Member of Parliament in this novel. Even before the three government ministers, implicated with the damning evidence, are sufficiently grilled in court, the Attorney General's office orders discontinuation of the hearings. By the time Gakeni & Company Advocates won the long legal battle to continue the prosecution, chaos were already underway. In this way, The Attorney General's office is found to have failed to protect its citizens (376). A long-serving Attorney General's failure to acknowledge the judicial report based on an enquiry into the violence is also mentioned in *From Terror to Hope* (47).

The few mentions of political and government forces in *The Last Villains of Molo* portray them as ineffective at best and complicit in adding to the distress of the citizens rather than alleviating it at the worst. A full month-and-a-half of coordinated attacks carried out by the militia on civilians continue without proper acknowledgement or leave-alone response from the government. Other than denying the violence its due attention, the provincial commissioner is suspected of aiding Kalenjin raiders (79). In the eyes of the victims, even the sitting president is aligned with the perpetrators, hence they chant 'Killer! Killer!' as the presidential convoy tours the area. His message to the victims to 'live in peace' with each other and *'Taangalia hiyo'* (I will look into it) does not convince the worried citizens (79). About a month later, a military aircraft is spotted in Ndoinet forest on a reconnaissance mission for Kalenjin warriors (94). Similar aerial support and ground transport for raiders by the government are noted in *From Terror to Hope*. In *A Friend of The Court*, one police officer tries to save lives in El Molo by scaring away militia but he explains to a Member of Parliament that saving lives is not his official brief. His orders are to ensure that roads going into the area of the clashes in El Molo stay closed to anyone who might interfere with the ongoing onslaught (319).

For their part, the police are not favourably presented in *The Last Villains of Molo* either as individuals or as enforcers of law and order. From the Administration police, whom no IDP will trust for any protection once they are resettled (110), to the night patrol police who are taking Ngeta to the mortuary even before ascertaining whether he is really dead (184), ineptitude emerges as the general character of the police. But when it comes to the council askaris who sodomize street children at night (118) or Senior Superintendent Rotich and his squad of corrupt police who frame Bafu with robbery and shoot him (138), their character degenerates into outright criminality. In *A Friend of The Court*, however, the police come just late enough, not to quell attacks but to promptly carry away the bodies of dead attackers, if any (323).

Of all politicians, Mr. Mungai, the local Member of Parliament for Molo is the only one who seems to realize that the situation is out of hand as presented in *The Last Villains of Molo*. He brings the matter to the nation's attention in the parliament. As a result, thousands of Nairobi University students riot in an attempt to forcibly enter the parliament buildings. The public attention accrued from these acts forces the government to send a record 15 district officers to the area (80). In *A Friend of The Court*, the Member of Parliament for El Molo, Paul Wamarema becomes involved only after being fired from the cabinet. He however makes up by giving evidence that incriminates three of his former colleagues. Even then, the narrator suspects that Wamarema only cooperates to secure himself votes in the coming elections, "...a politician's sense of self-preservation..." (380).

On the whole, the path to redemption as traced in *The Last Villains of Molo* and *A Friend of The Court* is not lined up with government agencies. It is instead marked with self-belief, determination, and the optimism of the young. Therefore, Kombani and Ndung'u seem to place the matter of a citizen's relations with his neighbour in the citizen's own unaided and unhindered hands, with Ndungu enlisting an independent judiciary. Ondego favours intervention by well-wishers, the press, and donors, a position that can at best favour only a few lucky victims.

Conclusion

Given the same conflict, the question this chapter has striven to answer therefore is, 'which of the specific possibilities and attitudes has each author found favourable?' The intention of posing such a question has been necessitated by the overall need to establish what Kenyan long fiction 'is saying' about ethnic violence in Kenya, which is the main objective of this study. Characters, in their symbolic representation of 'types' or entire 'tribes' operating in an ethnically charged setting, have emerged at the end of each of the stories as part of certain outcomes. These outcomes are the various possibilities that have been projected in the three texts and which constitute the voice of the Kenyan long fiction writer in the matter of 'how to resolve ethnic violence in Kenya'. In this chapter we have identified several scenarios towards which the individual authors have taken certain philosophical standpoints.

It has emerged that all the authors are optimistic about the outcome of ethnic violence. As seen above, all the protagonists in all three texts have made remarkable progress from the darkness of violence and hopelessness to achieve great heights. That is to suggest that, regardless of how exacting the ethnic violence quagmire may be, the three authors agree that eventually, good will win over evil. But this scenario is tied to several others that make a triumph possible. These include the encouragement of lifestyles devoid of ethnic polarity and the choice of compromise rather than winner-take-all resolutions. Also, inter-ethnic marriages are vouched for as one of the scenarios most unlikely to fuel further ethnic conflict. Both Kombani and Ndung'u present strong cases against the universal option of balkanization. Also strong among their possibilities is the suggestion that outsiders (mostly politicians) are more likely to fuel the violence than to quell it. On the contrary, Ogova has presented a case in which foreign benefactors are virtually responsible for the main character's recovery from victimhood and his propulsion into excellence. Finally, this chapter has coherently put together the sum of scenarios that the three authors have projected as suitable.

Works Cited

Fluck, Winfried. *Literature as Symbolic Action*. Heidelberg: Winter Location, 1983. Web.

Kombani, Kinyanji. *The Last Villains of Molo*. 2004, Nairobi: Acacia; Nairobi: Sasa Sema, 2012. Print.

Leech, Geoffery N., and Michael H. Short. *Style in Fiction: A Linguistic Introduction to English Fictional Prose*. London: Longman, 1981. Print.

Mulwa, David. *Redemption*. Nairobi: Longman, 1987. Print.

Ndungu, Muroki. *A Friend of The Court*. Nairobi: Focus, 1994. Print.

Ndirangu, Waiganjo. "Possibilities Projected in the Novels on Ethnic Violence: A Study of Kenyan Long Fiction," M.A. Thesis. Kenyatta University, 2014. Print.

Ogude, S.E. "African Literature and The Burden of History: Some Reflections." *African Literature and African Historical Experiences* (1991). Print.

Ondego, Ogova. *From Terror to Hope*. Nairobi: ComMattersKenya, 2009. Print.

Politi, J. *The Novel and Its Presuppositions*. Amsterdam: A. M. Hakkert, 1976. Print.

Selden, Roman. *The Theory of Criticism: From Plato to The Present*. London: Longman, 1988. Print.

Sollors, Werner. *Beyond Ethnicity: Consent and Decent in American Culture.* New York: Oxford University Press, 1986. Print.

Wa Wamwere, Koigi. *Negative Ethnicity: From Bias to Genocide.* New York: Seven Stories Press, 2003. Print.

Wright, Richard. *Black Boy: A Biography.* New York: Harper Perennial Modern Classics, 1945. Print.

———. *Native Son.* New York: Harper Perennial Modern Classics, 1940. Print.

Zanguil, Israel. *The Melting Pot.* New York: McMillan, 1901. Print.

7 Sycophants in a Cannibal State

Kenya in Ngugi wa Thiong'o's *Wizard of the Crow*

Wafula Yenjela

Introduction

While time and history heavily indict sycophants' and court jesters' legacies for their insincerity and hypocrisy that may have aided or abetted injustices, Ngugi wa Thiong'o's *Wizard of the Crow* intricately links their vocation with atrocity. The contingent of sycophants in dictatorial states is not limited to the political class but also from vital institutions such as the media and women's organizations that serve to camouflage regimented atrocities. This chapter not only establishes sycophants' instrumentality in perpetration of atrocities, but also explores their tragic fate as they too end up victims of the cannibal states they serve. The praying mantis analogy where a female mantis eats its male counterpart immediately after copulation is appropriated here to demonstrate the precarious relationship between gifted sycophants and cannibal states such as Kenya. Indeed, Kenya's turbulent political histories provide a rich archive from which the chapter dissects encodings of sycophants' annihilation of their souls and, by extension, the soul of the nation that they desecrate in their quest for tokens, for power embodied in autocrats, for their survival. Ultimately, the chapter asserts that Kenya's assassination histories are interlinked with tragedies that assail sycophancy.

Different types of sycophants who are masters of oratory and other hero-worship skills are pillars of dictatorial polities since they foster a façade of good governance in a space where everything meaningful that drives a society is crumbling. Sycophants are instrumental in such polities because, if one is to adopt a cynical stance, one of the preoccupations of the postcolony is "the production of lies and double-speak" (Mbembe 17). This would appear an uphill task for an autocrat to accomplish without lieutenants gifted in rhetoric and extreme subordination. The autocrat needs these special lieutenants to perform what Achille Mbembe refers to as a kind of "verbal trance" through which harmoniously arranged empty words enhance "a state of 'possession' and triggers the mind's voyaging; the space [that the state] creates through violence, [one] totally colonized by the *commandment*" (16). Sycophants are also key players in performances creatively orchestrated to validate a regime's power. According to Mbembe, such performances are manifest in "the body that [...] is willing to dramatize its subordination [through dances, dresses in party uniform, and assembling in multitudes] to applaud the passing of presidential procession" (Mbembe 25). These are the figures that have made the postcolony "a world of narcissistic self-gratification [in their] quest for profit or favours" (Mbembe 21).

Yet, though sycophancy is known for easy socio-economic ascendancy, it degenerates into a struggle for self-preservation and inevitable doom. Histories of sycophants from cannibal states such as Kenya powerfully establish the category's precarity. Through an ironical gaze that this chapter adopts, absurdities of the vocation of sycophancy are underpinned. The absurdities of this vocation are not only embodied in the perilous machinery of dictatorial states, but mostly in the inevitable loss of sycophants' and, by extension, a nations' dignity. In comparison with representations of martyrs who choose to die for a noble reformist cause, sycophants – the bedrock of dictatorial regimes – accelerate the decomposition of any conceivable gains towards freedom and respect for human rights. Hence, when they are consumed by a cannibal state, they seem to elicit the least empathy from readers aligned to social justice. In the novel, the fates of sycophants and the autocrat are not only emplotted in the tragic irony trope that is evident for all of them, but also in the sinister cycle of state cannibalism seen in the Ruler's successor. As such, sycophants' tragedies unveil rich grounds for inquiry into archives of atrocities in post-independent states such as Kenya. Their zealous glorifications of Africa's strongmen mask ominous histories of predatory states. This makes them key agents of atrocities in the polities where they practise their vocation.

The chapter emphasizes the need to interrogate the kind of benefits despots provide for the political elites who sing the former's praises. In portrayals of sycophants' precarity, Ngugi embraces Frantz Fanon's profound observation in *The Wretched of the Earth* that the "bourgeois dictatorship of underdeveloped countries draws its strength from the existence of a leader [while] in the well-developed countries the bourgeois dictatorship is the result of the economic power of the bourgeoisie" (133). Fanon argues that it is in the "shelter [of the leader that] the thin and poverty-stricken bourgeoisie of the young nation decides to get rich" (Fanon 133). *Wizard of the Crow* rattles the 'shelter' that autocrats provide to their henchmen by saturating it with atrocities that, unfortunately, can be gleaned from Kenya's turbulent chambers of state power.

It is also apparent that the narrative encodes many historical events that have happened in Kenya. In "Ngugi's Concept of History", James Ogude, following Carol Sicherman, asserts that "Ngugi's narrative is steeped in Kenya's historical landscape and, indeed, at times borders close to direct allusion on actual historical personages and events" (88). Simon Gikandi, too, points out that "some readers will instantly recognize [Aburiria] as 1980s Kenya, [ruled by] an aging dictator, a former school teacher transformed into a messianic figure and his people's supreme leader" ("The Postcolonial Wizard" 158). The aging dictator in question is Daniel Toroitich arap Moi, who ruled Kenya for 24 years (1978–2002). Gikandi also observes that "[r]eaders familiar with the politics of this period [...] will also be familiar with the main events in Ngugi's novel" (165). But it should be noted that the novel further imagines, dissects, and challenges the histories of the Kenyan state. It is from the premise that Ngugi's *Wizard of the Crow*, as well as his other works, unsettle Kenya's histories that this chapter draws inspiration to link grotesque characters to personages in Kenyan state histories of atrocity. Since the focus is on sycophants, there are cases in the novel where characters represent vital institutions such as the media and its connivance with a criminal state. But it should be clear that onslaughts on such institutions involve/d deaths of individuals. Furthermore, the chapter does not limit the reading of events in the novel to the Moi era, it locates them across Kenya's historical continuum.

Sycophants' Problematic Victimhoods

In *Wizard of the Crow*, Ngugi wa Thiong'o presents a wide array of seasoned sycophants. Simon Gikandi refers to these disgraced figures as the "learned sycophants [...], professional sycophants [who hail the ruler as] the master of the world, the alpha and the omega of nation, the master of politics, and of philosophy" ("Postcolonial Wizard" 159). Through satire, the novel catalogues atrocities attributable to repressive state power witnessed in many contemporary African countries. Satirical portrayals of the unpredictable cannibal state unmask the flipside of the ruling class who pretentiously exhibit themselves to the citizenry as wielders of real power yet are engaged in cutthroat wars for their own survivals. The novel explicitly documents how atrocity consumes both the perpetrator and the victim, literally. The employment of satire is important as it implies the novelist's advocacy for reform through exposure and condemnation of the flagrant disorder facilitated by sycophants in a dictatorial polity. According to Leonard Feinberg, "the basic technique of satire is distortion, usually in the form of exaggeration, understatement, and pretense; and distortion implies disorder" (4). *Wizard of the Crow* stretches satire to its limit through the grotesque or the repulsively ugly. In a critique of Ngugi's *Devil on the Cross*, James Ogude sees Ngugi's use of "the grotesque as an instrument of social satire, specifically in his depiction of 'thieves and robbers' – the comprador bourgeoisie of the postcolonial state" ("Allegory and Grotesque" 79–80). Similarly, sycophants are the caricatured comprador bourgeoisie of autocrats in *Wizard of the Crow*; they are accomplices and at times instigators of atrocities in dictatorial polities. Through their powerful faculties of rhetoric, they rebrand and glorify repression, underdevelopment, persecution.

Ngugi satirically presents sycophants who enlarge parts of their bodies in their quest for power. The sycophants take great risks, some of which are outrageous, for the sake of demonstrating their loyalty and magnification of the Ruler's sovereignty. Body parts enlargements also strategically position them as tools for their master's use. Through the grotesque, the novel enables incisive critiques on how dictatorial states contrive atrocities, as the enlargements/elongations of body parts symbolize the potential excesses and overzealousness in exercising state power on their target ministries. The sycophants in the novel include Markus Machokali, Silver Sikiokuu, and Benjamin Mambo who rise to ministries of foreign affairs, state, and information, respectively, after enlarging respective parts of their bodies: Machokali enlarges his eyes, Sikiokuu elongates his ears, Mambo elongates his tongue and lips. The names of these three principal sycophants are allegorical – Machokali for 'sharp-eyed', Sikiokuu for 'huge-ear', and Mambo for 'information'. Machokali and Sikiokuu additionally mentor Titus Tajirika, and John Kaniuru, respectively, into sycophancy.

Furthermore, the Ruler coerces formerly hard-line revolutionists, Dr Luminous Karamu-Mbu-ya-Ituika and Dr Yunity Immaculate Mgeuzi to join the camp of sycophants. Here, both individuals represent intellectual elites associated with important bodies regarding the autocrat's political persuasion schemes: the writer and women's rights movement. Notably, Luminous is another grotesque figure, a scribe whose huge pen would have benefited humanity had he not redirected his energies to buttress autocracy. The grotesque scribe references writers who play significant roles in augmenting autocracy through their connivances with various cannibal regimes. In another work, Ngugi wa Thiong'o agonizes over politically desensitized writers, "cocooned in their class or being prisoners of the propaganda of the dominant class become insensitive to basic structural conflicts" (*Writers in Politics* 75). In this portrayal, it appears Ngugi is disturbed at the idea of Kenya's important writers such as Grace Ogot whom dictator Daniel Moi appointed Minister of Culture in 1985, a time when repression was at its zenith.

Yunity Mgeuzi who is appointed the chair of women's movement in the autocrat's regime is another stooge the autocrat uses to create the impression that he cares about the affairs of women in his polity. Her name, Yunity, plays on Moi's Nyayo philosophy of peace, love, and unity; Immaculate references Virgin Mary's 'sinless' conception emphasized by Catholicism; Mgeuzi is Kiswahili for revolutionary. In "Phallocracies and Gynocratic Transgressions", Grace Musila observes that *Maendeleo ya Wanawake*, the women's movement lorded over by the Moi regime, was "predictably deployed in the service of a patriarchal state power" since it "was more instrumental in garnering the female vote for the ruling party than in actually promoting women's development as its name would seem to suggest" (48). Thus, Yunity Immaculate Mgeuzi's name allegorizes the autocratic state's ingeniousness in swallowing revolutionary women's legacies leaving behind but shadows of their potential. In a review of the oral histories of Julia Ojiambo who was one of the founders of *Maendeleo ya Wanawake* but who was later compromised by various dictatorial regimes, Marciana Were placably writes:

> In the absence of a strong female movement to support women like her, the most powerful political symbol became the presidency. To survive this political sphere that glorified masculinity, Julia embraced a paternalistic filial relation to the state as a 'daughter of the nation'. (492)

Were intends that readers perceive her subject as a victim of patriarchy. However, Julia Ojiambo's adoption in an oppressive regime and her acquisition of the 'daughter of the nation' marker is representative of autocrats' ideal women who are tolerant of and submissive to the autocrats' vulgar power.

These figures invoke memories of sycophants who served Kenya's various dictatorial regimes. One all-time sycophant of the Moi era is John Joseph Kamotho, famously known as JJ Kamotho. Kamotho's death on 6 December 2014 revealed the absurdities of sycophants' legacies. From newspaper articles that looked back at his political career, it is apparent that eulogizing a sycophant is a ridiculous task. For instance, Kamotho is eulogized as a man who became "an irritating mouthpiece of what critics regarded [as] an oppressive and corrupt regime" (Ngwala *Daily Nation* n.p.). Another article shows that Kamotho, the songbird of KANU (Kenya African National Union), the party that was in power from 1963 to 2002,

> never tired in reminding Kenyans wherever he went that Kanu *ni baba na mama* (is father and mother), and Nyayo *juu juuu zaidi* (high higher highest)! Kamotho would praise Moi and say unrealistic things without blinking an eye to the extent that, some time in 1993, he [ticked] Moi to laughter at a public meeting in Karatina. (Omari *Daily Nation* n.p., parentheses added)

But Kamotho is not the only sycophant of the infamous Moi regime. Kariuki wa Chotara, Mulu Mutisya, Shariff Nassir, and Ezekiel Barng'etuny "were President Moi's loud and proud, yet trusted lieutenants and court jesters. They fought his wars viciously as if they were their own. They made their wars the President's and fought them just as ferociously" (Opanga *Daily Nation* n.p.). This claim signals a trail of destroyed olives and values sycophants leave behind in their political duels.

The interrogation of legacies of Kenya's outstanding sycophants provides rare insights into Kenya's troubled histories. While sycophants or court jesters' legacies are heavily indicted by time and history for their insincerity and hypocrisy that may have aided or abetted political injustices,

Wizard of the Crow intricately links their vocation with atrocity. The novel not only establishes sycophants' instrumentality in the perpetration of atrocities, it further explores their tragic fate as they too end up victims of the cannibal state. This constructs sycophants as tragic villains: as soon as the Ruler notices their sycophantic efforts, they become marked wo/ men, marked for death. This feature affirms the nature of atrocity – a double-edged sword that devours both the perpetrator and the victim.

Autocracy that Thrives on Media Reportage of Atrocity

In *The Spirit of Terrorism*, Jean Baudrillard demonstrates the significance that media coverage provides to terrorism. He taunts his readers by claiming that Americans would have forgiven the September 2011 terror attack on the World Trade Centre and Pentagon had it not been for media coverage, "we would pardon them any violence if it were not given media exposure [...]. But this is an illusion. There is no 'good' use of the media; the media are part of the event, they are part of the terror, and they work in both directions" (31). These controversial sentiments position the media at the heart of atrocity. The media's contribution to atrocity in dictatorial polities is undeniable. One of the ways this is accomplished is by coverage of the autocrat's hypocritical empathies to the victims of atrocities.

Even though Lewis Odhiambo asserts that the Kenyan media has been on the forefront in "influencing the pace of political change" (295) despite "weaknesses in constitutional provisions with regard to [...] freedom of the media" (296), Kenyan dictatorial regimes always succeed in co-opting revolutionary or lethal political critics into the regime especially through political appointments to serve as Statehouse Spokespersons or in the Presidential Strategic Communications Unit. Consequently, like the grotesque Dr Luminous Karamu-Mbu-ya-Ituika, such journalists devote their talents in the glorification of autocrats.

Wizard of the Crow begins with a spectre of the autocrat's atrocities against individuals and communities he regards a threat to his reign. The narrator observes:

> Even his yawns were news because, whether triggered by boredom, fatigue, hunger, or thirst, they were always followed by some national drama: his enemies were lashed in public square with a *sjambok*, whole villages were blown to bits or people were pierced to death by a bows-and-arrows squad, their carcasses left in the open for hyenas and vultures. It is said that he was especially skilful in creating and nursing conflicts among Aburirian families, for scenes of sorrow were what assuaged him and made him sleep soundly. (4)

This portrayal of the Ruler reveals a pathological killer – he is hungry and thirsty for blood. The media, which has over time transformed the Ruler into a fetish by reporting everything he does, and sanitizing his evils, features prominently in the atrocities that are recounted here. Apart from reporting everything the Ruler does, especially with interpretations suggesting everything about him as an act of benevolence for the nation, the media also thrives on reportage of atrocity. Unscrupulously, the media portrays instigators of Aburirian atrocities as champions of peace. This is enhanced through the media's unwillingness to interrogate the Ruler's discreet contrivance of atrocities but rather highlights the Ruler's appearances at sites of atrocity to speak about 'peace, love and unity'. Since atrocities occurring in states like the represented Aburiria are frenziedly reported the world over, the autocrat uses them to validate his rule; to construct a myth that without his firm grip on power, Aburiria would be wiped out by rebel elements.

The narrator's revelation that there are times when "whole villages were blown to bits" as part of the national drama that follows reportage of the Ruler's hunger, boredom, thirst, is reminiscent of atrocities such as the February 1984 Wagalla massacre that targeted the Degodia clan of the Somali ethnic group in Wajir, North Eastern Kenya. The four-day massacre at Wajir airstrip where over 5,000 people were killed by the Kenyan military "still remains the largest loss of life in any single atrocity in Kenya's history" (Anderson 659). In the aftermath of the atrocity, "the Kenya Government of President Moi mounted a campaign of misinformation and denial" (Anderson 659). Such campaigns of misinformation and denial are usually accomplished through a complicit media that uncritically affirms claims by sycophants with exceptional mastery of propaganda and oratory gifts.

On the issue of the bow-and-arrow squads that engage in piercing villagers to death, the narrator seems to memorialize the 1991/1992 instigated ethnic conflicts. In a review of the Kenyan state violence employed by dictator Daniel Moi during Kenya's transition from a one-party state to a multiparty democracy, Binaifer Nowrojee and Bronwen Manby reveal how state-sponsored militias armed with bows and arrows attacked communities identified with opposition politics while the police watched, indifferently (33). This pattern would repeat itself in the 2017 general elections when Uhuru Kenyatta sanctioned police brutality against the Luo community both in Nairobi and in Kisumu.

Countering Atonement with Atrocity

The Ruler who is possessed by 'power daemons', as the novel suggests, is rumoured to have hunted down a sacrificial goat, killed it together with the elders who sacrificed it to appease the land. Here is the analogy:

> It is said that some elders, deeply troubled by the sight of blood flooding the land, decided to treat this evil as they had epidemics

that threatened the survival of the community in the olden days: but instead of burying the evil inside the belly of a beast by inserting flies, standing for the epidemic, into its anus, they would insert the Ruler's hair, standing for the evil, into the belly of a he-goat through its mouth. The evil-carrying goat, standing for the Ruler, would then become an outcast in the land, to be driven out of any region where its cry announced its evil presence. (4)

Unlike the state media that portray the Ruler as the benefactor of Aburiria, this rumoured ritual bluntly attributes atrocities committed in the land to the Ruler. The ritual suggests the need for the removal of the Ruler as a step towards atonement of the victims of state atrocities in Aburiria. However, participants in this ritual who include "the goat, the [Ruler's] barber, the medicine man, the elders, and even the soldiers [who arrested the ritualists] were given over to the crocodiles of the Red River to ensure eternal silence about the curse" (4–5).

Through the he-goat analogy, the narrator clarifies the media's connivances with autocrats in the enforcement of amnesia. Earlier, I showed that the media purportedly reports the charitable acts of the Ruler. But on the ground, the elders are "deeply troubled by the sight of blood flooding the land" (4). At this point, it seems that the murderous states find sycophants quite vital to counter rumours amongst citizens, rumours that crudely expose state atrocities. The state media greatly needs sycophants to create stories of the former to broadcast to the world. Above all, sycophants take state atrocities to a higher level by advising autocrats to ruthlessly root out imagined enemies; by witch-hunting and killing each other; and by, finally, falling victims to assassinations.

Nods to Robert Ouko, Tom Mboya, and Josiah Mwangi Kariuki

Wizard of the Crow provides a platform from which to read Kenya's high-profile historical figures such as Robert Ouko, Tom Mboya, and JM Kariuki for what they were before their assassinations – sycophants. These figures' brief but tragic fallouts with the inner circle of state power seem insufficient to transform them into martyrs. As a key strategist in the Jomo Kenyatta regime, Tom Mboya was instrumental in the destruction of multiparty democracy. Indeed, David Goldsworthy, one of Tom Mboya's biographer, greatly recognizes Mboya's exceptional gifts:

> Tom Mboya was a major, and indeed brilliant, political figure; a man of extraordinary intelligence and dynamism; a prolific and protean achiever. [...]. Ultimately, the causes he fought for in Kenya and Africa were the most fundamental ones of all: freedom and development, as he saw them. (ix)

But Mboya seems to have compromised on this quest for freedom especially as he began endearing himself to Jomo Kenyatta, "what mattered most in these latter months of 1961 was the growth of his relationship with Kenyatta" (Goldsworthy 189). Furthermore, "Kenyatta clearly understood that Mboya's talents, experience, connections, labour base, and electoral appeal made him indispensable" (189). Having abandoned his quest for freedom in his adoption of Kenyatta's dictatorial regime, Mboya played a key role in stifling multiparty democracy.

On the other hand, JM Kariuki who was a special point-man in the Kenyatta regime became the regime's enemy when he launched an offensive against those he termed "ten millionaires in a country of ten million beggars". Among the ten millionaires was Jomo Kenyatta. Perhaps Jomo Kenyatta's sentiments on JM Kariuki upon the latter's assassination clearly demonstrates the liaisons: "after Kariuki's body was finally found, Kenyatta told a crowd the story of a fallen angel who was 'going bad, so God threw him away'" (Branch 118). In the case of Robert Ouko, one notes that till the last minute of his death, he was a pillar in the infamous Moi regime system. According to Grace Musila, the "Ouko murder is easily the most investigated murder in the history of Kenya's assassination" (*Julie Ward Murder* 40).

The demystification of the lives of Kenya's victims of assassination, several of whom can be interpreted as sycophants, is not a project seeking to justify state atrocities against such figures. Rather, it illustrates the cannibalistic tendencies of the Kenyan state that is as weird as the female mantis that eats up its male counterpart immediately after copulation. The haunting power of the assassinations of Josiah Mwangi Kariuki, Tom Mboya, and Robert Ouko, which converge into one, seem to be embodied in the stories created to condemn their brutal killings. It is difficult to separate representations of these figures in *Wizard of the Crow* since the grotesque figures Machokali and Sikiokuu exhibit characteristics that can be linked to JM Kariuki, Mboya, and Ouko, especially in their powerful oratory skills and their allegiance to the autocrat of their various times. JM Kariuki and Ouko also share the desecration of their remains by their assassins.

Ngugi wa Thiong'o and Rocha Chimera revisit the assassinations through representations of a macabre assassination of a brilliant foreign minister. For instance, in *Siri Sirini* (or Secret in the Secret) trilogy, Rocha Chimera focalizes the assassination of Mfawidhi, a character with a vast knowledge of international affairs. Mfawidhi eloquently articulates the histories and significances of international networks with his country to audiences abroad and at home. Due to suspicions and power struggles amongst advisors of King Daudi Mringwari of a Swahili ancient city-state of Shanga, Mfawidhi is abducted from his house, tortured, and speared to death and his body burnt. It is a herder who stumbles on his remains. Despite the atrocity, it cannot be lost to a keen reader of the trilogy that it is mainly through Mfawidhi's rhetoric that the oppressive monarchy of Daudi Mringwari kept renewing its validity in Shanga.

In *Wizard of the Crow*, Ngugi explores these histories through the grotesque figure Markus Machokali and Sikiokuu. In a very uncanny way, the novel reveals how sycophancy and atrocity are interlinked. Machokali is the Minister of Foreign Affairs who enlarges his eyes in London "to make them ferociously sharp [...] so that they would be able to spot the enemies of the Ruler no matter how far their hiding places" (*Wizard* 13). The paranoia seen in this obsessive search for the Ruler's enemy implies victimization and hasty exterminations of those imagined as enemies. The imagined enemies seem instigated by London, the seat of power of Aburiria's former colonial power. Ironically, the autocratic system sees Machokali from afar as an enemy within when he is suspected of harbouring presidential ambitions, suffused with his dalliance with the West. This leads to his assassination. Like his colleagues in the sycophant team, Machokali loses his dignity when the tyrannical system objectifies him to the point that there seems to be little difference between him and a telescope or CCTV camera.

Even though Machokali can be a fictionalized nod to Mboya, JM Kariuki, or Ouko, he seems more of Ouko whom Cohen and Odhiambo claim enjoyed favourable access to his local and national community and "also to President George H. W. Bush and Secretary of State James Baker in Washington, DC" (ix). According to the two historians, "Ouko was a 'golden boy' in George Bush's and Margaret Thatcher's circles and was being groomed by his country's Western allies as the next president of Kenya" (11). This 'romance' with the Western powers seem to have made him a risk to Moi's presidency. According to Cohen and Odhiambo, at the time of his assassination, Ouko was unearthing a major corruption scandal involving powerful people in Moi's administration (10). His efforts were aimed at reviving the "Kisumu molasses project, the largest capital investment in twentieth-century western Kenya" (10). However, Grace Musila contests sanitized portraits of Ouko: "Ouko has been sanitized and rendered a moral hero and innocent victim of state brutality and the violent paranoias of powerful politicians close to the Moi regime" (*Julie Ward Murder* 58). Musila's observation completely unsettles the reading of assassinations in Kenya. Whenever an assassination occurs, most Kenyans prefer to read it as an attack on the victim's ethnic community as they proceed to sanitize the victim through claims that he/she was unearthing a scandal involving powerful people in the government. As much as this reading can be valid in many ways, the perspective casts into oblivion the legacies established by the victims during their lives, especially if the track record of the victims points to sycophancy.

Edifices that Mask Stalled Economies

Wizard of the Crow provides readers with the advantage to revisit Machokali's contributions to autocracy before his assassination. For instance, Machokali's "Marching to Heaven" grand project which he launches with much fanfare as a national birthday gift to the Ruler is one way that sycophantic figures service the state – the female mantis mentioned above. During the launch, Machokali bizarrely claims that Aburiria would "raise a building to the very gates of Heaven so that the Ruler could call on God daily to say good morning or good evening or simply how was your day, God?" (16). The represented excesses of this postcolonial polity resonate with Frantz Fanon's postulation that dictatorial postcolonies "sink all the more into stagnation [because the ruling bourgeois] is preoccupied with filling its pockets as rapidly as possible but also as prosaically as possible" (133). Hence, to mask economic disgrace, the rulers "can find nothing better than to erect grandiose buildings in the capital and to lay out money on what are called prestige expenses" (133).

The Marching to Heaven project ostensibly exposes Machokali's desire for economic advancement. Yet there is an acute dearth of practical plans and action that thwarts these aspirations. The narrator juxtaposes the aspirations towards erecting an edifice for the Ruler's gratification with the starving, jobless citizens of Aburiria seen in the chapter titled "Queuing Daemons". For instance, despite being a holder of Bachelor of Arts in Economics and Master of Business Administration degrees from India, Kamiti, who later becomes the wizard of the crow, resorts to part-time begging as he searches for a job. Homeless in the city, he sleeps in a dumpsite, dresses in a suit before engaging in job-searching but would instantly change into rags to beg. Kaniuru, while stalking a man whom he had seen talking to Nyawira, his estranged lover, encounters a shocking incident and later narrates it to Nyawira: "I saw him with my own eyes go into the toilet; I stood guard at the entrance, and only a beggar dressed in rags came out. [...] The man had vanished into thin air" (*Wizard of the Crow* 112). Kamiti's 'double life' seems a commentary on the absurd lives led by the Aburiria's underclass.

Due to joblessness, Kamiti's fiancée Margaret Wariara abandons prospects of marriage for prostitution in Eldares, Aburiria's capital. While begging at Angels Corner tourist hotel in Eldares, Kamiti stumbles upon Wariara "dressed in a mini-skirt, high heels, and a brown wig [...] holding hands with a white tourist whose hanging belly was held in place by two suspenders" (*Wizard of the Crow* 70). These cases that underscore familial dysfunctionality in relation to political dysfunctionality are best articulated by Grace Musila who sees "the domestic home and the nation-home as ambivalent spaces marked by both the promise of healing and the terror of predation" since the "paternal figure of authority

[...] whether biological, religious or political, is either absent or variously fails to deliver on the inferred promise of protection" ("Familial Cartographies" 351). Furthermore, this is a country where police officers, "as if bewitched", hotly pursue beggars "covered in rags from head to toe" on suspicion that the bags the beggars tightly clutched as they escaped "were full of Buri notes the two had been collecting all day and night" (*Wizard of the Crow* 75).

The Ruler's humiliation when he travels with his entourage to solicit for funds from World Bank to implement the project exposes the absurdity of it all. Machokali's speech during the Ruler's birthday ceremony exposes impractical development plans since every idea is geared towards idolization of the Ruler:

> Minister Machokali was waxing ecstatic about how the benefits of the project could trickle down to all citizens. Once the project was completed, no historian would ever again talk about any other wonders in the world, for the fame of this Modern House of Babel would dwarf the Hanging Gardens of Babylon, the Egyptian pyramids, the Aztecan Tenochtitlan, or the Great Wall of China. And who would ever talk of Taj Mahal? Our project will be the first and only super-wonder in the history of the world. In short, Machokali declared, Marching to Heaven was the special birthday cake the citizens had decided to bake for their one and only leader, the eternal Ruler of the Free Republic of Aburiria. (17)

It is ironical that Aburiria is a Free Republic and yet it is ruled by an *eternal* Ruler. By idolizing the despot and implying that his satisfaction and luxury is all that matters in a country languishing in economic turmoil, Machokali, who ironically has eyes that can see far, embodies the destructive myopia of sycophancy. This sycophancy must continuously regenerate itself for survival in changing political times to remain relevant. Read with Kenyan histories in mind, the Marching to Heaven project appears a critique of the Moi regime's "plans to build a new headquarters in Uhuru Park for the ruling party and the Kenya Times newspaper, co-owned by KANU and Robert Maxwell" (Branch *Hope and Despair* 186). The KANU headquarters, designed to be over 63 storeys high, at "a proposed cost of [...] $200 million, [...] was a flagrant act of profligacy at a time when donors were expected to pick up an ever-larger share of public expenditure" (Branch *Hope and Despair* 186). The 2004 Peace Nobel Laureate Wangari Maathai used civil disobedience to stop the building, arguing that the edifice was an affront to the city's ecosystem.[1]

Nyawira, who is the leader of the underground revolution against the dictatorial regime, challenges Kamiti to reflect on the necessity for a revolution: "There are two kinds of saviours: those who want to soothe

the souls of the suffering and those who want to heal the sores on the flesh of the suffering. Sometimes I wonder which is right" (94). Here, Nyawira challenges the morality of ideologies that insist on docility and aloofness in a tyrannical state. Indeed, sycophancy fits squarely in such posturing because it seems to soothe the soul of a suffering state, but it does not heal. In the end, the state suppurates, and amputations become necessary thus leading to permanent disabilities. For healing, Nyawira suggests a revolution – a surgical operation that best intervenes in healing the diseased Aburirian state. Like Wangari Maathai in Moi's regime, Nyawira does this through civil disobedience whereby members of her movement disrupt the Ruler's public rallies.

More poignantly, *Wizard of the Crow* portrays the cabinet in a dictatorial polity as an orchestra of sycophancy hence a progenitor of unprecedented excesses of power. Here, the cabinet is a space in which rivalry for power invested in the ruler flares up in unprecedented proportions. In one of the incidents in which the narrator shows a duel between Machokali and Sikiokuu, sycophancy is used to validate and entrench the Ruler's claim to sovereignty. Sikiokuu unknowingly attempts to separate the country from the Ruler. For this 'crime', Machokali leads the chant:

> *His Mighty Ruler is the Mighty Country and the Mighty Country is the Ruler.* Led by Big Ben Mambo, the other ministers also stood up and chanted, *The Ruler and the Country are one and the same,* and soon it became a call-and-response ceremony led by Machokali. (161, original emphasis)

At this point, sycophancy appears inseparable from worship; it fetishizes the Ruler to the point that he becomes a form of religion. In fact, Sikiokuu atones for his 'crime' by stating while on his knees: "I am a firm believer that you are the Country and the Country is You, and I propose that this fact be stated in the constitution. I swear before Your Mighty Presence that I shall myself make a motion in Parliament to amend the constitution accordingly" (161). The suggestions to amend the constitution as a way of showing loyalty to the Ruler show grievous consequences of sycophancy to aspirations for democracy, for freedom. Sycophancy of this stature gives a ruler carte blanche over the destiny of the country, suspending any pretence to accountability. Here, Ngugi appears to be making a commentary on various Kenyan despots who made themselves fetishes in the Kenyan social imaginaries. Sycophants like JJ Kamotho mentioned above seem to have made Moi believe he was an extraordinary being.

Sycophants' Deadly Rivalries

Sycophancy also embodies malicious tactics the political class employ class in their rivalry. Sikiokuu, the minister of state in the Ruler's office, uses strange ways to appease the Ruler's ego. For instance, when members of the Movement of the Voice of the People use plastic snakes to disrupt the public during the celebrations of the Ruler's birthday, Sikiokuu degrades himself in attempts to appease the Ruler for his (Sikiokuu's) failure in intelligence gathering. Sikiokuu sends his first, second, and then his third wife to the Ruler as sexual offers, all of which the Ruler ignores: "[f]inally, he sent his two daughters. It was only then that the Ruler softened and he started seeing Sikiokuu again, but then only to vent his anger on the hapless minister" (23). Ironically, these extreme forms of indignities in which the female body is sacrificed on the altar of sycophancy, where morals and ethics are also torn apart, are geared at the sycophant's quest for obscene powers to crush democratic reform crusaders. In this portrayal, the narrator unmasks the moral hollowness of Aburiria, or Kenya's political elites.

It appears sycophants' suffering in the bizarre mechanisms of the autocrats pay out when their master gives them powers to commit atrocities. For instance, after Sikiokuu has undergone various indignities, he is granted some powers. The narrator shows that Sikiokuu "fell to his knees and lowered his head" (135) his ears actually touching the Ruler's shoes. "I beg Your Mighty Excellency please give me more powers to smoke out those who are behind the latest plot to dishonour your person and government" (135). To this request, the Ruler gives him orders "to use all means, necessary and unnecessary, to bring [his] enemies dead or alive" (136). With these excessive powers, Sikiokuu sycophantically intones:

> I swear by my two ears and before you, My Lord on Earth and Heaven, that I shall do everything within the powers you have now given me to crush the members of this so-called Movement for the Voice of the People. [...]. O My Lord, their cries for mercy will be heard in all corners of the globe. (136)

In this promise to torture the state's 'enemies', I read Kenyan state histories of violating human rights of the citizenry such as the Nyayo House torture chambers of the mid-1980s that attracted global outrage (see Musila, "Phallocracies and Gynocratic Transgressions" 49). This underpins the link between sycophancy and the histories of torture in Kenya.

The novel invokes the Nyayo House torture chambers in the depictions of the Ruler's sacred chamber in the State House in which the

> skulls of his most hated enemies hung on the walls and others from the ceiling, bone sculptures, white memories of victory and defeat. The chamber was a cross between a museum and a temple, and every morning the Ruler, after first bathing in the preserved blood of his enemies, would enter, carrying a staff and a fly whisk, and then walk about quietly, looking at various exhibits one by one... (11)

The flywhisk and the staff are possibly nods to Kenyatta's and Moi's respective symbols for visible performance of power. These objects are "'accessories of power' [because they] are symbols of traditional authority and are the focus of numerous popular legends which impute almost fetish-like power to them. To be hit with any of these objects was to suffer a great curse" (Ogola 151). The atrocities that the Ruler has committed in his country seem a constant presence. He is condemned to commune with victims of his atrocities every waking day. In the statement that the chamber was located between a museum and a temple, the narrator reveals the Ruler's desires to exhibit absolute power over history, but his kind of history should be sanitized. This is seen in his oscillation from the temple to the museum. There is a contradiction between the histories that the temple should archive, what is in the chamber of skulls, and what should be taken to the museum. A glimpse into this ominous chamber seems symbolic of opening classified state secrets to the public. Inside it, one encounters horrendous atrocities that sycophants mask by flaunting the greatness and benevolence of the Ruler.

The torturers of dissidents, political prisoners, and other sociopolitical reform crusaders construe their crimes as patriotic acts. Sikiokuu who is at the centre of these histories of torture in Aburiria draws much pleasure from his duty. He is joyful to be tasked with crushing those deemed enemies of the state: "[t]he state would now strike back, and he, Sikiokuu, was thankful that fate had chosen him to be the instrument of the Ruler's revenge" (219). Yet, the novel also unmasks the complex nature of sycophancy and how it relates to settling personal scores with one's political enemies. Sikiokuu concentrates his newly acquired powers on his rivals – Machokali and his allies. This results in subjecting Vinjinia to "the secret grip of the State" (230). Vinjinia is Titus Tajirika's wife, and Tajirika is Machokali's closest political ally. When the Ruler is out of the country, Sikiokuu also kidnaps Tajirika and tortures him with the intent of forcing him to produce a statement implicating Machokali in unfounded claims of treason. The contrived charges of treason against Machokali are meant to show how loyal Sikiokuu is to the Ruler, and possibly grant him (Sikiokuu) more powers.

Conclusion

This chapter shows a powerful interlink between sycophancy and assassinations in a dictatorial state. Sycophants sanitize state violence with political propaganda, but they end up as victims of the very system they construct and shield. After spending their lives glorifying the Ruler even in the most humiliating of circumstances, Machokali, Sikiokuu, Big Ben Mambo, and Dr. Luminous Karamu-Mbu among others, are eventually assassinated. Karamu-Mbu is assassinated for showing evidence, in the Ruler's biography he writes, of having known too much concerning the

Ruler. His revolutionary criticism of autocracy that he perfected while in exile is no longer remembered, and never rewarded. Ben Mambo is assassinated for delivering a speech to the public while standing on a military tanker. It seems Mambo was getting too familiar with state apparatuses. To a paranoid state, this act indicted him of fantasies for a coup against the Ruler. Sikiokuu is assassinated for possessing suits like the Ruler's which he secretly wore behind closed doors, an indication that he was entertaining secret ambitions of ascending to the Ruler's throne. Machokali, too, is assassinated for being the West's preferable presidential successor of the Ruler. These key architects of dictatorial regimes end tragically in a way suggesting that they are villains.

Acknowledgement

This chapter is a revised version of my PhD thesis's section titled "Sycophancy in the Moi Regime: Ngugi wa Thiong'o's *Wizard of the Crow*" (82–92), a section in Chapter Three: "Literary Reconfigurations of Kenya's State Histories". The thesis itself is titled "Narrated Histories in Selected Kenyan Novels, 1963–2013". I'm indebted to my supervisors Prof Grace A Musila and Dr Godwin Siundu whose views were instrumental in the preparation of the earlier draft.

Note

1 In 1986, University of Nairobi "students collaborated with Wangare Mathaai's Green Belt Movement (GBM — a local environmental NGO) and succeeded in protecting Uhuru Park from the KANU political party, which wanted to appropriate part of the park for a sixty-story headquarters" (Amutabi, "Crisis and Student Protest in Universities in Kenya" 174).

Works Cited

Amutabi, Maurice N. "Crisis and Student Protest in Universities in Kenya: Examining the Role of Students in National Leadership and the Democratisation Process." *African Studies Review* 45.2 (2002): 157–177.

Anderson, David M. "Remembering Wagalla: State Violence in Northern Kenya, 1962–1991." *Journal of Eastern African Studies* 8.4 (2014): 658–676. Taylor & Francis. doi:10.1080/17531055.2014.946237.

Baudrillard, Jean. *The Spirit of Terrorism*. Ed. Chris, Trans. Translation Turner. Verso, 2002.

Branch, Daniel. *Kenya: Between Hope and Despair, 1963–2012*. Yale University Press, 2012.

Cohen, David., and Atieno Odhiambo. *The Risks of Knowledge: Investigations into the Death of the Hon. Minister John Robert Ouko in Kenya, 1990*. Ohio University Press, 2004.

Fanon, Frantz. *The Wretched of the Earth*. London: Penguin Books, 1963.

Feinberg, Leonard. *Introduction to Satire*. Iowa: The Iowa State University Press, 1967.

Gikandi, Simon. "The Postcolonial Wizard." *Transition* 98 (2008): 156–169.

Goldsworthy, David. *Tom Mboya: The Man Kenya Wanted to Forget.* Heinemann, 1982.

Mbembe, Achille. "Provisional Notes on the Postcolony." *Journal of the International African Institute* 62.1 (1992): 3–37.

Musila, Grace. *A Death Retold in Truth and Rumour: Kenya, Britain and the Julie Ward Murder.* London: James Currey, 2015.

———. "Familial Cartographies in Contemporary East African Short Stories." *Journal of African Cultural Studies* 25.3 (2013): 349–363. doi:10.1080/1369 6815.2013.766585.

———. "Phallocracies and Gynocratic Transgressions: Gender, State Power and Kenyan Public Life." *Africa Insight* 39.1 (2009): 39–57. http://search.proquest. com/docview/856404773?accountid=14609%5Cnhttp://gq8yy6pb7j.search. serialssolutions.com/ ?ctx_ver=Z39.88-2004&ctx_enc=info:ofi/enc:UTF-8&rfr_id=info:sid/ProQ:socabsshell&rft_val_fmt=info:ofi/fmt:kev:mtx: journal&rft.genre=article&rft.jt.

Ngwala, Mike. "Joseph Kamotho: How Kanu's 'Cockerel' Perfected Art of Political Survival." *Daily Nation.* December 2014. www.nation.co.ke/news/pol itics/joseph-kamotho-kanu/-/1064/2548348/-/bsfs8r/-/index.html.

Nowrojee, Binaifer, and Bronwen Manby. "Divide and Rule." *Africa Report* 38.5 (1993): 32. doi:10.1177/136843198001001005.

Odhiambo, Lewis. "The Media Environment in Kenya Since 1990." *African Studies* 61.2 (2002): 295–318. doi:10.1080/0002018022000032965.

Ogola, George. "Popular Culture and Politics: Whispers and the 'Dramaturgy of Power' in Kenya." *Social Identities: Journal for the Study of Race, Nation and Culture* 11.2 (2005): 147–160. doi:10.1080/13504630500161581.

Ogude, James. "Allegory and the Grotesque Image of the Body: Ngugi's Portrayal of Depraved Characters in Devil on the Cross." *World Literature Written in English* 36.2 (1997): 77–91. doi:10.1080/17449859708589276.

———. "Ngugi ' s Concept of History and the Post-colonial Discourses in Kenya." *Canadian Journal of African Studies* 31.1 (1997): 86–112.

Omari, Emman. "The Kamotho I Knew: A Man for All Seasons." *Daily Nation.* December 2014. www.nation.co.ke/lifestyle/DN2/Remembering-Joseph-Kamotho-Kanu-apologist-No-1-/-/957860/2556072/-/5ywn5/-/index.html.

Opanga, Kwendo. "In Barng'etuny and Mulu Mutisya, Moi Was in Good Company." *Daily Nation.* 22 December 2013. http://mobile.nation.co.ke/news/ In-Barng-etuny-and-Mulu-Mutisya-Moi-was-in-good-company-/1950946-2121758-format-xhtml-11wel2/index.html. Web. 20 Sep. 2016.

wa Thiong'o, Ngugi. *Wizard of the Crow.* East African Educational Publishers, 2007.

———. *Writers in Politics.* Nairobi: Henemann Educational Publishers Ltd., 1981.

Were, Marciana Nafula. "Kenyan Women in Androcentric Political Culture: From Julia Auma Ojiambo to Affirmative Action." *Social Dynamics* 43.3 (2017): 487–504. Routledge. doi:10.1080/02533952.2017.1416975.

Yenjela, David Wafula. *Narrated Histories in Selected Kenyan Novels, 1963–2013.* no. March, Stellenbosch University, 2017. http://scholar.sun. ac.za/handle/10019.1/101185.

8   Mediating the Vicious Cycle of Political Atrocities in Ngugi wa Thiongo's *Wizard of the Crow*

Charles K. Rono

Introduction

This chapter analyzes the vicious cycle of political atrocities in Ngugi wa Thiongo's *Wizard of the Crow*. The chapter shows how Ngugi mediates political atrocities in dictatorial societies through a regime's loyalists and indicates that those who bear the brunt of a regime's atrocities are ironically the devotees and not necessarily the rebels. Espousing Michael Humphrey's (2002) theorization of political violence, the chapter reads Ngugi's *Wizard of the Crow* as a serious indictment on the dangers of absolute power in society as demonstrated by the Ruler's and syco- phants' bizarre bodily metamorphosis in order to continue to mete out violence on innocent victims. Paradoxically, as this chapter shows, the devotees who the regime expects to perpetrate torture to the rebels are undergoing self-torture within and amongst themselves so as not only to remain in the "good grace" of the dictator but also to evade punitive measures that can be meted out to them in case they are suspected of de- fying the Ruler. The chapter shows that both the devotees and the Ruler suffer from psychological torture leading to the deformation of their own bodies. The chapter goes beyond physical atrocities and argues that bodily harm is only a manifestation of real and mental torture of one's own body. It is important, at this juncture, to point out that negotiation in this chapter alludes to the ways that victims devise to mitigate or sur- vive various political atrocities.

The chapter contextualizes political atrocities in Ngugi's *Wizard on the Crow* by first taking a quick look at how creative works of art document the violation of human rights committed by Jomo Kenyatta's (1963–1978) and Daniel Toroitich Arap Moi's (1978–2002) regimes. Atrocities by the two regimes are creatively documented in various post-independent biographies and autobiographies such as Jaramog Oginga's *Not Yet Uhuru*, Waweru Kariuki's *We Lived to Tell: The Nyayo House Story*, and Wanyiri Kihoro's *Never say Die* among many others. In these texts, both real and imagined rebels are mostly represented as victims who bear the brunt of the regime's heinous acts and little has been said on the suffering of those known to have been so devoted to these dictatorial systems. In her discussion of how self and history intersect in Kenyan autobiographies, Jennifer Muchiri argues that "autobiographies of political detainees after independence demonstrate the pain and dehumanization of the supposed 'enemies' of the state during Moi and Kenyatta's governments" (89). Muchiri's observations are anchored on the autobiography's supposed fidelity to historical truth, which is critical for this chapter as it examines how Ngugi weaves and uses history to foreground political atrocities in his *Wizard of the Crow*. The chapter argues that, in the novel, exaltations of the repressive leadership by the Ruler's disciples are not because they uphold and have fidelity to the law but because they want to shield themselves from atrocities that they would be subjected to if they defy the Ruler. At this juncture, the relevance of Plato's ideas on governance and justice as articulated in *The Republic* cannot be gainsaid. In theorizing the meaning of justice and injustice, Plato insists that people can be unjust only if they can get away with it without being punished. While challenging Socrates to prove the goodness of being just, he observes that the highest category of just and goodness is that of things that are both good in themselves *and* because of their consequences. Plato further argues that justice is *only* valuable because of its good *consequences* and not because of what it is inherently worth (Plato 32). In *Wizard of the Crow*, devotees venerate the Ruler by proposing torture of their own bodies not because they are so loyal to him and his autocratic rule, but because they fear the consequences of being rebellious to the Ruler's regime.

Reading Ngugi's *Wizard of the Crow* as a Dictator Novel

In a way, Ngugi's *Wizard on the Crow* can be read as a dictator novel in Kenya. Though writing on the dictatorship in Africa is not such a new phenomenon; dictator novels as a genre in the continent is relatively new compared to other continents such as Latin America. Dictator novels primarily examine, albeit creatively, the relationship between power, dictatorship, and writing. Largely drawing from history, dictator novels focus on the power wielded by the dictator over his subjects foregrounding how direct confrontations with the dictator are met with brutal force, torture, and arbitrary detentions and imprisonments. While exposing the dictatorial tendencies of the tyrannical rulers, writers explore the role of a section of the citizens who are abetting and perpetuating dictatorship. This situation could be said of Ngugi's *Wizard on the Crow* where a section of the citizens, the devotees, team up with the Ruler to perpetuate dictatorship. Taking a cue from Robert L. Colson (2011), this chapter examines characters close to the Ruler in its attempt to unearth how the regime's disciples shield themselves from political atrocities by deifying the dictator and his rule. In *Arresting Time, Resisting Arrest: Narrative Time and the African Dictator in Ngũgĩ wa Thiong'o's*

Wizard of the Crow, Robert L. Colson argues that "one of the striking features of Ngũgĩ's latest novel is the amount of attention that he pays to the ruling elite, exposing their infighting, insecurities, paranoia, and fear" (135). This chapter seeks to further Colson's observations by showing the mutual relationship between negotiating atrocities, 'deifying' and 'defying' in the dictatorial context and by juxtaposing the effects of dictatorship not only on devotees (represented by Machokali, Sikiokuu, and Big Ben Mambo) but also on the Ruler, whose terror unleashed on innocent citizens finally turns against himself.

First written in the Agikuyu language in 2004 under the title *Murogi wa Kagogo* and translated to English in 2006, *Wizard of the Crow* is a story about the aristocracy of the second Ruler of the Free Republic of Abuiuria. Though the narrative begins by referring to the strange illness of the Ruler, the rumoured illness has not yet occurred when the novel begins. In fact, he started ailing the very moment the Global Bank denies his government a loan to finance the Marching to Heaven Project. The Ruler's regime is aided by three trusted advisers who constantly try to prove their devotion to him. The three advisors are depicted as engaging in bizarre activities in order to catch the eye of the Ruler. For instance, Machokali earned his ministerial position after having a plastic surgery to have his eyes "enlarged to the size of electric bulbs" (53) leading Sikiokuu to follow suit with the enlargement of his ears so that he would be able to hear even the most private conversations of citizens in a bid to protect the Ruler. The three cabinet trustees are the novel's protagonists while Kamiti wa Karimiri and Grace Nyawira are the antagonists with the magic of the wizard, whose powers can bring down even the crows from the sky, revolving around their lives. The novel's fidelity to post realist writing precisely fits into the genre of dictator novels that not only thematize power but also rejects the formal structure of conventional realism. Though Gĩchingiri Ndĩgĩrĩgĩ' sees Ngugi's use of magical realism as a safety valve for readers to comfortably read even while in dictatorial regimes, this chapter argues that magical realism in the text faithfully captures the events that are too traumatizing for readers to imagine. The moments of torture in the text are presented in such a manner that makes readers question their very existence.

The removal of the ruling party, KANU from power in 2002 allows former political detainees and prisoners to reveal how the former regime used to torture them as a means of extracting confessions on alleged crimes committed, or worse to implicate an individual perceived to be a dissident. *Wizard of the Crow* reads like a documentary on the occurrences evidenced in Moi's regime. The Nyayo House torture chambers came into existence in the early 1980s and were housed at the basement of Nyayo House. During the Moi era, any hint on the existence of these torture chambers would be dismissed as untrue by the authorities. Though former president Daniel Moi was more than once referred to as one of Africa's dictators, he stood his ground by telling off his critics that they mistook discipline for despotism. Moi was vehemently critical of a ceremonial president asserting that this kind of ruler does not even have a political voice which is a prerequisite for running not only the party's political affairs but also in articulating issue of the national importance. In Moi's KANU, political order and discipline found a perfect home and which culminated at the formation of the famous KANU Disciplinary Committee in 1986 and the secret existence of the Nyayo House Torture Chambers. The presence of Torture Chambers and its subsequent reflection in *Wizard of the Crow* fortifies the chapter's argument that the Ruler's disciples deify him and his rule.

Deification of the dictator in *Wizard of the Crow* is brought about by the use of the term deity, together with its synonyms like Almighty among others, by the Ruler's followers. Though the followers use the term in order to seek his favours, it is worth noting that it is the Ruler himself who occasions the use of these terms since he compares his powers to that of God, the Almighty. While reprimanding Rachael's 'false' accusation that he sleeps with girls who are young enough for him to be their father, he tells her that he has "power, real power over everything including...yes...Time", (34). The Ruler, here, exposes his mightiness when he tells Rachael that he is so powerful that he can control everything including time! Indeed, in order to demonstrate his powerfulness, the Ruler manages to freeze Rachael's time. Though the Ruler successfully stopped it, his proclamations on time undermine Biblical teachings that God alone has total authority over time. Additionally, the Marching to Heaven Project clearly demonstrates how the Ruler is elevated to God's level. The building will be raised "to the very gates of Heaven so that the Ruler could call on God daily to say good morning or good evening or simply how was your day today, God?" (61).

Worth noting is the fact that the Ruler is glorified by his disciples in order to win his favours. The conversation between the Ruler and Machokali in which the Minister for Foreign Affairs accuses his counterpart of failing to arrest Nyawira serves as a classic example. At this point, Machokali refers to the Ruler as "Almighty Esteemed Father" (747). For his part, Tajirika refers to the Ruler as "Your Lordship" (1706). While responding to the two voluminous typescripts, "The Kaniürü Report on the Origins of the Queuing Mania and Its Possible Connection with Anti-government Activities" and "A Secret Report on Acts of Treason" (1603), Sikiokuu swears before the Ruler, "I swear before you, the Almighty one on Earth" (1603.). These utterances serve to affirm the fact that the Ruler's disciples are doing this to shield themselves from punitive actions that might befall them in case they are seen to defy The Ruler. Though Nyawira and Kamiti shield themselves from the Ruler's political atrocities with their own tactics, their evasion is not necessary since it is not intertwined with the act of deification as that of the devotees.

Political Atrocities in Ngugi wa Thiong'o's *Wizard of the Crow*

Michael Humphrey, in *The Politics of Atrocity and Reconciliation: From Terror to Trauma*, says that acts of face-to-face violence to torture and mutilate victims is a political strategy. He argues that atrocity threatens life by cruelly disfiguring human bodies. Atrocities horrify and terrify when they produce wounded and mutilated bodies. The self-torture that Ruler's devotees undergo as they seek his favours mirrors Humphrey's postulations on atrocity as a political strategy. Despite the fact that they feel unsafe in the Ruler's precincts, the devotees wish not to be out because it's not an option. This is so because opting out of the regime will turn out to be their detriment as they could be victims of the brutal regime. It is clear from the novel that the survival and wishes of the Ruler's devotees depend greatly on the whims of the Ruler himself. The novel says that Members of Parliament in the Ruler's regime wish to alter their bodies depending on what services they wanted to render the Ruler (56). Three members of the cabinet do their level best to deform their bodies and sure enough, according to their wish, they win the Ruler's favours. There is a need to state at the very outset that the three devotees proclaimed self-torture as a means to cope with the mental torture they suffer from. The body deformation therefore is a physical manifestation of the psychological torture that the Members of Parliament suffer from.

Benjamin Mambo agonized over the best bodily change that would land him the Defence portfolio. It is reported that he chose to have his tongue elongated so that in echoing the Ruler's command, his words and threats would reach every soldier and corner in the country. He emulated Sikiokuu and went to Paris but there was some misunderstanding about the required size, and the dog-like tongue now hung out way beyond his lips, rendering speech impossible. Machokali came to his aid by arranging for him to go to a clinic in Berlin, where the lips were pulled and elongated to cover the tongue, but then it was not done competently and the tongue protruded even now just a little. Silver Sikiokuu, the Minister of State in the Ruler's office, secretly sold his father's plot and borrowed the rest to buy himself a flight to France and a hospital bed in Paris so as to have his ears enlarged. Markus, the Minister for Foreign Affairs, went for an eye surgery in one of the major hospitals in England in which his eyes were enlarged "so that they would be able to spot the enemies of the Ruler no matter how far their hiding places" (53) and so he earned the name, Machokali. Later on, in the novel, the readers get to know that even the Ruler himself gets entangled in the web of body deformation when he suffers from Self-Induced Expansion, a condition that saw the expansion of his body after getting the reports that the Global Bank Ministry rejected the plans to finance the Marching to Heaven Project.

The politics of Self-Induction is best exemplified by the acts of the three members of the cabinet who proposed self-torture as a means to win the Ruler's favours. The word 'Self' in the text is used more than once, especially when the text is making a connection to how characters' dispositions impacted on themselves. The inflections on the 'Self' are furthered by the Ruler's Self-Induced Expansion, his disciples' Self-Induced Tortures and finally Machokali's Self-Induced Disappearance. Inspiring in all these 'Selves' is how torture executed by perpetrators of the atrocities turns against them. Ngugi in *Wizard of the Crow* dexterously weaves the narrative to reflect this self-inflicted suffering as a way of suggesting that though political atrocities affect a regime's rebels its agents become the greatest recipients of the regime's brutalities. For instance, Machokali was accused of planning and executing the Queuing to Heaven Manna and as the novel ends, we are told that the minister has disappeared. It is said that the private detectives the Ruler hired from abroad reported to him that Machokali's disappearance is a case of self-induced disappearance. The Ruler is convinced that Machokali is behind the Movement for the Voice of the People, a scheme that the Ruler tells parliament that is "so absurd as to boggle the mind" (2147). Though the Ruler sees Machokali's disappearance as a payback for his misdeeds, the chapter reads this as a kind of self-torture that he prescribed against himself. Earlier on in the novel, Machokali cursed himself by swearing that may his eyes turn against him if he "not telling the truth" (55). His Self-Induced Disappearance could then be read as fulfilment of the curses he brought on upon himself. Machokali initiated this self-torture when he proposed to have plastic surgery done on his eyes and though this devotion was acknowledged, the Ruler makes it clear that his security forces would hunt 'rebels' like Markus Machokali down and bring them to justice.

In *Wizard of the Crow*, Ngugi subtly captures excesses of brutality through the symbolic arrest and subsequent interrogation of Titus Tajirika, the Chairman of the Marching to Heaven Building Committee. Tajirika's ordeal at the hands of his interrogators paints a picture equivalent to that of President Moi's heinous regime, particularly the dispensation of KANU Disciplinary Committee. In examining the politics of populism in Moi's first decade in power (1978–1988), Bethwell Allan Ogot and William Robert Ochieng' observe that President Moi suggested that the party should establish a disciplinary committee to deal with party members who contradict the party's standpoint. According to the historians, the disciplinary committee rapidly developed into the party court of justice where both the accusers and the accused were heard in the open before the committee passed its judgment (206). Readers can make a veiled connection between the Ruler's devoted ministers and the politicians in Moi's era. Members of the cabinet and close associates in Moi's era used the Disciplinary Committee to seek Moi's favour by throwing muck at each other.

The novel's Commission of Inquiry into the Queuing Mania is synonymous with the Disciplinary Committee. When Titus Tajirika disobeyed the sermons to appear before the Kaniuru-led Commission, he was arrested, blindfolded, and thrown into a dark chamber and was later subjected to a concatenation of interrogations led by Assistant Superintendent Elijah Njoya, Superintendent Peter Kahiga, Sikiokuu, and Kaniuru among others. As Tajirika goes through the interrogative session, what punctuates the process is the forced confession; "For my part, I can make sure that the confessions you make in this office will be sent to the Commission of Inquiry to be made part of its records" (1220). What the interrogators are simply doing is to win each other's favour because they are quite conscious of the fact that everyone is under surveillance and the slightest misconduct would reach the Ruler. While in the torture chamber, Titus Tajirika swore his innocence in the name of his ancestors, his children, God, anything that might give him after wizard of the crow temporary respite from needles in his fingers and cigarette burns on his body, (809). Tajirika knows nothing about the Queuing Mania, but his interrogators force words into his mouth that if he confesses, then it is tantamount to appearing in the august body freely and willingly and all this amounts to "full cooperation with the commission" (1221).

In dictatorial contexts, innocent citizens are compelled to 'cooperate' for failure to means excessive torture. Conscious of the kind of brutality which awaits him if forwarded to the Ruler, Tajirika pleads with Sikiokuu, "Help me; please do whatever you can to make sure that this matter does not reach the ears of the Ruler" (1220). We have to remember here that Titus Tajirika is one of the Ruler's steadfast servants whose loyalty prompted his appointment as the chairman of Marching to Heaven, as well as CEO of Eldares Modern Construction and Real Estate. Tajirika's high profile could have made him immune to brutalities that are inflicted on those who rebel against the Ruler. However, he like other devotees becomes the victims of the brutal regime they devoted and served with all their energies. Later on in the text Sikiokuu, who was initially implicated in the crime of Queuing to Heaven Mania, turns against his fellow minister Machokali and victimizes him by putting words in Tajirika's mouth thus: "at different times and occasions you heard Machokali express his longing for the highest political office in the land, often with the conditional *if the Ruler were not there...etc.*" (1229–1230).

The accusations and counter-accusations that devotees cast on one another are just but gimmicks that they employ in their bid to both venerate their Ruler and shield themselves from any punitive measures that can be taken against them for not being the Ruler's trusted eyes. Ngugi framed the novel with the backdrop of dehumanizing political orientations in post-colonial African nations where statements were interpreted at will so as to incriminate the imagined state rebels. Though Tajirika truly suffered from the '*if*' disease, the disease that expresses his wish of becoming white, Sikiokuu interprets this white-ache as an implication of power. In fact, it is shocking that he further interprets this malady of words as Tajirika's shock occasioned by Machokali's wish to become the ruler, a dream that Ruler himself claims that it will only be dreamt by the person who has not been born (45). Sikiokuu further complicates the interpretation by saying that when Tajirika later tried to recall the implications of the sentiments, his larynx rebelled and refused to give words to those thoughts. Later on in the novel, we learn that Sikiokuu himself suffered from the same '*if*' disease after wizard of the crow confesses that his shadow has a lot of powers. Sikiokuu's desire to know the destiny of his own shadow became an irresistible hunger for more signs, but because he could not clothe his thoughts in words, he suddenly started barking, "*If*". Every time he tried to say something, he would simply mutter, "if" (1272). When the wizard cured his malady of words, Sikiokuu reveals that he dreams of becoming the Ruler one day. Though rebels are usually brutalized and repressed by dictatorial regimes, *Wizard of the Crow* subverts this popular assumption by portraying how devotees are mostly affected by heinous acts of tyrant leaders. In a scenario where Kamiti, the wizard of the crow, was arrested with a view to shedding more light on the Queuing Mania, he meets with Tajirika in the same cell. Tajirika thought that the fellow prisoner has been sent to kill him, he started screaming: "Don't kill me. I beg you, don't kill me. I have committed no crime. Have mercy on me. I have a wife and children. Please don't spill innocent blood because of money. Whatever they have given you, I promise to double it" (1157). This shows the kind of humiliation and mental anguish that the devotees go through once they fall out of favour with the Ruler.

Conclusion

This chapter has shown to the popular notion that rebels in dictatorial regimes suffer the most while devotees enjoy the comfort of the dictator, the dictator's faithful servants also bear the brunt of the despot's brutal rule. As shown in *Wizard of the Crow*, the devotees went further than expected to deform their bodies so as to win the Ruler's favors. Benjamin Mambo, for example, was given the Ministry of Information after a surgery that saw the elongation of his tongue, while Silver Sikiokuu's enlargement of the ears earned him State portfolio in the Ruler's office. On his part, Markus Machokali went for eye surgery in one of the major hospitals in England where his eyes were enlarged "so that they would be able to spot the enemies of the Ruler no matter how far their hiding places" and he was named the Minister for Foreign Affairs. The chapter has argued that because these disciples are conscious of the heartlessness that they can be subjected to when they rebel against the regime, they please the Ruler by not only outdoing themselves but also doing unimaginable things like deforming their bodies. These acts of deformation, as the chapter has demonstrated, serves as a means of negotiating the political atrocities in Ngugi's post-colonial dictator novel. However, the regime's devotees did not escape the vicious cycle of political torture when their turn came calling. The trustees were subjected to the same brutalities that they subjected the regime's rebels, a case of the hunter becoming the hunted.

Works Cited

Citizen for Justice. *We Lived to Tell: The Nyayo House Story.*

Colson, Robert. "Arresting Time, Resisting Arrest: Narrative Time and the African Dictator in Ngũgĩ wa Thiong'o's *Wizard of the Crow.*" *Research in African Literatures* 42.1 (Spring 2011): 133–153.

Foucault, Michel. *Discipline and Punish: The Birth of the Prison.* New York: Vintage Books, 1979.

Humphrey, Michael. *The Politics of Atrocity and Reconciliation: From Terror to Trauma.* New York: Routledge, 2013.

Muchiri, Jennifer. The Intersection of the Self and History in Kenyan Autobiographies. *Eastern African Literary and Cultural Studies* 1.1 & 2: 83–93.

Mutahi, Wahome. *Three Days on the Cross.* Nairobi: East African Education Publishers. 1991.

Ndĩgĩrĩgĩ, Gĩchingiri. Spectacle and Subversive Laughter sin Ngũgĩ wa Thiong'o's *Wizard of the Crow. Canadian Review of Comparative Literature.* 2010. 280–294.

Ogot, Betwel A., and William R. Ochieng. *Decolonization and Independence in Kenya 1940–1963.* Nairobi: East African Educational Publishers, 1995.

Plato, G M. A. Grube, and C D. C. Reeve. *Republic.* Indianapolis: Hackett Pub. Co, 1992.

Spencer, Robert. Ngũgĩ wa Thiong'o and the African dictator novel. *The Journal of Commonwealth Literature* 47 (2): 2012. 145–158.

9 Gender-based Atrocity in Kenyan Urban Women's Novel after 2000

Alina Rinkanya

Introduction

Couched in post-colonial feminism and urban development theoretical stances (the latter as presented in the study of J. Roger Kurtz), this chapter examines how gender-based atrocity spreads far beyond the domestic sphere, curbing women's agency and fundamental rights in all ambits of life, such as professional, social, and political among others. Kenyan urban women's novel after 2000 reflects sensitively all aspects of gender-based atrocity in various spheres of life creating images of role model characters, who resist gender-based atrocity at all levels. The chapter demonstrates that various forms of gender-based atrocity, as depicted in Kenyan women's urban novel after 2000, intertwine and stimulate each other creating the "environment of atrocity" as part of a social landscape of post-colonial Kenya – the environment which the authors, through their mouthpiece characters, are trying to do away with. The modern urban environment and the women's urban mentality are read as twin enablers of the modern women's struggle for self-emancipation from gender-based atrocities.

Gender-based violence has been one of the main topics of gender studies around the world, on all levels and in all spheres, for several decades. In the theoretical field alone, there have emerged a variety of approaches, some of which are instrumental to this study. Among those, we would mention the "women-blaming" theory, which relies on the expectations of appropriate or "unacceptable" female behaviour posed by a male partner, based on cultural attitudes towards gender inequality and male entitlement, which Hotaling and Sugarman (1986) call an "effort to explain male behaviour by examining characteristics of women". Another notable theoretical stance is, of course, feminism (see also below), which focuses on social conditions that support gender inequality and male privilege, and generally asserts that gender-based violence exists as a part of patriarchal social structures, and is an intentional pattern of behaviour utilized to establish and maintain power and control over a female (e.g., Bograd 1988, 1993). As related to it one may consider the theory of "social ecology", where violence in human society is understood through the interaction of various factors at each level of the social ecology – individual, family/relationship, community, society/culture (as its founding work, see Bookchin 2005).

It should also be mentioned that fundamental research on gender-based violence has been carried out by international organizations, such as various branches of the UN, WHO, and others. Suffice it to mention that in 1993 the UN General Assembly passed the declaration on the elimination of violence against women. Then in 1994, at the International Conference on Population and Development in Cairo, and in 1995 at the Fourth World Conference on Women in Beijing, organizations from around the world advocated ending gender-based violence as a high priority. WHO also acknowledges gender-based violence as a violation of human rights and a constraint to development throughout the world (WHO 1999).

Various research organizations and scholars have come up with an array of definitions of gender-based violence, especially violence against women. The Declaration on the Elimination of Violence Against Women, adopted by the UN General Assembly in 1993, defines violence against women as "any act of gender-based violence that results in, or is likely to result in, physical, sexual or mental harm or suffering to women, including threats of such acts, coercion or arbitrary deprivation of liberty, whether occurring in public or in private life" (UN Declaration 1993).

According to Neft and Levine (1997), gender-based violence takes place throughout the life cycle and can be grouped into five main categories: (1) Sexual violence, for example, sexual harassment, incest, rape, forced prostitution, and sexual slavery; (2) Physical violence, like wife battering and assault, female infanticide, child assault by teachers, and gay bashing; (3) Emotional and psychological violence, such as threats of violence, insults, and name-calling, humiliations in front of others, blackmail, and the threat of abandonment; (4) Harmful traditional practices, including female genital mutilation, denial of certain foods and forced or early marriage, (5) Socio-economic violence, such as discriminatory access to basic health care, low levels of literacy and educational attachment, inadequate shelter and food, economic deprivation, armed conflicts, and acts of terrorism.

An almost similar definition is proposed by the European Institute for Gender Equality, which states that

> direct violence against women includes violence in close relationships; sexual violence; trafficking in human beings, slavery and sexual exploitation; harmful practices such as child and forced marriages, female genital mutilation, and crimes committed in the name of so-called 'honour'; emerging forms of violations, instigated or facilitated through the use of information and communication technologies, stalking, and bullying; psychological and economic violence.

Along with that, indirect violence can be understood as

> a type of structural violence [...] characterised by norms, attitudes
> and stereotypes around gender in general and violence against
> women in particular. Indirect violence operates within a larger so-
> cietal context; institutions, and the individuals within and outside
> these institutions, are all engaged in the production and reproduction
> of attitudes which normalise violence against women. (EIGE 2018)

In Kenya, gender-based violence, especially against women, has a long-
reaching history and remains one of the burning problems of today, although several legislative acts against it have recently been passed on
the governmental level (e.g., the Protection Against Domestic Violence
Act, 2015, and Policy on Sexual and Gender Based Violence by National
Gender and Equality Commission 2017). Kenyan scholars have made a
substantial contribution to the research on the subject. To mention just a
few and relatively recent ones, we would refer to the studies by Kameri-
Mbote (2000), Kaluyu (2007), Saidi et al. (2008), Aura et al. (2010),
Kniss (2016). These publications cover various aspects of the problem,
from medical to social; but the problem definitely calls for further research on various levels and in various fields, one of them being the representation of gender-based violence (and other forms of gender-based
atrocity) in creative arts, as a sensitive mirror of any society.

J. Roger Kurtz, in his seminal study *Urban Obsessions, Urban Fears:
the Post-Colonial Kenyan Novel,* acknowledges that "the development
of a significant tradition of writing by women is one of the most important recent developments in Kenya's literary history" (Kurtz 154). And
throughout the chapter dealing with women's literature, Kurtz deliberately stresses the inseparable connection between the concept of female
emancipation and the urban lifestyle.

> [Kenyan novels] suggest that the city, because it disrupts traditional
> social patterns, and despite its customary nature as a male environ-
> ment, can be a place where women are able to create some measure
> of personal emancipation. Women can free themselves from depen-
> dence on fathers, husbands, or other men—particularly if they can
> find employment. The city may be historically male, but it is a com-
> plex enough place to allow some maneuvering room for women.
> (Kurtz 137)

And further: "City offers some hope for women, allowing them to create a space for themselves in ways that the patriarchy of rural social
structures cannot" (Kurtz 157). An embodiment of the ideas of personal
emancipation, independence, "manoeuvring" and, finally, gender equality and empowerment reveals

a line of strong female characters [...] who have appeared in novels from Kenya, especially in novels from women writers. While such characters were relatively scarce during the first generation of writers and even during the booming period of the 1970s [...] they have multiplied during the post-Kenyatta years. In fact, their appearance may be classified as one of the most significant recent developments in the Kenyan novel. (Kurtz 137)

The critical role of the urban environment and the instruments of social and personal advancement have been stressed in quite a number of scholarly works. Marie Kruger in her study of East African women's literature notes,

> For women, literacy has always been of particular appeal, for it promised an escape from the confining grasp of poverty and patriarchal domination. The desire for social mobility through education informs the novels of FEMRITE writers [...]; it dominates the fiction of established Kenyan writers, beginning with Grace Ogot, Asenath Odaga, Pamela (*sic*) Ngurukie, and Margaret Ogola; and it resurfaces in the work of new writers (Wairimu Kibugi Gitau and Florence Mbaya). (Kruger 10)

Later in the text, commenting on the spiritual and social growth of Elizabeth, one of the heroines of Ogola's renowned novel *The River and the Source*, she notes that Elizabeth's marrying a clerk, becoming a teacher, and moving to Nakuru "signifies the transition from arranged marriages to individual choice, from relationships defined by social and spatial proximity to those extending beyond familiar social networks, and from communally negotiated contracts to the risks of personal decision making" (Kruger 65). Likewise, John Kuria in his thesis "The challenge of feminism in Kenya", speaking about the resistance to gender-based violence portrayed in Kenyan women's short stories, poses an example of Rosa, a heroine of Asenath Odaga's eponymous story, "who fights and kills her assailant, Dan, [and] is set free on grounds of self-defence". Her self-courage and fighting spirit are stipulated by the fact that

> Rosa is not only a financially independent career woman but also a gender activist who, knowing the violent nature of men, has prepared herself by training in karate for self-defence. Because of her education, economic empowerment and experience, Rosa is careful to record Dan's previous visits and threats on an audio-cassette as well as in her diary. (Kuria 125)

Could that all have been possible but for Rosa's urban upbringing – would, we believe, remain a rhetorical question at best.

The rapid growth of Kenyan women's novel and the development of its "strong female characters" has become even more significant in, rephrasing J. Roger Kurtz, "post-Moi" years, that is, in the first quarter of the current century. And one significant feature that brings these characters together is that, unlike the novels of the previous decades, in which many of the female heroines came to the city from the rural areas (a classical example is Paulina in Oludhe-Macgoye's *Coming to birth*), the novels written after the year 2000 feature a different type of main character – urban-born, urban-grown, educated, working, middle-class women, with the widest range of professions. Some of these heroines have a village background, but their formation since their primary school years has been shaped by the city life, and they are the bearers of specifically urban mentality, moulded by university education, urban employment, and generally the whole complex of behavioural patterns pertinent to an urban lifestyle. These women, as depicted in these novels, since their formative years (mainly through schooling) have absorbed the ideas of emancipation, independence, and gender equality; they are trying their best to use these ideas as their guidelines in life – and this, naturally, brings these women into sharp confrontation with the "traditional social patterns", particularly with traditional concepts of gender roles and female behaviour. J. Roger Kurtz in his study asserted that "the most over-riding tension in contemporary Kenyan narrative is the dichotomy between tradition and modernity and that this dichotomy is manifested most fully in the city" (Kurtz 158). In Kenyan women's novels this dichotomy is mainly manifested in the conflict between gender equality and female empowerment, embodied by female protagonists, and traditional patriarchal gender patterns, embodied by antagonistic male figures. This conflict reveals itself in all spheres of life, from domestic to educational, professional, and political among others, and in its sharpest exertions, it is frequently characterized by various forms of atrocity – from sexual and physical violence to more subtle psychological torture.

This chapter, therefore, investigates atrocities accruing from gender conflicts as portrayed in recent novels by Kenyan women writers, and ways in which these writers deem instrumental to resist and neutralize gender-based atrocities. Various forms of gender-based atrocity, as depicted in Kenyan women's novel, intertwine and stimulate each other, creating an "environment of atrocity" as a part of the social landscape of post-colonial Kenya – the environment which the authors, through their characters, are trying to do away with. The chapter focuses on recent novels by women authors with female characters as main characters and a specific focus on women's problems. For these reasons, Yvonne Owuor's novel *Dust*, though undoubtedly a major event in recent Kenyan female writing, was deemed not suitable for the purpose of this chapter since the novel has male characters as central characters powering its polyphonic nature and varied thematic concerns.

Gender-based atrocity, as depicted in women's novels, is exercised in three main spheres – family (people bound by blood kinship), marriage, and profession, and its forms vary from "primitive" sexual and physical violence to a more sophisticated psychological mistreatment, and in some cases, these forms combine. In all these spheres, all these diverse occasions of gender-based atrocity have different consequences, but all of them in the end serve as a major trial for the main woman character – the trial which, in all cases, the woman victim is put into a dire state, physically, mentally, and socially; but this trial, in all novels, is successfully overcome, and in the long run serves for the strengthening of the heroine's personality, her personal and social empowerment, and independence.

Gender-based Atrocity in the Family

Atrocious actions of male characters against their female relatives permeate the fabric of Kenyan women's novels. Again, the forms are multiple, but the source is a single one – the concept of a female relative (or a relative's friend) as a "third-rate creature", a "disposable material" existing for the satisfaction of male's needs, from housework to sexual pleasures. In order to affirm this standpoint, different forms of gender-based atrocity are effected – and they provoke different forms of resistance.

The atrocious attitude of her relatives nearly ruined the life of Seith, one of the main characters of Georgina Mbithe's novel *Arise and Shine*. Being an orphan, she was mistreated through her childhood years by her malicious aunt and grandma; but her male relations inflict much greater pain on her, even more so because her first offender, her young uncle Peter, for several years was the only person who was making her life slightly more bearable, helping her with her domestic chores and school work. But when at the tender age of sixteen Seith developed a friendship with Tom, her classmate, the uncle, feeling that the girl of his lust may slip away from him, after unsuccessful attempts to talk her out of this friendship and even declaring his love to her, makes the final move – he waylays Seith in the forest and, after a long and painful struggle, rapes her. The fact that he, tortured by conscience, commits suicide immediately after his deed, only aggravates Seith's state of fear and depression. Furthermore, her next torturer – and her potential relative – appears to have no remorse at all: when after two years Seith, already a university student, decides to marry Tom, they temporarily share the house with Tom's brother Jared and his family of a wife and two children. Right on the eve of the wedding, Jared, coming home earlier in order to catch Seith alone, rapes her, leaving for Tom and his suffering bride the only option – to leave his house. Even Tom confesses that "incriminating him with the offence was not a choice" (116) – because, with all his honesty and affection to Seith, the authority of his elder brother matters more

to him, than the dignity and safety of his unmarried bride. A couple of
weeks later traumatized and frazzled Seith receives the final blow – she
loses Tom in a car accident. "I often felt as if I had lost love irrevocably.
I believed that death was my destiny. I didn't have any hope for life". Her
friend Nancy, the novel's main character, tells the readers about Seith:

> She explained she could not love after that. She wished to either die
> or kill every man. [...] She was in the sea of guilt and self-dislike,
> which almost culminated in suicide. She did not mind dying like a
> dog, but our love was strong and real [...] With encouragement from
> us she began thinking positively. (117)

Yes, only love of her friends – Nancy and Charles, the student CID officer and her future husband – saved Seith from the state of destruction
inflicted on her by her male relatives.

A similar plight befalls Ann, the heroine of Ketty Arucy's novel *Captive of fate*. The fifth child in a poor family, she lives in the house of her
rich aunt, who pays for Ann's schooling in exchange for Ann's services
as a housemaid. Morally mistreated by her aunt and cousins, Ann, however, receives real abuse from her aunt's husband, Mr. Tumbo. For six
years that she lived in his house, Mr. Tumbo "normally had treated her
more than an object than a human being. If he talked to her, it was either
to reprimand, rebuke, insult or give orders" (17). However, when at the
age of 19 Ann's beauty bloomed, Tumbo decided that it was time to reap
the harvest. His first attempt to rape Ann was unsuccessful – she lost
her consciousness, frightening the rapist (he thought the girl had died).
"Would it be right to narrate the ordeal to her aunt? [...] Her aunt will
never believe it. The possible reaction could be worse than the ordeal
itself [...] She resolved to shut her mouth on the issue and pretend that
it never happened" (21). Inspired by Ann's behaviour, Tumbo made the
second attempt; she resisted fiercely, which infuriated Tumbo so much,
that "taking advantage of his superior strength, he turned her round to
face him and slapped her face" (24). "She wanted to faint but some voice
inside urged her to steady herself and fight on. Don't give in. This man
will defile you and kick you out. Resist, if possible, to the point of death"
(25). After Tumbo's next slap Ann spat into his face, after the third one
she hit his head with an empty wine bottle, leaving him half-conscious,
and escaped. However, her courage did not save Ann from punishment.
As Ann had predicted, the verdict favoured her offender. After long
heart-breaking interrogation, the blame ended up on her side" (27). She
was to suffer severe penalties, which included two days of confinement
in the servant's quarter without food or drink. [...] No one had reproved
Tumbo for the crime. Not even his wife whose trust he had betrayed.
She had transgressed against the master and had to suffer the consequences. [...] She wished she could answer the ceaseless inward questions:

"Why?" and "For how long?" (27). Only Ann's soon-followed enrolment to the university saved her from her further advances from her "uncle" – however, as we will see, not from other assaults from the "mighty sex".

Wairimu Ben, the main character of Martha Mburu's novel *The Mistress*, in her young years almost repeats the fate of the two described female characters above. Orphaned at teenage, she is adopted by her uncle Joseph, who first secured Wairimu a good school, but then

> he started hitting on his niece. After all [...] since she was young he had been dying to bed her. After a few unsuccessful attempts to get Wairimu to sleep with him, uncle Joseph finally raped her. After all [...] it was his right to be the first to taste this beauty. In retaliation, Wairimu hated her uncle with a passion, but knew if she ran away, she would have nowhere to go and no money. So she let uncle Joseph have his way. One day she would revenge for taking advantage of her. Time flew, and before she knew it she was through with High School into Egerton University with a full tuition scholarship. Soon she was working as a financial controller at an insurance agency.

After that, Wairimu's revenge did not take long:

> The day Wairimu moved her belongings out of uncle Joseph's house, she put a sachet of cocaine in one of his jacket pockets. Then she reported to the police that the uncle was a drug dealer and they would find the evidence in this house. Sure enough they searched his house and found the cocaine. Uncle Joseph was arraigned in court and sentenced to jail for 10 years. Yes, Wairimu thought, let him languish with the bad boys for some years. She had finally gotten her sweet revenge. (18)

A high-school student Abigail, heroine of Florence Mbaya's novel *Sunrise at Midnight*, receives her first, and the harshest, lesson of male atrocity from a "near relative" – Richard, the elder brother of her best school friend Claire. "Richard has shown a lot of interest in her, and Abigail, happy to be appreciated, especially by someone she thought very handsome and from a good family, had accepted his amateurish advances" (10). Once, after a quarrel with her mother, Abigail ran to Richard's house – "She had felt he was the only one who cared" (13) – and he decided that the condition is ripe. Giving a poor girl a sleeping drug disguised as aspirin to cure her headache, Richard then took full advantage of fully unconscious Abigail. The horror of teenage pregnancy was aggravated for Abigail, among other factors, by the fact that she did not know how it all happened. Later, after Abigail's life changed positively, Richard, after a long absence, came to her house to ask for forgiveness and in their conversation told her that "I got this stupid idea... how to have sex with a girl without trying too hard... I got it from some friends" (186). For Richard, although a very young man, the female body initially was also a "disposable material" created for his pleasure – and only harsh life lessons pushed him into changing his mind. For Abigail, salvation lay in the tender and understanding attitude of her relatives – first of all, her mother and her female cousin Constance – and her own determination to overcome all the hardships that befell her so suddenly, to bring up her newly born child and to complete her education.

As could be seen from the above-quoted episodes, the authors allow their heroines to use all the possible and available ways to cope with the violent advances of their male kinsmen – from the assistance of caring friends and relatives, as in the cases of Seith and Abigail, physical resistance, as in the case of Ann, or, in the case of Wairimu, even paying with criminal methods for an equally criminal deed. In all cases, self-courage and determination play a founding role. It is also notable that education is thought by the authors as a primary recipe for deliverance from the abusive family ties – the heroines of three above-mentioned novels get the opportunity to change their life only after moving from their relative's houses to campus hostels, and acquiring further independence through a university degree; higher education is also Abigail's dream, who passes her high school exams with flying colours, in order to avoid a lamentable future of a single-mother-housewife.

Psychological violence in the family circle, as portrayed by Kenyan women authors, is also deeply rooted in the patriarchal concept of a male as the head and the sole ruler of the family. Primarily, this kind of gender-based atrocity is executed by fathers towards their daughters. The opening chapter in Margaret Ogola's *Place of Destiny* tells about an unenviable life of Warigia, who becomes pregnant at the young age of seventeen – only to face growing abhorrence from her authoritarian and tyrannical father.

> Perhaps things would have been different if her mother had shown some spine in at least trying to regulate the balance of power within the family. However her father was the ultimate despot, the absolute and unquestionable monarch. He was not only above the law, he was the law itself. Her mother on the other end was a timid mouse at the periphery of existence whose use had ended with her capacity to bear children. She had two other children apart from the girl. The oldest of the three was a girl who had perfected the art of survival by causing no ripples and being as invisible as a shadow [...] The youngest was a fifteen year-old-boy who suffered grimly and silently, because his father considered him not only a born loser, but also effeminate, because he did not display such admirable male attributes as uncalled-for aggression, total selfishness, disregard for other people's feelings and untrammeled acquisitiveness. (11–12)

"They lived in the great big house like refugees in a camp. [...] So one day she wrapped up her six-month-old bundle of sorrows and left the house" (12). The despotism of their father ruins, in this or that way, the lives of all of his offshoots – Warigia, after running from father's house, becomes a prostitute and is killed by a client; his elder daughter Tetu gets married for the purpose of leaving her father's house and never returning – her hatred towards her father proves to be that deep, and even the marriage of his son, Magu, is also destroyed by the despotic old man. Magu's wife also immediately develops a deep feeling of execration to her father-in-law and leaves.

Amor Lore, the main character of the novel, also recalls her childhood in a village as the realm of male dominance.

> Though we had two brothers, I don't remember them doing any-
> thing heavier than holding a stick and following our small herd [...]
> to the grazing fields where they would laze their weekends away
> playing games [...] This was the village norm. Indeed upon growing
> up they, like my father and most of the males around, would never
> engage themselves in anything actually as strenuous as wielding a
> hoe. That was woman's work. Even as a little girl, I found it odd
> that most things that were tedious, boring, repetitive or tiresome
> but necessary for survival were considered woman's work – unless
> somebody was willing to pay for it, at which point the work would
> [...] be elevated to the high status of man's work. [...] This, as well
> as hanging around the market centre all day, discussing *important
> matters* whose fruits and benefits were never forthcoming. (18)

Amor, however, follows the same route as the heroines of other novels – she chooses education as the trail to a new and better life. "Soon, I was in high school as a boarder and at least my family didn't have to deal with my rebellion on a daily basis" (22). Her efforts really paid off:

> I have a Master's degree in Business administration and a post-
> graduate Diploma in Human Psychology, both of which I received
> on the run while working and raising a family at the same time. [...]
> I *am* a woman and it is by thinking as a woman that I have built,
> from the ground up, one of the most reputable and successful busi-
> nesses in its field of operation. (17)

Sasha Nzioka, the main character in Monica Genya's novel *The Wrong Kind of Girl*, also remembers her childhood as the darkest time of her life – in fact, due to the efforts of both her parents.

> She grew up as the daughter of Jackson Nzioka, a prominent busi-
> nessman, and his beautiful socialite wife, Lucy Nzioka. [...] Growing

up in the Nzioka household was a nightmare. Lucy alternated between resenting Sasha's presence and actively hating her. Jackson
simply couldn't be bothered to acknowledge Sasha's existence most
of the time, and when he did, it was usually to criticise her, a thing
that he did constantly and with relish. (178)

As implied in the text, the pain of birth made even a thought of having
another child unbearable for Lucy; for Jackson, therefore, the perspective of having a son is also out of question – thus his deep rejection
of his only child of the "wrong sex". Sasha tries, therefore, to find
her consolation in studying – although even this does not satisfy her
ever-nagging dad.

She was to think why her father disliked her so much and why he
found her so stupid. She was to ask herself why when she brought
home a report card with straight A's, he perused the marks and commented that instead of an average of 88, she should be scoring 90.
But Sasha did not want to think. Thinking made her feel upset and
useless. So she studied instead. She studied like her life depended
upon it. And maybe, in a way, it did. (179)

The final blow comes when her father's partner, a businessman named
Ochieng Omondi, " a member of Parliament and a rising star in the
Kenyan Government" (179), tries to seduce her in her parents' house in
their absence. "He grabbed her by the arm to turn her around to face
him and she snapped. Her hand flew up of its own accord and before she
knew what she was doing she had slapped him, her nails drawing blood
as they raked down his face" (189). Her father's reaction – "Jackson
apologised for the stupid, embarrassing behaviour of his daughter" and
"declared that if he were going to lose the deal he had been trying to cut
with Ochieng because of his ugly daughter's stupidity, then he would
kill her" (181) – draws Sasha to suicide attempt, after which she realized
two things: "one that she wanted to be a doctor, and two that she never
wanted to see her parents again" (181). To pursue this, she demands
from her parents to "deposit money on my account for me to live on until
I can stand on my own two feet" – otherwise she will sell the story of
Ochieng's advances towards her to the newspapers, which "were always
looking for juicy stories like that" (181–182). "Jackson blustered but
gave in. He had too much at stake, money-wise, to risk the kind of exposure that Sasha threatened" (182). Sasha finishes the medical school,
becomes a successful neurosurgeon, and finally reconciles with her parents after a ten-year absence.

For the father of Raelle, one of the major characters in Florence
Mbaya's novel *Heritage High*, the daughter is simply a commodity,
which he intends to use to increase his wealth. As Raelle confesses to her

school friend Jesse, "I discovered my father had committed me to something without my knowledge. [...] My parents have someone lined up for me for marriage already" (11). Mayeke, Raelle's father, is not deterred by the fact that his daughter is only 14 years old. To her friend's comment, that this is against the law, Raelle answers bitterly: "My father is the lawmaker of our family, our clan actually, and he will use customs and traditions to do and get what he wants" (12). As it turns out, what he wants is money – and he is rather unwilling to waste it on his daughter's school fees: "I think he is greedy", Raelle said.

> If it was not for my elder married sister, who was also married off at thirteen, I would not be in school. She paid for my first term tuition fees, and perhaps out of shame, or pride, my father has been paying, but reluctantly. [...] When it comes to tradition, a girl's education doesn't count for much. (13)

Jesse gives Raelle a piece of valuable advice: "The only way you can refuse, or escape, is for you to strive to make it to university. Even the most entrenched tradition cannot survive the onslaught of an educated woman" (13). Raelle tries her best to follow her friend's guidance, but her father has different plans – being afraid that his daughter's university dream may one day become a reality, he simply kidnaps Raelle from school and hands her over into the custody of her prospective husband. However, the idea of the "onslaught of an educated woman" is already deeply rooted in Raelle's mind – she escapes from the shed, where she is confined by her kidnappers (in the process hits one of them severely on the head), and reports the case to the police. Her father is arrested and imprisoned for ten years; the relatives disown Raelle, and she resides with her sister. She successfully passes the school examinations and hopes to make it to the university one day – her dream is to become a veterinarian.

As seen from the above, the authors offer to their heroines the same recipe – to leave, by all possible means, their paternal houses, where they have become the objects of all kinds of abuse, and determine their lives on their own conditions; even if these attempts are not successful, as in the case of Warigia, it is still better than to live "in the great big house like refugees in a camp". However, most of these women succeed in not only releasing themselves from the patriarchal yoke, but also in shaping up their lives according to their own ideas and aspirations. Personal courage and determination are crucial factors that guide them; the woman characters are using the opportunities offered to them by city life; and education (especially higher) and further employment are the greatest of those opportunities, establishing independence of a woman, elevating the social status, and putting her on an equal, and frequently superior, step of the social ladder with men.

Gender-based Atrocity in Marriage Relations

In the sphere of married life also gender-based atrocity, as shown in the works by Kenyan women writers, takes a variety of forms. Among those, sexual violence is, however, the rarest – although the cases of "marriage rapes" are well known in real life, they are very rarely depicted in Kenyan women's novels; presumably, because their writers figure that such a case in a life of an educated urban woman is a rarity. Instead, many novels feature a "reverse" case of sexual mistreatment – wives being ignored by their husbands, as a result of general deterioration of their married life (mostly due to husband's efforts). However, an illustrative case of "sexual blackmail" is shown in Georgina Mbithe's novel *Arise and Shine*, where the heroine's university mate, boyfriend and prospective husband, Mike painstakingly pushes Nancy towards physical "consummation" of their relations. Nancy declines variously, and finally openly tells Mike that she is a virgin and will give her body only to her husband, "to the man with whom I will share my life" (39), implying that only marriage will give him the right to such relations with her. Mike's response is predictable; disappointed, he shifts his efforts to Nancy's schoolmate Jane, whom he beds easily, thinking that this would arouse Nancy's jealousy and make her give in to him in the end, – but ends in fact in only bringing his relationship with Nancy to complete ruin.

Episodes of physical violence, unlike sexual, are more frequent in the stories of married life portrayed in Kenyan women's novels. Most of these episodes have one and the same scenario: during a quarrel a husband hits his spouse in order to stress his masculinity – in a real sense, mostly because of being defeated by her in the argument and thus hating her for "outsmarting" him. Frequently, these episodes have dire consequences for a woman's health or even life, as in Mbithe's novel, where Seith, one of the main characters, at the tender age of three suffered the demise of her parents. Her father Mase, "the richest man in our village [...] traded in jewellery, animal skins, and rumour had it that he headed a drugs cartel [and] also dealt in ivory and rhino horns" (107). His wife, a woman with a strong character, did not like his dangerous illegal business, openly and frequently telling him about it, and their quarrels were increasing. One day, after two weeks of absence, Mase returns home, a quarrel ensues immediately, and after a harsh argument in defence of his male ego – "I live my life the way I choose. Since you accepted me, you have to accept me the way I am" (108) – he knocks his wife down; she hits the edge of the bed with the back of her head and dies on the spot after bleeding profusely. Seized by remorse and fear, Mase commits suicide, which leads to Seith's becoming an orphan and creates further problems in her life.

A similar situation is portrayed in Ketty Arucy's *Captive of Fate*, but there the case of the husband's physical violence against his wife (also with dire consequences) is preceded by a full-fledged theoretical argument about the traditional and the modern – "male" and "female" – concepts of gender roles and rights. In fact, the larger part of chapter 26 – which starts with Henry, the husband of the main character Ann, coming home drunk at two in the morning – is dedicated to their heated debate over the subjects of feminism, women's rights, emancipation, and tradition, in which debate Henry fiercely defends the latter, whereas Ann holds the opposite views. In the course of the argument Henry becomes sober, but then, feeling intellectually defeated by his highly educated wife, resorts to insults, and then to violence.

> Overcome by fury, he began to shake. And then, as if he had lost his mind, he moved and struck her hard on the face. Realising that she was not responding to it, he threw a kick at her stomach without considering her state. [...] The kick sent Ann across the table. She landed on the wall opposite and knocked her head on the wall so hard that she lost consciousness. (157)

The state that Henry was supposed to consider is that his wife is seven months pregnant with their child. Fear for her life completely sobers him, he brings Ann to the hospital, but it is too late – she loses the child, and this ends their marriage. After recovering, Ann moves to the house of her old friend Faith, who helps Ann to get a job at a bank in Eldoret, where Ann meets her old flame Dan, a former university don turned preacher.

Physical violence between married couples portrayed in novels by women authors is often preceded, or accompanied, by psychological violence, which is also variegated in its manifestations. Henry, the husband of Ann in *Captive of Fate*, manages to turn even his unfaithfulness to his wife into an instrument of psychological torture – he not only admits the fact that he sleeps with other women, but even tries to substantiate theoretically the necessity of side affairs for their marriage. When Ann reproaches him for infidelity, he is almost genuinely surprised:

"But why, Ann? [...] You're much too wise to be troubled by the few amusing hours I spend elsewhere. If I drunk heavily [...] or abused you in any way, you would have a reason to be unhappy, but..."
"You abuse me. You demean me. You destroy my ego."
He began to sound angry. "What Freudian nonsense is that? You have a beautiful mansion, expensive clothes and jewels [...] You have security, social position and a husband who's proud of you. What more could a woman want?"
"Fidelity, perhaps".
"Fidelity? I think you are using the wrong word.[...] No my dear, you mean Christian monogamy. That's what you think you want: one woman for one man all the time. [...] My visits to some feather-brained

creature are no more significant to me than an evening at the theatre. They keep me from becoming dull and stodgy.[...]"
He could hear choked back tears in Ann's voice. "Am I dull and stodgy because I am faithful to you Henry? Is it different for women? How would you feel if you knew I was with another man [...]?"
There was ghostly silence, and then Henry said, "Dearest, you're being ridiculous. You are a lady. There's no comparison between physical urges of sexes. We've been over this a hundred times." (148–149)

Another form of psychological torture often inflicted by male characters on their wives or partners is demeaning their self-esteem. Two cases of such demeaning behaviour are depicted in Monica Genya's novel *The Wrong Kind of Girl*. One victim is, Sasha, unlucky (at least initially) but the courageous heroine of the book. Sasha releases herself from the "nightmare" of her father's house to a new and exciting world of the university – only to find herself bound by no less torturous and miserable relationship with Brian, a well-known campus gigolo. As narrated by Sasha, "Brian turned on his charm and I fell for him like a ton of bricks. [...] For the first time in my life I had a boyfriend.[...] The first thing that went wrong when was that Brian started asking me for money [...] Before I knew it, I was paying for our dates, buying his clothes, giving him money to drink and to impress his friends with [...] The only problem is that by this time I was not accepting money from my parents anymore [...] I had to tell Brian that I could not afford to give him all the money that he was asking for [...] Brian told me that he knew I had rich parents and [...] basically gave me an ultimatum – either to come up with the money that he needed, or forget about the relationship. [...] I decided that I didn't want to go back to being that obscure fat girl with no boyfriend. [...] I decided to go to Brian's place immediately to patch up our quarrel [...] I found him in bed with another woman. I was devastated. Even more so when [...] he said he was tired of pretending to be in love with me when in actual fact I was ugly and I made his skin crawl" [...] (220–221). This drives Sasha to her second suicide attempt, which she also, fortunately, survives. "I never saw Brian again after that night. I never wanted to" (222). Sasha finds her further salvation in studies and work – and soon, as the action unfolds, her true love appears.
Another case of psychological humiliation is presented in the novel by the character of Alex, the elder sister to Sasha's colleague and friend Chris. Alex is a talented artist with an unhappy start in life. As Chris tells Sasha about his sister:

"her private life has been completely disastrous. She married a guy who was only after the family money. For years she lived a miserable life trapped within a terrible marriage to a guy who didn't love her even one bit. He just used her and treated her badly."

"He abused her?" she asked in disbelief.

"Never physically. That wasn't his style. He was much better at putting her down emotionally. He convinced her that she was worthless and that nobody could ever love her. He even derided hei artwork and for years she hid her paintings where nobody could see them. [...] He had numerous affairs, which quickly became common knowledge, and he made Alex believe that she was to blame for this as well. She lived like this for five years without letting any of us know" (7).

As in Sasha's case, emotional torture from her husband brings Alex to a suicide attempt; saved by a friend, she goes through a long period of psychological convalescence under the care of her friends and family, after which she successfully focuses on her career as a painter, becoming a celebrity in Nairobi art galleries.

The occurrences of physical and psychological violence, as described in the highlighted novels, lead in each case to a cathartic event that proves to be a watershed in the life of the main female character – loss of parents (Seith), loss of child (Ann), or the suicide attempts (Sasha and Alex). After this event, however tragic it may be, these women unexpectedly receive a chance to start their lives from a clean page (the only exception among these cases is Seith, who loses her parents at a tender age). Ann, Sasha, and Alex, although paying for it dearly, leave behind a load of previous tribulations and sorrows inflicted by their male partners, and begin their lives anew – and again, the fact that they are urban women comes to their rescue, offering them opportunities for a new independent life in the form of furthering their studies (Sasha), employment (Ann), artistic career (Alex). All these women will soon start an alternative relationship – Ann with her long-lost flame Dan, Sasha – with Chris' elder brother Tony, Alex – with their charming neighbour Bobby. It is symptomatic, though, that when Ann declares her feelings to Dan, she says: "I want to be your neighbour, your keeper, your companion and nurse" (175). The word "wife" is not mentioned – apparently, the horrors of her past marriage impel Ann towards a free relationship rather than to the fetters of matrimony.

Gender-based Atrocity in Professional Sphere

Education as a remedy and the strongest potion for female emancipation has been mentioned in sufficient detail in the preceding sections. However, as it turns out, educated women often encounter atrocious attitude in their working sphere, and these atrocities are demonstrated by those men who refuse to recognize either the professional or any other aspects of equality of their women colleagues, – atrocity again based on patriarchal notions of male superiority. Educated women are no longer a "curious rarity" in Kenyan society, they are not treated as "anomalies", and such "picturesque" cases as in Grace Ogot's classic short story "Elizabeth" – when a boss rapes his secretary in his office – are not described in modern Kenyan novels. Still, male bosses and colleagues use other, more subtle approaches for pushing their female workmates into sexual relationships –approaches which, as this section demonstrates, do not always work.

An almost "classical" case of sexual harassment inflicted over a female subordinate by her male boss is presented by Wanjiru Waithaka in her first novel *The Unbroken Spirit*. Young and intelligent woman Tessa has worked for three months in a company as a research executive, and her boss Mr. Kibuchi was sexually harassing her. Mr. Kibuchi is a senior director of the company and a much-respected member of the staff. Tessa approaches the managing director Mr. Kirubi and asks him to talk to Mr. Kibuchi so that he stops harassing her. This doesn't go well with Mr. Kibuchi; he denies everything and warns Tessa: "This is the corporate world Tessa, a man's world, with men's rules. For a while, I thought you were an intelligent ambitious woman [...] You are naïve and foolish. If I had my way, you wouldn't be working here again." An intelligent and ambitious woman must necessarily provide sexual favours to her superior – this implication made by Mr. Kibuchi infuriates Tessa, but she finds it increasingly hard to fight with her boss' malicious attempts. Twice Tessa is denied a promotion by Mr. Kibuchi. When she finally confronts him, he fires her on the spot. She approaches the chairman of the company, and he, impressed by Tessa's logical and honest self-defence, gives her another chance, which luckily corresponds with Mr. Kibuchi's transfer to the Uganda office with a larger pay. On hearing about this, Tessa's friends, although congratulating her with getting the job back, are still annoyed – apparently Kibuchi "got away with it". But as Tessa tells them,

> you feel I tried to fit into the system instead of fighting it. But doesn't the fact that I fought my own battle and won mean something? It is a small victory and may not change anyone's future but my own, but the fact is I didn't give up or run. (112)

Margaret Ogola in *Place of Destiny* depicts a similar situation around Lanoi Sompesha, an intelligent and ambitious university graduate who decides to resign from her first employment. Her boss, as she herself tells,

> had taken it for granted that my job description included listening to him drone on and on about the political situation, the country going to the dogs and anything else that caught his ire. I finally quit when it became apparent that he also expected me not only to fetch and carry for him, being after all only a woman, but to accommodate his penchant for young flesh as well. I decided that I'd rather starve

first and quit in a towering rage of righteous indignation one early morning after only three months of employment. (35–36)

Her school friend helps her to get an appointment for an interview at the company of Amor Lore, the novel's main character, and from that day Lanoi's life undergoes a qualitative change. "I love my job. I am devoted to the company. As for Amor, I hold her in awe – she is a mentor, a guide, an act to study and imitate [...]; I even try to look at things the way I think she would." (40).

Psychological mistreatment of females as "inferior gender" along the professional lines also is a not-so-rare occasion in inter-gender relations. Sasha Nzioka, the neurosurgeon heroine of Monica Genya's novel *The Wrong Kind of Girl*, is subjected to serious psychological abuse several times in her life – as mentioned above, she was an unwanted child for her parents, she suffered from the gigolo-ism of her boyfriend Brian, and throughout several chapters she has been literally terrorized by the man who, ironically, will later become her loving and devoted husband. Tony, a well-off and self-made businessman, elder brother of Sasha's colleague Chris, initially sees in Sasha a "gold-digger" – a pretty and unscrupulous city woman hunting at wealthy man, and treats her accordingly, once even nearly calling her a prostitute. Later, appreciating Sasha's likeable personality and sharp mind, he in every way expresses his regrets that Sasha is not properly educated (of which he has not the slightest doubt), and finally goes as far as offering to pay for Sasha's studies. He does not allow even a single thought that Sasha may be as educated as himself – not to mention higher; in Tony's view, it is simply impossible, because Sasha is a woman. Sasha does not rush to fight with Tony's male chauvinism – she waits for the moment to come, and it soon happens. When Chris's fiancée Alicia seriously damages her head, it is Sasha who takes all the necessary medical measures and later performs a complicated brain operation; and it is Tony who, crushed by Sasha's sudden grandeur and his own guilt and stupidity, abjectly asks for forgiveness.

A picturesque case of psychological mistreatment in professional sphere is described in Martha Mburu's *The Mistress*, when Wairimu, the heroine, goes with her two male partners (she is the head of a real estate company) for a prospected bargain in Mombasa. Their counterparts in Mombasa are also male – but while one of them, a German named Reinhardt, is joyful and hospitable, his Kenyan partner Omamo eyes Wairimu with loathing, and finally asks her confident Chege "why he had bothered to bring this 'malaya' along for such an important meeting. Chege looked at him and replied sternly: Wairimu is the company MD, she makes the decisions and we follow." [...] Wairimu had encountered such men before. She was merely amused by his obvious difficulty in dealing with a strong female presence. He was the kind that shrank at a mere hint of a female being in charge. These men got a kick at putting women down and often ended up being abusers. [...] Wairimu remarked: "I'm sorry to have wasted your time, bwana Omamo, but there is nothing really concrete to discuss." "Excuse me?" Mr Omamo said coldly, wondering how this mere figurehead would dare to address him, a Kenyan man, and a typical Kisii for that matter, like that. [...] Wairimu decides to give him a piece of her mind. "Why don't you first overcome your fear of women, it makes you look very stupid and weak and doesn't reflect well on a man like you, then give us a call. This meeting is over." (48–49).

Involvement of women into the ever-troublesome political profession is treated in recent novels by Kenyan woman writers with surprising infrequency, although the real experience of Kenyan women in politics has become rather rich. Of the novels highlighted above, only Florence Mbithe in *Arise and Shine* rewards her main character Nancy Mue with a promising political career – but already at the initial stage of it, she faces the opposition and contemptuous attitude of the male politicians in the figure of Honourable Komu, Nancy's rival at the regional elections. Annoyed by Nancy's overwhelming victory, Komu asks her for a meeting, to which Nancy agrees – "I needed to understand his strengths and weaknesses" (138). She comes to his place, Komu invites her into his office – he is already drunk after a party with his supporters – and straightforwardly asks her to give up politics in favour of becoming his mistress.

> You are such a beautiful girl. So attractive, you would make a great man like me happy. Why are you indulging in politics, a man's dirty game? Come to me. Don't mess up things for me, please. Be my third wife. [...] I have lots of money. More will come from donors. [...] Nancy, what do you say? (138–139)

When Nancy, who "couldn't believe that our leaders had degenerated to such a level", sharply refuses and storms for the door,

> it was then that I noticed him charge at me with hands on his trouser zip. Was it his way of teaching me who the man in the room was? [...] As a potential leader I needed more action than mere words. I grabbed a camera from my handbag, I was glad I had it with me [...] I managed to capture a series of spectacular moments. Zip open, trouser falling. (139)

Nancy's supporters, who were waiting outside, were alerted by the noise in the house and rescue her from any further attempts by Komu, whom Nancy appropriately warns – "I made it absolutely clear that I would expose the photographs, and since our people had no place for such men, his political sunset had arrived" (140).

On all the described occasions, the authors provide their characters with the same recipe – to hold firmly to their convictions and principles. Personal courage and consistency pay again – Tessa gets back her almost lost job, Lanoi gets a better one in a company headed by a woman that she adores, Sasha and Wairimu gain a personal victory over the diehard male chauvinists (Sasha even manages to turn her foe into her most devoted worshipper), and Nancy deservedly tramples her political rival. Again, city space offers these women "enough place to allow some maneuvering", and this is used by the heroines in full – their troubles are overcome, their lives become better, their future is promising, and their aspirations high.

Conclusion

"At the start of the twenty-first century, it seems likely that the African city will continue to be the most important site and symbol of social change on the continent. Writers will continue to discuss, analyze, and affect our understandings of the urban landscape in conscious and unconscious ways", wrote J. Roger Kurtz in his above-mentioned study (Kurtz 159). This chapter demonstrated how the urban space, as presented in several novels by Kenyan women authors written exactly at the beginning of the twenty-first century, was used in two different ways according to the characters' gender orientations. Many male characters were trying to turn this space into an "environment of violence" against women – for the purpose of satisfying their needs, both material and spiritual, which are largely based on patriarchal concepts of "male-the-ruler" and the inferiority of "the fair sex". The fact that many of these male characters who perpetrate this viewpoint are also the products of urban life matters not so much – they may be very "modernised" in other fields of life, but they readily "unearth" their patriarchal views at their convenience.

Contrary to that, the female heroines of these novels use the urban space and their urban mentality for resisting varied forms of gender-based atrocity, inflicted on them by men, and for the long-term purpose of their emancipation, empowerment, and the achievement of general equality, equity, and mutual respect between genders. In this noble task, they are assisted by "different" male characters, those who are ready to build their relationship with the opposite sex on the mentioned principles. Each of the discussed novels, thus, has a hopeful, inspiring and promising finale, in which the female characters manage to solve their social and matrimonial problems with a perspective for a brighter future, both on the personal and societal levels.

The above-discussed novels by Kenyan female writers, apart from giving a variegated and detailed picture of the various form of atrocity inflicted upon women in different spheres of life, reveal a standpoint common to all the writers. Casting an overall glance at the novels high-lighted in this chapter, it would not be too difficult to notice, that the views and orientations expressed by their authors are firmly based on feministic stance – namely, a variety of it known as "postcolonial feminism". According to Mishra,

> The matter of fact is that postcolonial women refuse to remain passive and continue to bear male-oppressive environments. These women seek to emancipate themselves through education, struggle, and hard work. The postcolonial men re-colonized the bodies and minds of their women in the name of preserving their cultural values. Postcolonial feminism is primarily concerned with deplorable plight of women in postcolonial environment [...] Postcolonial feminists argue for women emancipation that is sub-alternized by social, cultural, or economic structures across the world. (132–133)

And thus: "Postcolonial feminism [...] comprises non-western feminisms which negotiate the political demands of nationalism, socialist feminism, liberalism, and ecofeminism, alongside the social challenge of everyday patriarchy, typically supported by its institutional and legal discrimination: of domestic violence, sexual abuse, rape, honour killings, dowry deaths, female foeticide, child abuse" (130). Exactly for the purpose of altering this "deplorable plight of women in postcolonial environment" and fighting "the social challenge of everyday patriarchy", Kenyan women writers depict in their works various cases of gender-based atrocity, with different consequences, but for one purpose – to affirm the role-model character of an urban, educated, working, middle-class woman, who, with all the probable differences, feature basic common traits: she is independent, capable to defend herself and others, rules her own life – and all this largely owing to her urban mentality, which breeds the "feministic" concepts from the formative age. The authors through these characters advice their readers to terminate at will all the abusive relationships – familial, matrimonial, or professional, and thus to dissolve the "environment of violence" in favour of more constructive purposes.

Works Cited

Arucy, Ketty. *Captive of Fate*. Zapf Chancery, 2007.

Aura, Ruth. Rose Odhiambo and Tom Ojienda. *Pursuing Justice for Sexual and Gender Based Violence in Kenya*. Nairobi: ACORD, 2010.

Bograd, Michele. "Strengthening Domestic Violence Theories: Intersections of Race, Class, Sexual Orientation and Gender." *Journal of Marital and Family Therapy* 23.3 (1999): 275–289.

Bograd, Michele, and Kersti Yllö. (Eds). *Feminist Perspectives on Wife Abuse.* Sage Publications, 1988.

Bookchin, Murray. *The Ecology of Freedom: The Emergence and Dissolution of Hierarchy.* AK Press, 2005.

Forms of Gender-Based Violence. European Institute for Gender Equality. www.eige.europa.eu/gender-based-violence/what-gender-based-violence/forms-gender-based-violence. Accessed July 2018.

Genya, Monica. *The Wrong Kind of Girl.* Nairobi: East African Educational Publishers, 2004.

Hotaling G., and Sugarman D. "An Analysis of Risk Markers in Husband to Wife Violence: The Current State of Knowledge." *Violence and Victims* 1.2 (Summer 1986):101–124.

Kaluyu, Veronicah Kaindi. *Causes, Consequences and Management Strategies of Gender Based Domestic Violence: A Case of Central Division of Kitui District, Kenya.* Nakuru: Egerton University. Unpublished Master of Arts thesis,, 2007.

Kameri-Mbote, Patricia. *Violence against Women in Kenya: An Analysis of Law, Policy and Institutions.* Nairobi: International Environment Law Research Centre, 2010.

Kniss, Jennifer. *Masculinity and Violence against Women in Simenya, Kenya: Engaging Men as Part of the Solution.* Nairobi: School of International Training – Kenya, 2016.

Kruger, Marie. *Women's Literature in Kenya and Uganda: the Trouble with Modernity.* Palgrave Macmillan, 2011.

Kuria, John. *The Challenge of Feminism in Kenya: Towards an Afrocentric Worldview.* University of Leeds, School of English, Doctor of Philosophy Thesis, 2001.

Kurtz, J. Roger. *Urban Obsessions, Urban Fears: the Post-Colonial Kenyan Novel.* London: James Currey, 1998.

Mbaya, Florence. *Heritage High.* Nairobi: East African Educational Publishers, 2011.

———. *Sunrise at Midnight.* Nairobi: East African Educational Publishers, 2014.

Mbithe, Georgina. *Arise and shine.* Nairobi: The Jomo Kenyatta Foundation, 2007.

Mishra, Raj Kumar. "Postcolonial Feminism: Looking into within-beyond-to Difference." *International Journal of English and Literature* 4.4 (2013): 129–134.

Mburu, Martha Nthoki. *The Mistress.* Nairobi: Samir Khan Publications, 2015.

Neft, Naomi and Levine, D. Ann. *Where Women Stand: An International Report on the Status of Women in 140 Countries.* Random House, 1997.

Ogola, Margaret. *The River and the Source.* Nairobi: Focus Books, 1994.

———. *Place of Destiny.* Nairobi: Paulines Publications Africa, 2005.

Oludhe-Macgoye, Marjorie. *Coming to Birth.* Nairobi: East African Educational Publishers, 1986.

Owuor, Yvonne. *Dust.* Nairobi: Kwani Publishers, 2009.

Saidi, H., K. O. Awori, and P. Odula. "Gender associated violence at a women's hospital in Nairobi, Kenya." *East African Medical Journal* 85.7 (2008): 347–354.

154   *Alina Rinkanya*

United Nations General Assembly. *Declaration on the Elimination of Violence against Women.* Proceedings of the 85th plenary meeting, 1993. Geneva. www.ippf.org/resouce/gbv/ma98/cultural.htm. Accessed July 2018.
Waithaka, Wanjiru. *The Unbroken Spirit.* Nairobi: East African Educational Publishers, 2005.
World Health Organisation. *Putting Women's Safety First: Ethical and Safety Recommendations for Research on Domestic Violence against Women.* WHO/EIP/GPE/99.2. WHO, 1999.

10 Reading the Politics of Violence and Impunity in *Pango* and *Kufa Kuzikana*

Simiyu Kisurulia

Introduction

Around the world, politics is a major attraction to many. Those who wish to attain political positions and ascend to power through politics along with their supporters create a lot of euphoria and tension that many a time ends up being atrocious to the general citizenry. Yet because politicians have turned politics to be about personal power, not much is done to stem the violence that ensues. It is in this light that this chapter examines the politics of violence in *Pango* (Wamitila 2003) and *Kufa Kuzikana* (Walibora 2003). Content analysis and social dominance theory have been used to explore the reasons behind violent politics in the two novels. Jim Sidanius and Felicia Pratto (1999) posit that social dominance theory argues that intergroup oppression, discrimination, and prejudice are the means by which human societies organize themselves as group-based hierarchies, in which members of dominant groups secure a disproportionate share of the good things in life and members of subordinate groups receive a disproportionate share of the bad things in life. Understanding the cause and effects of violent and negative politics is of great social significance as it helps society realize the means used by dominant groups (herein politicians) to gain power and use it to serve their own interests. Consequently, the general citizenry is called upon to beware of such selfish politicians and resist their evil machinations to divide society and cause disharmony.

The United Nations defines political violence as "organized violent activity for political goals" (*International Affairs Review*). In this analysis, violence is considered political if it is politically motivated and its purpose has political gain. Specifically, the analysis looks at politics based on social differentiation, which is built around ethnicity and/or other social groupings. The two writers analysed in this chapter are Kenyans and their narratives certainly emanate from the experiences of ethnic violence that characterized the 1992 and 1997 general elections. In their works, the two writers unveil the politics of violence, explore its effects and propose possible solutions to forestall similar occurrences in the future. As such they document, in a literary way, the horrors of

political violence so that future generations can learn from them the futility of political ambitions. In order to unravel the politics of violence,
this chapter deploys social dominance theory to unpack intrigues of the
dominant group (for instance politicians) and to understand why the
subordinate (the ruled or subjects) group behaves the way it does when
violence ensues.

Pango (which loosely translates to *A Cave*) is metaphorically used to
denote a country in Africa. The plot is set around jostling for power
pitting the old against the young generation. On the one hand, the old
generation is seeking to reassert itself in power as having unquestioned
authority to lead because they are 'wise' while on the other hand, the
young generation is out to claim its place in political leadership. The
young generation feels that the old generation is running down the country economically by engaging in economic malpractices and failing to
anchor the development of the country in sound political and economic
practices. It is against this background of inter-generational conflict that
the narrative exposes a political clash between the two generations.

In *Kufa Kuzikana* (which loosely translates to Friends Forever), as is
the case in *Pango*, the conflict revolves around the struggle for political
power through political manipulations by powerful politicians of two
ethnic communities living in the same district. It is important to note
that the title, "Kufa Kuzikana" is also metaphorically used. Useful for
the current analysis is the fact that the title refers to 'social closeness'
between the two communities that have coexisted for ages (the Kanju
and Korosho). Having coexisted for such a long time, the members of
the two communities have built strong bonds amongst themselves that
only death can possibly 'break'. As such, the writer satirizes any attempt
at creating animosity between the two communities and anyone who
attempts to break the bond exposes himself to danger. In fact, the writer
uses names 'Kanju' and 'Korosho' to refer to the two communities to
project his point of view because the two names almost mean the same
thing; a type of fruit tree and its fruit. Metaphorically, the writer desires
to emphasize the importance of universal brotherhood but the actual situation is that there are those who are intent on disrupting this harmony.
It is as a result of the selfish and evil machinations of one politician that
tribal hatred is fanned leading to horrendous ethnic clashes between the
Kanju and Korosho.

An Overview of Social Dominance Theory

Jim Sidanius and Felicia Pratto state:

> according to the social dominance theory intergroup oppression,
> discrimination and prejudice are the means by which human so-
> cieties organize themselves as group-based hierarchies, in which

members of dominant groups secure a disproportionate share of the good things in life and members of subordinate groups receive a disproportionate share of the bad things in life. (418)

This argument supposes that a class structure arises in society due to social groupings. In the current discussion the dominant group is the political class while the subordinate group is the rest of the citizens who have no stake in leadership. In the political arena, there exists all manner of intrigues by politicians, some of which end up being violent. The violence is meant to subdue the subordinate group so that the dominant group remains in power. In effect, politicians apply certain strategies to achieve their dominance over their subjects. Whereas some of the strategies are instituted by individual politicians, others can be seen to emanate from state apparatus like the police. The dominant group ascends to power, controls state power and resources, enjoys good facilities and above all controls and rules over the subordinate group. As a result, the subordinate group receives poor infrastructure, poor health services, is exposed to social tension, and worse still, denied self-progression. Thus, social dominance theory avers that disproportionate allocation of resources as determined by the dominant group is the cardinal source of social discrimination. Often the dominant group does everything possible to justify the unequal distribution of resources. What follows out of this act is a number of behavioural tendencies among the subordinate group in society. First, the subordinate group tends to accept its subordination. And second, subordinate group engages in behaviours that damage the dominant group. These two tendencies form the basis for analysis in this chapter. The analysis attempts to show how dominant groups maintain their dominance over the subordinate group. Strategies that are used by the dominant groups to maintain the imbalances in society are uncovered and discussed. While the dominant group basks in glory and privileged positions, the subordinate group slumps into a sorry state of poverty, self-pity, and self-acceptance. This relationship is viewed in this discussion as a perpetuation of atrocity. The behaviours of the subordinated group which function to maintain the status quo of subordination are also analysed in this study. The above suppositions will form the backbone of the discussion in this chapter in order to reveal the nature and consequences of violent politics in the society, as represented in the two texts.

A Note on Politics of Violence

Howard-Hassmann (21) argues that the main reason behind violent politics is the desire of politicians to win political positions and remain in power for as long as they choose. Citing the example of Zimbabwe, Howard-Hassmann states that President Robert Mugabe of Zimbabwe

deprived Zimbabweans of free and fair elections in the 1980s, undermined the free press, intimidated and threatened the remainder of the
independent judiciary, and used murder, torture, and rape to intimidate
and punish his opponents (178). All these acts meted out against those in
opposition are meant to instil fear in them so that they do not raise any
objection to the ruling government. When such fear and decimation is
applied, the subjugated group recoils and is made impotent politically.
Such occurrences are not new in Africa or elsewhere in the world. In
Sudan and South Sudan, for instance, wars based on jostling for political
power have been witnessed for far too long. Jostling for power led to the
horrendous genocide in Rwanda in 1994. The case is not different in the
Democratic Republic of Congo as President Joseph Kabila struggles to
remain in power beyond the official limit of two terms. In fact, in Bu-
rundi, the same violence ensured President Pierre Nkurunziza remained
in power after the lapse of his two terms in 2015.

Political positions come with prestige and this is one of the underlying motivations why politicians aggressively seek these positions. In
repressive regimes, the president has the final say in the country on
multiple aspects. This could be the reason why this seat is so attractive
and is sought after by so many and by all means possible. Yet prestige
is not the only thing that pushes politicians into seeking these offices
but their desire to control state resources. Once in power, they make
decisions on how state resources are used and as such find opportunities to, albeit corruptly, benefit immensely from these resources. Ap-
propriating state resources for personal gain in such regimes is meant
to assure the leaders' opulent lifestyles as well as adequate financial
and material resources for subsequent election campaigns. Selfishness,
the quest for prestige, and control of state resources seem to be the
main motivations for violent politics as depicted in the two novels.
Some politicians find that they are not popular enough to ascend to
power on a popular vote and through peaceful means. The option that
is left for them is using violence based on ethnic affiliation to assure
them of a win in political competitions. Consequently, they whip up
support from their ethnic communities by turning them against the
"Other" ethnic communities. It is this whipping up of emotions which
results in political violence. For example, in *Pango*, Ngwese fights his
way to the top political seat in his country through bribery and violence. Similarly, in *Kufa Kuzikana*, Johnstone Mabende wins a political seat by inciting the Korosho against the Kanju. In this latter case, a
section of the country is plunged into a civil war whose effects are too
horrendous to speak about. Both Ngwese and Mabende are motivated
by selfishness in their quest for political power. They use any means
at their disposal to ascend to power regardless of the effects of those
means on the common citizens. Inciting one community against the
other is in itself selfish.

The Nature of Violent Politics in *Pango* and *Kufa Kuzikana*

For one to easily understand the events recounted in both *Pango* and *Kufa Kuzikana*, it is helpful to understand the background to the two novels. The clamour for multiparty politics in Kenya in the early 1990s ushered in a wave of ethnic animosity and what came to be generally christened as "land of ethnic clashes". In these clashes, some communities violently lashed out on their neighbours whom they believed would not vote for their preferred political candidates. This spate of clashes would only spring up around the electioneering period then die till the next electioneering period. Such violent instances were witnessed in Kenya in 1992, 1997, and 2007/2008. This forms the context of the two novels as events therein measure up quite close to what occurred in history.

Kufa Kuzikana, for example, illustrates the height of literary prophesying as it was published a few years before the 2007 general elections, which was marred by violent clashes that caused the death of over a 1000 people. The text depicts a situation that happened later after its publication, which points to the unique character of literature of being able to speak into the future. It also points to a writer's intuition following occurrences in a society he has lived in for some time.

In *Pango*, the political contest pits the elderly generation represented by Ngwese against the youthful generation represented by Katango. The political duel is to be decided through social factors held dear by the community of *Pango*. One such belief is that political power belongs to the elderly. They are the ones suited for leadership due to their experience in life. Within this argument is another underlying selfish notion among some families that have held traditional leadership positions: that leadership belongs to only certain lineages in the community. It is from these two standpoints that Ngwese campaigns to be elected as the leader of *Pango*. As advanced by Social dominance theory, this is a clear case of using the social beliefs and practices of one group to dominate the other. On her part, Katango argues that political leadership should be accorded those who merit it because they understand how to run the affairs of the country to achieve greater development. To her, the younger and educated generation is best placed to run the affairs of their country. Political tension therefore builds up in *Pango* due to these two dichotomies.

During the campaigns, Ngwese is driven by underlying cultural factors that favour him. One such belief is that traditionally, men are the ones who hold political positions. Two, he is from a lineage that produces leaders, and finally, he has the economic muscle to turn things around. These factors give him an advantage over Katango who has the same factors working against (*Pango* 11). She is female, hails from a family little known for producing leaders, and has no economic muscle. Evidently, this campaign is a big test for Katango and her supporters, the youth. Tension is built between the elderly and the youth, between those who support the status quo and those who are for change to a new brand of leadership based on ability and desire to turn the economy of the country around. For both sides, it is a war of the titans. In view of the Social dominance theory, this is a case of those who are dominant in society both politically and economically pitted against those who are subordinate to them.

Ideologically, Katango wins the support of the youth since her campaign is based on ideas and issues meant to bring about change and development in the country (31). Again, the youth are campaigning in protest against the elderly who have permanently used the saying that the youth are 'leaders of tomorrow' as they (the elderly) run down the country's economy (39). And this 'tomorrow' has never come to pass. In speech dotted with several short oral narratives at the end of Katango's campaign, it is evident that she has won the support of the majority as one of her supporters, Kikubi, asserts [*Aisee, ni wazi ushindi ni wa nani*! / It is obvious we are winning] (45). So when it is the turn of her opponent, Ngwese, to make his final speech and aware of the danger of losing his seat to Katango, he uses all means possible to ensure he wins back the support of the masses. To start with, he acknowledges that the elderly generation could have faltered in their leadership in the past and promises that they are ready to correct this. All the pleadings by Ngwese do little to change the mood of the masses which evidently is against him and the older generation. Sensing the prospect of losing the elections, Ngwese goes raw in his campaign strategies. He bribes the masses with 'fruits' [read money]. This trick works for him because instantly Katango's supporters represented by Mbabekazi and Kauleni abandon her and join Ngwese's supporters. This act points to rampant bribery common in many African countries, Kenya being no exception. This act of political bribery in *Pango* is also cited in Ngugi's *Petals of Blood* where politicians, as symbolized by Nderi wa Riera, the politician (Member of Parliament), come around during campaigns to issue a few coins to the electorate who "faithfully" or helplessly vote him, only to disappear into thin air like a vulture, just like his name implies. This means that Kenya as a nation has been experiencing such political atrocities since independence.

Ngwese is not new to corruption as Kauleni reminds him that he (Ngwese) helped him get the plot where he has erected his shop and is running a business. He also helped Kauleni get a license for his business when he found it difficult due to widespread corruption in government offices (*Pango* 29). Thus, Ngwese uses bribery as a means of winning the political seat. This is a common political malpractice that occurs not only in Africa but all over the world. Voter bribery is common political malpractice which, unfortunately, is hardly pursued and punished by courts of law. Apart from voter bribery, Ngwese uses two goons to assault Katango (*Pango* 31–35). They also indecently touch her to scare her out of the race for the leadership of Pango. The two goons have covered their faces with hoods meaning they had planned ill intentions against Katango. Such kind of terror is also common during political campaigns as evident in the case of Zimbabwe quoted earlier on.

What we see in *Pango* is a build-up on existing ideologies. The society has been made over time to believe that only the elderly can ascend to positions of leadership and that only certain lineages are endowed with leadership abilities. Ngwese employs such social ideologies in his campaign and indeed it works in his favour. To support such ideologies, the dominant group has acquired a disproportionate share of wealth, which it uses to get anything they want through bribery, placing themselves in a position that the subordinate find tricky to eject them from. The narrative therefore helps to reveal the violence and impunity that characterizes African politics.

Events in *Kufa Kuzikana* are more violent compared to those in *Pango*. From the outset, the main politician, Johnstone Mabende, is clear on how he plans to remain in power. He represents the Baraki region in the parliament. Baraki is populated by two communities, the Korosho and the Kanju. The Korosho are indigenous in Baraki whereas the Kanju only settled there through purchasing land from the local Korosho community (*Kufa* 29). However, the Kanju are more enterprising and are better off economically compared to the local Korosho (businesses belonging to the Kanju are doing better and even their farming is more productive, *Kufa* 75). Mabende comes from the Korosho community. His politics is based on the strength of numbers of his ethnic community. In order to endear himself to his community, he creates tension between the two communities. By using this strategy, he seeks to dominate the mental universe (Wa Thiong'o 16a) of his ethnic community, the Korosho, with divisive feelings of hatred against their neighbours, the Kanju. He reckons that once this is achieved, he will win the votes of his ethnic community and thus continue to be the Member of Parliament for Baraki constituency. One day while addressing a public rally at Baraki market he says, "*Hatutaki 'madoadoa' hapa. Wakanju sharti wahame warudi kwao Kanju*"/We do not want undesirable elements here. The Kanju must relocate back to their country, Kanju (*Kufa* 2). This is tantamount to inciting one community against the other. Later events in the text are based on this incitement. Such discrimination, one can argue, lies squarely in the Kenyan nation. The political class champions inter-ethnic discrimination leaving some of the communities suffering and feeling helpless in their own country.

The campaigns, the text shows, get nasty with anybody showing signs of equal treatment being eliminated. For instance, soon after Mabende's speech, one Korosho man is found dead. The late Teacher Alex, though a Korosho by ethnicity, was a believer in universal brotherhood and was the only one who vehemently opposed Mabende's divisive politics publicly at Baraki (*Kufa* 2). For this reason, his fellow Korosho people were against Teacher Alex for supporting the Kanju. It is, therefore, not surprising that when he is found dead, the Korosho point an accusing finger at the Kanju. If anything, circumstances point to the fact that it is possible he was murdered by his fellow Korosho people who may have felt offended when he opposed their leader in public. All the same, the Korosho circulates messages of incitement on leaflets that are dropped all over the villages. The leaflets carry the message, "*Wakanju mume-chokosa nyuki kwa kumuuwaa Mukoroso. Ama muondoke au mufe muzingani*"/Kanju people have rubbed us the Korosho the wrong way by murdering one of our own. You either chose to leave or you face death (*Kufa* 5). This threat, coming in the wake of the speech by their member of parliament at a public rally, suggests that political leaders are the key perpetrators of violence in independent African states. Such careless talks are often witnessed in Kenya throughout electioneering periods, making life unbearable for those that get intimidated. Such intimidation is a form of atrocity in itself.

A state of denial and protection of atrocious acts by the ruling class is also evident in *Kufa Kuzikana*. While on a visit to the capital city of his country Kiwachema, the main character, Akida Sululu, gets the news that there is ethnic fighting back at home in Korosho district. Akida and his friend Tim get this news through the television bulletin (*Kufa* 28). Yet the government is quick to deny this. The Minister for internal security, Panga Lutulia, objects to news chapter reports to the effect that there is ethnic fighting in Baraki, Korosho district. According to the minister, such news is only meant to cause animosity between the communities that have coexisted in Baraki peacefully for long. This news report gets the two young men by surprise as they never expected anything of the sort to happen and therefore they become keen to get the truth. They switch to BBC London radio station, which reports that fighting has broken out in Korosho district and that the government has banned both local and international journalists from covering the events in the district. Only humanitarian aid agencies are allowed to enter the area. As Humphrey (ix) argues, in internal wars the politics of atrocity produces 'body horror' as a central strategy to terrorize a target population. This is clearly evident in this case as many people are killed, many more are injured and many houses are razed down (*Kufa* 28). In this instance 'body horror' is seen in the dead, the maimed, and by extension in the property that is destroyed. The Korosho are out to scare the Kanju out of Baraki, which would benefit their leader Mabende as it would endear the Korosho to him even more. Fortunately, the reach of global communications technology (in this case BBC London radio) and the presence of outsiders (aid workers) help in unearthing the horrors that occur in Baraki despite government efforts to block reporters from covering the events (Humphrey ix). Such episodes on fictional narratives help weave together actions that have taken place in the Kenyan society, especially during the electioneering periods which helps the reader to conceptualize the reality of violence and impunity in the Kenyan state. Such narratives are alternative commentaries of performing power and in addition, misuse of power and state machinery.

The idea of misuse of power and state machinery is further explored in the text when on a visit to Tandika referral hospital, Tim and Akida learn that Mabende is deeply involved in the conflict. They gather this from one of the victims of the ensuing ethnic violence, Mzee Uledi, who they find admitted at the hospital. He says that the Korosho are being led by their member of parliament, Mabende, in fighting the Kanju (*Kufa* 75). It is here that we learn that this is government-supported violence. From Uledi's statements, we gather that Mabende has convinced other government officials to let the violence go on. This is why even the police just stand by watching the Korosho set houses belonging to the Kanju on fire. This makes Uledi feel less of a human being compared to his counterparts, the Korosho, who are left to do as they wish. As Wolfe (2) opines, Uledi and his fellow Kanju people are left feeling that they do not have the same rights, protections, or opportunities as their counterparts, the Korosho. It is as if the state has indicated that the Kanju are to be excluded from society whereas the Korosho is to be included. We grimly learn that in this case the state has sponsored this atrocity against the Kanju. This is made even clearer when Tom, a Kanju, goes to bury his father in Baraki. Whereas he is offered police escort, the police stand by and watch as he is attacked and left for dead by a group of marauding Korosho warriors who are also escorted by government police officers as captured in the following words by one police officer:

> "Wewe ungefanya nini?" askari aliyekuwa akivuta sigara aliuliza. "Eeh! Ungefanya nini na wavamizi wanakuja wakiongozwa na **boss** wako mwenyewe? Kisha anakuamuru uwaache wafanye watakavyo."/"What would you do if you were the one?" The policeman who was smoking asked. "Eeh! What would you do when the group of warriors that attacked Tom was being escorted by your own **boss**? The same **boss** then orders you to let them accomplish whatever they wished to." (*Kufa* 103)

From the above quotation, it is clear that the government machinery is behind the violence in Baraki. It is evident that the police commander referred to in this excerpt simply as 'boss' is under instructions to aid the Korosho in their murderous mission, which is done for political reasons – to benefit the reigning politician, Johnstone Mabende. Mabende uses violence and terrorism as a weapon to gain support from his Korosho ethnic community so as to remain in power. He is pleasing his community by ensuring the Kanju leave so that the land they bought from the Korosho reverts to them. The violence that rocks Baraki can, therefore, be seen as institutionalized intimidation against the Kanju (Sidanius and Pratto 437). In part, the intergroup conflict witnessed has to do with conflict over the power to allocate social and economic resources. The social resource at stake is that of the power of leadership while the economic one is what accrues from that power in terms of finances as well as being able to control other natural resources like land. In spite of all the atrocious conflict fanned by a well-known politician, no legal action is taken against the planners, Johnstone Mabende and his accomplices! The violent attack on the Kanju community is planned by Mabende and his cronies. Surprisingly, it is also sponsored by, among others, church leaders such as Pastor John Njalala thereby showing how intergroup conflict can operate without boundaries.

Whatever is exposed in *Kufa Kuzikana* is so atrocious and disturbing for both the victims and observers that it is inconceivable how the state would let such events to go on. It can be equated to the physical torture that the slaves underwent in parts of the world, such as America where whipping, burning, maiming, imprisonment, starvation, and hanging were some of the methods of punishment devised and effectively used to instil fear and compliance among slaves (Sum and Kisurulia 42609). When the people travel to the countryside to bury Tom's late father, the main character (Akida) and the entourage witness many corpses strewn all along the road in Baraki, with dogs feeding on them. Such atrocities according to Humphrey (1) are designed to engender horror and disrupt confidence among the affected community (in this case the Kanju). This way, Humprey (1) opines, the politics of atrocity challenges the very basis of modern political life: the belief in the sacredness of human life, of bodily inviolability in law, and that our humanity confers rights which stand in opposition to the political sovereignty of the state. It is apparent that some political leaders act in total contravention of what they have signed to and taken an oath to protect. Such acts are often witnessed in many African states. These events in the text demonstrate that violent politics in some countries in the world is fomented by self-seeking politicians out to ascend to power and remain in power. The tension that is created leads to ethnic violence resulting in socio-economic disruption in society.

Socio-economic Effects of Violent Politics

The socio-economic status of any country in the world is driven by structures which help boost the well-being of its citizens. Unfortunately, the politics of the day, characterized by violence, affect the economic status of many countries especially in Africa. This often happens because politicking is directly related to economic development since the political leaders are the chief designers of the economy. In the end, the social well-being of the nation also gets affected negatively, which is the case in the two novels. The effects of violence in Korosho district in *Kufa Kuzikana* are summarized in a journal written by a human rights group (*Kufa* 160–162). Akida, the main character, gets this journal from another character, Jerumani, who is mentally challenged. The journal documents the horrors and plight of the people following the violent ethnic skirmishes. About 1000 lives are lost, including Akida's and Tom's father. Akida's father, Sululu, is killed by his close neighbour and a long-time companion, Zablon Mapisi, who is the father to Akida's close friend, Tim Mapisi. Such happenings demonstrate how irresponsible politics can make social relations deteriorate.

The ethnic clashes result not just in deaths, but in the internal mass displacement of persons who get scattered all over the towns and cities of Kiwachema. They have no shelter, no food, and lack many other basic social amenities. As a result, there is an abrupt increase in social vices such as begging, prostitution, and robbery. Consequently, life in the Kiwachema towns and cities becomes a nightmare as beggars and robbers rule the streets, the majority of who are from the subordinate group, the Kanju. This is a clear case of behavioural asymmetry as propounded by the social dominance theory. In rural Korosho, government institutions (schools, hospitals, and ministry of Agriculture) and other services are disrupted as government workers who are from the Kanju community flee for their lives. Many schools close down due to lack of teachers and agricultural productivity slows down. Donor countries stop giving aid to Kiwachema and this worsens the already bad economy of the country. Inflation has hit the rooftop and the government is unable to pay its workers. As a result, services at government and local government institutions are hardly rendered. What we see here is a picture of a country that is on its knees because of irresponsible politics that is driven by violence. Through these occurrences in *Kufa Kuzikana,* Ken Walibora succinctly captures the happenings that took place in the post-election arena in Kenya, especially after the 2007 general elections, reiterating my earlier argument that fiction has the capacity to narrate the happenings in the society, including what might happen in the near future. Violence caused by politics is therefore like a recipe for deterioration in economic growth.

In *Pango*, we gather that politics that is dictated by violence results in the election of self-seeking leaders. After his election as the leader of Pango, Ngwese does not attend to duty (*Pango* 50–51). His responsibilities go unattended even to the disdain of his own wife. Additionally, he is involved in corrupt deals (*Pango* 54, 87), which shows political irresponsibility bears inept and corrupt leaders who cannot steer their countries to greater heights of socio-economic development. In other words, violent politics is disruptive to the social, economic, and political tranquillity of a country. It leads to social tension and animosity among citizens who have coexisted peacefully for long, leading to civil strife, consequently bringing the economy down and denting the image of the country.

Protesting against Irresponsible Politicians

When the subjugated find that they can no longer stomach the intrigues of political machinations, they use whatever power they have to protest. Their protest can either turn out to be another round of violence or a soft form of protest. In *Kufa Kuzikana*, the protest against irresponsible politics is seen through the action of Johnson Muyaka, a mentally challenged character, also known as Jerumani. Jerumani steals his father's private firearm and disappears for many days, until one day it is announced over the radio that Johnstone Mabende, the politician who fanned the violence that claimed many lives in Korosho, has been murdered by a mentally challenged person called Johnson Muyaka (*Kufa Kuzikana* 221). What we see here is that violence breeds violence. Other than Jerumani, who decided to solve the problem violently (he is mad and he neither fears nor cares) all the internally displaced people rule the streets, rob, engage in prostitution, and do all kinds of odd jobs to eke out a living. They are protesting 'quietly' against their government for failing to stop the violence that brought them to this sorry state of affairs. The subordinates realize that they have their agency which has not been taken away by the dominants (Sidanius and Pratto 432).

Conclusion

The main purpose of this chapter was to show how literary artists depict the nature and effects of violent politics in society. The chapter has shown that violent politics is disruptive to social life: it causes death, destruction of property, brings the economy of a whole nation to its knees, and brings disrepute to the affected nation internationally. Violent politics is depicted as one of the major reasons why probably some nations have failed to record positive socio-economic development. It is the reason that makes most towns in some African countries unsafe since the streets have been invaded by protesters who have been dispossessed of their property hence the only place they can live in is the streets. It becomes a vicious circle of robbery where government servants rob the citizens through bribery and other corrupt means whereas the landless and those who have run away from tribal animosity literally rob the civil servants what they have robbed from the government. As this cycle of events goes unattended, the country is held to ransom, and it fails to progress economically. The social tension that is left unattended to creates other social ills making the life of all citizens unsafe.

Kufa Kuzikana is arguably an atrocity narrative. Nayar (237) argues that an atrocity narrative is 'double-voiced': it is located within a discursive structure specific to a time and place, thus ensuring that the atrocity is made recognizable, and the demand for rights is made part of a universal schema of values. Indeed, in *Kufa Kuzikana* we see the writer exposing the effects of political atrocities and calling for respect of human rights. In this novel, therefore, the writer consciously speaks against a divisive class society. He reawakens society by compelling it to take a stand against the dominant group which espouses negative tendencies (Wa Thiong'o 6, 7b).

In *Pango*, the younger generation is galvanized by Katango to protest against the older generation that has refused to let go of the reins of power. The youth have always been told they are 'leaders of tomorrow' the 'tomorrow' that has hitherto failed to come as the older generation in positions of leadership continues to plunder the country's economy. Though the younger generation fails in its bid to take over power, they have stated their dissatisfaction with the way the older generation is running the affairs of the country. The two texts discussed in this chapter can therefore be said to be not just channels of exposing the ills of misguided politics, but also read as avenues for sensitization. Literature, therefore, plays an important role in bringing to light what would otherwise have been swept under the carpet. It helps to uncover the ills of rogue regimes therefore accomplishing one of its purposes as propounded by Aristotle namely to instruct (Fergusson 55). Besides mere instruction, literature shapes people's attitudes to life by making them view reality from a certain angle of vision (wa Thiong'o 6b). Therefore, one can rightly argue that through fiction, literary artists sensitize and instruct the society to abandon evil and selfish desires and instead seek a peaceful life that is meaningful to all.

Works Cited

Eagleton, Terry. *Literary Theory: An Introduction.* Oxford: Blackwell, 1983.

Fergusson, Francis. *Aristotle's Poetics.* New York: Hill and Wang, 1961.

Hawthorn, Jeremy. *Studying the Novel.* 6th ed. New Delhi: Atlantic Publishers and Distributers (T) Ltd, 2010.

Heczkova, Mgr Jana. *In The Wake of Atrocity: A Comparative Study of Native American and African American Narratives of Trauma.* Diss. Masarykovauniverzita, Filozofic kaFakulta, 2009.

Howard-Hassmann, Rhoda E. "13 Historical Amnesia, Genocide And the Rejection of Universal Human Rights." *Human Rights at the Crossroads* (2012): 172.

Humphrey, Michael. *The Politics of Atrocity and Reconciliation: From Terror to Trauma.* London: Routledge Taylor and Francis Group, 2002.

Hussen, Andreas. "Present Pasts: Media, Politics, Amnesia." *Public Culture* (2000): 21–38.

Kiage, Patrick. "Prosecutions: A Panacea for Kenya's Past Atrocities." *East African Journal of Human Rights and Democracy* 2 (2004): 104.

Moss, Simon. "Social Dominance Theory". Sico Tests. www.Sicotests.Com/Psychapter.Asp?Id=237

Nayar, Pramod K. "The Poetics of Postcolonial Atrocity: Dalit Life Writing, Testimonio, and Human Rights." *Ariel* 42.4 (2012): 237–264.

———. "Indigenous Cultures and the Ecology of Protest: Moral Economy and 'Knowing Subalternity' in Dalit and Tribal Writing from India." *Journal of Postcolonial Writing* 50.3 (2014): 291–303.

Peters, Julie Stone. "'Literature', the 'Rights of Man', and Narratives of Atrocity: Historical Background to the Culture of Testimony." *Yale Journal of Law and the Humanities* 17.2 (2013): 3.

Sidanius, Jim, and Pratto, Felicia. *Social Dominance: An Intergroup Theory of Social Hierarchy and Oppression.* Cambridge: Cambridge University Press, 1999.

Sum, Robert Kipkoech, and Simiyu Kisurulia. "The Psychology of Slavery: A Literary Discourse." *Elixir International Journal, Literature* 98(2016). www.elixirpublishers.com

The Elliot School of International Affairs at George Washington University. *International Affairs Review*, Xxiii (2016).

Wafula, Richard Makhanu, and Kimani Njogu. *Nadharia Za Uhakiki Wa Fasihi.* Nairobi: Jomo Kenyatta Foundation, 2007.

Walibora, Ken. *Kufa Kuzikana.* Nairobi: Longhorn Publishers, 2003.

Wamitila, Kyalo Wadi. *Pango.* Nairobi: Focus Publishers Ltd, 2003.

———. *Kamusi Ya Fasihi: Istilahi Na Nadharia.* Nairobi: Focus Books, 2003.

Wa Thiong'o, Ngugi. *Decolonising the Mind: The Politics of Language in African Literature.* Nairobi: East African Educational Publishers, 1981a.

———. *Writers in Politics.* Nairobi: East African Educational Publishers, 1981b.

———. *Moving the Centre: The Struggle for Cultural Freedoms.* Nairobi: East African Educational Publishers, 1993.

Waters, Timothy William. "Killing Globally, Punishing Locally?: The Still-Unmapped Ecology of Atrocity" *Still-Unmapped Ecology of Atrocity* 55 (2008): 1331–1370.

Wolfe, Staphine. "Atrocity: The State and Reparation Politics", *Politics of Reparations and Apologies.* Ed. Staphine Wolfe. New York: Springer, 2014. 1–18.

11 Political Atrocity in Kenyan Swahili Novel after the Year 2000

Mikhail Gromov

Introduction

Political atrocity has been a major theme in Kenyan fiction from independence and fiction produced in Swahili language being no exception. Since the mid-1970s, when Swahili writing in Kenya had established itself as an integral part of national literature, Swahili-writing authors have applied themselves to the ever-changing political climate in the society. Anchored on Karauri's (2012) notion of the political novel, this chapter investigates the representation of political atrocities in the works of selected authors such as Mwenda Mbatiah, John Habwe, Kyallo Wamitila, and Ken Walibora, showing varieties of depicted cases of political repressions and violations. Noteworthy is the fact that all the selected fall within the category of Kenyan Swahili novels written after 2000 and they show multimodal ways of portraying political atrocities in the Swahili novel.

The last quarter of the last century witnessed an upsurge in the number of Swahili works of fiction dealing with Kenyan politics at different levels and in different modes. Some of these works depict political matters in an allegorical and satirical manner such as Katama Mkangi's *Mafuta* (Oil) and *Walenisi* (Them-like-us). In Mkangi's works, Kenya's political situation is disguised as a fantastic country, where the poor are exploited by the privileged class either through lies, as in *Mafuta* or by direct oppression, as in *Walenisi*. Other novels use realistic modes of representation such as Rocha Chimera's *Nyongo mkalia ini* (The bile on the liver) and Mwenda Mbatiah's *Upotevu* (Prodigality). The two novels, though set in the 1970s and 1980s respectively, show a "society enmeshed in a web of moral turpitude, corruption, unemployment, lethargy, generational conflict and revenge" (Bertoncini et al., 64).

The beginning of the twenty-first century saw tangible changes in the country's political and social situation. These changes are, almost on an equal scale, reflected in Kenyan's Swahili literature. Alongside the unprecedented growth of the number of published titles, new literary forms have come into being such as the "new" or "experimental" novel, and a new generation of writers has emerged. Works of this new generation of Swahili writers surpass their predecessors both in terms of their literary merits and their social potential. In these works, thematic concerns related to politics, at different levels, scales, and dimensions are high-lighted in different modes and styles. Needless to say, political atrocity, in its various forms, stands out as one of the major themes in these works. In this regard, this chapter examines novels that show various forms of political atrocity on various levels, including, "high politics" – in other words, those works that can be qualified as "political novels".

The definition of a political novel is always a contested construct. Morris Edmund Speare, in *The Political Novel*, defines a political novel saying that, "It is a work of prose fiction which leans rather to 'ideas' than to 'emotions'; which deals rather with the machinery of law-making or with a theory about public conduct than with the merits of any given piece of legislation; and where the main purpose of the writer is partly propaganda, public reform, or exposition of the lives of the personages who maintain government, or of the forces which constitute government" (Speare 1924, ix). This chapter, however, relies on Speare's definition of a political novel as espoused and expounded by Mathew Karauri, thus:

i   Has the high-level politics (politicians and the state political process, machinery of law-making, political parties, voting, legislation, courts of justice, armies, etc.) as its principal theme or one of the main themes.
ii Reflects the political situation in the society critically (by an exposition of the lives of the personages who maintain government, or of the forces which constitute a government, by presenting the inside life of politics, disclosing political machinations, abuse of power, etc.).
iii Propagates, openly or implicitly, the writer's ideas about a better political organization for the society.
iv Presents these and other ideas in the form of characters, with their distinct personalities, physical and psychological features, and the actions that comprise the plot. (Karauri 8)

Novels discussed in this chapter demonstrate that politics and political atrocity in various modes are, conditionally, labelled as "historical", "allegorical" and "experimental", or "new". Each of these modes is characterized by its own stylistic and narrative particularities, but all of them hold the same purpose – to represent a certain sociopolitical reality and, in the long run, "propagate, openly or implicitly, the writer's ideas about better political organization of the society" (Karauri 8).

"Historical" Novel: Atrocity in a Familiar Setting

It is important to point out from the onset that the word "historical" is in quotation marks because the novels that fall in this category deal with the recent history of the country – for example, the 1990s or early the

2000s. These novels, as is in the historical novel, reproduce sociopolitical realities with a high level of precision, depicting known and recognizable places, events, certain occasions, and even historical figures. These novels, while referring to a specific period in Kenyan history, depict various forms of political abuse easily recognizable and memorable to readers.

Mwenda Mbatiah's novel *Vipanya vya Maabara* (Laboratory Mice) gives a bitter account of the hardships of what is considered to be the "Nyayo generation." This is a generation of young people whose adolescence and youth periods fall in the 1990s when the action of the novel is set. Throughout the novel, the author juxtaposes two plans. On the one hand, he tells about the solidarity of the poor people and its inspiring results (e.g., in Chapter 7 he tells how the public protests in 1991 assisted in adoption of multiparty democracy – "the people's struggle was not lost in vain, for the government was obliged to change the constitution and to allow the political parties to register. New era in Kenyan politics began" 94[1]). This solidarity is also manifested by the main characters, a group of youngsters from different social and ethnic groups, who throughout the novel support each other.

On the other hand, using high political posts for socially destructive activities, the author shows how high political figures injure the social fabric that holds society together. High political figures are typified in the novel by the character of Rashidi Hamisi, the Kenyan Minister of Defence, who deploys state defence structures to cover his own criminal activities. It is not lost on the readers that Rashid Hamisi is a large-scale drug baron. His criminal endeavours are harmful to all the social layers – while his main clients are the children from rich and affluent families, his distributors mainly come from the lower social classes. One of such distributors, a school-dropout named Swaleh, narrates his patron's illegal activities to his friend Bob Kerogo, the main character of the novel, who works as a driver, and even introduces him to the minister. Coincidentally, Bob in one of his rounds notices the minister's car parked on a deserted roadside and witnesses the minister trying to get rid of a body of an unknown white woman, and secretly photographs this. Later, from the newspapers, Bob learns about the sudden death of the daughter of a US senator. It was reported that the lady was doing social research in Kenya, in the process, discovered the minister's criminal business. It was further reported that she was raped and killed. The Senator organizes a mighty search campaign for his daughter's murderers. Bob, with his unmistakable evidence, plays a crucial role in this search and is rewarded handsomely. The "Hollywood-ish" end of the novel appears, however, to demonstrate Bob's (and the author's) mixed sentiments. On the one hand, there is pride and satisfaction from a "little man's" crucial role in unearthing and exposing hidden activities of a criminal of a high political calibre. On the other, there are regrets that such a mighty villain could only be overcome by the much-superseded might from across the ocean.

Kyallo Wadi Wamitila *Harufu ya Mapera* (The Smell of Guavas) and
John Habwe *Pamba* (titled by the name of the main character) do not
precisely indicate the historical period that they are set in. However,
inferences to the different historical and political references present in
the two texts points to the undeniable fact that actions in the two novels
take place in the first decade of the current century. Wamitila's novel
tells the story of a heated political rivalry between two presidential
candidates, the authoritarian Pipo Kenya and the much more liberal
"people's candidate" Jude Kinya. These political rivalries are accompanied by "routine" gathering of evidence against each other. Pipo's
project of destroying guava farms, belonging to poor peasants, for the
purpose of building profitable mines, is discovered by Jimna, the adopted son of Jude, and this starts a long row of vicissitudes at the family
and the state level.

John Habwe's novel *Pamba* (titled by the name of the main character)
at first glance stands farther from the political novel than Wamitila's
and Mbatiah's novels. Its characters do not include high political figures. However, the novel depicts long evidence of political atrocity –
atrocity of the government towards Kenyan intellectuals, particularly
university dons. Thus, the novel is a bitter lament about the miserable
state of public universities, represented in the novel by Chiromo Centre
(presumably its prototype being the University of Nairobi) and one of its
lecturers, Professor Pamba, a talented mathematician. Pamba, a locally
and foreign-educated scholar, initially gets a high-profile position at a
prestigious non-government organization but resigns from it when he
gets an opportunity to head a newly founded centre for mathematical
research at Chiromo centre. The centre "was hoping to change the ways
of constructing computer devices in its mathematical calculation. It is
the development which was intended to influence the whole world and to
bring to the country of Kenya big reputation worldwide" [2] (Habwe 48).
The centre worked successfully, but the state of the university and its
lecturers became more and more destitute. Even foreign-financed projects, no matter how well done, did not bring the desired increments –
everything was taken by the state structures. Classes and laboratories
did not have any equipment, lecturers lacked money. Pamba is thrown
out of his house in Kileleshwa and was unable his aged father's medical
bills. But when the teachers decide to defend their rights, the repressive
machine strikes, and their efforts go up in smoke:

> Teachers were annoyed with their small salaries. Those who were
> [the most] annoyed because of the various oppressions decided to
> create an organization for their defense.
>   [...]
> The purpose of creating a party caused four teachers being ex-
> pelled from their jobs. They were fired, packed their things and went.

The thrill of teachers was subdued for the time being. But like water it excited again after a certain time. The teachers were demanding the rights to be represented equally. They saw they were left behind in terms of salary, allowances, basic equipment for work. Teachers were not working, were not doing research.[3] (Habwe 56–57)

Brought to the end of their tether, the teachers decided to organize an all-university strike. The government responded by implanting spies into their ranks and arresting ten important members of the teacher's organization – among them was Miheso, the secretary, who disappeared without a trace. The strike was joined by students, who organized their own protest against the pitiful state of the teachers. Student protests were quelled by the police. Ironically Pamba, who for all his long-exercised caution towards the actions of his colleagues, was arrested and accused of inciting students to join the striking dons. When he eventually gets released, he decides to participate fully in the strike. The striking dons are brutally scattered by the police, Pamba is arrested again, and spends three days in a police cell. The strike goes on, with threats to withhold the teachers' salaries and more sackings. Among the sacked ones was Pamba himself. His further efforts to get employed in private and foreign universities go in vain. In the end, desperate, Pamba, deprived of his lifetime work and deserted by his family, commits suicide in his Chiromo office. Habwe's novel, obviously echoes recent events in the Kenyan society, particularly the strike of public universities in 2004. It therefore serves as a bitter documentary of atrocity committed by the state structures against the nation's intellectual potential – and, arguably, the first novel in Kenyan Swahili literature having this "intellectual atrocity" as the main subject.

"Allegorical" Novel: Atrocity in a Symbolic Setting

Again, at the outset, it is important to point out that the word "allegorical" is in quotes because novels in this category hardly rely on allegory as their main narrative mode. But allegorical in these novels refer to their settings. Events in these novels are set in imaginary or unnamed countries, whose political reality, however, is allegorical of not only Kenya, but many African countries. Wamitila's novel *Msimu wa vipepeo* (Season of butterflies), for instance, narrates a story "of the unhappy marriage of a young woman who divorced her loving but poor husband and married a government minister, whose wealth, however, fails to change her life for the better" (Bertoncini et al., 73). But Wamitila's writing skills allow him to interweave the main plot with numerous other storylines, which, taken all together, conjure up a vast panorama of the social and political life in an unnamed African country during the first decade of the twenty-first century.

The principal place in the novel is given, non-conventionally, to the figure of the antagonist, the government minister named Mkurutu. Mkurutu enhances his popularity among the masses by initiating, together with his foreign partners, various public-salutary projects: the girls' orphanage, delivery of food to the drought-stricken areas of the country, and builds in his constituency the Papilio Butterfly Centre – a farm for the breeding of exotic butterflies. He promises to sell the cocoons abroad and thus increase the living standards of the villages. In all his ventures, Mkurutu is joined by his old friend Fabio Mkalla, the country's Attorney General.

However, through the efforts of a young courageous journalist, Kalulu, the public slowly learns the true purpose of Mkurutu's charity. He sold many of the country's historical sites to his foreign partners for their private use; that the poor girls from the orphanage are sent abroad not to be educated, but to be sold to brothels; that the food delivered to the drought-stricken areas is dog food, which Mkurutu had been bribed to import from abroad and which is, moreover, toxic; that for the building of the butterfly farm he has used the state money intended to cater to the needs of HIV/AIDS victims. In the end, Mkurutu and Mkalla are about to face the court. It is apparent that the novel is "staffed" with various occasions of political atrocities. From the above-described anti-social practices Mkurutu is enabled to not only pursue his high political status, but also persecutes daring journalists, and uses parliamentary authorities to shut down unwanted press outlets. What is, however, even more notable is that although quite a few of the events described are reminiscent of recent ones in most African countries like Kenya, the author deliberately avoids direct historical-political allusions.

Ken Walibora in his novel *Kidagaa kimemwozea* (His small fish has caught a rot) tells the story of Amani, a young man from a poor background but rich personal virtues and his, not in any way less virtuous fiancée, Imani. Amani makes his journey to the city of Sokomoko, the capital of Tomoko, to seek justice. We are told his father was murdered, his land grabbed, his uncle unlawfully imprisoned, and he himself expelled from the University on a flimsy pretext. Instead of justice, he faces further atrocities of a tyrannical government, led by a dictatorial figure of Mtemi Nasaba Bora, the country's ruler. However, Amani's personal talents and support from his friends and the people allow him to topple the regime and give his countrymen hope for a new and brighter future.

The novel presents the 'collective image' of the modern African states and a large part is played by a highly "generalized" image of political atrocity, which, in Walibora's depiction, permeates all the levels of Tomoko's life. One of the novel's central plotlines is the story of the government minister, brother to the dictator, who had stolen the manuscript of Amani's book. It is no surprise, therefore, that after the demise of the dictator, the masses looking for a country's new leader invite Amani to take the reins of the government– which he declines. Regardless of all the temptations and snares of power, he prefers a peaceful family life with his beloved Imani (thus the symbolism of names: peace – *amani* – and faith – *imani* – always go together). The novel ends with the reunion of all their unjustly offended relatives.

In a "parable-like" manner, the political life in an imaginary African country of Bondeni is described in Swaleh Mdoe's novel *Mwanasiasa* (The Politician). An imaginary African country named Bondeni ("in the ravine") is ruled by a selfish and corrupt ruler Bwana Mkubwa ('the big master"). In a simplified, but convincing manner, Mdoe describes mechanisms of political forgery and economic exploitation, which Bwana Mkubwa uses to retain his power. All politicians of lower rank are totally subdued by Bwana Mkubwa, even his trusted deputy Mwangome "was not able to cut any decision related to the Bondeni country if Bwana Mkubwa was not at his side. But Bwana Mkubwa was rarely absent" (22). The autocratic leadership of Bwana Mkubwa, thinly disguised as democracy, is opposed by a former petty trader Mwarupia – a real man of the people, who represents the interests of the oppressed majority. Mwarupia unanimously wins elections for the post of the capital mayor and from that point he openly wages a struggle against Bwana Mkubwa's policies, calling upon the unity of his people. He is not stopped by the repercussions, ensuing imprisonment and torture – when the authorities, thinking that "he had enough" (116), they release him. Mwarupia leads the people in their last march against the dictatorship, which forces Bwana Mkubwa and his henchmen out of the country. Mwarupia calls the people to erect "a building of people's power" (124), because "we want equality for all the people of Bondeni. Everyone will make the living by his sweat" (125). Mwarupia is shown in the novel as an ideal figure. He is an exemplary husband and father, daily eats "only pieces of fried shark" (41), and spends his salary for aiding the working people like himself. It may be assumed, though, that the author's main purpose was not to create this rather conditional image of an ideal politician, but more – to provide a nimble and rounded criticism of current political mechanisms in modern African societies.

"New" Novel: Atrocity in an "Experimental" Setting

The word "experimental" is used alongside "new" in reference to that stratum of Swahili novels that show "a conscious formal and thematic split with the previous tradition of novel writing in Swahili" (Gromov 2014: 40). The setting that these novels depict is an innovative merge between a realistically painted "earthly" social situation and a fantastic "other-world" one, in which the main character goes on a quest of a specific mission. Characters in these novels vary from humans from various social spheres to fantastic creatures, such as giants, spirits, and prophets among others depicting in allegorical, metaphorical, and parabolic terms various social trends and political orientations.

Equally "experimental" is the depiction of various forms of political atrocities in these novels. In Wamitila's novel *Bina-adamu!* (Wonderman!), for example, an unnamed village boy, the hero of the novel, is searching for three 'male-female' kids (*wasichana-wavulana, huntha*). The three are children of the village prophet and if he manages to find them, life in his village will change for the better. During his long journey, the hero, assisted by a mysterious voice and a supernatural female being named Hanna, he makes discoveries in different parts of the world that he visits. He discovers that Europe, 'lives in yesterday', industrial Asia, 'lives in hope' and Africa, lives 'on the outskirts of the global village' and is devastated by famine and wars (134). Everywhere he goes, he comes across irrational and inexplicable deeds committed by a mysterious being known only as P.P. In Europe PP defeated fascism, in Asia he dropped an A-bomb over Hiroshima, and in Africa, using a stone, he knocked the brains off politicians' heads (70). By the end of his journey, the hero manages to find P.P. in America – *Bustani ya Eden ya pili* (The Second Garden of Eden) and he turns out to be none other than "Peter Pan, 'a giant with a baby's face', 'a worthy heir to Yanguis, the Kaiser, the Fuehrer, Franco, de Gaulle, Hirohito and Churchill' (99), the pillar of globalization and of the new world economy" (152).

The hero is surprised to learn that P.P. committed all his evil deeds merely by being playful, for he loves to play. Thus, the author implies that the imperialistic powers of today consider the whole world as their playground. In spite of this, the hero makes his choice: from this day on he will struggle against P.P. and for African unity. The Voice agrees with him, stating that "only unity and a new knowledge of yourselves will help you leave the outskirts of the global village" (154). The lengthy rendition of the novel's plot, nevertheless, helps readers to acknowledge the complexity of its style and structure. Equally complex are the manifestations of political atrocities found in the text, ranging from the "conventional" to the fantastic. When the hero visits different parts of the world, he witnesses P.P.'s various activities: in Europe P.P. and his accomplices breed Neo-Nazi movement, in Africa there are dictatorial regimes that sell their resources to foreigners, and on the global level, they pollute the ocean with oil and radioactive waste. But the fantastic forms of political atrocity appear even more frightening. In America P.P. and his yes-men are creating "the man of the future" (129). This is a human-like creature who doesn't remember his origins or his history, who doesn't bother to think and whose main concern is the consumption of industrial products; this creation of theirs, as they plan, will soon take over the world.

In Wamitila's novel *Musa leo!* (Moses of today) allegory is presented in a different dimension and subtly interwoven with realistic narration. The action is set in an unnamed country which is ruled by the tyrannical hand of the mysterious Mzee, the bearer of countless titles, one of which is 'Moses of today' because "he saved his people from the captivity of culture and history" (65). The country's realities such as political ambition, police repressions, and shattered economies resemble closely that of many African countries in recent decades.

The main hero, Mugogo Wehu, a young intellectual, is taken to a transcendental world in a quest to discover the true origins of Mzee. His findings reveal that Mzee is a hypocrite. Being the descendant of colonial yes-men, his power is built on fear and assistance from his overseas masters. In order to serve these masters, he has denied his kinship to his sister, Mamanchi, "Mother of the native land" (48). Mugogo's courage brings to his country the winds of change which have "blown down the Berlin Wall" and "demolished the palaces of many previously famous rulers" (66). Mzee's rule is over, and he returns to his native village, from which he had been expelled sometime in the past, to die. The novel is also soaked in allegorical allusions to African and world history, as well as modern and classical philosophy.

Political atrocities in the novel wear multiple faces ranging from police repressions, surveillance of dissidents, persecution of intellectuals, a ban on the books by Mzee's secret service and bodies of censorship. Again, the most threatening is its fantastic forms – Mzee decides to penetrate into the very brains of his subordinates using various methods so that the idea of his superiority remains in their minds even after his death. However, it takes the efforts of Mugogo and his friends to enlighten the people so that Mzee is unmasked and dethroned, and his plan of "global brainwashing" made ineffective.

Tom Olali's debut novel *Mafamba* (Underhand doings) features a rather innovative setting. Although the action is set in the year 2500 and its preceding decades, it describes a universe, consisting of several planets, inhabited by various types of human-like creatures, headed by dictators competing for power. The three main characters of *Mafamba* are planetary beings named Maotad, Limioe, and Amrao vying for power on an imaginary planet called Nuka. The course of events described in the novel reflects the happenings in the Kenyan political scene within the last two decades, roughly up to the post-election violence of 2008. Although the novel can be qualified as a rather thinly disguised political satire, the above-mentioned date—the twenty-fifth century—is significant. It appears that the author hints at the fact that even in a distant future and on distant planets the descendants of Africans (Kenyans) will retain the vices of the present-day situation in the country. Drawing this largely dystopian picture, the author at the same time offers no remedy—the novel ends with a set of rhetorical questions about the nature of political evils and social ills. (Gromov 2014: 46–47)

Nakuruto (Nakuruto 2009) by Clara Momanyi is deemed as the first female contribution to the realm of the "new novel". The novel follows

the quest structure similar to that of Wamitila's *Bina-adamu!* The female heroine Nakuruto, possesses magical abilities and assisted by mysterious powers, is sent through the history of Africa from pre-colonial,
through colonial, and to post-colonial times. Nakuruto declares that her
aim is "to search for the lost way" (kuisaka njia iliyopotea, Momanyi
11) and "to change things which are not pertinent to human nature"
(kubadilisha mambo yasiyotaalaki utu wa binadamu, Momanyi 31). But
if for that purpose in the pre-colonial days she has to deal with the destructive forces of nature (she saves the people of the village that accommodated her from the impending flood), then in colonial time she has
to lead the people's rebellion against the invaders, who in the novel are
called Wanguzu (anagram of Wazungu). Nakuruto's desire to liberate
people is strengthened by the atrocious deeds that the Wanguzu commit
against the indigenous inhabitants of her land. Wanguzu are forced out
but after the victory, it becomes evident that the riches they were using,
and which belonged to the people, are now appropriated by the former
henchmen of the colonizers. These new rulers use their freshly acquired
powers to grab people's lands, close schools, and burn churches that
impede their self-enriching exertion.

Equally transparent is the author's allegory of neo-colonialism – the
people, especially those who were supporting the Wanguzu in colonial days, are poisoned by the wax that Wanguzu had, but took with
them, leaving only its scent – and even this allows them now to dictate
their terms to the people of formerly colonized lands, because the scent
makes them addicted. This wax is the symbol of advanced technology
and higher living standards, which the neo-colonizers only allow the
Africans "to smell". Understanding the necessity of the wax itself for
the decent living, people of the country of Maboni (a symbolic name
for Africa) decide to build a high stairway, which will allow them to
reach the wax; but even at the initial stage the building is complicated
by discordance and theft; moreover, the building is supervised by the
specialists from the land of Wanguzu. In the end, those are the women
(especially the young ones) who manage to mobilize the people of Maboni to continue the construction against all odds; Nakuruto expresses
her hope that these women will manage to help the people to find their
lost ways.

Conclusion

This chapter has presented a brief survey of the portrayal of political
atrocities in selected novels by Kenyan writers of Swahili expression.
Along with depicting the atrocious deeds of particular politicians and political systems at different levels and different scales (e.g., intra-national,
continental, and global), the authors give different images of negative
and destructive political forces and situations. In realistic novels, the

political evil is pictured as criminal-type politicians (Mbatiah and Wamitila), or faceless structures harming the intellectual potential of the
nation (Habwe); "parable-like" novels of Walibora and Mdoe create vil-
lainous larger-than-life characters, representing augmented "collective
images" of African dictatorial governments. Finally, the "new" novel
features an intimidating and loathsome image of globalized political
evil, embodied in no less intimidating and loathsome semi-fantastic figures of Mzee, P.P., and other agents of imperialism, neo-colonialism,
and global plutocracy represented as possessing equally semi-fantastic
fiendish powers.

It may also be assumed that the reading audiences that are being targeted by the authors of these books are also sufficiently different, and the
authors represent their own understanding and interpretation of political forces according to the creative facilities of their audiences (or, using
modern terminology, "interpretative communities"). If such novels as
Vipanya vya maabara, *Pamba* or *Msimu wa vipepeo* are more appealing
to the readers of the "old school", brought up on predominantly realistic
fiction (e.g., teachers and lecturers in Swahili), then novels by Wamitila,
Olali, and Momanyi, full of parabolic, periphrastic, and metaphorical
images, richly alluding to world literature and history, are likely to target highly educated but younger audiences, familiar with modern literary styles and trends. The works of Walibora and Mdoe, judging by their
simpler structures and the higher level of language, especially in terms
of vocabulary and phraseology, may be oriented towards a certain audience cadre – high school students.

At the same time, all these novels appear to pursue the same main
aim – by reflecting the political situation in society critically. These novels, therefore, "propagate, openly or implicitly, the writer's ideas about
better political organization of the society" (Karauri 8) increasing political and social awareness of the readers, gradually turning them into
a creative force in society. This noble task has been intrinsic to Kenyan
literature, including its Swahili branch, since its formative years, and the
new generation of writers appears to carry it with honour.

Notes

1 Lakini harakati za wananchi hazikupotea bure kwani serikali ililazimika
  kubadilisha katiba na kuruhusu vyama vya kisiasa kusajiliwa. Enzi mpya katika siasa za Kenya ikaanza (all the translations from Swahili are mine – MG).
2 Ulinuia kubadili jinsi ya kujenga mtambo wa kompyuta katika ukokotozi
  wake wa hesabu. Ni maendeleo ambayo yalinuia kuathiri ulimwengu mzima
  na kuletea nchi ya Kenya sifa kubwa ulimwenguni.
3 Pamba hakutaka kuamini alijiuzulu kazi yake ya SAIDIA Kenya kujiunga na
  chuo cha namna ile. Hapakuwa na haki. Hapakuwa na uhuru. Hapakuwa
  na usawa. Ama ni kweli nyumba nzuri si mlango. Walimu walikereka pale
  kwa ajili ya mishahara midogo. Na wale waliokereka kwa ajili ya maonevu
  mengine waliamua kubuni chama cha kuwatetea.

"Vipi nyinyi wataalam mnaanzisha chama kama vibarua?" Watu waliwauliza.
"Kwa sababu hali yetu na wale wafanyakazi ni sawasawa," walimu walisema [...]
Lengo la kutaka kuunda chama lilisababisha walimu wanne kufukuzwa kazi. Walipigwa kalamu wakafunga virago vyao wakaenda zao. Msisimko wa walimu ulinyamaza kwa muda. Tena kama maji ulichipuka tena baada ya kipindi fulani. Walimu walidai haki ya kuwakilishwa kisawasawa. Waliona wameachwa nyuma katika mishahara, katika alawanzi, katika vifaa muhimu vya kazi. Walimu walikuwa hawafanyi kazi, hawafanyi utafiti. Ni malalamishi yaliyoendelea kumiminwa hapo Chiromo Centre. Huu ndio ulikuwa wakati na majira. Karama alivua nguo akakubali kuoga maji haya. Aliteuliwa kuwa mwenyekiti wa chama cha walimu Taaluma. Miheso akawa sekretari. Chombo cha walimu nacho kikaingia majini kuanza utetezi wa haki, usawa na uhuru. Ilikuwa vigumu wao kupewa ruhusa hata kukutana na wakuu wa chuo kwani waliwadharau.

Works Cited

Bertoncini-Zubkova, Elena, Mikhail Gromov, Said Khamis, and Kyallo Wadi Wamitila. *Outline of Swahili Literature: Prose Fiction and Drama*. Leiden: Brill, 2009.

Gromov, Mikhail D. "Visions of the Future in the 'New' Swahili Novel: Hope in Desperation?" *Tydskrif vir letterkunde* 51.2 (2014): 40–51.

———. "Women Characters in the Novels of Ken Walibora: Victims or Winners?" Pathways to African Feminism and Development. *Journal of African Women's Studies Centre, University of Nairobi* 1.3 (2015): 1–13.

Habwe, John. *Pamba*. Nairobi: The Jomo Kenyatta Foundation, 2011.

Karauri, Mathew. *Political Novel in Kenya: The Works of Wahome Mutahi*. Nairobi: University of Nairobi, Unpublished Master of Arts thesis, 2006.

Mbatiah, Mwenda. *Vipanya vya maabara*. Nairobi: The Jomo Kenyatta Foundation, 2007.

Mdoe, Swaleh. *Mwanasiasa*. Nairobi: East African Educational Publishers, 2014.

Momanyi, Clara. *Nakuruto*. Nairobi: Longhorn, 2009.

Olali, Tom. "Some Say I'm a Dreamer, But My Style Is to Tell it As I See It." *Daily Nation*, Saturday, 29 March 2014.

———. *Mafamba*. Nairobi: The Jomo Kenyatta Foundation, 2008.

———. *Watu wa Gehenna*. Nairobi: The Jomo Kenyatta Foundation, 2012.

Speare, Morris Edmund. *The Political Novel*. Oxford: Oxford University Press, 1924.

Walibora, Ken. *Kidagaa kimemwozea*. Nairobi: Target Publications, 2012.

Wamitila, Kyallo Wadi. *Bina-Adamu*. Nairobi: Phoenix Publishers, 2002.

———. *Musaleo*. Nairobi: Vide-Muwa, 2004.

———. *Msimu wa vipepeo*. Nairobi: Vide-Muwa, 2006.

———. *Harufu ya mapera*. Nairobi: Vide-Muwa, 2012.

Part 2

Narrating Mau Mau Violence and Trauma in the Kenyan Novel

12 Textual Subversion in the Representation of Mau Mau Atrocities in Settler Writing in Kenya

Colomba Kaburi Muriungi

Introduction

Colonial settlers were among the first group of writers to attempt narrating the nature, the causes, and the atrocities associated with the Mau Mau movement in Kenya. This was probably because they had a first-hand encounter with the Mau Mau rebellion. This settler writing was often coloured with myths about black people with regard to their traditions and actions especially in their confrontation with colonial systems. This chapter examines the representation of violence occasioned by Mau Mau activities by colonial settler writers in Kenya through a reading of Robert Ruark's *Something of Value*. Focusing on characters' actions and the author's narrative technique, the chapter posits that Robert Ruark's narrative not only presents scenes that reveal settler notions of black people and the Mau Mau in particular, but it also presents scenes that subvert the writer's ideology. Analyses in this chapter are grounded on suppositions by Barber (1987), Bakhtin (1990), and Cooper (1992), who agree that there are multiple competing voices in a text and it is by unveiling these voices that an author's ideology is rendered visible, and that it is through these same voices that an author's ideology gets subverted.

While analysing how Robert Ruark represents the Mau Mau movement in *Something of Value,* the chapter examines the possibilities of reading other discourses in the text in addition to the main ideology that the author seeks to project. Ideology is taken in this chapter to loosely mean the belief that is held by the author [read white settlers] towards the Mau Mau and the black people in Kenya in general. Gavin Grindon observes that "subversion is usually understood, broadly, as a matter of the reversal of established values, or the insertion of other values into them" (1). The chapter examines how Robert Ruark projects the activities of the Mau Mau such as the oath-taking or the killings they executed, and how he discredits Mau Mau leaders as careless bloody drunkards. While analysing how he represents cultural practices of the black people in Kenya as savage, the chapter demonstrates that Ruark's settler characters are caught up in the same backward and atrocious activities of the Mau Mau, which brings the idea of subversion.

184 Colomba Kaburi Muriungi

A Note on the Mau Mau Movement

The historical phenomenon in Kenya known as Mau Mau was a product of complex socio-economic determinants that it defies any straightforward categorization and interpretation. Scholars the world over have studied the Mau Mau and have come up with varying interpretations and images of this movement. Robert Buijtenhuis posits that some scholars have wondered whether the Mau Mau is a corruption of the Kikuyu word for oath which is "muma", while others have speculated that the letters M.A.U were intended to be reversed to give the initials for Underground African Movement (11). Maughan-Brown echoes the difficulties experienced in defining the Mau Mau movement when he states that there is a general tendency by scholars to wonder whether the Mau Mau movement was a revolt, a revolution, or a rebellion (18). Teresa Paterson observes that all these different interpretations of the term Mau Mau imply that anyone writing about Mau Mau appropriates the meaning that supports that narrator's cause (135). Though its interpretations are varied, Buijtenhuis argues that the Mau Mau movement remains "one of the first African liberation movements of modern times" (13). It is an organization that is generally attributed to the 1940s that was formed to protest the seizure of land by the colonial government for the white settlers in Kenya (Lonsdale 417). The movement was largely an attempt to reclaim the Kenyan people's freedom from colonial rule and was mainly organized in the present-day central region of Kenya mainly populated by the Agikuyu tribe. The Mau Mau movement invoked passion that has rarely been equalled in the history of decolonization in the African continent. However, what has been written about the Mau Mau, especially by settler writers has been coloured by myths because the origin, character, and effectiveness of Mau Mau as a phenomenon are very complex. Specifically, the colonialist viewed the Mau Mau rebellion as having been triggered by the failure of the Agikuyu to adapt to civilization (Buijtenhuis 45). An official delegation to Kenya from Britain concluded in a report to the secretary of state for colonies that "Mau Mau intentionally and deliberately seeks to lead the Africans of Kenya back to the bush and savagery, and not forward into progress" (Buijtenhuis 44). Bruce Berman argues that the Mau Mau was depicted [by colonialists?] as a savage, violent, and depraved tribal cult, an expression of unrestrained emotion rather than reason, that sought to turn the Kikuyu back to the "bad old days" (182). Maloba Wunyabari posits that missionaries in Kenya saw Mau Mau as a fight between the forces of light and darkness. They conceptualized the Mau Mau as possessing the dark forces that had to be confronted and defeated by Christianity (9). Wunyabari further argues, "The writings about Mau Mau, at the time when it occurred, were essentially undertaken by ... enemies of the movement" (9) and that these enemies were essentially local white settlers who painted the Mau Mau as dark and satanic in content and inspiration. This therefore means that the earliest view about Mau Mau to the rest of the world was from the binoculars of the colonial settler who held the view that the movement was a complete rejection of civilization.

The history of Mau Mau written by settlers and their sympathizers was determined by the ideological need to find and focus exclusively on an interpretation of the Mau Mau which would exonerate colonialism from any responsibility. Such history relied on anti-Mau Mau sources. Thus, the term Mau Mau is one that perhaps, more than any other signifies for many white settlers in Kenya the atavism, savagery, and primitivism of darkest Africa. Some of the well-known colonial settler writers such as Robert Ruark and Elspeth Huxley propagated this settler ideology of the Mau Mau movement in their writing. These writers are involved in what this chapter terms as "selective narration" of Mau Mau atrocities, where they preferred to focus on the negative native practices by Africans and the crude activities of the Mau Mau. These settler writers could not find any justifiable reason that would drive Africans to resist the alleged incoming civilization other than savagery. However, this chapter argues that as much as such writers try to voice this white ideology, there is an underlying contradictory narrative that counters the main narrative that they seek to narrate.

Methodology and Theoretical Perspective

This chapter relies on a close textual reading of Robert Ruark's *Something of Value* in order to unravel the writer's ideological standpoint. A close analysis of character portrayal and author's narrative point of view is central to this chapter because these two aspects provide insights to the author's perception of the Mau Mau and the black people in general. Maughan-Brown asserts that fiction reveals or "renders visible" the structure of the ideology within which it is produced (106). In reading the settler novel in Kenya, one can certainly decipher the author's main intention in narrating the Mau Mau story.

Mikhail Bakhtin posits that texts have multiple competing voices that he calls "ideologues" and each of them presents a kind of consciousness in the text. Bakhtin's argument is that a word does not belong entirely to the speaker, but rather the speaker has to appropriate it (263). Meaning (in a text) is therefore never created but constantly negotiated, hence it is constantly changing. Bakhtin further argues that there are two forces that act on meaning: the centripetal forces that unify meaning and the centrifugal forces that stratify meaning, but both are important for understanding any text (270). Thus, because of these two forces, a text is prone to limitless readings. It is on such readings, suggested by Bakhtin, that discussions in this chapter are grounded. Quoting Fredrick Jameson, Brenda Cooper asserts that no interpretation can effectively be disqualified in its own terms. Instead, she suggests that interpretation should take place within a Homeric battlefield in which a list of interpretive options is either openly or implicitly in conflict (4). However, when a text is subjected to these multiple interpretations that Bakhtin and Cooper talk about, it will end up not only portraying an ideology but other aspects of meaning because it contains "seeds" that expose conflicting ideas thus subverting the ideological position (Cooper 11). But it is not the author's intention to subvert his own idea. Instead, textual resistance to ideology occurs because subversion may not be an overhaul of things or actions in the text. It is the fictional underground that sets up another story within a dominant story (Cooper 12). It is on such theoretical background that this chapter discusses textual subversion in Robert Ruark's *Something of Value* in order to reveal how settler writing in Kenya often purposed to reveal negative aspects about the Mau Mau atrocities.

Textual Subversion in *Something of Value*

Discussions in this section starts by taking note of the kind of orientation given to readers in the foreword of *Something of Value* concerning the Mau Mau:

> In order to understand Mau Mau it is first necessary to understand Africa, and the portion of Africa in which Mau Mau *was allowed to flourish* is only just fifty years old as we reckon civilization. To understand Africa you must understand the basic impulsive savagery that is greater than anything we "civilized" people have encountered in two centuries. (7) [Italics Mine]

This quotation exposes the authorial ideology of Africa. Maughan-Brown argues that the use of the phrase "was allowed to flourish" shows that Ruark is taking sides with the settler in accusing the government of being blind to the dangers of Mau Mau movement and incompetent in dealing with it (116). In the foreword, Ruark gives readers the kind of actions to expect from the Mau Mau. Ironically, the way Ruark associates Mau Mau activities that he promises to describe as not necessitated by the need for action, but that killing is in the very nature of the African: "There is much blood in this book. There is much killing. But the life of Africa was washed earlier, by blood, and its ground was, and still is, fertilized by the blood of its people and its animals" (7). The idea of Africa being washed by blood finds its fulfilment in the text by the manner in which Mau Mau loyalists hack down anti-Mau Mau Africans, white settlers, and even animals. Although it is a fact that a lot of killing occurred when the Mau Mau movement was active, the manner in which these killings are described in *Something of Value* is exaggerated. However, on the one hand, Ruark succeeds in presenting his myth of the Africans and the Mau Mau in particular as backward, atrocious, uncivilized, and as people who are possessed with longing for blood and torture. On the other hand, consciously or unconsciously, Ruark presents white characters as people who are caught up in the Mau Mau animosity.

Peter McKenzie, the hero of the text, is used as one of Robert Ruark's mouthpieces because his articulations can read as the author's own standpoint. For instance, he is used to giving new arrivals in Kenya an account of how Africans have lived in the past and what they (arriving whites) may expect during their stay:

> Before we came less than fifty years ago – they [African] were eating each other and murdering each other for fun. Disease kept the population down and the lions... and the tribal wars kept population down.... Then we came roaring in and civilized'em.... We threw'em a pair of pants and said that over yonder was a church, where a much stronger God than their Ngai lived. (205–206)

McKenzie perpetuates the myth of the superiority of the white race over the black race, which suggests that colonialism had rendered the service of drawing Africans into the mainstream of civilization and away from pervasive barbarism (Wunyabari 1). We cannot deny that western influence played a role in changing the Africans' way of life, but utterances such as the one cited above serve to betray an ideology that the author wishes to further in the novel. McKenzie adds, "you send one of these chaps [Africans] off to fetch your hat, may be, and if he sees a butterfly he forgets the hat and chases the butterfly" (206). This implies the obvious superiority of the white man over black man in terms of memory. Although McKenzie speaks ill about the black man, earlier in the novel the narrator tells us that he was in love with Africa and its animals (166) and that he was brought up by Karanja's wife (an African) after the death of his mother. Additionally, Karanja's son, Kimani, was Mckenzie's childhood playmate, which contradicts Peter's negative articulations about Africans. In fact, one is forced to question why Peter McKenzie turns against the Africans towards the end of the narrative. This contradiction serves as evidence for textual subversion.

The fact that Africans are viewed as inferior to the whites is further confirmed by the way settler servants in *Something of Value* are constantly referred to as boys. Peter McKenzie says, "blacks are damned well inferior in the white man's world as we know it out here" (210), while Jeff, Peter's brother-in-law says, "These people just aren't out of the tree long enough. They were eating each other ... just yesterday" (48). Utterances like these are what Brenda Cooper calls "clues and pointers" (7) that help to uncover the ideological standpoint of any author. Through such assertions by the characters it is possible to argue that Ruark sees the Mau Mau as having flourished because of the savage nature of the Africans.

The ideology of Africans being backward and thus killing aimlessly is shown further when Ruark associates actions of the Mau Mau with communism in using a Russian and an Indian as advisers to the Mau Mau. In an incident where these advisors appear, they are accompanied by a black man whom the narrative voice describes as "The well-educated and travelled man" (293). In his advice to the Mau Mau leaders, wa-Russia says:

> What he wants is organization...those who are with us are bound forever to be with us; those who are against us should die, and as painfully as possible...If a white man befriends you kill him.... If a kikuyu presents an obstacle...kill him as coldly as you would kill a snake but more slowly. (295)

By allowing the Russian to convey and elaborate the Africans' course of action, Ruark is suggesting that the Mau Mau are brutal and violent not because of their own initiative, but because they are aided by outsiders. Paradoxically these outsiders are themselves white people. This suggests that Africans are incapable of thinking on their own why they have to conduct violent campaigns for their freedom. Often in this narrative, Ruark does not allow blacks to convey their thoughts independently but makes somebody speak for them. Even the kind of narrative voice that the novel assumes shows that in most incidences Mau Mau actions are reported while the white settlers are allowed to speak out, again pointing to partial gagging of the black person in the narrative. But the fact that the fighters continued to wage a war in the absence of the outsiders mentioned above, shows that the Mau Mau were independent in their actions and that they knew why they had to fight.

Subversion in fiction is brought about by contradictions, which remain visibly inscribed in a text and thus contribute to its irregular development (Cooper 3). In *Something of Value* Robert Ruark perpetuates the settler myth about Mau Mau movement through "selective narration", which is protective to the whites and condemnatory to Africans. In the process, he fails to acknowledge some facts about the Mau Mau and hence sticks to specificities of selected memory. This is attributed to the fact that when memory is suppressed it produces unfinished narratives (Werbner 9), and this suppressed memory may resurface (though unconsciously on the part of the author), bringing contradictions in text hence the subversion. To Ruark the Mau Mau war was one between savagery and civilization and he invokes African beliefs. For instance, when Kimani is slapped by Jeff, a white man and he does not hit back in revenge, it becomes a curse (Thahu) according to the Kikuyu traditions (70). As if in confirmation of the curse, Karanja's wife delivers a child feet-first, which is another curse. One thing leads to another and Karanja ends up in jail, which is still a curse. Kimani therefore decides to kill Jeff to "wash away" the curse from his family. He strikes Jeff with a spear and assuming he was dead, Kimani runs away into the forest and ends up as a Mau Mau. By showing Kimani's actions as ignited and propelled by Thahu (curse), Ruark underplays other dynamics of the struggle by giving whites confidence in their myths about Africans. Maughan-Brown comments on the attitude held by settler writers towards Africans when he argues that it was "unthinkable" for settlers [like Ruark], that the Mau Mau could have resorted going into the forest for socio-economic reasons (112). Ruark suggests that Africans were so immersed in their traditions that these traditions seemed to dictate how they acted.

The paradox of Ruark's narrative is evident when the white soldiers, having failed to extract information from the alleged Mau Mau members resort to the same "savagery" that is supposedly for the Africans. For instance, after his capture, old man Njogu refuses to confess that he was the sole giver of the oath. However, he confesses after Peter McKenzie cunningly refers to the power of the Mau Mau oath and further convinces Njogu to take a cleansing oath by telling him he would reincarnate into a hyena if he died without having undergone the cleansing and confession. Ruark shows that having had close contact with Africans for long and learnt their beliefs and way of life, Peter McKenzie "goes native" in his attempt to get the truth from Njogu. He uses the very beliefs of the Mau Mau that he and the other settlers term as backward for the purpose of getting a conviction. Although the confessions of old man Njogu are instrumental in the victory of the British over the Mau Mau, the actions of Peter McKenzie should be read as one way in which the text subverts itself. It was not likely that the settlers admired these beliefs anyway. Ruark is therefore getting short of his own ideology by the very fact that his "civilized" characters resort to "backwardness" in order to win the Mau Mau.

The inclination towards Africans' values and hence the subversion of white supremacist ideology is not just seen in the fight against the Mau Mau. Early in the novel we witness Peter McKenzie relying on a sorcerer to have a curse lifted after he had failed to shoot any animal in his hunting expeditions. Matheka a local tracker from Kambaland advises Peter McKenzie to have the curse removed so that he would be able to shoot (34). At first Peter McKenzie viewed African beliefs as paltry which could not be relied on for the purpose of success. However, after some time he finds no rewards in his hunting, which forces him to rely on the same beliefs that he despised and he sends for the sorcerer, thus questioning the alleged barbarism and primitivism of the African ways, in white man's view. Further in the text, we get a highly inaccurate and mythologized account about Africans and the Mau Mau when Peter Mackenzie informs Tom and Nancy Deanne that Africans "... have no sensitivity of inflicting pain, or receiving pain because their whole religion is based on blood and torture of animals and each other.... They think nothing's funnier than a wounded animal or a crippled animal.... I don't think they themselves feel pain the way we do" (209). Such statements serve to justify the infliction of physical violence and torture on Mau Mau victims by the whites in the text. Peter asserts that "Blacks are Liars", and thus torture is the only act that can make them tell the truth; and since the blacks do not feel pain, there is no need to worry about the pain inflicted on them. What Robert Ruark fails to acknowledge however is that blacks may not be natural liars, but lying is one of the strategies that the Mau Mau used in such a context (of torture) to keep themselves together in order to successfully fight for their land and freedom. In fact, those who do not lie betray the movement and lastly lead to its downfall. While Peter further claims that "Wogs [Africans] don't think like us, they don't react like us and they are too newly introduced to civilization" (207), the civilized lot paradoxically spend time searching for the Mau Mau leaders without success. Old man Njogu, for example, plays tricks on his employer by acting "the innocent good boy" for a long time without his employer ever realizing that he (Njogu) was the chief Mau Mau oath giver.

The myth of the Mau Mau being backward is also subverted by the fact that some Mau Mau loyalists lived with settlers as informants, thus demonstrating the author's failure to adhere strictly to this schema. On the one hand, settlers in *Something of Value* assume that their servants are genuine, but the servants pretend and assume two different identities (of "good" servants and as Mau Mau loyalists) as a result of the complex relationship of the war. On the other hand, the settler farmer gains in exploiting the black man and giving him food and other little benefits. Either group believes it is gaining from the other. However, the servants help the fighters in the forests to track the movements of the Masters, subsequently breaking into the houses and getting away with anything that they thought was of value to the war, and sometimes killing the settlers. The fact that the Mau Mau fighters would many times skilfully and successfully raid the settlers' homes and kill the whites without being captured, subverts the settler myths about Africans and the Mau Mau being less knowledgeable.

It is worth noting that Ruark discredits Mau Mau leaders by presenting them as people who are possessed by greed and violence. The leaders charge 90 shillings for the oath of which 30 shillings would belong to the oath giver. They are shown to overindulge in beer drinking, maybe, by the mere fact that they are irrational according to Ruark. Kimani and Njogu, for example, have plenty of beer in the cave where they hide, which is brewed by Njogu's daughter who is Kimani's wife (311). This representation of Mau Mau tallies with that of Louis Leakey who analysed the Mau Mau as "a perverted religious cult that was manipulated by its cynical, greedy and evil leaders" (Quoted in Berman 183). Berman posits that Leakey was believed to be the person who was supposed to know the Africans in Kenya more than the other settlers because he was born and raised

in Kenya and spoke the Agikuyu language fluently. However, his description of the Mau Mau is also informed by settler ideology. Ogot, however,
argues that the Mau Mau leaders firmly believed that "their cause was
sanctioned by God who was on their side: that they had been wronged
by the enemy invaders; the Europeans, who had stolen their land" (283).
It is therefore important to take cognizance of the fact that the mythologized account of the Mau Mau in *Something of Value* could be inaccurate because evidence shows that these fighters stated in their hymns that
what they needed was to get their land and freedom. Ogot for instance,
explicates some of the hymns that the Mau Mau fighters used to sing and
expressed the aims of the fight as those of education, land, freedom, and
deliverance from other types of discrimination based on the race.

Ruark exemplifies a supposition put forward by Lonsdale that the
whites thought of the Mau Mau as callous beings who used savage and
atrocious methods of killing (379). This comes clear in the way he presents the oath-taking scenarios by the Mau Mau fighters, especially their
leaders who were responsible for oath giving:

'This is your son", Njogu said looking down to the wounded man...
"I have no doubt he is the pride of your squinted eyes..." And Njogu
took the panga in one hand and seized the boy's hair with his left. He
tilted back the boy's chin by pulling on the hair. The panga swished,
and now Njogu held the boy's head in his left hand. The headless
boy fell twitching, blood pumping from his neck, across the body of
his father.... "These are ingredients of the oath", Njogu said. "The
new oath calls for the corpse of a man and a boy" (330)...Kimani
took the panga and split first the skull of the man, making a vertical
and then horizontal cut just above the eyes...Laid back the bone...
and scooped out the gray brains. (331)

Kimani later kills his own brother Kibarara wa Karanja, which though
painful and traumatizing had to be done because he was bound by the
Mau Mau oath to kill anybody who was anti-Mau Mau (337). The old
man, Njogu, also kills those who refuse to take the oath in the most
brutal manner:

Njogu swung the panga. It sliced into the old man's neck, cutting
through the spine and nearly removing the head. The old man fell
down, blood spurting thickly from his severed jugular. Njogu struck
with the Panga again, and the head toppled to one side.... Then he
(Njogu) wiped his hands and panga in grass. (281–282)

The Mau Mau leaders like Njogu and Kimani are presented as people
possessed by violence, perfectly conforming to the settler's idealized
concept about the blacks who are dancing faithfully to the stereotype.
The author however, seems to be possessed by this "pornography of

violence" judging from the way the description of the killings is given and the way Mau Mau oaths are administered because he appears to enjoy it. A closer reading of the context in which the described actions take place further represents Africans as people who have no feelings for each other because as the killing is taking place, other Mau Mau loyalists are singing and dancing as they watch. The reader is left whether such scenes are supposed to be enjoyed and this is what forces one to argue that the author is also possessed of this violence. The Mau Mau animosity is further demonstrated when they attack the settlers' homes and chop the cows' udders, strangle cats, and kill many other animals and remove their eyes (390). The inclusion of cats' and dogs' eyes in the oath and the brutal killing of those who refuse to take the oath, presents the blacks as having a natural and irresistible inclination towards evil. Such actions by the Mau Mau echo Peter McKenzie's words that Africans love killing, and that their religion is based on torture of animals and their own kind (202).

However, Ruark's ideological depiction of the Mau Mau's actions is subverted by the fact that Peter McKenzie, like the Mau Mau adherents kills in a manner that is equally beastly:

> The man rolled his eyes upward at McKenzie as Peter took him by the hair and passed the panga blade against his throat.... He sawed steadily with the knife, and after a while the head came free in his hand (470)

At some point in the novel, Peter McKenzie condemns himself thus, "God almighty forgive us, Peter thought. Look at me. A bloody-handed murderer, as bad as Mau Mau, may be worse, because we do it absolutely coldly" (473). Such sentiments imply that settlers were also gripped by the alleged "savage madness" of the Mau Mau, which I have read as textual subversion.

Conclusion

The thrust of this chapter has been the representation of the Mau Mau narrative in colonial settler writing. The chapter has shown that although colonial settler writers represent Mau Mau as barbaric and as having not secured any physical victory against the colonialist government, its contribution towards the process of decolonization cannot be downplayed or suppressed. The tactics employed by Mau Mau adherents helped to destabilize white settlers' beliefs and misconceptions about the movement. The chapter has shown that the author's overall ideology is rendered visible within his creative process agreeing with Lennard Davis who argues that "novels are agents of inculcating ideology... they embody ideologies; and they promulgate ideology" (25). However, while fiction renders ideology visible, it does so with contradictions because "the intention to produce a work of literature does not guarantee an autonomous text, since the signifiers always exceed and thus undermine intention" (Bennett 69). This is a constant that causes meaning in *Something of Value*, to differ with the intention of the author in perpetuating the settler ideology about the Mau Mau as an essentially destructive, illogical, barbaric, and unwarranted group (Wunyabari 9). In this text "the fictional underground sets up another story within the dominant story which generates "surplus": meaning that goes beyond the author's ideological suppositions and thus subverts the intentions of the work" (Barber 4).

Works Cited

Atieno-Adhiambo, Elisha Stephen "The Production of History in Kenya: The Mau Mau Debate", *Canadian Journal of African Studies* 25 (1991): 300–307.

Bakhtin, Mikhail, M. *The Dialogue Imagination: Four Chapters*. Austin: University of Texas Press, 1990.

Barber, Karin. "Popular Arts in Africa". *African Studies Review* 30.3, 1987: 1–78.

Bennet, Tony. *Outside Literature*. London: Routledge, 1990.

Berman, Bruce. "Nationalism, Ethnicity and Modernity: The Paradox of Mau Mau". *Canadian Journal of African Studies* 25 (1991): 181–205.

Bathwell A. Ogot. "Politics, Culture and Music in Central Kenya: A Study of Mau Mau Hymns". *Kenya Historical Review* 5.2 (1997): 275–286.

Cooper, Brenda. *To Play These Secrets Open: Evaluating African Writing*. Cape Town: David Philip, 1992.

Davis, Lennard, J. *Resisting Novels: Ideology and Fiction*. New York and London: Methuen, 1987.

Grindon, Gavin. "Subversion." *The Encyclopedia of Literary and Cultural Theory*. Ed. Ryan Michael. Hoboken: Blackwell Publishing, 2011.

Kanogo, Tabitha. *Squatters and the Roots of Mau Mau*. London: James Curry, 1987.

Kenyatta Jomo. *Suffering Without Bitterness: The Founding of the Kenyan Nation*. Nairobi: East African Publishing House, 1968.

Lonsdale, John. "Mau Mau of the Mind: Making Mau Mau and Making Kenya". *Journal of African History* 13 (1990): 393–421.

Maloba, Wunyabari, O. *Mau Mau and Kenya: An Analysis of Peasant Revolt*. Bloomington: Indiana University Press, 1993.

Maughan-Brown, David. *Land, Freedom and Fiction: History and Ideology in Kenya*. London: Zed Books, 1985.

Mbembe, Achille. "Provisional Notes on the Postcolony." *Africa* 62.1 (1992): 3–37.

Paterson, Teresa. "Mau Mau Remembered: How Narratives Transform and Reflect Power and Identity in Kenya". M.A. Thesis, Wesleyan University, 2016.

Ruark, Robert. *Something of Value*. New York: Buccaneer, 1955.

13 Grotesque Images of Colonial and Mau Mau Violence in Ngugi wa Thiong'o's *Weep Not, Child* and *A Grain of Wheat*

Benon Tugume

Introduction

The chapter presents a comparative analysis of the colonial era and Mau Mau violence, and the consequences that the two forms of violence have on personal relations of individual characters in Ngugi wa Thiongo's *Weep Not, Child* and *A Grain of Wheat*. The two novels depict, albeit artistically, the history of imperialism in Kenya, where land is of central concern. The anti-colonial violence carried out by Mau Mau as portrayed in *Weep Not, Child* and in *A Grain of Wheat* is essentially about freedom, identity, and restoration of land to the Africans. The focus in this chapter is on colonial violence of annexation of territory, the psychological violence of colonial education, and the anticolonial violence of the Mau Mau struggle for political independence. The anticolonial struggle is exploited by the colonial state to promote brute force, indiscriminate killings, and lawlessness. Ultimately, the chapter shows that what is more severe and lasting amidst the destruction of human life and property is the traumatic experience of violence and subsequent hopelessness of individual characters as portrayed in *Weep Not, Child* and *A Grain of Wheat*. Thus, the two texts discussed here have been selected not only because they are concerned with colonial experience in Kenya but also because of their portrayal of the atrocities and trauma that various characters experienced.

Ngugi, in the two novels, portrays the dispossession of Africans of their land by the colonial government in order to create land for white settlers to engage in commercial farming and industrial development. Consequently, landless Africans were forced to supply cheap labour in white-owned farms. As he puts it in *Homecoming,* "the white man rationalized this exploitation of African land and labor by claiming he was civilizing a primitive people" (26). The usurpation of land and the proletarization of Kenyan peasants were constant sources of tension between the Kenyans and the colonial state. Eventually, it became increasingly clear to the colonized Kenyans that the colonial government spoke the language of pure force. The violence unleashed by the colonialists sparked off counter-violence in the form of the Mau Mau, described in this chapter as revolutionary violence because the aim was to destroy the colonial state in order to usher into the country complete political and socio-economic change. The chapter starts by examining colonial violence under which it analyses physical and psychological violence executed by the colonial system and its effects on individual characters. Subsequently, the chapter looks at revolutionary violence and domestic violence, and their traumatic effects on characters.

Colonial Violence

Representation of colonial violence in Ngugi wa Thiong'o's fiction is manifested first, in the physical violence of forceful acquisition and occupation of territory using the gun, and second in the psychological violence of colonial education. Ngugi in *Decolonising the Mind* asserts: "Berlin of 1884 was effected through the sword and the bullet. But the night of the sword and the bullet was followed by the morning of the chalk and the blackboard. The physical violence of the battlefield was followed by the psychological violence of the classroom" (9). Whereas physical violence of the battlefield was to dispossess Africans of their ancestral land and force them into acceptance of colonial designs, the psychological violence of the classroom was meant to colonize the mind of the African child.

Physical Violence

As a form of colonial violence, physical violence in *Weep Not, Child* and *A Grain of Wheat,* is demonstrated in the eviction of Africans from their ancestral land to demarcated arid areas by the colonial state. The omniscient narrator in *Weep Not, Child* tells us that "you could tell the land of the black people because it was red, rough and sickly while the land of the white settlers was green and was not lacerated into small plots" (7). Only Africans who collaborated with colonialists were allowed to own land. Jacobo is the only African in the area who collaborated with the colonial state and is allowed to own land where he grows pyrethrum, making him rich compared to other Africans. Through the land alienation policies, the colonialist created new social classes different from the age group stratification of pre-colonial Africa.

The conflict in *Weep Not, Child* revolves among the families of Ngotho, Howlands, and Jacobo and is about who owns the piece of land that these three families occupy. Although Ngotho is a squatter on this land, he claims customary ownership because he inherited it from his father who occupied it before the British Colonial government annexed it. He says:

Mugo had told the people of the coming of the white man. He had warned the tribe. So the white man came and took the land. But at first not the whole of it. Then came the war. It was the first big war.

I was then young, a mere boy although circumcised. All of us were
taken by force. We made roads and cleared the forest to make it possible for the warring white man to move quickly. The war ended. We
came home worn out. We wanted to go back to the soil and court it
to yield. But 'Ngo'. The land was gone. My father and many others
had been moved from our ancestral lands. He died lonely, a poor
man waiting for the white man to go. (25)

The colonial government takes away land from Africans in order to create big chunks of land for white farmers and their African collaborators.
Mr. Howlands, the District Colonial officer, establishes a farm on this
land that belongs to Ngotho and employs him as *shamba* boy. Ngotho's
loss of land affects him and his family spiritually and materially. In the
African context, the land has from times immemorial been the key factor in the unity, cohesion, and strength of the family linking the living
and the dead. Ngotho's family had lived in harmony before the taking
away of his land, which is explained by the omniscient narrator:

The feeling of oneness was a thing that most distinguished Ngotho's
household from many other polygamous families. Njeri and Nyokabi went to the shamba or market together. Sometimes they agreed
amongst themselves that while one did that job, the other would do
this one. This was attributed to Ngotho, the centre of the home. For
if you have a stable centre, then the family would hold. (40)

The situation in Ngotho's family changes after land deprivation. His
demand for the restoration of land is not only meant to address his economic needs but also to regain the unity and stability of the family. The
dispossession deprives him of his sense of self and violates his integrity
as it brings him into collision with his wife and children. Ngotho feels
he has failed to play his customary and traditional role as husband and
father. Boro, his son, returns home from the Second World War only
to find the family land already occupied by Mr. Howlands. This makes
him lose confidence in his father and his generation for not resisting the
White man's land alienation scheme. He, therefore, opts to go to the
bush to fight the white man, despising Ngotho for his inaction to save
the family land.

In both cases, Ngotho has been robbed of the essence of his existence.
As the omniscient narrator states:

And yet he felt the loss of the land even more keenly than Boro,
for him it was a spiritual loss. When a man was severed from the
land of his ancestors where would he sacrifice to the creator? How
could he come into contact with the founder of the tribe, Gikuyu
and Mumbi. (74)

Ngotho defines ownership of the land by tracing his ancestry to Gikuyu and Mumbi, the founders of the tribe. His special relationship with the land is beyond economic, it is both cultural and spiritual. The land is sacred and thus it defines his existence. Denying Ngotho his land and his sense of attachment to it is equal to renouncing his spirituality and obliterating him as a human being. Although Ngotho loses his land, he continues tending the crops on it hoping that one day he would recover it. For Ngotho's white employer, Howlands, land was like his god, as the narrator informs us that "he worships the farm he has created, the land he has tamed" (75). Ironically, this land unites Howlands and Ngotho:

> Ngotho felt responsible for whatever happened on this land. He owed it to the dead, the living and the unborn of his line, to keep guard over this *shamba*. Mr. Howlands always felt a certain amount of victory whenever he walked through it all. He alone was responsible for taming this unoccupied wilderness. (37)

Howlands claims the land by right of conquest. He is an occupier responsible for taming what he calls 'unoccupied wilderness' while Ngotho has a spiritual attachment to the land by birth and heritage. For Ngotho, the presence of Howlands reminds him of his spiritual loss and the subsequent poverty that engulfs his family. His endless waiting for the white man to go combined with Boro's criticism drives him into anxiety and eventually despair. His confrontation with Jacobo demonstrates his anger and frustration towards the situation the coming of colonialism had created in a once peaceful land. Ngotho dies on the same night that his son Boro kills Howlands, demonstrating that land alienation begot violence whose results were undesirable.

Similarly, in *A Grain of Wheat*, Ngugi portrays the process of land alienation in colonial Kenya. Through flash back, he depicts the magnanimity of the Gikuyu towards the first white man by giving him a place to build a shelter. As the narrator says: "they gave him, the stranger with a scalded skin a place to erect a temporary shelter. Hut complete, the stranger put up another building yards away. This he called the house of God where people could go for worship and sacrifice" (10). Eventually the white man wins more converts and acquires more land to meet the growing needs of his position. The elders protest this action but he ignores them. This prompts Waiyaki and other warriors to take up arms, which is the earliest sign of counter-violence in the text. Waiyaki's resistance which is eventually defeated by the white man through the use of the gun is precursory to the Mau Mau war led by Kihika.

The colonialists used the Bible and the gun to subjugate Africans. The Bible was used to soften the people to accept colonialism as an act of God's providence while the gun was used to force those who appeared unconvinced into the colonial situation. The successful eviction of

Africans from their land using the gun results in effective occupation and entrenchment of colonial rule. In order to maintain a tight grip on the territory, the colonial government introduces an educational system which is meant to change people's perception about colonialists.

Psychological Violence

Psychological violence in this article is understood as the forceful inculcation of Western culture into the mind of the African child through the medium of English language. This is carried out through the educational system that the colonialists introduce. The purpose of psychological violence is to imprison the mind of the African child because in the mind of the colonialist, to use Ngugi's words in *Decolonising the Mind*, "economic and political control can never be complete or effective without mental control" (16). The white man establishes a school in the two texts as an ideological centre meant to hold the mind of the African captive and make the conquest and exploitation permanent. The main vehicle through which this policy is effected is the school curriculum. The curriculum is designed to glorify Western culture and take African culture like a museum piece for amusement. Emphasis is put on the study of the English language because first, the colonialists want English to be the official language of communication, and second, the English language is a carrier of Western culture. Through the use of English language children are taken further and further from themselves to the white man's land, from their world to the white man's world.

Ngugi in *Weep Not, Child* depicts the administration of corporal punishment to children by teachers in order to force them to learn the English language. Teacher Lucia is an epitome of terror to pupils. The description by the omniscient narrator of Lucia's appearance while administering corporal punishment to students shows that she is an authoritarian teacher:

> The teacher wore a white blouse and a green skirt ... Njoroge however, feared her, when two days later she beat a boy, whack, whack! (bring the other hand) whack, whack! The stick broke into bits. Njoroge could feel the pain. It was as if it was being communicated to him without physical contact. The teacher looked ugly while she punished. (14)

Njoroge is a newcomer to the school. The young boy who bullies Njoroge is transferring aggression to force him to do his will. The young boy has learnt from teachers the use of force on weaker human beings to get what they want in life. The use of violence in the school environment has a psychological impact on Njoroge, who now fears Teacher Lucia and learns his lessons with fear not to make a mistake as this dialogue illustrates:

TEACHER: What are you doing?
NJOROGE: (thinly) You are standing up.
TEACHER: (Slightly cross) What are you doing?
NJOROGE: (clears his throat, voice thinner still) You are standing up.
TEACHER: No, no! (to the class) Come on. What are you, you doing?
NJOROGE: was very confused. Hands were raised up all around him. He felt more and more foolish so that in the end he gave up the very attempt to answer
TEACHER: (pointing to Mwihaki) stand up. What are you doing?
MWIHAKI: (head bent on to one shoulder) I am standing up.
TEACHER: Good. Now Njoroge. What is she doing?
NJOROGE: I am standing up
    The class giggled
TEACHER: (Very annoyed) Class, what is she doing?
CLASS: (singing) You are standing up
TEACHER: (still very angry) I am asking you…what is she doing?
CLASS: (afraid, quietly singing) you are standing up
TEACHER: Look here you stupid and lazy fools. How long do you take to catch things? Didn't we go over all this yesterday? If you come tomorrow and find that you make a single mistake I'll punish all of you severely. (45)

Ngugi depicts the teacher as an authoritarian who does not take time to get to the learner's level. The pupils feel intimidated and the fear of punishment in case of a mistake while learning makes Njoroge and other children feel nervous while learning. Teacher Lucia beats them whenever they make mistakes; for instance, she beats the whole class for making mistakes while greeting the European woman visitor:

When the European went away, the children regretted the incident. Lucia beat them to cool her rage and shame. In future, they were to know the difference between 'a morning' and 'an afternoon' and that between 'a sir' and 'a madam'. (47)

As an African teacher serving in the colonial educational system, Lucia is herself dissatisfied and insecure before the European visitor and makes the children suffer because of her own job insecurity. She uses the weapon of coercion, a familiar colonial weapon, to force the children to do her will. She provides no space for any questioning by the children for the assertions she is making. The school system is modelled on the colonial model of unquestioning subservience.

Similarly, Ngugi in *A Grain of Wheat* portrays Teacher Muniu using the Bible to preach against African culture to African Children. He calls the circumcision of women a heathen custom. Kihika challenges him by saying that the Bible does not say so. But as Kihika says it, "Some of the boys hid their faces, excited yet fearing that the wrath of the teacher might reach them" (86). This does not go down well with the teacher and the church elders as the omniscient narrator states:

> 'For who are we to say that the word from God's mouth is a lie?' his deep voice boomed across the building. However after discussing Sunday's incident with the church elders, he had decided to give the boy a chance to save his soul. The teacher had therefore decided to whip the boy ten times on his naked buttocks in front of the whole assembly-this for the sake of the boy's own soul and of all others present. After the beating, Kihika would have to say thank you to the teacher and also recant his words of last Sunday. (87)

The teacher contemplates meting out corporal punishment to communicate to Kihika and the rest of the children the supremacy of the teacher's opinions and beliefs. The punishment is also meant to scare children from asking questions and so kill their cognitive abilities to question the supposed sanctity of western education and Christianity. Kihika rejects this punishment whose purpose is to humiliate him and destroy his personal dignity. He therefore abandons school when it becomes a centre of dogmatism. With this experience as a young boy and having learnt from the elders the history of colonial rule in Kenya with its attendant land alienation scheme, Kihika decides to take up arms to fight colonial rule.

Revolutionary Violence

Ngugi in *Weep Not, Child* and *A Grain of Wheat* depicts in artistic form, the history of the Mau Mau armed resistance to foreign domination in Kenya. Because colonial rule relies on violence, the struggle for Kenya's independence by the Mau Mau inevitably becomes what Fanon calls "a violent phenomenon" (27). The aim of the Mau Mau Movement was to replace the colonial masters with indigenous leaders and change the colonial social structure. Frantz Fanon argues, "The native who decides to put the programme into practice is ready for violence at all times. It is clear to him that this narrow world strewn with prohibitions, can only be called in question by absolute violence" (29). Fanon's theory of violence is evident in the choice of characters in the two novels. The main characters are revolutionary and speak the language of violence. For example, Kihika in *A Grain of Wheat* carries out a massive awareness campaign among peasants and workers in order to arouse class consciousness and prepare them for an armed confrontation with the colonial state.

Ngugi draws much of the leadership of the Mau Mau from Second World War veterans such as Boro in *Weep, Not Child*, and General R and Lt Koinandu in *A Grain of Wheat*. These returnees from the Second World War participated in the struggle for freedom in other parts of the world and therefore they find it justifiable to struggle to liberate their own country. Ngugi celebrates the Mau Mau heroes and their struggle for Kenya's independence. In an interview published in a book edited by Sander and Lindfors Ngugi says:

> We, as writers, as historians, as Kenyan intellectuals must be able to tell these stories, or histories, or history of heroic resistance to foreign domination by Kenyan people. Doing so, we shall not be looking at ourselves as people who were weak in the face of foreign domination, threats, aggression, but as a people whose history shines with the grandeur, if you like, heroic resistance and achievement of the Kenyan people. (87)

Ngugi's *Weep Not, Child* and *A Grain of Wheat* portray the tumultuous and violent period in Kenya against colonial rule. As he further states, "The highest peak of this heroic tradition of resistance is the armed struggle initiated and carried out by the Kenya Land Freedom Army (KLFA), otherwise widely known as Mau Mau" (97). This essentially is a war about land, identity, and freedom. The question of the restoration of land to the Africans defines the major aim of this struggle for independence.

The Mau Mau revolutionary violence in *A Grain of Wheat* revolves around the immersion of character in a historical setting. This is because individual characters play a very important part in shaping social and political movements. Ngugi lauds Kihika for his unwavering determination to mobilize a corporate will to achieve social justice. Kihika ably articulates peoples' problems that accrued from colonialism and abhors the reactionary character of the colonial state. He urges people to reject Christians' hypocrisy that the dispossessed Africans should lay their treasures in heaven while the white man lays his on earth. He calls upon people to unite and make sacrifices in order to regain their land. To justify the struggle against colonial rule, Kihika refers to the history of resistance to imperialism in Africa and other parts of the world. He argues that through sacrifice Mahatma Gandhi won freedom for the people of India. His awareness campaign, courage, and farsightedness recruit all kinds of people into the struggle. Women such as Wambui and Njeri and the disabled Gatu play important roles in the struggle. Wambui participates by carrying bullets to freedom fighters in the bush. Out of love for Kihika's insight, Njeri joins him in the bush. She is later shot dead in the battlefield. Gatu while in detention comforts and keeps up the detainees' spirit of resistance by narrating to them the imprisonment of

Gandhi, the American war of independence, and Napoleon's campaigns in Europe.

In spite of the numerical strength of the oppressed, Karanja in *A Grain of Wheat* doubts the ability of the Mau Mau to defeat the colonialists. He tells Kihika: "They have got guns and bombs, see how they whipped Hitler" (87). But Kihika responds: "it is a question of unity...the example of India is there before our noses" (88). As Frantz Fanon asserts:

> There are individuals who are convinced of the ineffectiveness of violent methods; for them, there is no doubt about it, every attempt to break colonial oppression by force is a hopeless effort, an attempt at suicide, because in the innermost recesses of their brains the settler's tanks and aero planes occupy a huge place. When they are told 'Action must be taken', they see bombs raining down on them, armoured cars coming at them on every path, machine-gunning and police action...and they sit quiet. They are beaten from the start... They have remained in the same childhood position. (49)

The argument Fanon makes in the above passage is that in the struggle against colonial rule, there are individuals who have been terrorized by state machinery and therefore feel powerless to change the status quo. Kihika abhors this kind of defeatism as expressed by Karanja and insists that revolutionary violence negates the element of fear. He launches the Mau Mau armed rebellion knowing that violence liberates the oppressed.

The Mau Mau insurgency against colonial rule prompts the colonialists to use brute force to quell the insurgency because in their belief Africans are savages who only understand the language of violence. In Sicherman's *Ngugi wa Thiong'o: The making of a Rebel*, Baldwin, the only American who fought the Mau Mau war describes Mau Mau fighters as " a gutless bunch, 'bloody wogs' wild beasts of the forests, diseased animals who could be cured only by death" (337). Ion Leigh in *In the Shadow of Mau Mau* reiterates:

> Today they are fighting not for self-government which to most of them is merely a word whose significance they do not understand but because it is their nature to fight and because they are ready to listen to those who urge them to fight. The fact that they are committing the most savage and brutal murders is simply because brutality is part of the native character. It is prevalent in all Africans. (9)

By referring to the fighters as beasts, savages, these whites are asserting racial superiority over Africans. With this perception, the colonialists eliminate Mau Mau freedom fighters and suspects without showing any remorse. Mugo, in reference to the torture and death of political prisoners by the colonial officers at Rira camp in *A Grain of Wheat* says to

Mumbi, "Now I know that a Mzungu is not a man – always remember that he is a devil – a devil" (184). Mugo repeats the noun 'devil' to metaphorically refer to the viciousness of the white man's killings in Kenya. It is interesting that Mugo subverts the image of the devil utilized in the colonizing mission to refer to the ways of Africans and applies it to the colonialist. The intensification of Mau Mau insurgency against the colonial state prompts the government to institute curfew laws that limit people's movement and assembly. As the narrator in *Weep Not, Child* states:

> No one could tell when he might be arrested for breaking the curfew. You could not even move across the court yard at night. Fires were put out early for fear that any light would attract the attention of those who might be lurking outside. It was said that some European soldiers were catching people at night, and having taken them to the forest would release them and ask them to find their way back home. But when their backs were turned they would be shot dead in cold blood. (84)

Under curfew laws, the entire population is gripped with fear as innocent people are picked and killed in cold blood by soldiers and home guards. There is an escalation of police repression, imprisonment of suspected insurgents and indiscriminate killings of people. The colonial government uses brutality and violence as a means of suppressing a people's will to liberation. The war situation is exploited by the oppressor to promote lawlessness, brute force, indiscriminate killing. Killing however is not only done by the colonial officials. The Mau Mau fighters too kill. But whereas the colonial military officers and home guards wantonly kill innocent civilians and suspected Mau Mau loyalists, the Mau Mau freedom fighters only target the enemies, the representatives of the colonial state such as D.O Howlands and Jacobo, the home guard. In *Weep Not, Child*, the Mau Mau insurgency is associated with the darkness that falls and destroys Njogore's dreams of attaining education to salvage the family from poverty and landlessness.

Ngugi's ideological transformation to a revolutionary Marxist-Fanonist ideologue who believes in revolutionary violence as the highest form of struggle to dismantle the oppressive system as is witnessed in the character traits he assigns the Mau Mau leaders beginning with Kihika in *A Grain of Wheat*. Kihika is an insightful and dynamic character capable of taking on leadership challenges in post-independence Kenya. His close association with elders enables him to learn and discern the history of colonial Kenya. He is intelligent in that whereas the colonizer uses the Bible to justify subjugation, he uses it to champion liberation. He is a great orator who emphasizes the need for armed struggle against colonial oppressors.

Kihika argues that the days of organizing processions are over because these processions did not restore their alienated land. Instead, the people were met with the animal brutality of the police who shot many people to death in cold blood. He emphasizes action backed up by sacrifice in order for them to get freedom. In fact, he globalizes the Mau Mau struggle for independence when he places it in the context of the successful armed struggles for independence in Burma, Egypt, Palestine, and America. He justifies his flight to the bush by saying to Mugo, "We don't kill anybody...We are not murderers. We are not hangmen-like Robson-killing men and women without cause or purpose...We only hit back. You are struck on the left cheek. You turn the right cheek" (191). Kihika's decision to go to the bush is premised on the context that colonial rule is imposed, sustained, and legitimized by violence and therefore the inevitability of violence as an antidote to colonial brutality must be used where all other means have failed. He launches a guerrilla campaign against the white man because of the oppressor's superior weapons which make conventional warfare impossible.

In retaliation to the white man's oppression, Kihika and his band of freedom fighters target and kill whites and their African collaborators. He therefore attacks and destroys the Mahee police post, shoots D.O Robson dead, and eliminates traitors such as Chief Muruithia and Reverend Jackson of the revivalist movement for preaching against the Mau Mau freedom fighters. These actions by the freedom fighters prompt the colonial government to declare a state of emergency that denies individuals the right of movement and assembly. The state of emergency marks the period of violence between the loyalists of the colonial order and those opposed to it. Thabai village is completely destroyed as people's houses are set on fire and the people forced into concentration camps: "...old Thabai village had tumbled down: mud, soot and ashes marked the spots where the various huts once stood" (142). Gikonyo's family is one of the victims of this heinous act as Mumbi watches helplessly her husband being led to the detention camp and her house set on fire. She together with other women, children, and the elderly are driven into concentration camps in order for the colonial government to deny freedom fighters support in terms of food and information. Gikonyo, Gatu, Mugo and other able-bodied men who are suspected to have taken the oath of unity with the freedom fighters are driven into detention camps in order to force them to denounce the oath and as Ngugi states in *Detained: A Writer's Prison Diary* "instill into a community of millions the culture of fear and the slave aesthetic of abject submission to tyranny" (49). Life in both concentration camps and in detention camps is characterized by a high level of violence. Soldiers and home guards in the concentration camps beat up people to dig the trench as Mumbi recounts to Mugo:

> The trench was to surround the whole village. After you were taken
> away, beating was not isolated to one person here, another one there.
> Soldiers and home guards entered the trench and beat anybody who

raised their back and slowed down in any way...We were prisoners in the village and the soldiers built their camps all round to prevent any escape. We went without food. The cry of children was terrible to hear. The new D.O did not mind the cries. He even permitted soldiers to pick women and carry them to their tents. (144)

The soldiers and home guards are permitted to pick women and carry them to the tents for sex. The women are raped because they are forced into sex against their will. One day, as women were digging the trench that was to surround the concentration camp, one of the home guards beat up Wambuku to death just because she rejected his sexual advances. The omniscient narrator says that Wambuku, "...refused, so it is said the advances of this particular home guard who got his chance for revenge during the trench. She never recovered from that beating and died three months later, in pregnancy" (137). This particular home guard stands out to represent the callousness, remorselessness, and inhumanity of colonial chiefs. He uses his position to exact vengeance on the innocent woman. Wambuku's death ultimately symbolizes her resistance to the dictatorship of the colonial system as well as an assertion of her sexual rights as a woman.

In detention camps where men are confined, the detainees are subjected to forced labour, tortured in order to confess the oath. Gatu, one of the detainees is hanged at Yala camp because he had become a symbol of collective resistance by preaching sacrifice and resilience to the detainees. At Rira Camp detainees are subjected to terrible beatings when they go on strike and demand the right to be treated as political detainees, not criminals. Eleven men died in that single night. In fact, a lot of innocent lives are lost in this war of independence. As Sicherman states:

The (settler) was given power (under emergency regulations) to "shoot to kill" any African who refused to stop when challenged. Here again who was to say whether the victim was innocent, guilty, frightened, chased away or simply shot? Dead bodies do not speak... In a population equal to a fifth of that of Scotland the forces had been killing twelve people every day, seven days a week, for three and half years. In the process they put one person in every twenty five into a concentration camp (where land owners can get them for slave labor), destroyed homes...(and) whole villages, killed cattle, sheep and goats, confiscated vehicles and other property, raped women after arresting their husbands and allowed thugs both white and black, to torture, kill and pay off grudges on the innocent population. (366)

Ngugi describes a similar situation in *A Grain of Wheat*. The dumb and deaf Gitongo is shot dead in cold blood as soldiers and home guards shoot indiscriminately to enforce emergency laws. The irony is that soldiers declare him a Mau Mau terrorist. These extra-judicial killings continue unabated but they do not deter Kihika and his freedom fighters from intensifying the struggle for freedom. Kihika is finally captured by the enemy and hanged in public after being betrayed by Mugo whom he presumed was a comrade not knowing Mugo was a psychopath. Thompson, the District Officer who hangs him displays raw terror to discourage others from waging war against the colonial state. But the attempt by the oppressor to instil fear and break Mau Mau resistance fails because the armed struggle has reached a stage which Fanon calls "the point of no return. Always it is marked off by a huge and all inclusive repression which engulfs all sectors of the colonized people" (70). The deployment of terror by D.O. Thompson does not yield results instead the situation worsens.

Having failed to cow down the restive masses, the colonial government grants independence to Kenya. This is political independence which General R. doubts is likely to lead to the full realization of democratic governance. He sounds this fear because he has seen that those who are in charge of political parties are the African elite who took refuge in schools and not Mau Mau freedom fighters who went to the forest to fight for freedom. As Gikandi asserts: "while decolonization seemed to function as the eschatological moment of revelation foretold by the cultural nationalists in the 1920s, it was to bring with it renewed doubts about the exact nature and meaning of this revelation and thus the possibility of its betrayal" (28). As Appiah observes:

> The national bourgeoisie that took on the baton of rationalization, industrialization, bureaucratization in the name of nationalism, turned out to be a Kleptocracy. Their enthusiasm of nativism was a rationalization of their urge to keep the national bourgeoisie of other nations – and particularly the powerful industrialized nations – out of their way. (150)

Instead of seeing independence as a moment of closure of the heroic and justifiable past, General R. is driven to a sense of bitterness and desolation by the betrayal of the ideals for which they fought. The betrayal is committed by the leaders of national political parties who have assumed the mantle of leadership at independence. The political parties are elitist organizations which do not aim at ushering in the newly independent country complete socio-economic and political change. As Frantz Fanon asserts:

> The national political parties never lay stress upon necessity of a trial of armed strength for the good reason that their objective is not the radical overthrowing of the system. Pacifists and legalists, they are in fact partisans of order...On the specific question of violence,

the elite are ambiguous. They are violent in their words and reformist in their attitude. (46)

Fanon's argument above reinforces General R's scepticism about the preparedness of the leaders of post-independence Kenya to overhaul the entire colonial superstructure, restore the land to the people, and provide social services. The leaders are reformist because they are products of Western education that opens their eyes to institutions in which capitalism survives. As a result, they cannot see alternatives to the very shrines created by forces of imperialism. Eventually the post-independence leaders form an alliance with the former colonial masters this time to indirectly continue the economic exploitation of human and material resources of the former colonies.

Domestic Violence

Both the colonial violence of land alienation and the anti-colonial violence of the Mau Mau disrupt the stability of African families. Ngotho in *Weep Not, Child* stripped of his manhood when his land is alienated by Mr. Howlands turns into a brute by demanding respect as a man and head of the family. The conflict between him and his wife Nyokabi about the impending strike for better wages reveals his intolerance of the wife's views that reject his participation as this dialogue shows:

'I must be a man in my house'
'Yes – be a man and lose a job'
'I shall do whatever I like. I have never taken orders from a woman'
'We shall starve...'
'You starve! This strike is important for the black people. We shall get bigger salaries'
'What is black people to us when we starve?'
'Shut that mouth'
'But he is paying you money. What if the strike fails?'
Don't woman me!' he shouted hysterically... Ngotho could bear it no longer...
He slapped her on the face. (52–53)

Nyokabi's fears expressed in the above dialogue stem from the need for survival. She has despaired and unlike her husband who has future expectations, she believes the little money her husband receives from settler Howlands is enough to keep the family going. Ngotho's violent reaction to Nyokabi's challenge is a manifestation of anxiety. He has waited for too long without a solution to the problem of landlessness and exploitation by Mr. Howlands. Ngotho's son, Boro has always criticized him for his inaction against land alienation by Mr. Howlands. This criticism has already made him nervous and Nyokabi's argument adds insult to the injury. Ngotho doubts himself and therefore he beats Nyokobi in order to reassert his authority and manhood in the family.

In *A Grain of Wheat* Ngugi portrays the impact of Mau Mau insurgency on the family of Gikonyo. Under emergency laws, Gikonyo is separated from his dear wife Mumbi and taken to the detention camp. Having denounced the oath of unity, Gikonyo is released and returns home to find Mumbi with Karanja's child. Mumbi has betrayed the marital bond and therefore life in the family changes as Gikonyo keeps to himself and hates his wife and the child: "kill her and the child...end all misery" (114). He does not ask what type of life the family went through; he kept dreaming, expecting everything not to have changed. The crisis in the family comes to a climax when the child comes running eagerly to tell Gikonyo a good story grandma has told him. Gikonyo with hatred sends the boy staggering and he falls down. This action infuriates Mumbi and words come tossing out of her,

> ...they came in floods, filling her mouth so that she could hardly articulate them. Shut your mouth, woman? He shouted at her, also standing.
> 'You think I am an orphan do you?'
> 'You think the gates of my parents' hut would be shut against me if I left this tomb?
> 'I will make you shut this mouth of a whore' he cried out slapping her on the left cheek and then on the right. (168)

The confrontation between Gikonyo and Mumbi as depicted in the above passage shows that each of the two is arrogant before the other. Mumbi calls the household "tomb" because Gikonyo has shut all avenues of communication between the two. Gikonyo uses the word "woman" to remind Mumbi of her status in the family. She is not supposed to speak to him as if they are equal. He also refers to her as a "whore" because she gave birth to a child outside her marriage. In effect, Gikonyo is re-echoing patriarchal ideology that conditions a woman to produce children only with her husband or else she becomes a whore. Eventually Gikonyo slaps her in order to assert his authority over her. The result of this violence is the disintegration of the family as Mumbi goes back to her parents. She reunites with her husband on the day of independence after Gikonyo has realized that war affected everybody and each person carries a guilty conscience including himself because he betrayed the Movement by denouncing the oath.

Conclusion

Ngugi wa Thiong'o's novels analysed in this chapter are historical works of art set in colonial Kenya. They portray in realistic detail the atrocities committed by the colonial state against Kenyans. The novels contain a mixture of fictional and historical characters that were involved in the conflict between the colonial state and Mau Mau freedom fighters. Like Ngotho's family in *Weep Not, Child*, Ngugi's family was caught up in the Mau Mau war. Boro in the same novel is the fictional version of Ngugi's brother Wallace Mwangi who joined the Mau Mau war against colonial rule. The events portrayed in the novels and discussed in this chapter such as colonial violence of land alienation, the psychological violence of colonial education, the Mau Mau insurgency against colonial rule, the state of emergency and the imposition of curfew laws, the atrocities committed by the colonial police and home guards in a bid to suppress the insurgency such as torture, indiscriminate killing of innocent civilians, sexual violence are fictional versions of what really happened in Kenya during the colonial period. Ngugi employs imagery to humanize these historical facts and render violence more perceptible to the reader.

Works Cited

Appiah, Kwame Anthony. *In My Father's House: Africa in the Philosophy of Culture*. Oxford: Oxford University Press, 1992.

Barber Karim. "African Language, Literature and Post-Colonial Criticism". *Research in African Literatures* 26.4 (1998), Indiana University Press.

Cook, David, and Okenimkpe Michael. *Ngugi wa Thiongo: An Exploration of His Writings*. 2nd ed. Nairobi: Heinemam 1997.

Fanon, Frantz. *The Wretched of the Earth*. Harmondsworth: Penguin, 1967.

Gikandi, Simon. *Ngugi wa Thiongo*. London: Cambridge University Press, 2009.

Leigh, Ion. *In the Shadow of Mau Mau*. London: W.H. Allen, 1954.

Ngugi wa Thiongo. *Weep Not, Child*. London: Heinemann, 1964.

———. *A Grain of Wheat*. London: Heinemann, 1967.

———. *Home coming*. London: Heinemann, 1972.

———. *Detained: A Writer's Prison Dairy*. London: Heinemann, 1981.

———. *Decolonising the Mind: The Politics of Language in African Literature*. London: James Currey, 1986.

———. *Dreams in a Time of War: A Childhood Memoir*. Nairobi: Kenway, 2010.

Ogude, James. *Ngugi's Novels and African History: Narrating the Nation*. Sterling, VI: Pluto Press 1999.

Sander, Reinhard, and Lindfors Bernth, eds. *Ngugi wa Thiongo Speaks: Interviews with the Kenyan Writer*. Oxford: James Currey, 2006.

Sicherman, Carol. *Ngugi wa Thiongo: The Making of a Rebel: A Source book on Kenyan Literature and Resistance*. London: Hans zell, 1990.

Simatei, Tirop. "Colonial Violence, Postcolonial Violations: Violence, Landscape, and Memory in Kenya Fiction". *Research in African Literatures* 36.2 (2005), Indiana University Press.

14 Emergency-era Trauma in Ngũgĩ wa Thiong'o's *A Grain of Wheat*

Gĩchingiri Ndĩgĩrĩgĩ

Introduction

The narrator in Ngũgĩ's *A Grain of Wheat* begins chapter nine with these prophetic words: "Learned men will, no doubt, dig into the troubled times which we in Kenya underwent, and maybe sum up the lesson in a phrase. Why, let us ask them, did the incident in Rira Camp capture the imagination of the world?" (127). This chapter digs into these euphemistically labelled "troubled times" by focusing on Mugo, a character traumatized by the detention experience at Rira. The chapter probes Mugo's struggles to find a frame of reference that would make three overlapping layers of his traumatic experience comprehensible, underlining the inadequacy of a phrase to sum them up. It further explores a social turn in trauma witnessing by his connection to a community of fellow victims, in the text. The chapter concludes by pointing out that the public performance that Mugo is forced to stage on Independence Day lifts the burden of guilt for Kihika's betrayal without articulating the experiences that produced victims still acting out their trauma and crying to be heard.

Giorgio Agamben reminds us that although survivors of traumatic experiences may remember, "the value of testimony lies essentially in what it lacks; at its center it contains something that cannot be borne witness to and that discharges the survivors of authority. The 'true' witnesses, the 'complete witnesses', are those who did not bear witness and could not bear witness" (*Remnants of Auschwitz*, 34) because they are dead. Still, in a nod to Dori Laub's path-breaking research on trauma witnessing, Agamben amplifies difficulties of bearing witness to trauma by survivors. As Laub himself states, reality continues to elude the subject who lives in the grip of trauma and unwillingly undergoes its ceaseless repetitions and re-enactments: "The traumatic event, although real, took place outside the parameters of 'normal' reality, such as causality, sequence, place and time. The trauma is thus an event that has no beginning, no ending, no before, no during and no after" ('Bearing' 69). Agamben himself argues "language, in order to bear witness, must give way to non-language in order to show the impossibility of bearing witness" (39). These descriptions fit Mugo in Ngũgĩ wa Thiong'o's *A Grain of Wheat*, an obviously traumatized victim of the repressive measures taken to contain large populations in Central Kenya during the British colonial government's imposed State of Emergency in the mid-1950s. Tens of thousands of Kenyans were trucked to detention camps like Hola, the fictionalized Rira Camp where the 'incident' referenced in the quotation above took place. Eleven political detainees were bludgeoned to death there in 1959.

Playing off Agamben and Laub, this chapter argues that Mugo is a paradoxical victim given his initial complicity with his victimizers when he betrays Kihika, the character who would qualify as Agamben's true witness. The chapter closely reads three significant overlapping traumatic experiences Mugo undergoes: first as a child living with an abusive aunt, second when Kihika intrudes into his space and Mugo is forced to make the difficult choice to betray him, which ironically leads to Mugo being brutalized by John Thompson, and a third when he is brutalized in detention for not confessing to an oath that he did not take. However, this trauma has lain latent in Mugo, manifested only in his avoidance and withdrawal from the world. The community's invitation to speak at the Independence Day celebrations triggers memories that force Mugo to finally confront his trauma. By accepting responsibility for Kihika's betrayal, Mugo and his judges participate in a juridical process with moral overtones. While Mugo's confession essentially supplies the missing testimony regarding the missing narrative behind Kihika's betrayal, and satisfies the juridical need by the local community that was traumatized by the enforced participation in the spectacle of his hanging (17), the story of detention is untold, and remains an event without a true witness. This chapter concludes that Mugo's testimony is significant for its 'social turn', in that he moves from his alienation into some sort of traumatized community seeking to be heard. This move illuminates social and political underpinnings of his traumatic experiences precipitated by the colonial state crisis and deprivileges the talking that helps individuals by forcing them to turn inwards for the liberating force. The social turn pays keen attention to the social world that produces individual and collective traumatic experiences and foregrounds collective approaches to overcoming trauma.

In *Weep Not, Child, A Grain of Wheat, Petals of Blood, Matigari*, and in almost all his essays, Ngũgĩ has persistently evoked the trauma caused by the state of emergency in 1950s. The most noteworthy fictional characters who best embody that trauma are Njoroge (*WNC*), Mugo (*AGOW*), and Abdulla (*POB*). A discussion of Mugo's character allows us to see Ngũgĩ's most sustained handling of traumatized characters, and he amplifies Mugo's trauma as part of a larger social trauma that has gone unprocessed. While it is tempting to see Mugo as either a traitor or a victim, Ngũgĩ complicates his characterization by presenting him in his duality. Before discussing the novel, however, a brief discussion of the related conditions of trauma and Post Traumatic Stress Disorder (PTSD) is appropriate.

Cathy Caruth indicates that "[i]n its most general definition, trauma describes an overwhelming experience of sudden, or catastrophic events, in which the response to the event occurs in the often delayed, and uncontrolled repetitive occurrence of hallucinations and other intrusive phenomena", of which the soldier's numbed response to death around him and his re-experience of it in nightmares is the most recognizable symptomatic image ('Unclaimed Experience', 181). The American Psychological Association describes trauma as "an emotional response to a terrible event like an accident, rape or natural disaster. Immediately after the event, shock and denial are typical. Longer term reactions include unpredictable emotions, flashbacks, strained relationships and even physical symptoms like headaches or nausea" (Web). While these symptoms may occur immediately, Ngũgĩ presents characters who are dealing with repressed memories that more easily fit under the label of PTSD. The American Psychiatric Association describes PTSD as "a psychiatric disorder that can occur in people who have experienced or witnessed a traumatic event such as a natural disaster, a serious accident, a terrorist act, war/combat, rape or other violent personal assault. PTSD is a real illness that causes real suffering" (Web). Further, they isolate four categories of symptoms that may be inter-related:

i   Intrusive thoughts such as repeated, involuntary memories; distressing dreams; or flashbacks of the traumatic event. Flashbacks may be so vivid that people feel they are re-living the traumatic experience or seeing it before their eyes.

ii Avoiding reminders of the traumatic event may include avoiding people, places, activities, objects, and situations that bring on distressing memories. People may try to avoid remembering or thinking about the traumatic event. They may resist talking about what happened or how they feel about it.

iii Negative thoughts and feelings may include ongoing and distorted beliefs about oneself or others; ongoing fear, horror, anger, guilt, or shame; lesser interest in activities previously enjoyed; or feeling detached or estranged from others.

iv Arousal and reactive symptoms may include being irritable and having angry outbursts; behaving recklessly or in a self-destructive way; being easily startled; or having problems concentrating or sleeping. (Web)

A cursory review of the four symptoms given above reveals that Mugo suffers from all of them. All the major characters in the novel exhibit the same symptoms, though in varying degrees, attesting to the communal nature of emergency-era trauma calls for public witnessing that would form the core of the Truth and Reconciliation Commission hearings in South Africa and Rwanda.

From the beginning, we see that Mugo suffers from intrusive thoughts and distressing dreams (3), and his effort to repress these produce disinterest in the farming work that previously gave him joy (5). Mugo is a victim of an abusive aunt (4–5), and that abuse engendered feelings of shame, inadequacy, and withdrawal but Kihika misread this withdrawal as a sign of his trustworthiness. Intrusion by the village elders produces arousal marked by his 'unproductive' trip to the latrine (9). In their presence, he stutters and is unable to concentrate (20), and the final visit arouses negative feelings that find vent in his seemingly inexplicable horror that the villagers were asking him to celebrate the man "he had so treacherously betrayed", a revelation he willingly makes to himself in his interior monologue (65). Mugo reacts with distorted feelings when Gikonyo shares his Emergency-era trauma in detention, thinking that Gikonyo was trying to trap him into revealing his guilt for Kihika's betrayal by telling him the story of his own betrayal of the oath of allegiance to the freedom struggle. But after listening to Mumbi relive the trauma in the same Emergency village in which Mugo insulated himself – Mumbi paints the picture of imminent annihilation (139) – Mugo belatedly re-experiences his trauma: he feels "an irrational terror" after he leaves Mumbi, and he is hyper-vigilant as he walks (167). He reflects: "Yesterday, this morning, before Mumbi told her story, the huts had run by him, and never sang of the past" but now that Mumbi's story "had cracked open his dulled inside and released imprisoned thoughts and feelings" (167), he experiences the vivid flashbacks that characterize PTSD. He sees "the white face" of the man who tortured him in detention, the barbed wire enclosing the detention camps, death, he hears the sound of the galloping horses' hooves that he fears, and all these involuntary memories merge into an image that concretizes "the terror of an undesired discovery" (167).

Unlike many people who suffer from unresolved trauma, Mugo cannot resist the urge to return to the site of one of his traumatic experiences rather than avoid the painful reminders. As Caruth suggests in her reading of Freud, "[t]he experience of trauma, the fact of latency, would thus seem to consist, not in the forgetting of a reality that can hence never be fully known; but in an inherent latency within the experience itself ..." (187). In shock, the traumatized person appears to forget the event as it happens, and then relives it so that

> it is only in and through its inherent forgetting that it is first experienced at all... For history to be a history of trauma means that it is referential precisely to the extent that it is not fully perceived as it occurs; or to put it somewhat differently, that a history can be grasped only in the very inaccessibility of its occurrence. (187)

Not having been fully conscious during the actual event, Mugo thus re-experiences his trauma as history. He goes to the trench where he staged his lone act of heroism and was subsequently detained, and we are told that "The whole scene became alive and vivid" (168). He relives the pain of the whip eating into the flesh of the woman he had tried to protect and the terror as he pushed forward to stop the woman's torturer. Mugo recalls that the scene remained "a nightmare whose broken and blurred edges he could not pick or reconstruct during the secret screening that later followed" (168). He dissociated from the trauma, answering with a voice "as from a dead body" questions as to how many oaths he had taken. He forgot some specific details of the torturer while he recalled others vividly (168), a classic reaction by trauma victims. We are shown that after Mumbi's confession about her adultery and her own suffering during the Emergency, Mugo finds it impossible to resume his 'limbo' state because of the community of empathy Mumbi establishes (169). Mugo later opens up to Mumbi about the torture he saw in detention, comparing it to "a darkness I could not penetrate" (179), and then confesses to having betrayed Mumbi's brother Kihika, leading to the latter's hanging (180). When he confesses at the public ceremony the following day, he "felt light. A load of many years was lifted from his shoulders" (231), but the chapter suggests that the load that has been lifted is only the ethical-juridical and not the weight of trauma. It is easy to misread Mugo simply as a traitor who callously betrayed the village hero, but the chapter reads Mugo as an unwilling conscript of Kihika's nationalist project who was traumatized by Kihika's intrusion into his life. The chapter teases out the (mis)readings of his heroism leading up to the moment of his confession.

When Kihika seeks shelter in Mugo's hut, he has made the general miscalculation that the apolitical Mugo is duty bound to forget the atrocities done in the name of Kenyan nationalism during the Emergency. Just before Kihika intrudes into his space, Mugo contentedly muses about the cocoon he has been able to fashion for himself: he often fussed over pushing the key into the lock on his door, because he saw the hut as "an extension of himself" (182). Mugo reflects upon having escaped "unscathed the early operations of the Emergency" for the past three years: "Some people had been taken to detention camps; others had run away into the forest; but this was a drama in a world not his own. He kept alone ... [awaiting] entrance into the other world" (182). After Kihika intrudes into his space and proudly talks about killing Robson and others while trampling on the weak "like a man possessed" (185–6), Mugo sits "rigidly in his seat" thinking that "Kihika was mad, mad... and the thought only increased his terror" (186). In other words, his world had been secure amid the turmoil, but Kihika's intrusion unsettles that security. As Kihika asks him to organize an underground movement in the village, Mugo "thought of running out" and shouting for help, "and then he remembered that Kihika had a gun. And that gun had just killed a man. He secured the door and went back to his place. He was walking in a nightmare" (187) and he denies the reality right before him in a way that illustrates Patrick Bracken's discussion of the ways "[t]raumatic experiences disrupt an individual's life by producing a block in cognitive and emotional processing" (48). Mugo is caught in this block: "It was not true that the man who had burnt down Mahee, the man who had just killed Robson, was actually in the hut" (187).

In speechless terror, Mugo accepts the appointment with Kihika a week later (188), and when Kihika leaves, Mugo feels like the ground under his feet is not firm. He resists bolting the door because "it was better to be without a door rather than it should be there and yet bring in cold and danger" (188). He hears voices and then realizes that they are in his head (188), manifesting the intrusive and hypervigilance aspects to trauma. The future becomes a blank as he sees prison and death:

> To be caught harbouring a terrorist meant death. Why should Kihika drag me into a struggle and problems I have not created? Why? He is not satisfied in butchering men and women and children. He must call on me to bathe in the blood. I am not his brother. I am not his sister. (188)

The words "terrorist" and "butchering" are straight out of the colonial government's propaganda machinery, attesting to Mugo's insulation from the social cause waged in his name. He dis-identifies with that community by emphasizing his individual kinship ties and their absence in his life. The following day, he tries to convince himself that Kihika's intrusion was a dream that connects with other nightmares he has had before (189), a way of protecting himself from the full knowledge about his traumatic encounter the night before:

> Night exaggerates everything—our fears, misery and despair. Bush and trees appear like men. Ha! Ha! Ha! But his ill-attempts at self-comfort could not undo the reality; Kihika's face was indelibly engraved in his mind; the unkempt hair, the shifting eye, banished Comforting illusions and made Mugo shiver in spite of daylight. (189)

Throughout the day, he cannot "forget Kihika's shadow behind him, waiting for an answer" (189), but this pushes him to recognize his existential crisis: "If I don't serve Kihika he'll kill me. If I work for him, the government will catch me … And they'll hang me. My God, I don't want to die, I am not ready for death, I have not even lived" (189). He again recalls that unlike him, Kihika had kin who would mourn his end, "who would name their children after him, so that Kihika's name would never die from men's lips" (189). In other words, Kihika's militancy was underwritten by his socio-centric organicism, to borrow Bracken's term from another context. Mugo, on the contrary, was the disengaged individual from whom the community could not expect anything just like he did not expect anything from them.

During the week leading to Mugo's "fatal" appointment with Kihika, he exhibits the classic symptoms of hyper-arousal. The thought of his kinlessness "obsessed him; it filled him with a foamless fury, a tearless anger that obliterated other things and made him unable to sleep" (190). He is unable to concentrate, and the appointed day "caught him undecided on a course of action" (190). It only gets worse from there as he walks to his farm in a daze, unable to discern anything in the village: "He was in that stage of exhaustion that comes from an accumulation of sleepless nights, heated, ceaseless, and directionless thoughts—that stage in which a man is irritable, ready to break at the slightest provocation without he himself realizing his danger" (190). He is agitated, he shakes and trembles as he walks, and his depression only becomes worse to the point where he feels too weak to walk (190). He recovers by repressing his anxiety and projecting his hyperactivity onto a cone-shaped pillar of wind that sweeps up debris around him, a wind which the local people attributed to possession by "women's devils" (191). It is in that state that he sees the poster offering a reward for Kihika's head. The face becomes larger "and more distorted the longer he gazed at it. The face, clear against a white surface, awakened the same excitement and terror he once experienced, as a boy, the night he wanted to strangle his aunt" (191). The poster links the two sources of terror in Mugo's life, Kihika and his abusive aunt. And thus, two panes of traumatic experiences merge in Mugo's dazed head in which, paradoxically, "thoughts acquired the concrete logic of a dream" (191). In the dream, he was Isaac being saved from sacrifice just in time because God had another purpose for him (191).

In his daze, Mugo fantasizes about what to do with the reward money: he would buy more land, build a big house, find a woman for a wife, and have children: "He would flash his victory before the eyes of his aunt's ghost. His place in society would be established. He would be half-way on the road to power" (192). In other words, this disengaged individual was only missing the opportunity to express himself as a social being in the community's value system. But in his delusional thinking, he would use the reward money—derived from getting even with one man who had just terrorized him—to exorcize the ghost of his aunt, the other person who traumatized him. It is an insightful representation of some of the distorted motivations that informed some of the atrocity experienced during the Emergency. For good *and* worse, John Thompson, the colonial officer to whom Mugo reports Kihika's possible location, chooses not to believe him immediately because in his racialized thinking, all

Africans are liars (194, 55). Instead of thanking him, Thompson spits in his face (55, 194) and then "slapped him hard, once" (194), thus sending Mugo back into his "nightmare" in which everything becomes distorted and "[h]e was nothing... With a choked cry, his body smashed on to the broken stones and jutting rock, at the white man's feet. The shock of discovery was so deep it numbed him. He felt no pain, and saw no blood" (194). Then everything around him spins and as he falls, it occurred to him that "[h]e did not want the money. He did not want to know what he had done" (195). He thus dissociates from the traumatic event as it happens.

Apparently, Mugo goes through eight years of constriction and avoidance in connection with Kihika's betrayal until the night the elders invite him to speak at the Independence Day celebrations in honour of Kihika. Naturally, this leads to the clashing symptoms of intrusion and avoidance discussed earlier, but in a complicated portrayal of the interpenetration of victims turned victimizers in the novel, Mugo later confesses to the juridical responsibility for Kihika's betrayal. Problematic as it might be, he gains articulacy in witnessing his betrayal of Kihika, but not to his own trauma. As he tells the gathered multitudes, "'You asked for Judas ... You asked for the man who led Kihika to this tree, here... Kihika came to me by night. He put his life into my hands, and I sold it to the white man. And this thing has eaten into my life all these years" (218). Further, the narrator tells us that Mugo "spoke in a clear voice, pausing at the end of each sentence. When he came to the end, however, his voice broke and he fell into a whisper. 'Now you know'" (218). Trauma studies scholars like Agamben, Laub, Van Alphen, and Yaeger consistently point to the inadequacy of language, and conventional form, to convey traumatic experience. Agamben reminds us that testimony is the disjunction between two impossibilities of bearing witness; it means that language, in order to bear witness, must give way to a non-language in order to show the impossibility of bearing witness ... It is necessary that this senseless sound be, in turn, the voice of something or someone that, for entirely other reasons, cannot bear witness ... [that] the 'lacuna' that constitutes human language, collapses, giving way to a different impossibility of bearing witness—which does not have a language (39).

Mugo's dutiful confession enables him to process his guilt, rather than his traumatic experience. For this, he is able to speak in a clear voice and his speech follows syntactical ordering. The voice that breaks at the end of the speech signals the return of the repressed traumatic experience that remains unarticulated. Tellingly, Mugo is 25 years old at the time when he betrays Kihika (183), and he is therefore 33 years old when he confesses his betrayal on Independence Day in 1963. Ironically, unlike Christ who died at the same age, he offers himself as a Judas figure, but he becomes the scapegoat for "the thing" that must be eating into the lives of his fellow villagers given their inability to look him in the eyes and the fact that they allow him to slink away.

Mugo's conflicting articulacy/inarticulacy as he confesses bears out Patricia Yaeger's reading of trauma victims' "inconsistent worlds [that] coexist simultaneously; foreground and background become interchangeable" and in whom "two or more memories come together that demand a shift between incommensurable domains" (409). That is why syntax and voice disappear at the end. It is important, then, to pursue the missing link to that experience where foreground and background merge. Surprisingly, we do not really know how Mugo ended up in detention and the community's haste to celebrate obvious heroes and heroines who fought in the forest, the entire detention experience and the dislocation of the village community become events without a witness. However, part of the problem is that we can only rely on Mugo to supply the missing link between his brutalization by Thompson at his office and his participation in Wambuku's defence at the digging of the trench. It is important to read the discordance between the Thabai villagers' reconstructed memory of Mugo's heroism as we build up to the climactic Independence Day celebration when they sing about his actions at the trench.

On the eve of Independence Day, we are told that the celebrants encircle the hut of the supposedly reluctant hero, Mugo:

> For more than an hour Mugo's hut was taken prisoner. His name was on everybody's lips. We wove new legends around his name and imagined deeds. We hoped that Mugo would come out and join us, but he did not open the door to our knocks. When the hour of midnight came, people broke into one long ululation. Then the women cried out the five *ngemi* to welcome a son at birth or at circumcision. These they sang for Kihika and Mugo, the two heroes of deliverance, from our village ... . (200)

There is some irony in the sense that the celebrants essentially hold Mugo prisoner on this dawn of independence even as they invent new legends to celebrate his imagined deeds. In this threshold hour, women trill ululations for the male heroes of the village. Left unsaid is the fact that a heroine would only get three trills, in a way that attests to the masculine symbolic content undergirding the new nation. Though women like Mumbi bore the brunt of terror in the Emergency villages—as we saw earlier, she tells us that they thought the world would end, a classic traumatic response (139)—none is celebrated in song or invited on Independence Day as witness to their trauma. Later we learn that at the precise moment that the villagers were singing his praises, the terrified Mugo was cooped up in his hut, fearful that having confessed earlier in the day to Mumbi, Kihika's sister, that he is the one who betrayed Kihika, he was now "vile and dirty" to her, another of the distorted views of the self that characterize PTSD:

> And then suddenly he heard the village people around his hut sing-
> ing Uhuru songs. Every word of praise carried for him a piercing
> irony. What had he done for the village? What had he done for any-
> body? Yet now he saw this undeserved trust in a new light, as the
> sweetest thing in the world. Mumbi will tell them, he thought. He
> saw the scorn and horror, not on Mumbi's face alone, but on every
> person in the village. The picture, vivid in his mind, made him coil
> with dread (231).

Ironically, the community ascribes greatness to Mugo for refusing to lead despite having suffered so much. On Independence Day, the local heroes Kihika and Mugo are again celebrated, and a delegation dispatched to Mugo to tell him that he had no alternative but to address the gathering. As they wait, they celebrate him in "the song of the trench"

> And he jumped into the trench,
> The words he told the soldier pierced my heart like a spear;
> You will not beat the woman, he said,
> You will not beat a pregnant woman, he told the soldier. (215)

We are told that "[b]elow the words of the song was the sound of something like a twang of a cord broken. After it, people became deathly
quiet" (215). The broken cord signals the broken string of a musical instrument. The harmony between the aural text and its instrumental ac-
companiment is broken, and the ensuing hollowness to the words rings
true for the reader who has been clued already that Mugo had not exhibited such heroism. Earlier, after Mumbi's confession to him releases "imprisoned thoughts and feelings" (167) and he dares to confront his latent
trauma, Mugo remembers working "a few yards from the [unnamed]
woman". When the home guard lashes her, he feels a somatic identification "yet he did not know her, had for three days refused to recognize
those around him as fellow sufferers". When no one else would save the
woman, we are told that "In terror, Mugo pushed forward and held the
whip before the homeguard could hit the woman a fifth time" (168).
He was beaten up as he was arrested but he never uttered a word. And
thus, the cord that binds the sign and its signified is broken and it is the
hollow link between the actions and their celebration that the narrator
foregrounds in the anti-climactic celebration.

After getting the women's "five Ngemi to a victorious son", Mugo
ruins the "drama" by identifying himself as the "Judas" who betrayed
Kihika. The man who has had a speech impediment like the Moses of his
delusional thinking now speaks in a clear voice and transmits a concise

message. Ironically, it is only Githua, the man we already know to be an impostor, who calls Mugo a liar (218). And thus, the triumphalist narrative of national liberation seems to end on a sour note as people now hide behind blank faces and a storm gathers in the sky. While we are invited to focus attention on the community's investment in a villain that they mistook for a hero, to the chapter takes a different approach here and explores how Mugo's action on this anti-climactic moment is remarkable for its ability to advance the idea of the nation as an organic community where everybody does his/her share, by foregrounding the fact that Mugo accepts the finality of his scapegoat status only after finding the equivalent of a community. It is only then that he comes to see the missing links of causality, sequence, and time that were absent when he was engaged in "acting out" the ceaseless drama that trauma scholars have foregrounded. In so doing, he has to become a witness to himself and relocate his traumatic experience from the individual to a communal setting.

There is a move in trauma studies to understand what is now called the "social turn", the move beyond focusing on the traumatized individual to the underlying cultural, political, and social conditions that produce the trauma. Patrick Bracken, for example, problematizes the "strongly individualist approach to human life, in which the intrapsychic world is emphasized, and society is understood as a collection of separate individuals" (40–41), whereas non-Western cultures have different notions of the self and its relationship to others (41). He faults the attempts to universally use "talk therapy" which focuses on the individual who is "capable of transformation in relative isolation from particular social contexts" (41), and he deconstructs the term PTSD of its Western baggage and its emphasis on cognitivism, the successful 'processing' of traumatic experience (42) steeped in the idea of reason central to the Enlightenment project (43). In contrast, in non-Western society the social context is more important than the personal (54), and Bracken posits that in these "sociocentric organic" societies, there is "less focus on the psychological realm" and more on the integration of "the individual with the natural, supernatural and social worlds" (54). Elaborating on the same dimensions, Margaret Rose Torrell argues that whereas trauma is understandably "inexpressible, irretrievable, and unhealable, the field often concerns itself with the extent to which the victim's giving voice to the trauma can be therapeutic, providing an outlet for some of the traumatic pain ..." (92). She faults trauma theory's "emphasis on the validation of pain and loss and the de-emphasis on trauma's relationship to socio-political representation and structures" (92). But as she recognizes, trauma studies have recently begun to "explore the ways that traumatic experience is mediated by culture and connected to oppressive social frameworks ... [a]s opposed to the understanding of trauma as inexpressible, inaccessible, and personal, the pluralistic approach situates it in a social landscape" (92). Amplifying Michelle Baelev, Terrell argues that "the pluralistic model considers that trauma's meaning can be located in the interactions between the real lived experience of trauma and its cultural causes and representations" (92). This chapter extends this social turn to the traumatized individual's ability to channel the social good by glossing Mugo's back story. Mugo admits his private guilt, thus manifesting Bracken's Western notion of the self as hidden, but he also helps us to understand his society's emphasis on kin connections, social worth, and its disruptions by colonialism. If colonialism was an economic, cultural, and political project, it reaches its ignoble end in Kenya by torturing the least privileged in the traditional society.

From the beginning of the novel, we are told that Mugo is a loner. An abandoned child, Mugo was brought up by his abusive aunt who suddenly dies before Mugo is old enough to take care of himself. Though he hated his aunt, Mugo misses her when she dies: "Whom could he now call a relation? He wanted somebody, anybody, who would use the claim of kinship to do him ill or good. Either one or the other as long as he was not left alone, an outsider" (8). With his aunt dead, Mugo substitutes organic life for the absent organic community:

> He turned to the soil. He would labour, sweat and through success and wealth, force society to recognize him. There was, for him, then solace in the very act of breaking the soil: to bury seeds and watch the green leaves heave and thrust themselves out of the ground, to tend the plants to ripeness and then harvest ... But then Kihika had come into his life. (8)

Later, we learn that to Mugo, Kihika had attempted to "draw me into the stream" of blood he was shedding (180), in an echo of Pheng Cheah's reading of the nation as organic community that holds itself together "by means of atavistic hallucinations and the violent and oppressive subordination of its members to the larger whole" (*Spectral* 17), with the individual seen as an abstraction that "must be subordinated to its function within the larger whole qua living organism" (*Spectral* 18). The chapter suggests that having feared and resisted subordination to the larger whole as a living organism, the moment Mugo discovers his organic vitalism prepares him to make the ultimate sacrifice for the community, the micro-social model of the nation. However, he does so on the basis of consent, not coercion, and as a move in juridical accounting for responsibility for a past wrong. The unfairness of it all is that he is the only one who is made to account for his wrong action. He offers that guilty private self as a witness to one layer of trauma in the society—the traumatized fence-sitters who ended up betraying those waging the militant struggle, but his fatalistic acceptance of his fate leaves the detention

story essentially untold, as colonial torture is erased from the performance of memory on Independence Day.

When the community first asks Mugo to speak at the independence
celebrations, it is out of a mistaken ascription of heroism only as a
relational act. In their version as told by General R., Kihika shot D.O.
Robson, was sheltered by Mugo on that night, Mugo was subsequently
arrested and sent to detention where he resisted confession about the
oaths he had taken (22–24), even though we as readers later find out
that he had taken none (187). Aware of his own betrayal, Mugo begs
off the speaking role but the supportive Gikonyo reminds him that it is
"not easy for any man in a community to be left alone" (24). Two days
later when he refuses to make the main speech and becomes lionized
for his refusal to lead, Mugo recalls the one speech he made on an
occasion celebrating the return of detainees, some of whom insisted
that he must speak at that gathering about his detention experience
at Rira. But even though he seemed to say all the right things, the
crowd wanted to hear, an inner voice tracked his thoughts: "I did not
want to come back; I did not long to join my mother, or wife or child
because I did not have any. Tell me then, whom could I have loved?"
(65). That recognition forces him to cut his speech short and walk
home. Like the traumatized man he was, as he walked "[h]is mind
would suddenly see his whole past in a flash – like when lightning cuts
the night in two. His whole life was compressed in that flash. Then
he would single out events trying to skip the ones that brought him
pain" (65). The call to make another speech opens that pain and he
wonders, could they really have asked him to carve his place in society by singing tributes to the man he had so treacherously betrayed?
(65). The important development in the novel is Mugo's change from
acknowledging the betrayal of Kihika to himself to acknowledging
the betrayal in public, thus forcing his community to interrogate its
binary reading of heroes and villains. At the end, even the hypocritical
Gikonyo celebrates him as "a man of great moral courage he stood
before much honor ... tell me a man who is willing to open his heart
to be pecked at .... (229–230).

The recovery of this moral courage comes from the connection Mugo
establishes with the community, as embodied in Mumbi.

After his confession, Mugo contemplates running away from his community and escaping punishment for his betrayal. But having confessed
to Mumbi earlier, he was unsure how he would ever be able to look
Mumbi in the face again (231). After he confesses in public, causality,
sequence, and responsibility are re-established in his mind (232), and
though he momentarily feels like fleeing again, he is then drawn towards
the house of the nearly blind Old Woman who lives alone, to whom he
is uncannily drawn for the way she reminds him of his aunt (232–233).

As she reaches out to him having mistaken him for Gitogo, her son who was killed by a colonial soldier in cold blood, she staggers back into her seat and dies. With the only person who had ever claimed him as kin dead, he resigns himself to his fate and he goes back to his hut. There, for once, "was nothing on the walls: no visions of blood, no galloping footsteps behind him, no detention camps" and even Mumbi recedes into the background (233). Mumbi's erasure here is of a piece with the incommensurable planes of Mugo's traumatic recall. A day earlier after confessing to her, "the picture of Mumbi merged with that of the village and detention camps. He would look at Mumbi and she would immediately change into his aunt or the old woman" (231). Mumbi has become joined with Mugo in an uncanny consanguine kinship. In the end, she is erased together with the traumatic experience of the detention camps. She becomes thus identified because she is the only one with whom Mugo engaged in "talk therapy": she shares her traumatic experience in the Emergency village and he shares the true story of his traumatic detention experience. In sum, Mugo's story is that of an abandoned child brought up by an abusive aunt. He is sucked up into an atomistic colonial order that privileges the individual at the expense of the community, but his attempt to play by its rules leaves him brutalized on a colonial officer's floor, tortured with beatings and waterboarding, stamped upon with hobnailed boots (168), and then hauled off to detention camps where he saw men "crawl on the ground ... like cripples because their hands and feet were chained with iron" and "bottlenecks were hammered into people's backsides and the men whimpered like caged animals ... at Rira" (179). While there, he saw a man's "manhood ... broken with pincers" and he "only looked into an abyss and deep inside [he] only saw darkness [he]could not penetrate" (179). This is the totality of his traumatic experience. However, it is not this story Mugo is invited to tell on Independence Day. Neither is Mumbi invited to tell hers. The story of the glorious fight in the forests deprivileges the story of terror in the Emergency-era villages and detention camps whose traumatized victims remain without a witness.

As Ernest Renan reminds us, the story of nationalism is riddled with violence that takes place at the origin of all political formations, and unity is effected by means of brutality, which all nations must subsequently forget (Bhabha, 11). While the nation-in-formation privileges certain stories, by talking through their traumatic experiences, the marginalized Mumbi and Mugo enact the social turn that bears witness to those marginalized from the triumphalist narrative on the basis of gender, class, and political consciousness. But if the story of nationalism is riddled with violence from its inception, in *A Grain of Wheat* we are called to witness the sheer barbarity of the colonial state in Emergency-era Kenya, and its ignoble clutch at empire as the spread of a great moral idea. In his *New York Times* Article titled "Atoning for the Sins of Empire", David Anderson continues his argument in *Histories of the Hanged* but from the vantage point of the court decision that awarded Emergency-era Kenyan victims of torture some token compensation in 2013. As he states,

> [i]n the detention camps of colonial Kenya, a tough regime of physical and mental abuse was implemented from 1957 onward ... [it] was sanctioned by Kenya's governor, Evelyn Baring, and authorized at cabinet level in London ... Empire was built by conquest. It was violent. And decolonization was sometimes a bloody, brutal business. (Web)

History seems to be finally catching up with fiction 40 years later, but the true victims of Kenya's Emergency-era trauma are long dead.

Works Cited

Agamben, Giorgio. *Remnants of Auschwitz: The Witness and the Archive.* Trans. Daniel Heller- Roazen. New York: Zone, 1999. Print.

American Psychiatric Association. https://www.psychiatry.org/patients families/ptsd/what-is-ptsd. Online accessed 11/26/16.

American Psychological Association. http://www.apa.org/topics/trauma/. Online, accessed 11/26/16.

Anderson, David. "Atoning for the Sins of Empire." www.nytimes.com/2013/06/13/opinion/atoning-for-the-sins-of empire.html?nl=today.

———. *Histories of the Hanged.* The Dirty War in Kenya and the End of Empire. New York: Norton, 2005.

Bhabha, Homi, ed. *Nation and Narration.* London: Routledge, 1990.

Bracken, Patrick J. "Hidden Agendas: Deconstructing Post Traumatic Stress Disorder". *Rethinking the Trauma of War.* Ed. Bracken and Celia Petty. London: Free Association Books, 1998.

Caruth, Cathy. "Unclaimed Experience: Trauma and the Possibility of History." *Yale French Studies* 79 (1991): 181–192.

Cheah, Pheng. *Spectral Nationality: Passages of Freedom from Kant to Postcolonial Literatures of Liberation.* New York: Columbia University Press, 2003.

Laub, Dori. "An Event Without a Witness: Truth, Testimony and Survival". *Testimony: Crises of Witnessing in Literature, Psychoanalysis, and History.* Eds. Shoshana Felman and Dori Laub. New York: Routledge, 1992. 75–92.

———. "Bearing Witness or the Vicissitudes of Listening." *Testimony: Crises of Witnessing in Literature, Psychoanalysis, and History.* Eds. Shoshana Felman and Dori Laub. New York: Routledge, 1992. 57–74.

Ngũgĩ wa Thiong'o. Ngũgĩ wa Thiong'o. *A Grain of Wheat.* London: Penguin, 1986 (2002).

———. *Matigari.* Trans. Wangui wa Goro. Oxford: Heinemann, 1987.

———. *Petals of Blood*: New York: Dutton, 1978.

———. *Weep Not, Child*: London: Heinemann, 1964.

Renan. Ernest. "What is a Nation?" *Nation and Narration*. Ed. Homi Bhabha. London: Routledge, 1990.

Torrell, Margaret. "Interactions: Disability, Trauma, and the Autobiography." *Life Writing* 13.1 (2016): 87–103.

Van Alphen, Ernest. "Symptoms of Discursivity. Experience, Memory, and Trauma." *Acts of Memory: Cultural Recall in the Present*. Eds. Mieke Bal, Jonathan Crewe, and Leo Spitzer. Hanover: University Press of New England, 1999. 24–38.

Yaeger, Patricia. "Testimony without Intimacy." *Poetics Today* 27.2 (2006): 399–423.

Part 3

Representations of
Atrocity in Popular Arts

15 Between Fait Accompli and Eruptions of Violence

The Kenyan Social Imaginary in Selected Stories of *Kwani?05*

Miriam Pahl

Introduction

The *Kwani?05* twin edition of 2008 is a literary interrogation of violence which erupted in Kenya after the December 2007 general elections and thus represents an important contribution to Kenyan's archives of atrocity. Published in the immediate aftermath of the violence, the twin edition represents an archive that questions and suggests how to integrate this episode in Kenyan history. Examining three selected literary texts from the twin edition, this chapter analyses how the Kenyan social imaginary is shaped and negotiated with respect to the global imaginary of Kenya and "Africa", on the one hand, and local perceptions of the Kenyan nation and ethnicity, on the other. It argues that, against the common perception of Kenya as a largely stable nation in the East African region and on the continent as a whole, the writers in the journal use the post-election crisis as an angle to access and negotiate the violent history of Kenya since independence. The widely used term "post-election violence" "legitimizes the idea that the 2008 atrocities were perpetrated purely because of the elections, a line of thought that is clearly vacuous given its refusal to acknowledge historical facts" (wa-Mũngai and Gona 20). The narratives analysed here contest this ahistoricism and examine the complex injustices of the past and present that led to the violence in 2007 and 2008.

Contextualizing *Kwani?*'s Kenya

Kwani? is a Kenyan literary magazine that exemplifies how young writers and other creatives contribute to shaping the social imaginary of Kenya and the collective memory of its history. The twin edition *Kwani?05* explores causes and consequences of the violence which erupted in Kenya after the 2007 general elections. As such, it represents an intervention to official narratives of the elections that tried to link the violence "confidently" and, arguably too simplistically to "tribalism" (Ochieng in Kakai Wanyonyi 32).

Kwani? was set up in 2003 by a group of creatives, among them were writer Binyavanga Wainaina, filmmaker Wanjiru Kinyanjui, and sculptor Irene Wanjiru (Maliti). Wainaina won the Caine Prize for African literature in 2002, an event that coincided with him having the opportunity to present the idea of *Kwani?* to the Ford Foundation who eventually supported establishing the journal, first as an online literary magazine which quickly made its way into print. The working theme for the first edition, "What does it mean to be Kenyan?" indicates the national scope of the magazine (Ligaga 46), and can be traced through to the latest edition to date, edition 08 published in 2015.

The journal created consciously outside academia promotes submissions that deviate from the conventional paths of literary creation. As such, Ashleigh Harris characterizes the journal as a site "exemplary of African cosmopolitanism, ... conversant with African everyday life and as such [a key site] in which we are seeing African writing shed the skin of its forebears" (8). According to Aurelie Journo, the aim of *Kwani?*'s events and the magazine "is to make literature 'young'" (1) a characterization that is also valid for the audience of *Kwani?* events and may tentatively be transferred to the readership of the journal. 'Young', in this context, is understood as a finite definition rather than a fluid description for a generation of creatives that set themselves apart from the "established cultural institutions" of literary production (Journo 1). In the editorial of *Kwani?*'s first edition, Binyavanga Wainaina calls this generation the "Redykyulass Generation" (a parody of the word "ridiculous") because "breaking new ground always provokes ridicule" (6). Dina Ligaga, writing about the first edition, demonstrates how the journal explores new literary spaces, a trajectory that later editions follow. Ligaga examines the use of E-mail, Sheng, and of matatu slogans and how these forms extend the scope of literary production in the journal (47). Thus, even though the journal seeks to blur and deconstruct the lines dividing "high-brow" literature from popular arts, it may be located closer to the latter field of production and consumption. The conflation of different writing forms in the composition of diverse stories and texts, but also within the individual texts, posit the journal as detached from the "established cultural institutions" of literary production (Journo 1).

References to popular culture like the use of Sheng and matatu slogans illustrate that the journal is tightly entrenched in the urban cosmopolitan space of Nairobi. Nairobi is the primary site of production and is often reflected in the stories and poems featured in the magazine. As a nodal point and centre for literary and cultural production in Kenya and Africa, this particular city determines the position of *Kwani?* as both local and global. It is the political, economic, and cultural centre of Kenya and the East African region, and thereby has to manage influences from smaller cities in Kenya and from beyond Kenyan borders. Its writers thus inhabit globalized urban spaces (and the internet), and are aware of the contrasting images of Kenya as an "island of peace" in the East African region, and the cliché of the "dark continent" (Mochama 211) that Kenya is part of and which still prevails in Western public discourses. In effect, they are positioned simultaneously in a global and local space of consciousness that informs their writing.

In light of the 2007 general elections, the *Kwani?05* edition pays special attention to the political aspects of Kenyan identity – "the individual's story as a citizen in the space called Kenya, his or her relationship to *serikali* or state, [...] the relationship between Kenyans and government" (Kahora 9). As Billy Kahora recounts in the editorial, the volume was already in progress with a focus on reporting the 2007 elections when the erupting violence demanded a reconsideration of how the edition could be set up. With regard to the violence after the general elections in 2007, the *Kwani?05* twin edition of 2008, "Maps and Journeys" and "Revelation and Conversation", which is the subject of this chapter, examines "questions of Kenyan-ness" and, as the journal's name suggests, seeks answers to the question "why?".[1] These questions touch on aspects of the Kenyan social imaginary as it is constructed within its national boundaries, relating to interlinking factors such as ethnicity, class, and gender.

Simultaneously, the two volumes seek answers about the image of Kenya as it is perceived in the African and global framework – The stories analyzed in this chapter present the image of the stable and peaceful Kenya as a myth that they undermine in their reconsideration of history. Billy Kahora evokes this impression of Kenya in the editorial that stands out on the African continent as its recent history has been largely devoid of conflicts and crises that other African countries have been confronted with in the last decades, and which they are often reduced to. Kahora recounts that somebody approached him with a morbid enthusiasm about the chance of the Kenyan writer to now contribute to "the great contemporary African themes" of war and conflict, themes that Kenyan contemporary writers, according to this rationale, have been excluded from until the eruptions in 2007/2008. Andia Kisia recalls the view of Kenya as stable and peaceful in her piece "Untitled", recounting that Kenya, for her generation that grew up in the 1980s, has always been "a fait accompli, immense, indestructible, unchangeable, a fact of life" (Kahora et al., *Kenya Burning 1* 196). By allowing Kenya to join "the machete and AK canon", the post-election violence represents a rupture in the global imaginary of Kenya, a country that has previously been "customarily hailed as a relatively peaceful and stable haven in the turbulent continent" (Kagwanja and Southall 260).

In its unique conflation of creative popular modes and styles, the journal represents an open forum that encourages questioning and discussing the events of 2007/2008, as well as an alternative to conventional archives of history. *Kwani?05* incorporates a variety of texts, poems,

and interviews that elucidate the events of early 2008 from many different perspectives. It seeks to create an alternative archive to the official
and public explanations of the post-election crisis. Kahora writes in the
editorial that "so far, our defining text, our national moments are the
politician's voice on the 9 o'clock news" and distances the literary works
in the edition from the one-dimensional narrative of politics. His singular use of "text" in this quote mirrors the perceived singularity and
shallowness that the editorial ascribes to the governmental narrative.
The "Interview with Siri-Kali"[2] between a journalist and Alfred Mutua,
a Kenyan government spokesperson, illustrates what Kahora alludes to.
Mutua blames the opposition party for the violence after the general
elections and denies a connection between the Electoral Commission
and the subsequent crisis. He also refuses to speak openly about the
great divide between the wealthy and the poor as a potential reason for
the violence unleashed (*Kenya Burning 2* 40–47). As a literary journal,
the magazine offers perspectives on historical events and makes sense
of social and political realities in a way that is different from other—
non-fictional—modes of writing. Literary writing insists on its emancipation from the official versions of history. The aim of the journal is to
extend the scope of this narrative through a "multiplicity of voices and
stories told, often contested, sometimes contradictory and incomplete"
(Muhoma 167).

The gulf between what *Kwani?* has created as an archive and the
official version narrated in the media becomes even clearer through
the story of the exhibition "Kenya Burning", a selection of 100 photographs, "human portraits that captured the spirit of brutality" but
never made their way "past the mainstream filters" (Kahora et al.,
Kenya Burning 1 61). A selection of the photographs from the exhibition
is featured in *Kwani?05*. The exhibition aimed to bridge the gap between "what reporters knew and what they were allowed to say" (*Kenya
Burning 1* 61) and to complement the narrative that was captured in
the news. Building a visual archive, the exhibition also represents "an
opportunity for all Kenyans to remember and reflect" (*Kenya Burning 1*
79). The directors of the GoDown Arts Centre, the place where the collection was exhibited for four weeks, report that "not a single member
of parliament visited the exhibit" despite repeated invitations, and that
requests to bring the collection to the Parliament buildings remained
unanswered. The unresponsiveness of Kenyan officials to this alternate narrative represents silent disapproval with what *Kwani?* and the
GoDown Arts Centre have created, underlining that the "versions of
'truths' from official political organs are in conflict with the 'truths' as
narrated in *Kwani?5*" (Muhoma 166).

The writers of the *Kwani?* twin edition use post-election violence to
disperse the view of Kenya as largely stable – economically, politically,
socially – and to reconsider Kenya's difficult history after independence

through this moment as their focal point. Against Kisia's evocation of Kenya as a "fait accompli", most writers do not represent the post-election violence as a sudden rupture but instead connect it to a complex set of factors that accumulated in the past and came to bear heavily on the 2007 general election. Tony Mochama, Kalundi Serumanga, and Billy Kahora use the post-election violence as a canvas on which they examine Kenyan history as discussed in detail subsequently.

Ethnic "Balkanization" or "Violence" in Tony Mochama's *The Road to Eldoret*

Tony Mochama's *The Road to Eldoret* reconsiders the view of Kenya as a peaceful, stable nation in comparison to other countries in Africa and, simultaneously, conjures the image of Kenya "on the brink, the precipice, of 'Rwandanisation'" (212), a contrast that the author tries to reconcile in the story. The narrative is divided into two parts, the first a fictional account of a character named "Mwangi" being murdered on his way to Eldoret, the second a non-fictional contextualization of the first part into a personal account of the author's experience of the day of the 2007 general election. The non-fictional account is interspersed with historical information that a Kenyan reader would arguably be familiar with which suggests that Mochama has a non-Kenyan reader in mind. However, the mockery of CNN and Western ignorance also invites Kenyan and African readers into the story.

The exceptionality of Kenya on the continent is summed up in the word "elsewhere" (207) as being the perceived locale of "burnt churches", "skeletons on the hard, sandy faces" and "ant-like lines of refugees" (207). Mochama ironically expresses the perception that Kenya, until 2007, was excluded from the image of the "dark continent" that dominates in the global imaginary of "Africa". However, the irony is rather directed at the misrepresentation of Africa in Western news. Mochama evokes and ridicules the image of Africa as the "dark continent" suggesting to "write us off, 'and will you, Melissa, kindly throw Africa out with the garbage, please?'" (211). The author reproduces the superficiality that dominates media coverage in Europe and America through keywords like "balkanization" and "ethnic tension" that he inserts into the narrative but denies to contextualize (207). This superficiality is set in opposition to the – equally superficial – glorifying description of Kenya as imagined for a wine box text – "the great deserts [...] the majestic Indian Ocean [...] the game ranges [and] its myriad mountain-ranges" – which emphasizes its beautiful landscapes and underlines the contrast to the "blood spilling in our country [Kenya] on that aftermath arid Friday" (210). Mochama takes up these contrasting representations of Kenya in the global imaginary and sets them in relation to socio-historical developments before the election 2007. The author thus contests the dominant conception that the post-election violence presents a rupture in Kenyan history, instead of summoning common representations of Kenya and Africa as superficial and shallow.

Mochama thematizes ethnicity as a key motivation for the 2007/2008 post-election violence, an aspect that both Kahora and Serumanga spare from their stories. The author's choice to call the character Mwangi, a very common Kikuyu name in Kenya, is the first invocation of ethnicity that possibly evades non-Kenyan readers. Mochama thus represents a generic, prototypical Kikuyu person and, in a problematic inflection, associates this ethnic group with victimhood. The first explicit mention of ethnicity comes from descriptions of the main character's hastiness to leave the hotel: "Mwangi was on his feet, and out of the hotel, before one could say the words 'balkanization' or 'ethnic tension'" (207). Ethnicity is thereby introduced as a secondary issue, one that is mentioned in passing and used to help describe the commotion in which the character finds himself. Ethnic disputes that are customarily mentioned as the primary reasons for the violence are thus pushed into the background. Mochama sticks to this pathway throughout his fictional account of "The Road to Eldoret" in which ethnicity is merely mentioned as an indication on Kenyan I.D. cards. Mwangi drives into an ambush but the mob realizes that "'Haka hakana pesa,' (this one has no money)" (208), so they ask him to show his I.D. card:

> In Kenya, the I.D.s not only come with your name and date of birth, but also your place of ethnic origin, or tribe. They were an invention of the British Colonialists to prevent Kenyans slipping from their tribal reserves (concentration encampments) at the height of the Mau Mau rebellion against British rule. (208)

In this story, the people at the roadblock look for money first and then look at their victims' ethnic identity. Mochama presents the looters as using the country's state of turmoil as an opportunity for their own financial gains, thus introduces the issue of poverty. He also represents ethnicity as a marker of identity that has been made relevant by British colonizers and integrates the 2007/2008 violence into Kenyan history. The discrimination upon which the 2007/2008 violence is based upon is traced back to the colonial legacy of categorizing individuals to ethnic groups. Ethnic identification, here, still has to draw on I.D. cards that were introduced in 1915 and fails as an obvious identity marker. The story thus promotes an argument that sees the roots of a rigidified ethnic consciousness in colonialism (Kakai Wanyonyi 38). Despite this fictional introduction that downplays the relevance of ethnicity in the violence, the non-fictional account explains Kenya's history along ethnic lines and thus reinstates the relevance of ethnicity that the story of Mwangi has undermined.

In the transition to the non-fictional account, Mochama makes clear that the fictional account is "based on actual events", thereby emphasizing the severity of the situation in the first days of 2008. He says "actual events" rather than "real life" (209) because the events were "surreal [...] as if a daemonic Salvador Dali had, overnight, painted Kenya over in dark and crimson hues" (209). Mochama thus detaches the violence from "normality", making clear that the atrocities cannot be integrated into an understanding of human societies. However, the narrator explains the political set-up and ethnic tensions before the general elections and incorporates disputes over land into the causes that led to violence in 2008. His visit to his brother who is in hospital after being beaten up because he "voiced his support for Kibaki in Kalenjin country" (214) points towards the tensions that had already erupted before the election and contributed to the climate of hate around them.

The combination of a fictional account of the violent clashes and the killings happening at roadblocks with a non-fictional report of the author's experience on Election day and its aftermath construct a very specific, individualized insight into happenings around the 2007 general elections. Mochama's text takes up shallow representations of "Africa" in Western media and sets them in dialogue with an individualized experience of the election and its aftermath. Interspersing his narrative with information about political and social realities in Kenya, both in history and in the present, he offers a deeper understanding of what happened before, during and after the 2007 general election.

Madness or Invisibility in Kalundi Serumanga's *Unsettled*

Kalundi Serumanga's story "Unsettled" examines the causes of the post-election violence through the tropes of madness and invisibility which he connects to Kenya's history since independence. Serumanga provides a detailed characterization of Kenyan society through these tropes before he relates them to the catastrophe that followed after the 2007 general elections. The narrator is a Ugandan refugee who "disappeared" (171) to Kenya in the 1970s and is thus able to provide a comparative view of Nairobi and Kampala, and of Nairobi in the 1980s and now. His former girlfriend and "would-be wife" serves as an entry point into the past, when he used to spend time with her in the 1980s and before she started to roam the streets of Nairobi, "shivering slightly and muttering to herself" (168). He is reminded of her when he wonders about people who do not mind the sewage that floods the streets and who "were sane, I am to believe" (170) while, in contrast, "she was mad, I am told" (168). The afterthought in both statements expresses distance and scepticism and invites the reader to reconsider what they mean – where does one draw the dividing line between sanity and madness. The afterthoughts challenge the dividing line which is further questioned in the course of the story.

The image of excrement flooding the streets of Nairobi projects the image of the city as filth, and together with the description that somebody "had used their shit to write ["Uhuru"] on the toilet wall" at the end of the story, frames the story with the imagery of disillusionment and depravity. The excremental imagery in relation to nation-building aligns the story with a long tradition in African literature, as John Esty has argued. The fact that at the beginning of the story, it is "the collective excrement of all those Nairobians who use flush toilets was now liberated to surge down the main road" (170) alludes to uneven development in the city in which the toilet "is a powerful symbol of technological and developmental superiority – one that has the corollary effect of intensifying, via a newly potent scientific language, the negative valence of shit" (Esty 29). The sewage in the streets is an indicator of the trope of poverty and inequality that is explored further in the course of the story. The final sentences of the story conflate the mundane lack of toilet paper – which symbolizes a larger deprivation in society – with the celebration of independence in a disgusting image of "Uhuru" written on the toilet wall with excrement.

Madness, in this story, is represented as an illness caused by events and experiences that are not processed. Mad characters in the story are not given the possibility to come to terms with atrocities that they experienced – they continue to exist although "power has decided you or your narrative should not exist anymore" (178). The girlfriend's uncle, for instance, is a survivor of the Mau Mau revolution who, according to the narrator, "went into detention sane, and came out crazy, or went crazy some time after" (177). The association of madness with suppressed narratives alludes to the failure of the public in Kenya to discuss the Mau Mau, a movement that is only slowly making its way into national memory. For example, the Mau Mau as a society was banned in Kenya by the colonial government and only legalized by the Kibaki government in 2003. The story, thus, reproduces the silence that it is attempting to expose, omitting what the uncle experienced in the British detention camps. The rhetorical question "why is it that in the Nairobi of the 1980s, nobody seemed curious about an ex-freedom fighter wandering around in a state of mental despair, while millions were spent on Uhuru Day celebrations?" (178) drives the point further. The opposition of mental despair and the celebrations underline the irony of this connection between past and present. It also links failure to come to terms with events that led up to Kenya's independence, and to the government which does not acknowledge the struggles that continue to haunt former freedom fighters. In effect, governmental efforts to emphasize the achievements while downplaying the losses and the violence connected to independence play a major part in the current state of the country, and consequently also in the post-election violence.

The girlfriend is another "mad" character who is equally subjected to a silenced biography. In her narrative, poverty is related to corruption and violence to which she was subjugated in the form of rape. Her mental illness, in succession, is caused by the denial of credence and attention from society. Her mother neglected her, and now, "people look on, but cannot help" (178). The narrator compares Nairobi to his "now mad would-be wife" (175), an "old friend who has since lost her mind to mental illness" (172), thus describing the changing character of the city. Nairobi as he sees it is mentally deranged and does not follow social codes of behaviour anymore. Instead, it is "trapped in a cage of madness" (178), abnormalities that are not addressed but shrugged off and silently accepted.

Another important characteristic that defines Nairobi in the eyes of the narrator is its orientation towards Europe and America. Nairobi "was the place you had to go to partake of the marvel of the white world, without having to leave the African continent" (170). British names of city districts demonstrate that "the whole city was named after whiteness" (171) and thereby continues to be defined via its colonial history. This persisting legacy is also showed in the stark supremacy of a white person in a lift that the narrator uses to emphasize this point. The Kenyan mzee – a figure that is conventionally associated with respect and authority (Musila 281) – in the lift becomes a "badly drawn caricature" (185) next to the white man who is dressed better. The white man is dressed "appropriately for the city built for him by his genocidal ancestors" (185), a historical fact that the city has not overcome since independence, according to the story. The narrator thus opens up a historical perspective on the development of the city and the country, which he calls "an atrocity a long time made and a catastrophe a long time coming" (186). The Mau Mau uprising and the violence of and caused by poverty are protracted and carried into the present, made invisible but still affecting the country's society. The silences and invisibilities create a Kenya "where the abnormal was normalised" (184). The trope of madness, similar to Mochama's characterization of the crisis as "surreal", sets the events apart from rational behaviour, however, in Serumanga's story, the trauma is not cured but tolerated and disregarded.

The madness caused by diverse forms of violence – physical, economic, ideological – is shown to translate into invisibility, a trope that dominates the second half of the story. The narrator lists a range of people that are "invisible" in Kenyan society: Street children that gather up rotting food from the garbage dump and go unnoticed, "queue-dwellers" in the post or immigration office who do not dare to protest against white people who naturally jump the line of people, former residents of the Limuru area who were replaced by the "endless carpet of green tea [that] was violently laid down" (183) and the *mzee* in the lift who is "properly dressed" but nevertheless offended in his "petty pride" by the mere existence of an even better dressed *mzungu*. In this narrative, economic inequality translates into a kind of apartheid that distinguishes between visibility and invisibility. There is a clear hierarchy of individuals, with rich white people at the top and poor children at the bottom.

Invisibility becomes a living condition and an instruction that invisible people have to adhere to. Invisible people, however, oppose this unspoken order to remain invisible and "get ahead by dressing and accenting oneself into visibility, through aping the culture of the settlers" (184). The story creates a tension between those who force others into invisibility, and the others occasionally trying to resist, a tension that erupts after the general elections in 2007. The tropes of madness – as a way in which the past controls the present – and invisibility are connected to the post-election violence of 2008 at the end of the story. The narrator explains that those made invisible by society and the government:

> had to attempt visibility by becoming a vast, rioting, murderous nuisance whose two week rampage gave rise to expressions of grief, shock, anger and disbelief from Kenyan intelligentsia, in a way that has left me truly mystified. Have they not been paying attention? (186)

In effect, the post-election violence is a result of inequalities that permeate Kenyan society and a total disregard of the injustices that a larger part of the population is and has been subjected to since independence. The 2007/2008 post-election violence is thus an eruption of accumulated tension between those pushed into silence and invisibility, and the resistance of those made invisible.

Gems of Wisdom from the Rwanda Genocide in *The Gorilla's Apprentice*

Billy Kahora's short story *The Gorilla's Apprentice* is set in the immediate aftermath of the 2007/2008 general election and, on a conceptual level, mediates the boundary between animal and human. Evoking this boundary in an African context, the story invites a reading that sets it into dialogue with colonial discourses that have located Africa in a "framework (or on the fringes) of a meta-text about the animal—to be exact, about the beast: its experience, its world, and its spectacle" (Mbembe 1). Kahora does not mention ethnic divisions in the story or evoke ethnic identities but the story examines the Kenyan social imaginary as a whole and with regard to the framework of Kenya in the world. The story revolves around Jimmy, an almost-18-year-old young man who spends as much time as possible close to his friend Sebastian, an old gorilla at the animal orphanage in Nairobi. A third important character is Charles Semambo, a professor who is portrayed as a genocidaire from Rwanda hiding in Kenya. Jimmy believes that Semambo is able to talk to the gorilla, an ability that he asks the professor to teach him. The story moves from the animal orphanage to a lecture theatre where Semambo delivers a lecture about gorillas, and on to Jimmy's destitute home. The post-election violence remains only as an allusion;

nevertheless, it serves as an important context for the questions that are examined in this story.

The threesome of Jimmy, the gorilla, Sebastian, and the genocidaire Prof. Semambo provides a number of points of access into the issues that the story negotiates. In opposition to Semambo and Sebastian who come from Rwanda, Jimmy as a Kenyan character seems to stand for the Kenyan nation as a whole. His birthplace and residence as a young boy on State House Road ties his individual identity to that of the Kenyan national collectively and simultaneously produces a sense of promise for his future and for Kenya. Nevertheless, after his father abandoned his family Jimmy experiences a steady social decline with his mother – a decline that is thus projected on Kenyan history after independence. His resilience and loyalty to his mother shed a positive light on Kenyans and their continuing belief in their country despite the failures and destitution that it has to offer. The description of the relationship between Jimmy and his mother – "Jimmy knew all about being watched. What his mum called love." (312) – further characterizes the relationship between Kenyans and the government as oppressive and un-loving. The story shows Jimmy at the brink of adulthood and Kenya at the verge of decline into destructive violence just shortly after the 2007/2008 general elections. Both Jimmy and the Kenyan nation, in the process of coming of age, are confronted with questions and have to make decisions at this point, determining their ways into the future.

Jimmy finds a doppelgänger in Sebastian, the gorilla. This is expressed through both of them having problems with their eyesight – Jimmy had to spend almost a year of his life in hospital because of a "blood clot [that] had blacked out his sight" (311) while Sebastian has cataracts, causing his eyesight to fail. The short-sightedness of both characters points beyond the mere physicality of seeing and understanding. This symbolizes that Jimmy and Sebastian are able to understand life not only through visible things. The dance the two share "small mimicking movements ... scratches and hand flutters, heads bowed forward and swaying from side to side" allows for a similar twist, demonstrating that they understand each other without words and language. It also underlines their duplicity.

Billy Kahora says that he feared that Kenya "could degenerate into a 'Rwanda' [which is] the kernel of the story" (Kahora in Brock). He suggests this even stronger by relocating two characters – the gorilla and the genocidaire – from Rwanda to Kenya in the story. Kahora describes it this way:

> But before all this I had always been gripped with the common idea that some Kenyan political elites in the 90s had been accused of harbouring Rwandese war criminals who were 'genocidaires'. Genocide was an idea that was being bandied around when the violence in

Kenya broke out. And that the very notion that we could degenerate into a 'Rwanda' was the kernel of the story. So I wondered, what if what was being perpetrated had something to do with certain 'expertises' learnt from the genocidaires? That was the main thread in the genesis of the story. (Brock)

The gorilla, Sebastian, represents the knowledge or wisdom that could have been gleaned from the genocide in Rwanda while the professor-cum-genocidaire stands for the perpetration of violence. Semambo is a genocidaire who "erased his past" (318) and started a new life in Kenya with a "title deed, four different Ugandan passports with appropriate visas and work permits, a pin certificate, an identification document and his new name" (319). The documents are provided by a middleman and authorized by "our old man" (319) who remains unidentified but, arguably, belongs to the political elite of Kenya. Kahora thus touches on one aspect of corruption that generally gains little attention – the fact that criminal immigrants may be allowed residence in the country if they are able to afford the bribe. Since post-election violence remains in the background of the story, and Semambo and the other characters are not shown to be involved, it may not be considered as a simple "import" from neighbouring countries. The story does not draw a causal relation between the toleration of criminals in the country and the violence erupting after the elections; however, the fact that the political elite is an important agent in allowing genocidaires into the country and the post-election violence implies a staunch critique of the Kenyan government. It calls into question issues of justice and international responsibility in the case of the Rwandan genocide, and represents the Kenyan government as corrupt and complicit.

Sebastian is "the oldest gorilla in the world [who was] captured and saved from the near extinction of his species after the genocide in Rwanda" (310). This link to Rwanda is established at the outset of the story, shedding a distinct light on "that last Sunday of 2007" (310) which coincides with the day the post-election violence broke out in Kenya. The description of Sebastian lends him an air of authority and wisdom, congruous with Jimmy's knowledge about "their [the gorillas'] sense of community, their empathy, their embracing of death" (313). Jimmy misinterprets Sebastian's reaction to Semambo, a reaction that is indicative of Sebastian's grasp and comprehension of humanity. Jimmy also has an undecided feeling of recognizing Semambo from somewhere but is not able to place him, "Sebastian bounded to the bottom of the wall standing fully upright, running in short bursts to the left and right, beating his chest as if he was welcoming an old friend" (315). Instead of welcoming, beating their chest is a display of threat and power to a perceived danger amongst gorillas, meant to discourage an individual from coming closer. The gorilla seems to be one step ahead of Jimmy, sensing the danger that Semambo represents while Jimmy cannot remember why Semambo seems familiar to him.

The introduction of the gorilla into the story and its close connection to the human characters serves to explore questions of humanity and animality, a boundary that is increasingly blurred. Giorgio Agamben elucidates the "production" of humanity, of what it means to be human in distinction to the animal. He writes:

> The division of life into vegetal and relational, organic and animal, animal and human, therefore passes first of all as a mobile border within living man, and without this intimate caesura the very decision of what is human and what is not would probably not be possible. (Agamben 15)

Agamben identifies a conceptual boundary between human and animal within the human being, this being a "field of dialectical tensions always already cut by internal caesurae" (Agamben 12). Thus, humanity, or being human, is produced through negation and expulsion of "animality", of features of non-humanity, of "undesired traits" that are assigned to the non-human other, the animal (Piskorski). In other words, both the concepts of "humanity" as well as "animality" are constructed categories that coexist within the human being, but the latter is excluded from the sphere of being human. It is important to realize, at this point, that the conceptual notion of being human can be different from the biological human being, and it is this flexibility that enables dehumanization of human beings. In this equation, colonial discourses have effectually located Africa and African human beings in the realm of animality, a realm that was expelled from the representation of the colonizer's self as civilized and advanced. The global imaginary that equates Africa with savagery and primitivism has persisted since then and is promoted through one-dimensional media coverage of conflicts and war on the continent. Kahora evokes this discourse of animality and violence as an African characteristic that finally also descends on Kenya. The implicit alignment of Kenya and Rwanda and the strong evocation of the Rwandan genocide contests the image of Kenya as a "peaceful and stable haven in the turbulent continent" (Kagwanja and Southall 260). Kahora dares to enter the territory of stereotypes and misconceptions of Africa by representing violence and evoking the Rwandan genocide. However, Kahora himself contests that this story bears the threat of perpetuating stereotypes of Africa:

> For me, a stereotype is basically an unwarranted idea, image or conclusion about a place, based on ignorance and generalisation. It would be flattering to think that this story will create or reinforce negative stereotypes of all the things that are discussed within

it. [...] This piece tries to tell a specific story about a young man, his mother, an older man and a gorilla within a specific time and space – I do not see the older man as really coming from outside or having a past that is outside the story. [...] But hopefully, the characters and time are as individualized and as specific as possible, sitting outside any generalized settings such as the Africa of the generalized lens. (Brock)

Instead of perpetuating the stereotypical representations that link Africa with violence and animality, Kahora problematizes the separation of humanity and animality or civilization and violence in the first place. Kahora emphasizes that Semambo and the violence he stands for are not foreign to the Kenya of the story; instead, he is part of a shared past that the society and the government have not come to terms with. As Semambo says, "we are in the abyss and the abyss is in us" (323). In this case, the atrocity of Rwanda reappears in another country, continuing to haunt the genocidaire himself and his surroundings.

Sebastian is a doppelganger of Jimmy, as shown above, but he also serves as a double of Semambo, sharing the country of origin and a similar biography of migration to Kenya. However, Semambo's identity as a genocidaire suggests that he should be the one behind bars, instead of Sebastian. The gorilla's sense of community and empathy makes him the better human from whom the crowd in the lecture theatre should learn. The story questions the order of human supremacy over animals, and thus questions the understanding of humanity as civilization. The carelessness of the tourists towards the animals in the sanctuary emphasizes this confusion. Jimmy's profuse interest in the gorilla and his eagerness to communicate with him might be understood as an attempt to cross the boundary between human and animal, and to access the wisdom that Sebastian presumably harbours. The last image of the story – Sebastian wrapping Semambo in an embrace in which "the two figures became one" (325) – ultimately blurs the boundary between human and animal. This image perseveres beyond the text and is projected to the context of the post-election violence in which the story was written; poignantly asking in which direction Kenya wants to move on.

Conclusion

A close reading of the three selected stories from the *Kwani?05* edition shows that the authors use the 2007/2008 post-election violence to examine Kenyan history in retrospect from this point in time. Against the common perception of Kenya as a largely stable nation, they represent the violence as a result and effect of Kenya's silenced history. Tony Mochama undermines dominant media representations of Kenya through ironical evocations of these images. He allows insight to his individual experience of Election day and thus provides the reader with a concrete account that leverages on stereotypes and speculations. Evoking the legacies of colonialism as a factor that manifests in ethnic identities, his fictional account represents the past as a significant aspect that has to be addressed in order to enable a peaceful present and future for Kenya. The protracted problems of the past also loom large in Kalundi Serumaga's story "Unsettled", in which individuals and their narratives are forced into silence and invisibility. The post-election violence, in this story, is explained via the resistance of the invisible, silenced individuals who protest against their voices being stolen in a rigged election. Both Serumaga's and Kahora's stories omit ethnic tensions or recent events during the general elections as explanations for the violence. Instead, they seek alternate and more complex explanations than those distributed by governmental institutions that integrate the violence as "ethnic clashes" into Kenyan history. Serumaga and Kahora ascribe the violence to economic inequality and persisting injustices of the past that divide the society of Kenya. The stories resist representations of Kenya as a stable, peaceful nation and the post-election violence as a rupture in an otherwise smooth course of history. Instead, they use the violence as an access point to the silences and injustices of Kenya's past, which they project as the main causes of the atrocities of 2007/2008. The three stories and the explanations they offer for the atrocities happening in early 2008 exemplify how *Kwani?* meaningfully contributes to the conversations about these events and the collective memory that has to integrate this episode in Kenyan history.

Notes

1 "Kwani?" is a "compression of two interrogative Swahili terms "kwa nini?" which literally means 'why'," as Ligaga explains (46).
2 Kalundi Serumaga, a Ugandan journalist interviews Alfred Mutua, the spokesperson for the Kenyan government from 2004 to 2012. "siri-kali" is the kiSwahili word for "state".

Works Cited

Agamben, Giorgio. *The Open: Man and Animal*. Stanford, CA: Stanford University Press, 2004. Print.

Brock, Ollie. Interview with Billy Kahora.

Esty, Joshua D. "Excremental Postcolonialism." *Contemporary Literature* 40.1 (1999): 22–59. Print.

Harris, Ashleigh. "Awkward Form and Writing the African Present." *The Johannesburg Salon*. JWTC, 2014. 3–8. Print. 7.

Journo, Aurelie Marion. "Hip-Hop Literature: A Case Study from the New Kenyan Literary Scene." *Postcolonial Text* 5.3 (2010): n. pag. *www.postcolonial.org*. Web. 25 Oct. 2016.

Kagwanja, Peter, and Roger Southall. "Introduction: Kenya – A Democracy in Retreat?" *Journal of Contemporary African Studies* 27.3 (2009): 259–277. *CrossRef.* Web.

Kahora, Billy. "Editorial." *Kenya Burning: Mgogoro Baada Ya Uchaguzi 2007/8 Edition 1.* Ed. Yasuyoshi Chiba et al. Nairobi: GoDown Arts Centre: Kwani Trust, 2009. 8–12. Print.

———, eds. *Kenya Burning: Mgogoro Baada Ya Uchaguzi 2007/8 Edition 1.* Nairobi: GoDown Arts Centre : Kwani Trust, 2009. Print.

———, eds. *Kenya Burning: Mgogoro Baada Ya Uchaguzi 2007/8 Edition 2.* Nairobi: GoDown Arts Centre: Kwani Trust, 2009. Print.

Kakai Wanyonyi, Pius. "Historicizing Negative Ethnicity in Kenya." *(Re)Membering Kenya: Identity, Culture and Freedom.* Ed. Mbugua wa-Mungai and George Gona. Nairobi: Twaweza Communications Ltd., 2010. 32–49. Print.

Ligaga, Dinah. "Kwani? Exploring New Literary Spaces in Kenya." *Africa Insight* 35.1 (2005): 46–52. Print.

Maliti, Tom. "Kwani Trust: Our History." N.p., 2012. Web. 27 Oct. 2016.

Mbembe, Achille. *On the Postcolony.* Berkeley: University of California Press, 2001. Print.

Muhoma, Catherine. "Versions of Truth and Collective Memory: The Quest for Forgiveness and Healing in the Context of Kenya's Postelection Violence." *Research in African Literatures* 1 (2012): 166. Print.

Musila, Grace A. "The 'Redykyulass Generation's' Intellectual Interventions in Kenyan Public Life." *Young* 18.3 (2010): 279–299. Print.

Piskorski, Rodolfo. "Animality, Animals and Racial Otherness." *Post Humanities.* N.p., 9 Apr. 2009. Web. 15 Jan. 2016.

wa-Mũngai, Mbũgua, and George Gona, eds. *(Re)Membering Kenya: Identity, Culture and Freedom.* Nairobi: Twaweza Communications Ltd., 2010. Print.

Wainaina, Binyavanga. *Kwani?01.* Nairobi: Kwani Trust, 2003. Print.

16 Confronting National Pain and Suffering through Judy Kibinge's Feature Film, *Something Necessary*

Jacqueline Ojiambo

Introduction

Using Judy Kibinge's feature film *Something Necessary*, this chapter explores how national crisis is depicted through cinema and examines questions that arise from a cinematic text. *Something Necessary* replays aspects of post-election violence that took place in 2007/2008 in Kenya. The film juxtaposes perpetrators with victims and takes the audience on a journey with them as they look for something necessary. In the process, the film asks pertinent questions like who caused the violence? Why did they do it? What does it feel like to be a perpetrator? How does the perpetrator reflect aspects of victimhood? While the film may not answer all these questions, its interrogation enables productive contemplation over historical injustices that nobody really wants to deal with. Thus, the chapter explores how the paradoxical dichotomy of perpetrator-victim facilitates confrontation of national pain and articulation of a national crisis. Particularly, the chapter examines how narrative strategies adopted in *Something Necessary* bring out the social, cultural, and political function of film. The author argues that such filmic narratives demand the audience's willingness not only to walk through the pain of communal loss but also offer an opportunity to question ideological mainstream modes of individual, collective, and national identity in relation to national loss and pain. Grounded on grid-group theory by Mary Douglas and various approaches to pain and trauma, this chapter sheds light on the perpetrator-victim relationship and how the film's narrative changes our sensibilities when we view the perpetrator as a victim as well.

It is estimated that over 1,000 people were killed and 600,000 displaced in Kenya over the course of the two months of post-election violence. This took place in an orgy of violence that arose among ethnic groups due to discontent over the December 2007 presidential election results. This monstrosity of violence was on a scale not witnessed since the 1992 ethnic clashes. Various artists have memorialized the events of the heart-wrenching violence in diverse forms such as Wanjohi wa Makokha's poetry collection *Nest of Stones*, Tony Mochama's short story *The Road to Eldoret* and on the film scene, Judy Kibinge's feature film *Something Necessary* and Zippy Kimundu's short film *Burnt Forest* and through a documentary *Give Me Back My Home*. These creative pieces among other similar works contribute in some way to answering the recurrent question: what went wrong in Kenya? In asking this question, this chapter allows readers to contemplate over the words of the fictional commission of inquiry facilitator who in *Something Necessary* says to her audience "[u]ntil we Kenyans understand what happened and why we did what we did to each other, we cannot move forward".

This chapter situates *Something Necessary* within the larger body of a distinct filmmaking within African cinema – one that collects and commemorates memories of violence. The largest collection memorializes the Rwanda genocide that took place in 1994. Several feature films such as *100 Days* (2001), *Hotel Rwanda* (2004), *Shooting Dogs* (2005), and *Shake Hands with The Devil* (2007) among others tell the story of the mass slaughter of the Tutsi's by the Hutu's. Mbye Cham observes, in "Film and History in Africa: A Critical Survey of Current Trends and Tendencies", that filmmaking alongside other creative forms "is a way of defining, describing, and interpreting African experiences with those forces that have shaped their past and that continue to shape and influence the future" (48). Through film, Kibinge contributes to national narratives by re-enacting past events as well as interrogating various national concerns. In the same article Cham (referring to the general body of African cinema) adds that "[t]hese films also take up history as a way of reflecting on, and coming to terms with, the many crises and challenges confronting contemporary African societies as well as the future" (49). This chapter aims to contribute to the larger body of interrogations which then enable productive contemplation over historical injustices that the hegemonies have failed to deal with. The film also helps to foster a cultural memory albeit a painful one. By closely examining *Something Necessary*, a film which has not been widely recognized by critics, this chapter attempts to shed new light on the perpetrator-victim relationship and how the films' narrative changes our assumptions regarding the perpetrator as a victim as well.

By looking into the past through memory, victims can walk through their traumatic experiences and denounce the atrocities committed to them. The directors, as part of the larger community of victims, view themselves as contributors to the process of reconstruction and remembrance. In an interview with Smart Monkey TV, Kibinge states that the film is "a record of a time we've been through as a nation, an everlasting testament". Kibinge positions herself as part of the community of victims by using the plural pronoun "we". She further states that it "was a hard film to make" revealing her difficulty in remembering the painful events that form the context of the film. Thus, the filmmaker contributes to nation-building through the creation of films that serve as a monument of this historic event. Maurice Halbwachs, argues that although it is individuals and not groups or institutions who remember, they are located in a specific social context, and therefore they remember their past in that context (22). The memory of the post-election violence is maintained through the piecing together of emblems within the films, alongside the protagonists' narratives. It preserves the events surrounding the violence and opens the possibility for us to make enquiry of how we got there so that hopefully in the words of George Santayana we are not "condemned to repeat" (*The Life of Reason*, 133) those experiences.

Brief Overview of *Something Necessary*

Something Necessary follows the lives of Anne and her son Kitur who are victims of the post-election violence. The film, through horrifying images of violence and pain experienced by the characters, appeals to our affective senses. Art historian Jill Bennet has argued that visual images do more than only representing images and experiences from the past, they relay to us an emotional or bodily experience by stirring up our own emotions (92). In the opening scene, for example, we see many people running with machetes/pangas, some others burning buildings and wounding people, and the police firing gunshots. After this scene, the film narrows our focus to the story of the protagonist Anne narrating the effects of the violence at a more personal level. The embodiment of this violence in a character helps show the reality of the violence.

The feature film explores various forms of violence prevalent in the 2007/2008 post-election atrocities. Anne experiences physical, mental, and sexual violence. She is subjected to physical abuse by the young men who attack the home she shares with her son, and her husband, Steve. The three are beaten, cut with machetes/pangas, their home looted, then set ablaze. Steve succumbs to his wounds and dies while Anne and her son are hospitalized. This leads to mental anguish as she is unable to get rid of the images of the attack that recurrently play in her mind. She tells Cherono, her nurse, "I see him (Steve) everywhere". Memories of happier times spent on the farm with her husband and son often remind her of her losses. Anne is raped by the men who attack her house and soon after her return to work she discovers she is pregnant from the rape. Anne refuses to remain a victim, overcoming a myriad of challenges and embarks on rebuilding her farm. Though her story is full of painful events, it is a story of the triumph of the human spirit.

As she rebuilds her farm, she receives unwavering support from Joseph. Joseph was part of the group that mobbed Anne's house during the post-election violence. Joseph is haunted by his involvement in the violent acts. He is often seen deep in thought, perhaps reflecting on his mistakes, a stance that makes his remorse believable. Anne and Joseph are linked together by their experiences of the violence, and each deal with their trauma in different ways. To exonerate himself, Joseph chooses to help Anne by putting up Kitur's swing and erecting a fence around Anne's property. Later in the film, we learn that Joseph has qualified to be admitted to the university, but his dream is hampered by a lack of finances. Kibinge offers an individual perspective on the perpetration of violence through the character of Joseph. This chapter reads Joseph as a representation of the victims not considered by official reports such as Commission for Inquiry into Post-Election Violence (CIPEV) since the focus is more on them as perpetrators.

Besides the direct victims, as represented by Anne and Joseph in the film, the Kenyan nation experienced collective trauma from the events surrounding the post-election violence. People suffered trauma by witnessing the events as they happened, watching them on various platforms or merely hearing of them. Joyce Nyairo and Johannes Hossfield observe that in the season following the post-election violence, there was tension in the air: "[s]ites of public assembly became places that one avoided lest you say something that annoyed the other, or you heard something that released your tenuous hold on an ugly tirade" (10). The fear and tension that gripped the nation stir our collective historical consciousness concerning the violence. The collective trauma experienced by Kenyans has elicited various communal responses including creative pieces such as this film. The film satirizes Leah who carries on with her life as if nothing happened, unmoved by her relative's long stay in hospital and grave losses. Through Leah, the film aims at nudging our conscience to get involved and be a part of the transformative process.

Ethnic Tensions and the Land Question: Key Concerns

Something Necessary foregrounds land as one of the main causes of conflict during the post-election violence. The director focalizes the predicament of displaced women and the challenge of resettlement of internally displaced people. The film highlights the gendered nature of violence by giving attention to a woman's experience during the post-election violence. Studies have shown that women and children were displaced the most during the conflict. Those who lost husbands and did not have title deeds to their land were bound to experience difficulties in the process of resettlement. This difficulty is due to discriminatory property rights and customary laws. Apart from the destruction of her farm and property and the loss of a spouse, Anne is shown to be at risk of losing her land. Anne's brother in law, Lesit, tries to dissuade her from returning to her "Haven" claiming that it would stir up bad memories for her and her son. Lesit cunningly offers to give her a flat in exchange for her farm. Invoking a patriarchal stand, he says that it is not right for a woman to run the farm on her own. Anne, however, resolves to rebuild her land even when she gets no assistance from her employer or her family.

In addition to focusing on women and the land issue, the film high-lights how the unresolved questions on land in the Rift Valley remain at the core of the recurrent cycles of violence. In the scene at the crime den, Chepsoi violently reacts to a television broadcast airing President Mwai Kibaki and Raila Odinga shaking hands after reaching a peace deal to end the violence. In anger he says:

> Why are these people shaking their hands as if nothing happened? This is bullshit! What the hell! Let me tell you we are not fighting because of those two. We are fighting because of our soil, our soil. Left to us by our forefathers. They have stolen our land now they have stolen the election. We will fight for it to death.

This response alludes to the unresolved historical injustices over land is-sues in Kenya. Chepsoi and the gang represent the Kalenjin who strongly feel that the Kikuyu took their land. This is inferred to when he says "they stole the election" meaning the Kikuyu represented by Mwai Kibaki whose election win is contested. Chepsoi points to the fact that it was more than just the election result that fuelled the violence. What also erupted amidst the contestation of the election results were the simmer-ing tensions that had not been dealt with over the years. The land issue is cited as one of the major causes of the violence; the CIPEV report records that the Kalenjin wanted to evict non-Kalenjin so that they could recover the land they believe the colonialists took from them. While a substantial amount of time and money has been invested in investigations on the land issue in Kenya, there seems to be a lack of political will from the government to get to the bottom of the matter. Karuti Kanyinga observes that settlement schemes and the land purchase contributed to ethnopolit-ical conflicts that date back to the1960s. Kanyingi's work traces Kenya's politics of land rights in the former white highlands from the 1960s to 2008. His findings are that "the land reform program in Kenya has not been sensitive to inter-ethnic relations nor has the 2008 political settle-ment that led to the formation of a coalition government addressed the land question" (342). Kanyingi's notion foregrounds inter-ethnic tension which is useful in discussing the unresolved land issue.

Ethnic mobilization plays a key role in the Kenyan political sphere. It is a known fact that ethnic divisions were among the issues that fuelled the post-election violence. Intimations to the ethnic tension are seen when Lesit tells Anne not to show him her "kikuyuness" which happens when she insists that she would not sell her land to him. Gathoni, Anne's sister constantly sees the Kalenjin as the evil "other" and is always sus-picious of the Kalenjin community into which her sister Anne is mar-ried. In one instance, she asks "what kind of people are these"? While acknowledging that ethnicity was a factor in the violence, the filmmaker is careful to avoid developing stereotypes. This is important because in trauma studies it is observed that the perpetuation of good versus evil narratives continues the cycle of violence. Carolyn Yoder writes against simplistic analysis of causes of pain and trauma because these result in "equally simplistic solutions" such as "if evil people or groups are the cause, then the solution is to separate ourselves from them, somehow get rid of them or even kill them" (41). Kibinge carefully balances her characters to avoid sustaining good versus evil narratives. To achieve this, she creates characters who offer alternative narratives about their communities, for example, Cherono, the kind and empathetic nurse who takes care of Anne and Kitur in the hospital. Cherono, a Kalenjin, is shown to be sympathetic to this family pointing to the fact that it was not communities at war but individuals. Also, to avoid narrowing the violence to only the Kalenjin and the Kikuyu tribes she weaves stories about people from other communities, like Atieno, the hairdresser, who lost her brother in the violence.

The film portrays the attitude of the public to the commission of enquiry as suspicious. The characters in the film view the commission as a public relations act just to show the citizens that something was being done about the violence and a tool for the politicians involved to avoid the International Criminal Court. One of the unnamed characters in the film, during an awareness campaign about the commission, says "[l]et me ask you will the commission give us back our land? Will it resurrect our relatives? First, resettle those who are stuck in the camps ...". These questions imply that the citizens are not interested in a window-dressing exercise and hope that the real issues would be dealt with. This attitude may be due to the history of numerous commissions of enquiry such as the Ndungu Land Commission (2003) and the Akiwumi Commission of Inquiry on Tribal clashes (1998) whose findings have never been acted upon.

Speaking the Unspeakable

In *The Body in Pain,* Elaine Scarry points to the limitation of language to convey pain. Scarry contends that "physical pain does not simply resist language but actively destroys it, bringing about an immediate aversion to a state anterior to language, to the sounds and cries a human being makes before language is learned" (4). Due to her pain and torture, Anne lacks the language to speak about it, the intensity is such that she is dumbstruck when it comes to the subject of her pain. On some occasions, she sits in a corner in her house in deep thought, and at other times she just weeps. Even when she goes to the tents set up by the government to collect information on the violence, she is unable to speak and walks away. Atieno, one of the hairdressers in the film, refuses to talk about the loss of her brother in the violence. While trying to understand her silence, her colleagues conclude that "it is difficult to talk about such things". Joseph is also portrayed to be contemplative most of the time, and he hardly speaks. These characters exemplify the loss of speech that occurs as a result of experiencing trauma and pain. At the end of the film, Anne gathers the courage to go to the Commission of Inquiry to give her testimony. When she takes the witness stand she is unable to open her mouth; she gestures as if to open it and then closes her eyes in deep thought. This strategy is employed by the filmmaker to demonstrate to the audience the intensity of Anne's trauma which renders her mute.

Something Necessary voices the unspeakable in two levels. The first level is Kibinge's depiction of a rape scene and an abortion scene. The second level is where Anne does not speak of these two events thus portraying them as unspeakable. The film then airs the rape and abortion to the audience by showing rather than telling. Anne's hesitation to speak about her rape can be associated with the stigma attached to sexual violence in Kenya. Stigma stems from the circulation of myths such as "[d]ressing a certain way or being seen visibly drunk invites rape" (Gqola, 149) which shift the blame to women. Women become objects of shame rather than victims. Unlike other forms of physical violence rape may not leave bruises or broken limbs but deep unseen wounds. This makes it difficult for women to seek justice because apart from the burden of the violation, they have to contend with the burden of proof. This and other factors cause women to resort to silence.

Kibinge brings to the fore sexual atrocities during the violence. Obioma Nnaemeka's research on the depiction of sexuality in various texts on the Biafran war, observes that "[i]n contrast to male writers who focus on consensual sex and raise moral questions about the promiscuity of girls during the war, women writers foreground painful and graphic depictions of sexual violence and rape as a weapon of war" (255). This scene can be read as a statement that rape should be of public concern. As Anne lays on her hospital bed, she is disturbed by flashbacks of events during her attack. In one of these flashbacks, we view the rape scene. The scene is presented among other quick cuts through which the director demonstrates the chaotic nature of the moment. In this scene, Anne is calling out Steve's name while pinned on the ground by two men, one lying on her side. This kind of filmmaking goes beyond demonstrating sexual violence, Kibinge engages with the consequences of this violence and how the aggrieved party deals with it.

Anne runs counter to Kenya's restrictive abortion law by choosing to abort her unborn child. This is a micro-political act that critiques Kenya's abortion law and society's moral stance on abortion. Implicitly, the film asks, given the socio-religious norms and the legal stand on abortion, how should women deal with pregnancies arising from rape? Abortions in Kenya are shrouded in secrecy, many performed illegally on the back streets posing a significant risk to women (Ankomah et al). The chapter concurs with Robin Steadman's observation in his review of the film, that "[b]y presenting Anne's decision to terminate her pregnancy as a personal one, contrary to both socio-religious norms and Kenyan law, the film takes a decidedly feminist stance on the issues of abortion and sexual violence" (288). Kibinge presents to the audience a new way of looking at these two problems. She exploits the opportunity the film offers to explore what Elizabeth Grosz puts forward as "[d]ifferent ways of knowing, different kinds of discourse, new methods and aspirations for language and knowledge need to be explored if women are to overcome their restrictive containment in patriarchal representation" (126). Popular discourse in Kenya offers various thoughts on abortion, the majority speaking against it and others for it. Anne makes it a personal choice. She neither consults anyone on whether she should do it nor does she seek anyone's help in procuring it. She makes it an individual process, staking a claim to her body. Thus, Kibinge upsets dominant moral codes imposed against women without consideration of the particular circumstance women find themselves in.

The chapter argues that Anne's decision to abort her unborn child is also a subversive act. Anne opts to cleanse herself of what would be a reminder of her rape. This act also ensures that she does not create an "invisible victim". The term invisible victim is used in the Human Rights Watch Silicon Valley (HRWSV) report to refer to children born out of rape during the violence. The report observes that these children face stigma and physical and verbal abuse. They are invisible because discourses on assistance to victims of post-election violence do not include them. Anne's choice is a way of stopping the cycle of victimhood. She does not want to reward the perpetrators by enabling them to achieve their goal which was to redraw ethnic boundaries by breeding children of their own kind. Her abortion resists and counteracts the rapists' intentions.

Anne's abortion is symbolic of a necessary soul-searching process that the nation should undertake. *Something Necessary* seems to suggest that the nation should not allow the seeds of violence and division to mature. Like the foetus in Anne's womb, implanted through an act of violence, the nation should not carry such seed to term. The abortion scene is prolonged to signify the symbolic value of the process. Anne checks herself into a hotel room and rids herself of the baby. She goes through pain and agony implying that the process to rid the nation of cycles of violence and other forms of discontent may be uncomfortable yet necessary. Chantal Kalisa, while tracing sites of violence in African Francophone and Caribbean women's literature, finds that "[a]bortion becomes a cleansing tool to eliminate traces of male invasion from a woman's body" (148). Like Anne in *Something Necessary* she argues that the female characters in Calixthe Beyala's *The Sun Hath Looked Upon Me* who have been violated preoccupy themselves with seeking a form of sanctification. Just as the abortion becomes "something necessary" that Anne does, the nation must also do "something necessary" to put a stop to violence.

Precarity and Victimhood

Joseph, one of the perpetrators of the violence meted against Anne's family, comes across as a young man lured into crime without understanding what the consequences would be. In the scene in the crime den, Chepsoi hands the youth money from the "big bosses". He explains to them that they must continue fighting for their land at all costs. Joseph hesitantly takes his money and appears troubled. Observing his demeanour, the gang members demand an explanation. He confesses that he is troubled by the violent acts performed on Anne and her family. At this point, he is made to drink to an unspecified liquid as an oath to show solidarity with the gang. Joseph courageously deserts the gang, though helpless and hopeless, he begins to rebuild his life. This state of hopelessness exhibited by Joseph is eloquently articulated by Tom Odhiambo as "[t]he state of permanent uncertainty about the future, the improbability of ever getting employment, of ever satisfying one's immediate needs and of ever planning for the future causes a sense of hopelessness for many young men and women" (np). Odhiambo's reading of the three Kenyan novels points to the causal relationship between the state of hopelessness among youth and their engagement in crime.

Joseph's hopelessness stems from his inability to progress in life; he appears to have reached a dead end. He obtains a good grade in high school, but he cannot forge ahead due to his inability to raise university fees. Joseph has minimal opportunity to survive. He has difficulty finding employment when he opts to leave the gang. *Something Necessary* offers a critique on the Kenyan society that continues to marginalize and exclude the youth from socio-economic opportunities. Due to lack of choices, the youth such as Joseph become the precariat of our times. Precarity has been defined by Judith Butler as "that politically induced notion in which certain populations suffer from failing social and economic networks of support and become differentially exposed to injury, violence, and death" (np). Just as the victims of the violence experienced trauma due to the horrific acts they experienced or witnessed, some of the perpetrators may have been equally traumatized by the hideousness of the acts of violence they engaged in. Joseph's guilt and shame bother him, and he opts to leave the gang despite the consequences. He is unable to face Anne neither speak to her, though he is often seen in her compound delivering building material. In shame, he avoids her gaze. He is burdened by his guilt and finds ways of making it up to Anne.

Joseph is unable to rebuild his life due to constant threats by the other members of the gang. When he leaves them, and finds employment elsewhere, they waylay him, beat him up and rob him of his day's earnings. Though he feels a sense of self-loathing, he is unable to seek help. When his girlfriend asks him to report Chepsoi and his cronies to the commission, he tells his girlfriend "what they did, I also did". This shows he is not only a victim but also a perpetrator. Butler argues that "those exposed to precarity are also at a risk of not qualifying as subjects of recognition" (np). Joseph exemplifies this state by his predicament, though he was used and now he is remorseful, who would listen to him? Finally, when the gang realizes that no amount of threats would deter Joseph from his determination to move on, they brutally murder him and dump his body outside his mother's house. Unfortunately, the likes of Joseph do not count in the estimated 1,500 dead who died because of the post-election violence.

Conclusion

Something Necessary provides a representation of the 2007/2008 post-election violence in Kenya. It engages with some of the causes of violence such as ethnicity and unresolved land issues, and the public's attitudes towards the Truth and Justice Reconciliation. Through its focus on the twin narratives of a victim and perpetrator, Kibinge humanizes offenders labelled as the perpetrator. She portrays Joseph as a victim of a wider scheme of perpetrators that employ vulnerable youth to commit heinous acts on their behalf. While critiquing the sociocultural and legal stance on abortion in Kenya, *Something Necessary* speaks powerfully on the issue of rape during times of conflict. The film suggests that the choice of what happens in and to a woman's body is ultimately her choice. Lastly, *Something Necessary* represents the many necessary things that have to be done for healing and rebuilding the nation. In so doing, Kibinge acknowledges the difficult task of prescribing a fixed set of solutions given the intricacies surrounding the violence. For Joseph, it was the acts of kindness that he unreservedly showed to Anne, contributing in a way to her healing process. For Anne, it was the resolve and courage to rebuild her farm despite the obstacles that stood in her way. She also musters the courage to face the commission and share her painful story. Kibinge suggests that Kenyans need to confront individually and collectively the things necessary for healing, rebuilding, and to preventing a repeat of such atrocities.

Works Cited

Ankoma, Augustine, Colette Aloo-Obunga, Magdalena Chu, and Alicia Manlagnit. "Unsafe Abortions: Methods Used and Characteristics of Patients Attending Hospitals in Nairobi, Lima, and Manila." *Health Care for Women International* 18.1 (1997): 43–53. Web. 4 Nov. 2016.

Assmann Jan, John Czaplicka. "Collective Memory and Cultural Identity". *New German Critique* 65 (1995): 125–133. Web. 29 Oct. 2016.

Bennet, Jill. "The Aesthetics of Sense-Memory: Theorising Trauma through the Visual Arts." *Trauma und Erinnerung/Trauma and Memory: Crosscultural*

Perspectives. Ed. Franz Kaltenbeck and Peter Weibel. Vienna: Passagen Verlag, 2000. Print.

Boehmer, Elleke. *Stories of Women: Gender and Narrative in the Postcolonial Nation*. Manchester: Manchester University Press, 2005. Print.

Beyala, Calixthe. *The Sun Hath Looked Upon Me*. Trans. Marjolijn de Jager. African Writers Series. Portsmouth nh: Heinemann, 1996. Print.

Branch, Daniel. Kenya: *Between Hope and Despair 1963–2011*. Yale: Yale Books, 2012. Print.

Butler Judith. "Performativity, Precarity and Sexual Politics". *Revista de Antropologia Iberoamericana*. 4.3 (Sept. 2009 University of Complutense Madrid. 8 June 2009). Web. 9 Nov. 2016.

CIPEV. *Commission of Inquiry into the Post-Election Violence*. Nairobi: Government Printers, 2008.

Cham, Mbye. "Film and History in Africa: A Critical Survey of Current Trends and Tendencies." *Focus on African Films*. Ed. Francoise Pfaff. Bloomington: Indiana University Press, 2004. Print.

Fletcher, Angus. *Allegory the Theory of a Symbolic Mode*. Ithaca: Cornell University Press, 1965. Print.

Forti, Daniel, and Grace Maina. "The Danger of Marginalisation: An Analysis of Kenyan Youth and their Integration into Political and Social Life". 55–85. Web. 22 July 5 2016.

Gabriel, Teshome. *Third Cinema in the Third World: The Aesthetics of Liberation*. Michigan: UMI Research Press, 1982. Print.

Gqola, Pumla. *Rape: A South African Nightmare*. Johannesburg. MFbooks: 2015. Print.

Grosz, Elizabeth. *Sexual Subversions: Three French Feminists*. St. Leonard: Allen & Unwin. 1989. Print.

Halakhe, Abdullahi. "R2P in Practice: Ethnic Violence, Elections and Atrocity Prevention in Kenya". *Global Centre for the Responsibility to Protect – Occasional Paper Series*. 4 (2013): 1–28. Web 3 Nov. 2016.

Halbwachs, Maurice. *On Collective Memory*. Translated by Lewis A. Coser. Chicago: University of Chicago Press. 1992. Print.

Horowitz, Jeremy. Policy Brief 3/2008: "Power Sharing in Kenya" Centre for the Study of Civil War, Pric. March 2008. Web 21 April 2017.

Human Rights Watch. "I Just Sit and Wait to Die" Reparations for Survivors of Kenya's 2007–2008 Post-Election Sexual Violence". 2016. Web. 2 Nov. 2016.

Jameson, Fredric. "Third-World Literature in the Era of Multinational Capitalism "Social *Text*, 15. (1986). Web. 12 Oct.2011.

Kagwanja, Peter, and Roger Southall. "Introduction: Kenya – A Democracy in Retreat?". *Journal of African Contemporary Studies* 27.3 (2009): 259–277. Web. 21 Apr. 2017.

Kanyinga, Karuti. "The Legacy of the White Highlands: Land Rights, Ethnicity and the post-2007 Election Violence in Kenya". *Journal of Contemporary African Studies* 27.3 (2009): 325–344. Web. 10 Nov. 2016.

Khalisa, Chantal. *Violence in Francophone African and Caribbean Women's Literature*. London: University of Nebraska Press, 2009. Bookfi. Web. 17 Aug. 2016.

Langford, Michelle. *Allegorical Images*. Portland: Intellect, 2006. Bookfi. Web. 19 Sep. 2016.

Mochama, Tony. "The Road to Eldoret". *The Road to Eldoret and Other Stories.* Nairobi: Brown Bear Insignia, 2009. Print.

Muhula. Raymond. "Horizontal Inequalities and Ethno-regional politics in Kenya". *Kenya Studies Review* 1.1 (2009): 85–105. Web. 03 Nov. 2016.

National Accord and Reconciliation Act No. 4 of 2008.

Nnaemeka, Obioma. "Fighting on all fronts: Gendered Spaces, Ethnic Boundaries, and the Nigerian Civil War". *Dialectical Anthropology* 22.3/4 (1997): 235–263 Web. 7. Nov. 2016.

Miller Nancy, and Tougaw Jason. Introduction. *Extremities.* Eds. Nancy K. Miller and Jason Tougaw. Illinois: University of Illinois Press. 2002. Print.

Nyairo Joyce, and Hossfield Johannes. Foreword. *(Re)membering Kenya.* Eds. Mbugua wa Mungai and George Gona. Nairobi: Twaweza, 2010. 10–15. Print.

Odhiambo, Tom. "Juvenile Delinquency and Violence in the Fiction of Three Kenyan Writers" Tydskrif *Vir Letterkunde* 44.2 (2007): 134. *Gale Virtual Library.* Web 3 Oct. 2016.

Ongalo, Otuma. "Coalition Rows Won't Fade If Kibaki Remains Suspicious and Raila Angry". *Standard Digital,* 18th April 2009. Web 21 April 2016.

Penal Code, Chapter 63. Laws of Kenya, Chapter 15.

Scarry, Elaine. Elaine. *The Body in Pain: The Making and Unmaking of the World.* New York: Oxford University Press, 1985. Print.

Steedman, Robin. Rev. of *Something Necessary* by Judy Kibinge. *African Studies Review* (2015) Web. 10 Nov. 2016.

Transparency International Kenya. *Kriegler Commission Report: An Audit of Its Implementation.* Nairobi. February 2013. Web. 12 Nov. 2016.

wa Makokha, Wanjohi. *Nest of Stones: Kenyan Narratives in Verse.* Bamenda: Langa Research and Publishing, 2012. Web. 4 Nov. 2016.

Yoder, Carolyn. *The Little Book of Trauma Healing: When Violence Strikes and Community Security is Threatened.* Pennsylvania: Good Books. 2005. Print.

Filmography

Something Necessary. Dir. Judy Kibinge. Prod. Tom Tykwer et al. 2013. Film.

Burnt Forest. Dir. Zippy Kimundu. Prod. Emily Wanja. 2013. Film.

Give Back My Home. Dir. Zippy Kimundu. Prod. Emily Wanja. 2013. Film.

17 Screening Violence and Reconciliation

The Production and Circulation of Films about the Kenyan Post-election Violence of 2007/2008

Robin Steadman

Introduction

Following the 2007/2008 post-election violence in Kenya, a 'critical juncture' (Forest and Johnson 2002) was formed in which ordinary voices could contribute to the construction of a new 'post-conflict' nation, perhaps contesting official narratives and histories while adding to processes of reconciliation and nation-building. The Kenyan creative seized this opportunity and there has been a remarkable ongoing output of creative production in varied media, including film, books, and photography. Yet, to date there has been no systematic examination of this volatile period on screen, despite the existence of several shorts, documentaries, and feature-length productions specifically on the post-election violence (*Togetherness Supreme*, *Pieces for Peace*, *Ni Sisi*, and *Something Necessary*). This chapter moves beyond the current scholarship that examines post-election violence on film (Mugubi 2014, Giruzzi 2015) by looking at contexts of production and circulation rather than simply at the filmic texts. Arguments in this chapter follow Dovey's (2009) postulation that for films to have an impact, they must reach an audience. While textual analysis methods are necessary to explicate the films and analyse the philosophies they put forward, a discussion on the 'public lives' (Modisane 2012) is also required to understand their tangible role in post-conflict reconciliation and nation-building. As such, this chapter focuses on feature-length films and is based on two periods of research in Nairobi (one month in Spring 2012; and eight months between October 2014 and June 2015). The chapter includes audience research and interviews with film-makers regarding their production and circulation of films addressing post-election violence. In this regard, the chapter examines the films' textual images as well as the intentions of the producers (the desired impact) and the actual contexts of their distribution and exhibition (circulation) both within and outside Kenya.

The 2007/2008 post-election violence was a moment of tremendous social upheaval resulting in at least 1,000 confirmed deaths and 300,000 internally displaced people – to say nothing of sexual violence, non-fatal injuries, and economic losses. The Kenyan election crisis took place after the disputed Presidential election where Mwai Kibaki was re-elected with his party, the Party of National Unity (PNU); Raila Odinga and his party, the Orange Democratic Movement (ODM) was defeated with a narrow margin. The Kenya Electoral Commission released the results of the presidential election on 29 December 2007 and the perception that these results were fraudulent was "the immediate contingent cause of the violence" (Anderson and Lochery 328–329). Violence spontaneously broke out as accusations of electoral fraud and malpractice spread, yet while the election may be seen as the 'trigger' of the violence "the spread of the conflict reflects long-term popular frustrations" (Cheeseman 170), particularly around the key issues of regionalism, land redistribution, and access to political opportunities (Branch and Cheeseman 3).[1] While there is a long history of political violence in Kenya[2] the "intensity and extent of the conflict" following this election was unprecedented (Anderson and Lochery 328). A power-sharing settlement was reached on 28 February 2008, with the help of international mediation, which saw Odinga take up the new post of prime minister.

In this context of violence, Kenya-based creatives were not content to sit by idly while there was the possibility that Kenya could descend into complete anarchy and violence and they began to use their diverse media and art forms to contribute towards peace and reconciliation. This remarkable creative output addressing post-election violence include feature fiction films, photography exhibitions *Kenya Burning*, twin editions of the literary journal *Kwani?*, the play *Ni Sisi*, multiple documentaries such as *Peace Wanted Alive* (Kibinge 2009) and *Peace: an Aftermath of the Postpoll Crisis* (SlumTV 2009), and short fiction films such as *Wale Watu* (Boy 2008). However, within this creative context, fiction films are a uniquely public art form with the potential for a mass audience that is not bound by location – a fact that has been recognized since the origins of independent African cinema when Ousmane Sembene began making films as a mode of reaching Senegalese and African audience beyond the elite. It is also a fact that continues to be recognized by creatives in Kenya, for instance, the play *Ni Sisi* was adapted to film so as to capture "the peace play for those who cannot see a live performance" (Trustee Report 4), which explicitly recognizes the potentially wider reach of films beyond art forms that must be seen live. As such, this chapter specifically focuses on the four works of feature-length fiction that have so far been made: *Pieces for Peace* (Bresson and Kimani 2008), *Togetherness Supreme* (Collett 2010), *Something Necessary* (Kibinge 2013), and *Ni Sisi* (Reding 2013). These four films were made within the same milieu by Nairobi-based filmmakers[3] within a five-year period. Textual analysis methods are necessary to explicate the films and analyse the philosophies they put forward. The chapter also presents a discussion on the 'public lives' of these films in order to understand their tangible role in post-conflict reconciliation and nation-building.

Producing Critique through Film

Film production addressing the post-election violence began almost immediately after the violence, and all four films were made and circulated prior to the next Presidential election in 2013. Creating in this deeply unstable context presented unique challenges to filmmakers wanting to impact on reconciliation with their films. Muhoma and Nyairo pose an important question that define the early milieu in which filmmakers seeking to address the violence were working: "How does one tell the story of events that are so traumatic and horrific when the perpetrators of the atrocities have neither been arrested nor charged in a court of law" and the painful events are so recent? (420). Made in the early period described by Muhoma and Nyairo, *Pieces for Peace* was the first post-election violence centred feature film to be released. It is a combination of two intertwining short films – "Tough Times" and "LR 45" – directed by Riverwood veterans Mburu Kimani and Robby Bresson respectively. It was produced in the immediate aftermath of the violence, and according to Kimani, was developed because they, as filmmakers, felt they had to participate in the reconciliation process (Kimani). In a different but not conflicting aim, Nathan Collett was inspired to make *Togetherness Supreme* because he "wanted to tell a realistic story about what happened" in the election crisis ("The Story Behind the Film").[4] The latter two feature films, unlike *Pieces for Peace* and *Togetherness Supreme*, were made within the context of much larger filmmaking or cultural projects. *Ni Sisi*, directed by Nick Reding, is a film by the Kenyan NGO and UK charity S.A.F.E., which uses street theatre, film, and community programs as a catalyst for social change in Kenya. The film is part of their peace program, which was developed in response to the post-election violence and has been in operation since 2010 ("Peace").

In the context of the aftermath of the post-election violence where there was no "sense of things having been dealt with properly" (Reding) S.A.F.E. decided to mobilize their resources to tackle the problem of violence and in so doing produced the play that would later go on to become their film *Ni Sisi*:

> We thought, well, what can a play do? I don't know, but we've got to try, and, well, it might not stop a civil war, but it might help... And we did a lot of research and a lot of talking, as we always do, and a lot of discussion about what the reasons for the violence were and what could be possible solutions to the violence, or to another outbreak of violence ... and we devised the play. (Reding)

Something Necessary developed in the context of a larger organization, but significantly not one devoted to creating cultural change. One Fine Day Films is a transnational filmmaking project in two parts – the first is a workshop master class and the second the production of a feature fiction film.[5] After participating in the master class, Judy Kibinge was selected as the director and the screenplay was then revealed. Kibinge would later receive an adaptation credit for her efforts in reworking the screenplay (Kibinge Q&A) – a clear sign of her authorial involvement in the project – and her focus was on developing a film that would avoid being "preachy" and "really make it an observation about two people … to try to make it a very human story" (Kibinge).[6] She was personally invested in the message of the film and felt a tremendous sense of responsibility working on the film in the intense period in the run-up to the next election (Kibinge Q&A).

In each of the films, the directors had a clear motivation to use their art to contribute to social change and peace-building in Kenya. However, authorial intention does not guarantee productive messages and as such the films must be carefully assessed for their critiques of violence and philosophies of reconciliation. Two structuring principles can be seen in each film: first, how the violence is explained and, second, how reconciliation is imagined as possible. Writing within the context of the Rwandan genocide, Mahmood Mamdani argues "we may agree that genocidal violence cannot be understood as rational, yet, we need to understand it as thinkable" (8). This chapter suggests that understanding the 'thinkability' of post-election violence is a key principle in the films. The most common popular explanation for the violence is that it was caused by 'tribalism.' In this scenario, the violence had no structural causes; instead, it was just another outburst of 'atavistic' 'tribal' hatred (Githongo 360). While both formal media and politicians have referred to the post-election violence in terms of "age-old hatreds" (MacArthur 228), this fails to explain either the causes of violence or the role ethnicity played in the violence. The films both perpetuate and subvert this common explanation in their attempts to make the violence 'thinkable.'

Pieces for Peace, for instance, focuses on imagining reconciliation rather than explaining the violence. The film shows ordinary Kenyans being swept up in violence. In "LR45" the main characters, a father and his two sons, are actually shown as being randomly confronted with violence when they venture into the city centre for unrelated business. "Tough Times" focuses on an inter-ethnic couple whose wedding is cancelled because of external pressure about ethnic purity. The critique the film makes thus focuses on reconciliation and togetherness in the face of unexplained violence and this plays out dramatically in the climax of the film. The couple of "Tough Times" is reunited in time for the birth of their child. The father names the child Kenya in a speech, set to the tune of upbeat music, where he says: "We will name him Kenya …

[be]cause he is a symbol of our togetherness. And a reminder of what we went through. It should not have happened. And it shall never happen again." While the same music plays, the brother of "LR 45" are then shown reconciling – the nuclear family metaphorically representing the 'national family' Kenya. In the following and final scene, the characters gather to watch the Kenyan flag being raised when they are interrupted by armed youth, yet, these youth are convinced to lay down their arms when an older man points to the flag and talks to them. Importantly, we cannot hear what the man says – the message of the film is not nuanced in words but rather focuses on major symbols like the national flag. The message is ultimately hopeful – that despite everything togetherness as Kenyans is possible – but this hopeful ending is predicated on eliding a nuanced explanation of the violence and does little to explain what made acts of violence 'thinkable' in the first place. However, as it was made and distributed almost immediately after the violence its focus on reconciliation, on ending violence no matter the reasons that caused it to start, is understandable.

While the title evokes 'togetherness' advocated by *Pieces for Peace*, *Togetherness Supreme* spends only its short epilogue on reconciliation after the violence and instead the film focuses on depicting the run-up to the violence where the outbreak of violence is the climax of the film. Its mode of understanding the 'thinkability' of the violence rests in understanding the violence's root causes. However, it explains the violence almost purely in ethnic terms,[7] which dangerously simplifies a complex situation in which violence "was not caused by ethnic difference per se, but rather by its politicization" (de Smedt 591). Whether or not ethnicity causes violence is often due to the way politicians mobilize and manipulate ethnicity to gain political support (Whitaker 111). The logic of the instrumental nature of ethnicity is that voters assume resources are more likely to come their way if the politician who controls those resources is from their ethnic group as politicians actively campaign on these grounds (Posner 1305), thus, voters are "trapped in an equilibrium where ethnic favouritism is the rule" and they cannot ignore the political and economic implications of this when voting (Bratton and Kimenyi 279).

Togetherness Supreme attempts a realist sensibility, though this is undercut by its simplistic understanding of the events it is attempting to realistically portray. The film is set entirely in Kibera and follows two young men – Kamau and Oti – as they campaign for ODM in the run-up to the election. Portraying young unemployed men as ardent believers in ODM's message is realistic as "much of ODM's support would come from disaffected youth, disillusioned by unfulfilled promises of employment by the Kibaki government" (MacArthur 233). However, the ground the film is built on – realistic depictions of historical events – is itself unstable for if a "filmmaker is to offer critique ... it is not sufficient to portray a situation realistically or authentically" (Dovey 98).

As Mamdani argues "violence cannot be allowed to speak for itself, for violence is not its own meaning. To be made thinkable, it needs to be *historicized*" (229, emphasis in original). *Togetherness Supreme* attempts historicization, but by avoiding analysis of politicized ethnicity it instead dangerously replicates reductive popular explanations of the violence.

In a significant departure from the ideals of realism, *Ni Sisi* is set in Kenya but not in a defined location and it invents ethnic groups rather than referring to the actual ethnic make-up in the Kenyan society. Its critique focuses on the role of rumour in inciting fear and violence, and particularly, on the way politicians manipulate rumour for their own personal gain. Talking specifically about Kibera, Osborn argues that prior to and during the post-election violence:

> Kenyans avidly passed on political gossip, while politicians happily deployed and exploited rumour and misinformation as part of the political process. Rumours and deceit were undoubtedly used to circulate propaganda and half-truths in hopes of mobilizing voters, and over the month following the polls this played its part in the story of violence and displacement in Kibera. (325)

While *Ni Sisi* is not set in Kibera but rather a fictional village it explores exactly these dynamics. Lies and half-truths are shown being spread from a political campaign and then from ordinary person to person through repeated montage sequences of whispering mouths. Tension builds throughout the film as the rumours become more and more violent and ultimately lead to violence at the end of the film's first act. Yet, the film is able to critique the violence rather than simply represent it through its use of a double plot structure with two climaxes.

The first half of the film ends without outbursts of violence – essentially depicting instances of violence that took place in Kenya in 2007/2008. The narrator (a character in the film) then wakes up and we realize the sequence of events we just witnessed were his, potentially prophetic, a dream. The central characters are then shown fighting against the divisive rumour mongering and lies of politicians that the film suggests led to the violence in the first place. The final climax of the film takes place in a church and involves a politician and the congregation (a synecdoche for the town) being confronted openly with the lies he had been spreading through recordings of his words being played through a loudspeaker. Rumour is confronted and overcome with rational facts and truth and through this engagement, the violence of the first act is avoided. Both *Togetherness Supreme* and *Ni Sisi* attempt their critiques by depicting fictionalized versions of the events of the post-election violence, but by moving beyond the conventions of filmic realism *Ni Sisi* can present a more nuanced political analysis.

Togetherness Supreme, Ni Sisi, and *Something Necessary* all suggests that only when conflict is understood can reconciliation happen – thus if the films want to encourage reconciliation they must explain the violence. *Something Necessary* does this through the use of two intertwining character arcs: the first focuses on Anne – a survivor of rape and a gang attack on her farm that left it in ruins, her husband dead, and her son comatose – and the second on Joseph, a member of that gang. Writing the character of Joseph was essential for Kibinge in creating her critique:

> Most importantly of anything for me was just to show that that violence was complicated. It wasn't simplistic; two tribes jumping at each other. And they only way to show that was to show perpetrator as victim. Which in many ways they were. And they are. And it's not easy thing to say when you know the horrible things that these guys did, or if you look at photographs from the Rift Valley that show the whole valley of young guys with bows and arrows just out for blood, the blood of people like Anne. And ... when you think of the sort of gang reactions: Do they really have a choice? Can they really choose not to be a part of these things? (Kibinge)

The film humanizes Joseph by focusing on the quotidian aspects of his life such as his relationship with his mother and that he is saving to buy his girlfriend a mobile phone, and through this we see that not all perpetrators of violence are inherently evil even if they participate in grotesque acts of violence. Joseph is a tragic figure and at the end of the film, he is beaten to death by the members of the gang he deserted when he started trying to atone for his and their actions. Quite simply, he is depicted as *both* perpetrator and victim. *Something Necessary* reflects the fact that the election crisis took place in the context of long-term structural violence – "the constant and humiliating reduction in the physical, intellectual and social life chances of people" through biased structures and practices (Uvin 614). By showing 'perpetrator as victim' Kibinge captures the nuance of "violence as process" and the fact that "violent acts may be spontaneous, but they are more often the product of a longer sequence of historical decisions and political actions" (Anderson and Lochery 328). Like *Ni Sisi, Something Necessary* works to explain the violence, and the critical impetus of both in this regard is understanding the involvement of 'ordinary' people; rather than Othering perpetrators they contextualize them and show that the socio-economic and political conditions in which their actions are rooted must be understood and addressed.

This corpus of films rises to the challenge Mamdani speaks of and attempts – through overlapping and conflicting reasons – to explain why the violence took place and how reconciliation can be imagined moving forward. However, following the groundbreaking work of Stuart Hall in his famed essay "Encoding/decoding" it is no longer possible to examine meaning purely in relation to texts (as previous scholarship on films on the post-election violence does) because meaning "does not always inhere in a text, but is negotiated, made and remade as the text moves" through time and space and is seen by different audiences (Nyaior and Ogude 238–239). Audiences are not homogenous – they interpret media differently, thus creating diverse "readings of the same material" (Diawara 846), which in turn supports the idea that meaning is "actively invented during the process of reception" (Askew 6). Thus, the intention of the filmmakers for their film to contribute towards reconciliation does not ensure that their films actually had this impact: the potential may live in the texts, but it can only be fulfilled if the texts meet actual audiences and hence their circulation must be accounted for (Dovey 59).

Public Lives: Activated Critiques?

As Muhoma and Nyairo argue, "every nation has a collective and public memory" that on one hand "is propagated by the state" and another that "springs unsolicited from the public" in many varied forms (412), furthermore, these repositories of collective memory may be in conflict. From the turmoil of the post-election violence both state and non-state actors worked to pull meaning from the violence and control the narrative. State attempts included forming two commissions of inquiry, the Independent Review Commission focusing on electoral conduct and the Commission of Inquiry into Post-election Violence (Muhoma and Nyairo 412), and it seemed as "though the political class was anxious to sweep the post-election violence under the carpet and sanitize Kenya as the haven of peace within the Horn of Africa, where armed ethnic conflicts, among other forms of violence, abound" (Muhoma and Nyairo 412). Yet, state attempts to quickly 'sanitize' the violence and project a specific image of peace and stability did not remain uncontested and creatives of various kinds also put forward their own narratives of the violence, its causes, and its aftermath. In order to understand this process of contestation it is necessary to look at what film scholar Litheko Modisane terms the 'public lives' of films: "the totality of the events and engagements in the circulation of films across time and space" (10).

The role of filmmakers in shaping this process and speaking back to the state's version of events can be understood through Forest and Johnson's theorizing on national identity formation at 'critical junctures.' A critical juncture is the "temporally and spatially limited" (527) period after a conflict or significant political upheaval where the pre-conflict identity of a nation is no longer tenable and must be refashioned. Crucially, what makes a critical juncture so 'critical' is the fact that the nation's past identity is no longer tenable, as it does not account for the post-conflict conditions in which the society exists. Forest and Johnson specifically study the role of physical sites of memory in the formation of nationalism in Russia post-USSR, but their arguments and approach can be adapted to the study of public discourse and the arts because they theorize the contest between elites and ordinary members of the public during these critical junctures. Arguably the violence of 2007/2008 opened a critical juncture in Kenyan political history where elites had to scramble to control the narrative and where ordinary citizens – including filmmakers – could contest these official narratives of history and reshape the nation. Rather than looking at public landscapes I am interested in public discourse and the struggle between elites and non-elites – in this case filmmakers – to control and contest narratives of Kenyan history.

While "political elites generally have far greater power than does the public to shape the physical and symbolic representation of national identity", non-elites can still contest this power because "the ability of the state or political elites to impose their intended meaning on an audience is limited by the active role readers play in the creation of meaning" (Forest and Johnson 536 and 538) or, as Modisane would put it, the "role" of a text "resides in its circulation and subjection to many uses over time" (9). Elites are constrained by public opinion because, despite the fact that they are far more powerful than ordinary citizens, they cannot impose meaning on events or locations if the public reads those sites differently. The interchange between elites and non-elites, whether collaborative or conflictual, produces certain definitions of the 'nation' and delineates the possibilities of what the nation can become. These dynamics of struggle always exist, but they become uniquely important during critical junctures:

> Not only do critical junctures loosen the normal, inertia-bound, path dependent ties among and within political and economic institutions, but they create the possibility for significant redefinitions of national history and identity as well. Powerful political actors thus have a rare chance to impress their conceptions of the national character onto the public landscape, and in doing so assert their right to lead the nation and the state into the new era. (Forest and Johnson 527)

Governments of changing societies seek to memorialize the past as a means of forming civic democratic national identity and this process is shaped by the struggles between elite groups and multiple publics each fighting for their own interests (Forest, Johnson, and Till). Yet, crucially, what happens at these critical junctures is not random; it has to fit within the "realistic" worldview of the citizenry (Cruz), meaning they have space to reform the image of the nation, but only insofar as non-elites 'buy-in'. With the concept of critical juncture in mind it becomes ever more important to examine the public lives of these texts to see how that opened space was seized by filmmakers and to what effect.

These films were all made and circulated both in the aftermath of the 2007/2008 post-election violence and prior to the next election in 2013. Films about the post-election violence can be divided into two circulation periods: first, the aftermath of the 2007 election (*Pieces for Peace* and *Togetherness Supreme*) and, second, in the immediate run-up to the 2013 election (*Ni Sisi* and *Something Necessary*). The relative proximity to each election shaped the way the texts were circulated. It is important to note that one of the major precipitating factors of the violence – the election – is a repeatable event. This gives a particularly urgent timeframe to filmmaking if the filmmakers are hoping to shape the future in some way (i.e. preventing another episode of massive violence). If films want to engage with Kenyan residents – as these four films do – then it logically follows that the films must be visible in Kenya. The production context of the films is essential to understanding their circulation in Kenya because these two factors are inextricably linked in the domestic film market where the infrastructure of distribution relies heavily on the production company's resources and connections, as such, production and circulation will be discussed in tandem here.

The producers of *Pieces for Peace* and *Togetherness Supreme* could mobilize different amounts of resources for the distribution of their respective films; yet, access to resources is only one factor impacting the spread of a film across time and space. According to co-director Mburu Kimani *Pieces for Peace* was screened in theatres in Nairobi (including suburbs like Kibera), Nakuru, and Mombasa, and its most predominant form of distribution was screenings at government forums (Kimani). The distribution of the film has been somewhat limited and Kimani speculated that had not been 'distributed as fully as possible' because the government thought the wounds from the violence were still too fresh to 'really put it out there' (Kimani). However, its circulation must be contextualized within the context of Riverwood, Nairobi's fast-paced vernacular film industry whose projects circulate along the same networks as pirated foreign films (Overbergh 2015, 99) where films tend to sell an average of 3,000 to 6,000 copies (Overbergh 107). Kimani and Bresson are both part of the filmmaking association Third Force who, while being part of Riverwood, self-consciously try to make 'professional' films that distinguish themselves from usual Riverwood fare. Yet, Kimani said he uses conventional Riverwood distribution structures and that he shares an audience with Riverwood: "the audiences are the same. I grew up in the village, I like to tell local stories. I come up with very common-man stories. These audiences are not very urbanized" (qtd. in Overbergh 107). In contrast to the other three features it was made without the backing of international institutions,

though it did receive some financial support from the Kenya Film Commission (Kimani). The ability for the film to 'activate' its message of
unity and reconciliation was constrained by the material limitations of
its circulation network.

While *Pieces for Peace* was made by two independent Riverwood
filmmakers working within a limited distribution network, *Togetherness Supreme* was made within the context of an internationally funded
and connected organization. Hot Sun Films is the for-profit film production company associated with the media NGO the Hot Sun Foundation,
which in turn is based in Kibera but "receives its primary funding from
Belgian government initiative Africalia" (McNamara 178). *Togetherness
Supreme* was produced by Hot Sun Films in conjunction with Bajo La
Manga Lab, Hot Sun Foundation, and CNAC (Venezuela) and directed
by Nathan Collett. Hot Sun Films' ability to potentially mobilize audiences greater than Riverwood's must be read within this context. According to its producers, by 16th December 2010, 35,000 Kenyans had
seen the film (Kibera Film School). According to their Facebook page[8]
this included the Togetherness Supreme Rural Peace tour with Child
Wellness Fund, from September 4, 2010 to September 10, 2010 held
in several locations across Kenya, and several screenings in Nairobi's
'slums' (e.g. one screening in tandem with SlumTv in Mathare ("Screening in Mathare"). Following these screenings, it transitioned to travelling
the international film festival circuit. *Pieces for Peace* circulated within
commercial and government forums to a limited number of Kenyan residents whereas *Togetherness Supreme* was able to leverage NGO networks and potentially take their film to a much bigger audience across a
larger geographic area.

However, Hot Sun's goals of showing "the film broadly across Kenya
leading up to the 2012 elections and be part of the dialogue for peace
and reconciliation" ("Togetherness Supreme wins at ZIFF"), seems
to have potentially been undercut by what can be read as their desire
to protect their copyright and therefore the potential to make money
from the film. In an anecdote recounted by McNamara "as social activist Abdul Kassim commented in Kibera during the film's release in
2010, the promotion of the film was so intense and its actual distribution
so non-existent he had mistaken the film's poster for another religious
positive-message campaign, failing to realise that it was a movie at all"
(180). This evidence, anecdotal as it is, reflects a fundamental issue in
Nairobi-based filmmaking: if filmmakers want to control the circulation
of their films, which means keeping them away from pirates, they have
a limited number of options for distribution and exhibition locally.[9] The
understandable intention to protect their film from illegal distribution
and thus guard their investment nevertheless limited the film's wider distribution and potential to participate in public conversations on reconciliation and nation-building.[10]

These distribution issues were negotiated very differently in the second phase of film circulation (in the run-up to the 2013 election). Production on the film adaptation of *Ni Sisi* began in 2012 with backing from HIVOS, a Minority Rights Group and Safaricom ("Trustee Report" 4). It was released in February 2013 leaving a narrow window for its distribution prior to the election. Unlike Hot Sun, which tightly controlled the release of their film, S.A.F.E. actively embraced pirate infrastructure as a way of increasing the film's circulation. In fact, one of their many distribution strategies was to actually give copies "to over 200 video pirates in Nairobi, Eldoret, Kisumu, Nakuru, Mombasa and Kilifi counties" ("Trustee Report" 5). Additionally, the film screened on free-to-air television twice, in cinemas in Nairobi and Kisumu, "at several community public screenings in 12 locations, reaching 7,500 people," and was distributed to a wide variety of stakeholders including the police, youth groups, "social gathering places", and businesses ("Trustee Report" 4–5). S.A.F.E. also launched a social media campaign to increase the visibility of the film ("Trustee Report" 5). S.A.F.E outright framed their film in the context of preventing future violence at the 2013 election. The DVD of *Ni Sisi* comes wrapped with a text that reads, "now that you have seen the film, spread the message of peace to your friends, family and community" alongside a list of suggested practical actions to do just that.[11] This DVD cover paratext acted as a "threshold" to "prime" the text for interpretation (Modisane 18). Clearly, S.A.F.E. intended their film to contribute towards a public discourse on non-violence and actively proposed strategies for peace-building during election times. *Ni Sisi* thus spread much more widely than either earlier film, and this spread was influenced directly by the upcoming election.

While it circulated in the same time period as *Ni Sisi, Something Necessary* took a different path – and this reflects its production story. *Ni Sisi* was made by a social advocacy charity whereas *Something Necessary* was produced by a film training group whose end goal was producing high-quality cinema and developing film industries and makers in Africa. Its production infrastructure was therefore not used to spread its message across Kenya like *Ni Sisi,* but to take the film to prestigious festivals outside the country such as the Toronto International Film Festival (TIFF). However, *Something Necessary* was popular locally and screened at Nairobi's Junction cinema for almost two months (Kibinge Q&A) and "across many of Nairobi's major cinemas" (McNamara 26) – a highly unusual feat as cinema space in the city is overwhelmingly dominated by Hollywood and other foreign films and locally made cinema is almost never screened in theatres outside of special one-off events. The film's public life transcended the primary goal of its producers as local demand to see the film clearly contributed to its abnormally long stay in cinemas. While organizations like S.A.F.E. and Hot Sun could mobilize larger distribution networks than independent filmmakers like Kimani and Bresson, resources are only one factor that impacting the circulation of the films. As the example of *Something Necessary* demonstrates, the public lives of films are influenced not only by producer intentions, but also by audience desires.

Films can play a valuable role in reshaping public discourse on violence and history and contribute to the democratic process, which matters because a stable functioning democracy was what was at stake in the post-election violence and in the 2013 election. Democracy has many meanings, but here it will be taken to infer, first, 'dissensus', meaning the right to express dissenting opinions (Willems 48), and second, the right to self-representation (Adamu 223–224). These conceptions are compatible as both argue that the right to express oneself is at the heart of democracy – even if that expression is non-conformist. The films discussed here offer conflicting and dissenting opinions to official narratives and express the rights of their filmmakers to represent their society in their own way. However, the films also provide material for ordinary people to think through their own 'dissensus' and 'self-representation' because they offer "a variety of material and stylistic sources for 'trying on' new identity options" (Narunsky-Laden 177). Films are but one part of this process and in Kibinge's words they are "part of many important conversations I think that we need to be having" (Q&A), but as uniquely public artworks, they have a rare potential power to contest official and elite narratives.

Conclusion

The past "is modeled, invented, reinvented, and reconstructed by the present" (Assman 210); the meaning of past events is never final, and therefore there is room for artists and state elites to "dredge meaning out of" it (Rollins 8) through cultural production and official narrativizing. As Rosenstone argues, "the past [films] create is not the same as the past provided by traditional history, but it certainly should be called history—if by that word we mean a serious encounter with the lingering meaning of past events" (5). The films discussed here explicitly aim to create meaning from the past and essentially present a different historical and political narrative from official explanations. I have argued that the election crisis opened up a 'critical juncture' where non-state actors – in this case filmmakers – could use their interpretations and representations of the past to contribute towards the formation of a new Kenya. They do not present a unified counter-narrative and they were all produced and consumed in different ways as I have shown, but this diversity and 'dissensus' is precisely the point in fostering democratic space and nation-building.

This chapter has discussed feature-length fiction films that focus their narratives specifically on the post-election violence all made and circulated between the election of 2007 and 2013. However, understanding the violence and its aftermath continues to be a critical project for Kenyan filmmakers as they continue to foster the conversation that, as Kibginge says, 'we need to be having'. For instance, Mbithi Masya included a subplot about a priest tormented by guilt over his role in the post-election violence in his new film *Kati Kati* (2016) because 'the post-election violence still haunts us [Kenyans] because we never dealt with it and Kenyans have a habit of not confronting our own actions as a country' (Masya Q&A). Muhoma and Nyairo boldly argued in 2011 that "It is the failure of Kenya to honestly "look to the past" that has given forth to the cycle of violence every five years" (422). As such, these films can be read, through their attempts to historicize the violence and make it 'thinkable', as an attempt to look beyond simplistic and reductive official narratives and confront the past in the hopes of transforming the future.

Notes

1 Kenya is among the "most centralized states in the world," (Ghai 225), and this extreme concentration of power among the executive has made the presidency a top prize, which has caused politicians and political parties to have "a winner–takes–all view of political power and its associated economic by–products'" (de Smedt 585).

2 Violence has become a routinized part of each election since 1992 (Anderson and Lochery 329) and it is reported with "little comment" in the formal media. For instance, almost 600 people were killed in the three months running up to the 2007 election and this went almost unreported (Cheeseman 170).

3 *Ni Sisi* and *Togetherness Supreme* were directed by non-Kenyans, but Reding and Collett are both based in Nairobi and the films' respective production companies are deeply embedded in local contexts militating against the idea that only Kenyan nationals can make powerful films that engage with local contexts. In addressing one of the major issues at stake in many 'foreign' films made in Africa Cieplak argues the "lack of Rwandan agency over their own representation on-screen have been reflected in the films made about the country," for instance the famed *Hotel Rwanda* was shot in South Africa and its truthfulness has been debated in Rwanda (75). The four films considered here negotiate these potential problems differently: for instance, *Togetherness Supreme*: "involved more people directly and indirectly that any other project in the history of Kibera. On any given day there were at least 70 people on location and up to 300 with extras for the crowd scenes" ("Impact"). Shooting lasted 30 days in Kibera ("Red One") and most of the material resources needed in the film shoot – including security, cooking facilities, wardrobe, props, and locations – were sourced from Kibera ("Impact"), so, unlike the films described by Cieplak, this film did engage strongly with the community it was trying to represent.

4 Nathan Collett wrote the screenplay "based on real-life experiences of the Kibera writer Evans K. Kamau" (Starkman 269).

5 One Film Day is "supported by the German-based DW Akademie, a media capacity building cooperation development group, and British-funded Nairobi-based organization Ginger Ink Films" (McNamara 2016, 26).

6 While Kibinge did not choose the topic for the film, she had systematically addressed the post-election violence in several previous films. Her 60-minute

documentary *Headlines in History* (2010), an exploration of Kenyan history as told through the corporate story of the Nation Media Group, concluded with the post-election violence. She also made a 12-minute short film for the Steps Why Democracy? series called *Coming of Age* (2008) where the climax is the violence. Finally, she made the 40-minute documentary *Peace Wanted Alive* (2009), which was explicitly about the violence.

7 This explanation is set-up from the very start of the film and then reinforced throughout. The opening titles set against establishing shots of Nairobi and then more specifically Kibera, read: "September 16th, 2007; President Kibaki, of the Kikuyu tribe, runs for re-election. Despite economic growth under President Kibaki, many have been left behind; Kibera slums; home to over 1 million people; many blame their situation on the political dominance of the Kikuyu tribe. Anger towards the Kikuyu tribe runs at an all-time high." The election is immediately and dominantly framed in the context of ethnic conflict.

8 Facebook is a commonly used publicity tool by film industry professionals and fans in Kenya, and even government organizations such as the Kenya Film Classification Board use Facebook as a primary mode of communication.

9 Films may show in cinemas (though this is rare), in international cultural institutions like the Goethe Institut and Alliance Française, the local arts and advocacy centre Pawa254, or in one-off screenings. Releasing a DVD for sale is widely believed to be a risky move given Nairobi's pervasive culture of DVD-based film piracy.

10 Thus, while I could acquire a copy of *Pieces for Peace* from a video store in the Central Business District I had to specially arrange a visit to Hot Sun's office in Kibera in order to view the film – a move predicated on the fact I already knew the film existed and had a vested interest in viewing it over and above the mass of films that are easily available in Nairobi.

11 The requested actions are:

> 1. Text 5 people with the message of peace from the film *Ni Sisi*; 2. Tell 5 people about what you learned about Post-Election Violence and keeping peace; 3. Vote peacefully; 4. Gender Violence is a crime. If you experience gender-based violence during the elections, seek immediate medical attention; report it to the police station; and visit or call your nearest Gender Violence Recovery Centre www.gvrc.or.ke; 5. On and after election day, send a text message to 3002, send an email to reports. uchaguzi@gmail.com or tweet @uchaguzi with any significant information about the election process.

> They then provide their contact information through links on twitter, Facebook, YouTube, email, and their website and a link to the Google Elections Hub where they could find up-to-date information about the election.

Works Cited

Adamu, Abdalla Uba. "Transnational Flows and Local Identities in Muslim Northern Nigerian Films: from Dead Poets Society through Mohabbatein to So..." *Popular Media, Democracy, and Development in Africa*. Ed. Herman Wasserman. London and New York: Routledge, 2011. 223–235. Print.

Anderson, David, and Emma Lochery. "Violence and Exodus in Kenya's Rift Valley, 2008: Predictable and Preventable?" *Journal of Eastern African Studies* 2.2 (2008): 328–343.

Askew, Kelly. "Introduction." *The Anthropology of Media: A Reader*. Ed. Kelly Askew and Richard Wilk. Oxford: Blackwell, 2002. 1–13. Print.

Assman, Jan. "Excerpts from "Moses the Egyptian: The Memory of Egypt in Western Monotheism" and "Collective Memory and Cultural Identity"." *The Collective Memory Reader.* Ed. Jeffrey K. Olick, Vered Vinitzky-Seroussi, and Daniel Levy. Oxford: Oxford University Press, 2011. 209–215. Print.

Branch, Daniel and Nic Cheeseman. "Democratization, Sequencing, and State Failure in Africa: Lessons from Kenya." *African Affairs* 108.430 (2009): 1–26.

Bratton, Michael, and Mwangi S. Kimenyi. "Voting in Kenya: Putting Ethnicity in Perspective." *Journal of Eastern African Studies* 2.2 (2008): 272–289.

Cheeseman, Nic. "The Kenyan Elections of 2007: An Introduction." *Journal of Eastern African Studies* 2.2 (2008): 166–184.

Cieplak, Piotr A. "Alternative African Cinemas: A Case Study of Rwanda." *Journal of African Media Studies* 2.1 (2010): 73–90.

Coming of Age. Dir. Judy Kibinge. STEPS International in association with Seven Productions. 2008. Short documentary.

Cruz, Consuelo. "Identity and Persuasion: How Nations Remember their Pasts and Make their Futures." *World Politics* 52.3 (2000): 275–312.

de Smedt, Johan. "'No Raila, No Peace!' Big Man Politics and Election Violence at the Kibera Grassroots." *African Affairs* 108.433 (2009): 581–598.

Diawara, Manthia. "Black Spectatorship: Problems of Identification and Resistance." *Film Theory and Criticism: Introductory Readings.* Ed. Leo Braudy and Marshall Cohen. Oxford: Oxford University Press, 1999. 845–853. Print.

Dovey, Lindiwe. *African Film and Literature: Adapting Violence to the Screen.* New York: Columbia University Press, 2009. Print.

Forest, Benjamin and Juliet Johnson. "Unraveling the Threads of Soviet History: Soviet Era Monuments and Post-Soviet National Identity in Moscow." *Annals of the Association of American Geographers* 92 (2002): 524–547.

Forest, Benjamin, Juliet Johnson, and Karen Till. "Post-Totalitarian National Identity: Public Memory in Germany and Russia." *Social and Cultural Geography* 5.3 (2004): 357–380.

Ghai, Yash. "Devolution: Restructuring the Kenyan State." *Journal of Eastern African Studies* 2.2 (2008): 211–226.

Giruzzi, Clara. "A Feminist Approach to Contemporary Female Kenyan Cinema: Women and Nation in *From a Whisper* (Kahiu, 2008) and *Something Necessary* (Kibinge, 2013)." *Journal of African Cinemas* 7.2 (2015): 79–96.

Githongo, John. "Kenya – Riding the Tiger." *Journal of Eastern African Studies* 2.2 (2008): 359–367.

Hall, Stuart. "Encoding/Decoding." *Culture, Media, Language: Working Papers in Cultural Studies, 1972–79.* Ed. Stuart Hall, Dorothy Hobson, Andrew Lowe, and Paul Willis. London: Hutchinson, 1980. 128–138. Print.

Headlines in History. Dir. Judy Kibinge. NTV. 2010. Feature documentary.

Hees, Edwin. "The Birth of a Nation: Contextualizing De Voortrekkers (1916)." *To Change Reels: Film and Film Culture in South Africa.* Ed. Isabel Balseiro and Ntongela Masilela. Detroit: Wayne State University Press, 2003. 49–69. Print.

Hot Sun Films. "Impact on Kibera." N.p., n.d. Web 7 June 2012.

———. "Red One Camera." *Togetherness Supreme.* N.p., n.d. Web. 7 June 2012.

Hot Sun Foundation. "Togetherness Supreme Wins at ZIFF 2011." *Kibera Kid.* Blogspot.co.uk, 25 June 2011. Web. 18 Aug. 2012.

———. "Screening in Mathare with Slum Tv." *Kibera Kid.* Blogspot.co.uk, 2 August 2010. Web. 29 August 2012.

Kati Kati. Dir. Mbithi Masya. One Fine Day Films. 2016. Feature Fiction.

Kibera Film School. "Hope and Reconciliation: Togetherness Supreme and the International Criminal Court." *Kibera Kid.* Blogspot.co.uk, 16 December 2010. Web. 29 August 2012.

Kibinge, Judy. Q&A at Film Africa chaired by Robin Steedman. London. 7 Nov. 2013.

———. Personal Interview. London. 6 Nov. 2013.

Kimani, Mburu. Personal Interview. Nairobi. 10 April. 2012.

MacArthur, Julie. "How the West was Won: Regional Politics and Prophetic Promises in the 2007 Kenya Elections." *Journal of Eastern African Studies* 2.2 (2008): 227–241.

Mamdani, Mahmood. *When Victims Become Killers: Colonialism, Nativism, and the Genocide in Rwanda.* Princeton: Princeton University Press, 2001. Print.

Masya, Mbithi. Q&A at Film Africa chaired by Isabel Moura Mendes. London. 3 November 2016.

Modisane, Litheko. *South Africa's Renegade Reels: The Making and Public Lives of Black-Centered Film.* New York: Palgrave Macmillan, 2012. Print.

Mugubi, John. "Violence as a Symbolic Tool of Enunciation: Film as an Artistic Response to Kenya's Socio-eco-political Realities." *Journal of African Cinemas* 6.2 (2014): 195–204.

———. "Deliniation of National Healing and Conflict Resolution in Film: A Case Study of Kenya." *International Journla of Music and Performing Arts* 2.1 (2014): 15–23.

Muhoma, Catherine and Joyce Nyairo. "Inscribing Memory, Healing a Nation: Post-Election Violence and the Search for Truth and Justice in Kenya Burning." *Journal of Eastern African Studies* 5:3 (2011): 411–426.

Narunsky-Laden, Sonja. "(South) African Articulations of the Ordinary, or, how Popular Print Commodities (Re)organize our Lives." *Popular Media, Democracy and Development in Africa.* Ed. Herman Wasserman. London and New York: Routledge, 2011. 174–187. Print.

Ni Sisi. Dir. Nick Reding. S.A.F.E., 2013. Feature Fiction.

Nyaior, Joyce, and James Ogude. "Popular Music, Popular Politics: Unbwogable and the Idioms of Freedom in Kenyan Popular Music." *African Affairs* (2005): 225–249.

Osborn, Michelle. "Fuelling the Flames: Rumour and Politics in Kibera." *Journal of Eastern African Studies* 2.2 (2008): 315–327.

Overbergh, Ann. "Kenya's Riverwood: Market Structure, Power Relations, and Future Outlooks." *Journal of African Cinemas* 7.2 (2015): 97–115.

Peace: an Aftermath of the Postpoll Crisis. Dir. SlumTv (Esther Wangiru, Cosmos Njanga, Pauline Awour, Benson Kamau). SlumTv. 2009. Participatory Documentary.

Peace Wanted Alive. Dir. Judy Kibinge. Seven Productions. 2009. Short Documentary.

Pieces for Peace. Dir. Robby Bresson and Mburu Kimani. XMedia Kenya and Hidden Talent Entertainment. 2008. Feature fiction.

Posner, Dan. "Regime Change and Ethnic Cleavages in Africa." *Comparative Political Studies* 40.11 (2007): 1302–1327.

Reding, Nick. Personal Interview. Nairobi. 3 April. 2012.

Rollins, Peter C. "Introduction: Film and History: Our Media Environment as a New Frontier." *Lights, Camera, History: Portraying the Past in Film.* Ed. Richard Francaviglia and Jerry Rodnitzky. College Station: Texas A&M University Press, 2007. 1–10. E-book.

Rosenstone, Robert A. "Introduction." *Revisioning History: Film and the Construction of a New Past.* Ed. Robert A. Rosenstone. Princeton: Princeton University Press, 1995. 3–13. Print.

S.A.F.E. Report of the Trustees for the Year End 31st December 2013. 1–16, n.d. Web. 14 Nov. 2016.

———. "Peace." S.A.F.E., n.d. Web. 13 Nov. 2016.

Something Necessary. Dir. Judy Kibinge. One Fine Day Films. 2013. Feature Fiction.

Starkman, Ruth. "A Review of Togetherness Supreme." *Peace Review* 23:2 (2011): 268–272.

Togetherness Supreme. Dir. Nathan Collett. Hot Sun Films. 2010. Feature Fiction.

Togetherness Supreme: The Story Behind the Film. Prod. Hot Sun Films. Vimeo. N.p., 2010. Web. 14 June 2012.

Togetherness Supreme. *Togetherness Supreme.* 2012. http://www.facebook.com/togethernesssupreme, accessed 12/6/2012.

Uvin, Peter. "Development Aid and Structural Violence: The Case of Rwanda." *Perspectives on Africa.* Ed. Roy Richard Grinker, Stephen C. Lubkemann and Christopher B. Steiner. 2nd ed. West Sussex: Wiley-Blackwell, 2010. Print.

Wale Watu. Dir. Cajetan Boy. Etc Cetera Productions. 2008. Short film.

Whitaker, B.E. "Citizens and Foreigners: Democratization and the Politics of Exclusion in Africa." *African Studies Review* 48.1 (2005): 100–126.

Willems, Wendy. "At the Crossroads of the Formal and Popular: Convergence Culture and New Publics in Zimbabwe." *Popular Media, Democracy and Development in Africa.* Ed. Herman Wasserman. London and New York: Routledge, 2011. 46–62. Print.

18 Bestial Zoosemic Labelling in Kenyan Political Songs
A Conceptual Metaphor Perspective

George Ouma Ogal and Titus Karuri Macharia

Introduction: The Connection between Cognitive Linguistics and Metaphor

The axiom that language propagates and sustains varied ideologies ranging from simple to ticklish issues in pursuit of speakers' stardom does not only reside in Kenya but is also the blast-off point in unpacking meaning where "backstage cognition" fills a lacuna traceable to the apparent mismatch between the artists' background and the consumer's limited linguistic resources. The deficiency of grammar necessitates a cognitive linguist's lens for a fuller explication of a text. Whereas the place of language in predicting strained relationships in a country has evoked international assiduity, there is a paucity of formally documented ethnic evidence in melodic compositions. Intellectual endeavours unclothing language and cognition cannot be controverted but the diligence paid to the study of zoosemy in Kenyan political lyrics within a cognitive-semantics perspective has hitherto been hemmed in. This chapter, therefore, analyses the Bestial Zoosemic labelling in Kenyan political songs. It identifies, classifies, and annotates the conceptual metaphors using descriptive research design within the Conceptual Metaphor Theory. The chapter established that animals are stratified source domains richly used to depict the characters in the songs. The authors conclude that culturally embodied zoosemic labelling in Kenyan songs fuels atrocity and need censoring before releasing it to the public.

The inability of grammar to fully hatch literary subjects was the basis for development of cognitive linguistics, an apparatus providing insightful inquiry into the mind, language, and the sociocultural experiences within a locality (Evans and Green 2006). Cognitive linguistics as a discipline helps provide meaning where "backstage cognition" fills a lacuna traceable to the misunderstanding arising from an artist's expressions and a reader's limited linguistic resources. According to Fauconnier (2001), language is not particularly a product of certain mental structures but of general cognitive principles used by humans to conceptualize all facets of reality. This premise shows the relationship between daily linguistic phenomena and literary expressions as cushioned by Freeman (2000, 253). He adds that the decoding of the experiences around us is shaped by language, mental processes, and the environment. This echoes Lakoff and Johnson's (1980) assertion that our understanding of the world leans on certain correspondences and mappings such as metaphor, analogy, and metonymy, all of which are masts of cognitive linguistics. In the words of Kövecses (2000), these pillars of cognitive linguistics are useful in making concrete sense out of mere abstractions.

Metaphorical studies are often excluded from generative language studies for lack of operational principles that would unearth the phenomena. The word 'metaphor' is derived from two Latin roots: "meta" meaning "over" and "pherein" meaning "to transfer" or to "carry beyond." The transference of one word to another normally takes the form of plants (plantosemy), animals (zoosemy), or objects (Kiełtyka and Kleparski 2005). The role played by metaphorical expressions, according to Freeman (2000), is to conceptually sustain reasoning and thought in the creation of social and psychological reality. This means that metaphors do not only apply to poetic language but also to conventional everyday discourse (Croft and Cruse 2004). The metaphor is therefore primarily a matter of thought and action and only derivatively a matter of language.

The principle guiding conceptualization of metaphors is referred to as the great chain of being proposed by Kövecses (2002). This premise arranges all things in the universe according to strict hierarchical order which is divinely planned. This order is vertically planned as a chain in which varied entities occupy places based on distinct properties and behaviour (Kövecses 2002). The transference and ontological mappings involved in metaphorical utterances are associated with at least one property of the elements in the hierarchical chain. In this order, therefore, the top position is occupied by God, then cosmos / universe, society, humans, animals, plant, complex objects, and natural physical things in this strict order (Kövecses 2002, 126–128). Each level is characterized by specific attributes which can be metaphorically inherited. According to Lakoff and Turner (1989), the great chain of being metaphor is "[...] a tool of great power and scope because [...] it allows us to comprehend general human character traits in terms of well-understood nonhuman attributes...." (172). Thus, the great chain of being metaphor helps appreciate people's inferred conducts and personalities as they are constructed in literary pieces like songs and books.

Language and Atrocity

The nexus between language and violence, which is the burden of this paper, perhaps resides in the proverbial admonition that "Death and life are in the power of the tongue: and they that love it shall eat the fruit thereof" (Proverbs 18:21, KJV). It is therefore apparent that language, which is majorly expressed through the tongue, could be a savour of life unto life or death unto death. In the words of O'Ballance (1979), the key cause of world violence is a piece of writing or speech whose language consists of half-chewed statements that prejudice a community against another. Deadly consequences are reaped when atrocious words are uttered by personalities who are oblivious of the consequences. Somerville (2011) chronicles that in Kenya, messages of incitement along ethnic lines that are likely to stir up violence have been to blame for cases of insurrection in the country.

Notably, Prothrow-Stith and Weissman (1991) observe that oftentimes, perpetrators of ethnic violence use their local tongues to propagate turbulence in various doses. It therefore means that one of the key causes of violence in a country is traceable to the kind of language used by those involved in the conflict. As posited by Somerville (2011), the structure of political discourses communicated in vernacular with many pseudonyms and fictitious characters that are metaphorically presented should be seriously investigated for in these reside inflammatory tribal animosity. Writing about the causes of violence in Rwanda in 1944, Schabas (2000) traces the pathway to genocide from the language of incitement used by the press which supposedly enjoyed the freedom of the media. He criminalizes the "willing executioners" for abusing both print and radio to proliferate ferocity in the genocidal food chain. Killingsworth (2005) notes that although artists enjoy poetic licence, some degree of reservation and censorship is necessary because absolute freedom may border on infringement of people's rights through abusive symbolic language. Thus, language is a potent tool for expressing unparalleled conflict fertilizing insinuations.

Rationale of the Study

The motivation for the present research was based on a number of factors. Firstly, the diligence paid to scholarly research bordering on cognitive linguistics in the country has been hemmed in (Gathigia 2014). Undertaking cognitive analysis of love metaphors, Gathigia (2014) postulates that the provisions of grammar are inadequate in unpacking the meaning of non-phraseological elements. Zhang (2009) advances that there is an apparent lack of research on the utility of cognitive linguistics in unearthing meaning of non-phraseological forms such as analogy, metonymy, metaphors, and counterfactual thinking. Accordingly, rigorous energy should be invested in this area. The scarcity of cognitive linguistics in decipherment of texts within the Kenyan locale is a key motivation for the current research.

Secondly, considering that metaphors could be referring to God, cosmos/universe, society, humans, animals, plant, complex objects, and natural objects, the present paper chose zoosemy (animal metaphors) due to a number of factors. Kövecses (2000) notes that humans often resort to animal characters to depict other humans because the behaviour of these animals is often overt. The conceptualization of humans in terms of animals is twofold – the attributes could either be desirable or distasteful (Kövecses 2002). Milić (2013) stresses that the position of an animal in the GREAT CHAIN OF BEING makes its transference positive or pejorative. In consideration of ethnic labelling in Kenyan political songs, the current paper chose the bestial (beastly) metaphors (e.g. dog and hyena) as these are the ones that stir insurrection as opposed to positive characters such as lion and bull (Kövecses 2000). Thus, it is imperative to consider the place of such zoosemic labelling in Kenyan songs.

Additionally, our motivation to study political songs was housed in Haas' (1990) aphorism that no amount of violence, however little, occurs without association with political catalysts in a country. On the other hand, Njogu, and Maupeu (2007) opine that political songs are quite captivating since they contain skilful praises wrapped in subtle tribal jibes that often carry the audiences away thus leaving them less cognizant of the language use since most concentrate fully on the rhythmic patterns of the renditions. Along these lines, we chew over animal metaphors in Kenyan political songs.

Theoretical Underpinning of the Study

The theoretical fabric on which this study is premised is a cognitive domain referred to as Conceptual Metaphor Theory (CMT). This apparatus was originally developed by Lakoff and Johnson in 1980 in a seminal publication *Metaphors We Live By*. CMT hypothesizes the universality of metaphor in both commonplace speech and literary expressions. Also, the theory qualifies metaphorical studies to be conceptual rather than linguistic thus requiring conceptual operations in unlocking the internal structures. This is the idea reverberated by Gibbs (1994) who argues that the brain retrieves certain information depending on the locality of expressions to make sense of non-phraseological elements such as metaphorical language. CMT advances that the transference of name from one entity to another is motivated by ontological mappings guided by certain domains. These include the *source domain* and *target domain* (Lakoff and Johnson 2009). Defining the two domains, Chung (2005) observes that abstract concepts are the targets while concrete ones are the source. Meaning is therefore constructed following mappings that build and sustain mental spaces as we talk and develop discourse structures. Fauconnier (1997) notes that CMT penetrates the mind and establishes connections "between our understanding of language and the way we comprehend human thought and activity in general" (11). In this apparatus, entities are likened to each other using sets of correspondences such as "copula" or "as" (Johnson and Lakoff 1980). That is to say, the target domain becomes the source domain. By way of example, Ethnic Group A is a frog (see Findings 18.1 and Discussions). Along these precepts, CMT becomes the most useful tool to investigate zoosemic labelling in Kenyan political songs.

Research Methodology

The present research utilized survey descriptive research design. This precursory system that informs the reader "of phenomena as experienced by investigators and interpreted in relevant contexts" was deemed best for the study (Bryman 2006). Expressly, the paper adopted a descriptive survey design because it sought to conduct a perusal of the Kenyan political songs before elucidating instances of protest speech and atrocious insinuations.

Eight political songs were purposively sampled for instances of bestial labelling. According to Tongco (2007), purposive sampling comes in handy where studies involving anthropological discoveries are required. Also referred to as judgement sampling, the paper used the method because it is cost and time effective. Also, content analysis, which is a constituent of qualitative research suggested by Creswell (2012), governed the research because the researchers are conversant with the vernaculars in which labelling is done in the Kenyan arena. Content analysis was used on the justification of its highly analytical structure in describing data which is impressionistic, intuitive, and interpretive.

Further, Krippendorff (2012) observes that content analysis gives a direct look at communication and discourses hence establishing the fundamental point of social interaction. Content analysis is superior because it is not unidirectional but involves moderately sized data which is both summative and directive. Rosengren (1981) echoes that profound textual analysis should use content analysis for a fuller explication of the text. Further, the current paper chose content analysis because it does not deal with haphazard data but relational themes which are flexible and occurring in different cultural contexts (Patton 2002). Four annotators (two assistants and the researchers) discussed the metaphors and established the inferred meanings based on the contexts of use.

Animal Metaphors in Political Songs in Kenya

In order to demystify the bestial zoosemic labelling in Kenyan political songs, it is important to borrow the GREAT CHAIN OF BEING analysis proposed by (Kövecses 2002) whose primary objective is to assign all things in the universe according to strict vertical protraction. The study established that beastly animal metaphors are stratified source domains related to characters in the sampled political songs. The general finding is that A HUMAN BEING IS AN ANIMAL. *Table 18.1* below summarizes the instances identified in the sampled songs.

Table 18.1 Animal metaphors in sampled political songs in Kenya and their "reliability measures"

No	Metaphor	Conceptual metaphor	Positive value	Negative value	Reliability measures				
					Coder 1	Coder 2	Coder 3	Coder 4	Total
1	Raila is a monkey	Animal		✓	0.25	0.25	0.25	0.25	1.00
2	Peter Kenneth is a hyena	Animal		✓	0.25	0.25	0.25	0.25	1.00
3	Isaac Ruto is a leopard	Animal		✓	0.25	0.25	0.25	0.25	1.00
4	Kibaki is a frog	Animal		✓	0.25	0.25	0.25	0.25	1.00
5	Moi is a mongoose	Animal		✓	0.25	0.25	0.25	0.25	1.00
6	Kikuyus are wolves	Animal		✓	0.25	0.25	0.25	0.25	1.00
7	The government is a snake	Animal		✓	0.25	0.25	0.25	0.25	1.00
8	Moi is a pig	Animal		✓	0.25	0.25	0.25	0.25	1.00
9	Luos are owls	Animal		✓	0.25	0.25	0.25	0.25	1.00
10	Kikuyus/Kibaki are baboons	Animal		✓	0.25	0.25	0.25	0.25	1.00

Raila Is a Monkey

The presidential hopeful Raila Odinga is conceptualized as a monkey. This transference of characteristics implies a number of meanings. First, a monkey, in the words of Haselhuhn and Wong (2011), is a member of the chimpanzee family with contorted facial expressions that would scare an individual. Thus, a monkey is a loathsome figure with an uninviting appeal. Reinforcing this point, Pruscha and Maurus (1976) reiterate that monkeys are "bad to the bone" and that their behavioural patterns are typical of any uncouth culture. Secondly, monkeys are known to be sharing the primate class with humans, a fact that creates some similitude to the lifestyle of humans. As Henazi and Barrett (1999) observe, there is perhaps no animal that tries to imitate the human lifestyle as a monkey. In light of the political heat in Kenya, Raila is therefore a monkey who, although eyeing the presidency, cannot succeed because his plans are viewed as ingenuine as compared to those of humans. Writing on the fascinating traits shared by monkeys and humans, Kappeler and Van Schaik (2006) stress that a peculiar fixation of monkeys is to make noise or tickle others to laughter in a jocular manner. The politician Raila is therefore a personality whose sole duty is to compose distractive hullaballoo through his distasteful 'Vitendawilis' (riddles) as government officials rule the country. Lastly, the conceptual metaphor monkey would mean one who constantly begs for food. As a member of the primate family, monkeys are known to either beg or snatch food from anybody nearby. Considering that monkeys are very destructive to crops yet they do not produce their own food, the metaphor implies that Raila is only able to benefit through stealing[1] (rigging elections) or begging for alms from the current government as was the case in 2007 when he settled for a prime minister's position. This is what Chapman et al. (2016) reinforce by suggesting that monkeys along Lake Nabugabo in Uganda have metamorphosed into snipers that terrorize the occupants of that region.

Peter Kenneth Is a Hyena

This monstrous labelling of the former Gatanga Constituency Member of Parliament (2002–2013) is quite embarrassing. A hyena, normally considered an animal worthy of contempt has been conceptually used to depict Peter Kenneth to reveal his traits. Writing on the impurity of hyenas, Kruuk (1972), notes that the feeding habit of hyenas that leans towards scavenging makes them impure animals. The artist, having likened Peter Kenneth to a hyena communicates that he is impure in terms of origin (the *singer says that Peter Kenneth is a product of raid and not a pure Kikuyu and should therefore not vie alongside Uhuru*). Therefore, a hyena is a person of hybrid parenting who comes out to be quite strange in the perception of natives and his presence should be treated with utmost contempt. Also, the conceptual metaphor hyena would mean a scavenger living off other people's sweat (Moleón et al. 2014). In many folkloric materials, hyenas are portrayed to be very wild and untameable. Drawing from the singer's implicative language, Peter Kenneth as a hyena would be an untameable beast because of his barbaric orientation and vying alongside Uhuru Kenyatta is tantamount to sabotage of the Gikuyu community.

Isaac Ruto Is a Leopard

The former Council of Governors Chairman Isaac Kiprono Ruto is depicted in one of the songs as a leopard. Drawing from the contextual information, it is imperative to infer that Ruto is a camouflaging character with calculated hunting behaviours (Bailey 1993). Writing on the hunting skills of leopards, Bailey adds that leopards, unlike cheetahs or lions are secretive and crafty cats whose opportunistic intelligence rips off the prey's skins (25). Therefore, the character Isaac Ruto is portrayed as a wily masquerader waiting to pounce on his enemies. Additionally, Martins and Harris (2013) accentuate that leopards are nocturnal feeders which kill by suffocation. In this light, Isaac Ruto would be a treacherous individual capable of strangling his colleagues if not keenly watched. Lastly, as the naturalists Rosen, Steklis, Caldwell and Hall, (2013) emphasize, leopards are capable of lynching preys that are way above their weight. This means that Isaac Ruto as a leopard is fitted for unimaginable manslaughter should his enemies joke with him.

Kibaki Is a Frog

Etymologically, the word frog is derived from the Old English term "frogga" which has a close association with the Germanic diminutives "frosc", "forsc", and "frox", later adopted by the British as a derogatory reference to an ugly and hoarse Frenchman (Sayers 2013). President Kibaki is therefore, according to this conceptual mapping, an ugly person. One more fascinating feature of frogs is that they may appear mild but produce unparalleled concentration of poison. Stynoski, Schulte, and Rojas (2015) confirm this assertion and add that certain frogs (especially those in South and Central America) can kill all predators using their poison. In this context, therefore, president Kibaki, though appearing calm and innocent, is capable of spewing venomous substance to wipe out his rivals.

Moi (Kalenjin) Is a Mongoose

A mongoose is a carnivorous terrestrial mammal primarily living in Africa. Some mongooses live in semi-aquatic areas or even treetops.

A striking feature of mongooses is that they are progressive feeders of varied organisms ranging from insects to bigger animals such as hens (Young 2015). In many African narratives, mongooses are symbolic of sluggards who live off others' efforts in a savage manner. Lewis-Williams and Lewis-Williams (2015) report that in the jungle, a mongoose utilizes its strong sense of sight and waits while some animal has maimed its prey. It then combatively drives away the predator and carries the hunt away. Conceptually, this metaphor means that Moi enjoys the fruit of his predecessor's labour regardless of the efforts involved. Alternatively, a mongoose is depicted in folkloric materials as a grabber. Klopp (2000) records crafty cases of pilfering of land engulfing the former President Moi in many parts of the country. A mongoose is therefore an animal which steals little by little to exhaustion. Lastly, a mongoose is an animal that can savagely fight for what it seeks to protect. As such, it relies on the support of a few allies to defeat the enemies (Cant, Otali, and Mwanguhya 2002). These naturalists also note that the greatest strength of a mongoose resides in its accomplices who have to cooperate or they receive ferocious bites. Thus, likened to a mongoose, Moi is a figure heavily relying on cronies to pass administrative dogma.

Kikuyus Are Wolves

In this metaphor, Kikuyu, the rival community to the artist is conceptualized as a wolf. Conventionally, a wolf is an animal of the dog family known for devouring other animals. Many researchers agree that wolves appear quite sociable and calm but deep inside, they are very lethal. Perhaps this is why Scripture warns against wolves. Murie (2011) advances certain detestable characteristics of wolves. First, they are sly and dishonest, a fact that perhaps gives credence to Jesus' admonition: "Watch out for false prophets. They come to you in sheep's clothing, but inwardly they are ravenous wolves" (Matt. 7:15, NKJV). The metaphor "wolf" therefore, insinuates gluttony and covetousness. This is alluding to Kihara and Schröder (2012) who postulate that a redundant *mchongoano*[2] session among peers features Kikuyus as avaricious and bluntly greedy. Secondly, a wolf is an animal with rare temperamental comportment. Miklósi et al (2003) picture wolves as cowardly animals with wavy emotions operating on the extremes of danger. Kikuyus are therefore very strange creatures capable of the most dangerous actions. Eliciting negative connotation, the metaphor wolf would also mean a person concealing his identity in order to satisfy selfish desires. Lopez (1978) writes that it is very difficult to read the intentions of wolves in a pack. He adds that occasionally, they disguise themselves as friendly neighbours just to win the confidence and friendliness of the preys before brutally devouring them. In this fashion, Kikuyus are depicted as pretentious personalities whose short-lived friendship results in either death or material gain.

Kikuyus Are Pigs

The metaphor pig can be demystified against the background laid by the singer (where money is squandered by some government officials). Derivationally, the word pig traces its roots to the Old English "picg" which loosely translates to "digger of furrow" (Wagner 2014). Because pigs dig with their noses in search of something edible, the conceptualization here would mean that Kikuyus are those who jab their noses into places where money is likely to be found. In their study on the behaviour of pigs, Pavlov and Hone (1982) note that pigs forage on a variety of foods in a gluttonous manner that justifies their fatness. Thus, the conceptual metaphor in this case would mean that Kikuyus are foragers (thieves) whose insatiable avarice often leaves them potbellied while others are on the verge of starvation. A pig is also depicted in many narratives as a very unchaste character. As Berman (1994) explains, pigs are often used in oral literature materials to stand for all that is murky, muddy, spotted, and unappealing to the sight. Another aspect closely related to this is what Englund and Leach (2000) describe as the unchaste habit of the swine. So, just like swine make themselves unchaste by rolling on all kind of morass, the Kikuyus are depicted to exhibit a similar tendency thus becoming morally impure especially where they have sniffed money.

The Government Is a Snake

Traditionally, the term 'snake' evokes feelings of fear and awe when uttered. Biblical evidence shows that "[...] the serpent was more subtle than any beast [...]" (Gen. 3:1, NKJV). This revelation shows that the snake is a beast. In relation to the government, the ethnic community from which the president comes is described as beastly by implicature. A distinct feature of snakes is that of producing venom. Bdolah (1979) postulates that snakes use their venom to both kill and digest their prey effortlessly. The Jubilee Government (which is in power at the time of the song) is therefore depicted as a snake that belches venom thus killing its innocent subjects. Additionally, the mention of the word snake often arouses feelings of consternation in the audience. Thus, the government, especially those in top positions are to be treated with suspicion since they can strike any time and cause untold anguish to the people.

Kikuyus (Kibaki) Are Baboons

The song from which this metaphor was retrieved is entitled *Bim en Bim (a baboon is still a baboon)* by the famous Daniel Owino Misiani who composed this psalm in castigation of the then president Mwai Kibaki who seemed to renege on his word after soliciting support from Raila Odinga. A baboon is an animal often associated with turbulent raids in villages and farms. Abie and Bekele (2016) reveal that constant war erupts in Ethiopian villages bordering the bush due to the invasion of the farms and even families. The baboons that have gone wild terrorize the village and leave every land upon which they pass bare. Thus, a baboon is a very uncouth, lewd, and uncivilized creature that cannot be trusted. This is what the singer attributes to Kibaki and his community. There seems to be some resemblance between baboons and humans. Strum (1987), in a passionate study of the baboons reports that these animals are "almost human" because of their orthographical orientation and the ability to almost read. If baboons are almost human, then the conceptual metaphor "baboon" would depict a person who is somewhere between an ape and a fully evolved Homo sapiens. The barbarity and immaturity of the baboons would therefore label one as he who belongs to the beast world or still has a lot of growing to do. Wallace and Hill (2012) admit that baboons can raid a village and kidnap "babies" that are not of their own species for children. This is the implicative effect of the song which seems to echo that as a baboon, a Kikuyu snatches even that which is apparently not allocated for them.

Luos Are Owls

The term owl is etymologically derived from "ule" in Old English, a term that diminutively refers to undesirably noisy habits and ugliness and ironic appearance of wisdom (Lilley 1998). Owls are associated with nocturnal noises that distract people sleeping at night. In the context of Luos complaining every time about the rigged election, the conceptual metaphor owl suffices because all their pleas are regarded as hullaballoos by the government. Sessions (1972) informs that an owl is a curious animal with explicit body language typical of a three-dimensional gadget revolving to discern trouble or mischief just like the binoculars. Lilley (1998) observes that perhaps the most constructive communication from owls take the form of whistles, hisses, screeches, and screams. On these lines, Luos are conceptualized as those whose best asset is noise. Fleay (1968) observes that in Africa, superstitious threats are attributed to the wailing of the owl but few people pay attention to these because there is no scientific basis for fear. Luos are therefore cowards who threaten but are incapable of doing anything to the government.

Conclusions

This study has established that animals are stratified source domains richly used to depict the characters in the songs. We, therefore, recommend that for a better appreciation of conceptual metaphors, it is salient to apply cognitive semantics to understand contextual language against the cultural, historical, and geographical backdrop. Further, conceptual metaphors are conduits of communication and should be explained using a cognitive linguistics approach. Finally, culturally embodied zoosemic labelling in Kenyan songs fuels atrocity and need censoring before release for public consumption. We therefore recommend that because such songs are likely to fuel atrocity in the country, a censorship board should screen the content before they can be released to the public for entertainment.

Notes

1 According to Kappeler and Van Schaik (2006), a monkey very keenly watches as someone eats and should one fail to pass a piece to it, it can grab it savagely. For more information on destructive behaviour of monkeys, see Conelly (1994) who notes that black monkeys seek recognition and feel nothing can happen without their effort.
2 Mchongoano is a very popular speech event in Kenya typical of "playing the dozens" in America. In this event popular among blacks in America, participants insult each other using resources that may border on prejudices until the other party gives up. This light moment is very hilarious but can at times become hurting.

References

Abie, Kassahun, and Bekele, Afework. "Threats to Gelada Baboon (Theropithecus gelada) around Debre Libanos, Northwest Shewa Zone, Ethiopia." *International Journal of Biodiversity*, 2016.
Babito, Queen. *Haki Yetu*. 28 July 2014. https://www.youtube.com/watch?v=FJ0Xdat-4Ms
Bailey, Theodore N. *The African Leopard: Ecology and Behavior of a Solitary Felid*. New York: Columbia University Press, 1993.
Bdolah, A. "The Venom Glands of Snakes and Venom Secretion." *Snake Venoms*. Berlin Heidelberg: Springer, 1979. 41–57.
Berman, Paul. Schiff. "Rats, Pigs, and Statues on Trial: The Creation of Cultural Narratives in the Prosecution of Animals and Inanimate Objects." *The New York University Law Review* 69 (1994): 288.
Bible, Holy. *The New King James Version*. Nashville: Nelson.,1982.
Cant, M. A., E. Otali, and F. Mwanguhya. "Fighting and Mating between Groups in a Cooperatively Breeding Mammal, the Banded Mongoose." *Ethology* 108.6 (2002) 541–555.
Chapman, C. A. et al. "How Do Primates Survive Among Humans? Mechanisms Employed by Vervet Monkeys at Lake Nabugabo, Uganda." *Ethnoprimatology*. Springer International Publishing, 2016. 77–94.
Chung, S. F., K. Ahrens, and C. R. Huang. "Source Domains as Concept Domains in Metaphorical Expressions." *International Journal of Computational Linguistics and Chinese Language Processing* 10.4 (2005): 553–570.
Conelly, W. T. "Population Pressure, Labor Availability, and Agricultural Disintensification: The Decline of Farming on Rusinga Island, Kenya." *Human Ecology* 22.2 (1994): 145–170.
Croft, William., and D. Alan. Cruse. *Cognitive Linguistics*. Cambridge: Cambridge University Press, 2004.

De'Mathew, John. *Ruhiu Rwa Guka*. 21 March 2015. https://itunes.apple.com/us/album/ruhiu-rwa-guka/id980853859.

De'Mathew, John. *Nyumba Mwinau*. 29 September 2008. www.youtube.com/watch?v=gQGN5fxWZDw&list=TLUyFJcGHPKVM.

Englund, Harri, and James. Leach. Ethnography and the Meta-Narratives of Modernity. *Current Anthropology* 41.2 (2000): 225–248.

Evans, Vyvyan, and Melanie, Green. *Cognitive Linguistics: An Introduction*. Lawrence Erlbaum Associates Publishers, 2006.

Fauconnier, Gilles. *Mappings in Thought and Language*. Cambridge University Press, 1997.

Fauconnier, Gilles. "Conceptual Blending and Analogy." *The Analogical Mind: Perspectives from Cognitive Science*. Eds. D. Gentner, K. J. Holyoak, and B. N. Kokinov. (pp. 255–285). Cambridge, MA, USA: The MIT Press, 2001Fleay, D. *Nightwatchman of the Bush and Plain; Australian Owls and Owl-like Birds*. Brisbane: Jacaranda Press, 1968.

Freeman, M. H. (2000). "Poetry and the Scope of Metaphor: Toward a Cognitive Theory of Literature." *Metaphor and Metonymy at the Crossroads: A Cognitive Perspective*. Ed. Antonia Barcelona, 253–281.

Gathigia, Moses Gatambuki. "Metaphors of Love in Gikũyũ: Conceptual Mappings, Vital Relations and Image Schemas." Doctoral diss., Kenyatta University, 2014.

Gibbs, Raymond. W. *The Poetics of Mind: Figurative Thought, Language, and Understanding*. Cambridge: Cambridge University Press, 1994.

Haas, Jonathan. *The Anthropology of War*. Cambridge: Cambridge University Press, 1990.

Haselhuhn, Michael P., and Elaine. M. Wong. "Bad to the Bone: Facial Structure Predicts Unethical Behaviour." *Proceedings of the Royal Society of London B: Biological Sciences* (2011) rspb20111193.

Henazi, S. Peter, and Louise. Barrett. "The Value of Grooming to Female Primates." *Primates* 40.1 (1999): 47–59.

Kappeler, P. M., and C. P. Van Schaik. *Cooperation in Primates and Humans*. Berlin/Heidelberg: Springer-Verlag, 2006.

Kiełtyka, R., and G. A. Kleparski. The Ups and Downs of the Great Chain of Being: The Case of Canine Zoosemy in the History of English. *SKASE Journal of Theoretical Linguistics* 2 (2005): 22–41.

Kihara, C. Patrick, and Helga Schröder. "A Relevance-Theoretical Analysis of Aspects of Mchongoano." *The University of Nairobi Journal of Language and Linguistics* 2 (2012): 63–78.

Killingsworth, J. J. "Licence and Poetic Licence: A Critical Examination of the Complicated Relationship between the CRTC and Specialty Channels." *Canadian Journal of Communication*, 30.2 (2005).

Klopp, J. M. "Pilfering the Public: The Problem of Land Grabbing in Contemporary Kenya." *Africa Today* 47.1 (2000): 7–26.

Kövecses, Zoltan. *Metaphor and Emotion: Language, Culture and the Body in Human Feeling*. Cambridge: Cambridge University Press, 2000.

Kövecses, Zoltan. *Metaphor: A Practical Introduction*. Oxford: Oxford University Press, 2002.

Krippendorff, Klaus. *Content Analysis: An Introduction to Its Methodology*. Thousand Oaks, CA: Sage, 2012.

Kruuk, Hans. The Spotted Hyena: A Study of Predation and Social Behavior (No. Sirsi) a102104.1972.

Lakoff, George, and Mark Johnson. *Metaphors We Live By*. Chicago: University of Chicago Press, 1980.

Lewis-Williams, J. D., and J. D. Lewis-Williams. *Myth and Meaning: San-Bushman Folklore in Global Context*. Walnut Creek: Left Coast Press, 2015.

Lilley, G. M. "A Study of the Silent Flight of the Owl." *AIAA Paper* 2340 (1998): 1–6.

Lopez, B. *Of Wolves and Men*. New York: Simon and Schuster, 1978.

Martins, Q., and S. Harris. "Movement, Activity and Hunting Behaviour of Leopards in the Cederberg Mountains, South Africa." *African Journal of Ecology* 51.4 (2013): 571–579.

Miklósi, Á., et al. "A Simple Reason for a Big Difference: Wolves Do Not Look Back at Humans, But Dogs Do." *Current Biology* 13.9 (2003): 763–766.

Milić, G. "The Treatment of Zoosemy in Conceptual Metaphor and Metonymy Theory." *Jezikoslovlje* 14.1 (2013): 197–213.

Misiani, Owino. Daniel. *Bim en Bim*. 14 February 2014. https://www.youtube.com/watch?v=Hr26mIFnWHE.

Moleón, M., et al. " Humans and Scavengers: The Evolution of Interactions and Ecosystem Services." *BioScience*, biu034, 2014.

Murie, A. *The Wolves of Mount McKinley*. Washington, DC: University of Washington Press, 2011.

Njogu, Kimani, and Harvey. Maupeu. *Songs and Politics in Eastern Africa*. African Books Collective, 2007.

O'Ballance, Edgar. *Language of Violence: The Blood Politics of Terrorism*. San Rafael, CA: Presidio Press, 1979. 136.

Onyi, P. J. *Raila Jakom*. 7 January 2015. https://www.youtube.com/watch?v=h_52_UJYWyA.

Patton, Michael *Qualitative Evaluation and Research Methods*. Newbury Park: Sage Publications, 2002.

Pavlov, P. M., and J. Hone. "The Behaviour of Feral Pigs, Sus Scrofa, in Flocks of Lambing Ewes." *Wildlife Research* 9.1 (1982): 101–109.

Prothrow-Stith, D., and M. Weissman. *Deadly Consequences*. New York: HarperCollins, 1991.

Pruscha, H., and M. Maurus. "The Communicative Function of Some Agonistic Behaviour Patterns in Squirrel Monkeys: The Relevance of Social Context." *Behavioral Ecology and Sociobiology* 1.2 (1976): 185–214.

Rosen, P. C., N. Steklis, D. J. Caldwell, and D. H. Hall. Restoring Leopard Frogs and Habitat in Sky Island Grasslands (Arizona): Final Report. *National Fish and Wildlife Foundation, project2010–0023-000 grant, 18411*, 2013.

Rosengren, K. E. "Advances in Scandinavia Content Analysis: An Introduction." *Advances in Content Analysis*. Ed. K. E. Rosengren. Beverly Hills, CA: Sage, 1981. 9–19.

Sayers, W. "Speculations on Substratum Influence on Early English Vocabulary: Pig, Colt, Frog." 중세르네상스영문학 21.2 (2013): 159–172.

Schabas, W. A. "Hate Speech in Rwanda: The Road to Genocide." *McGill LJ*, 46 (2000): 141.

Sessions, P. H. B. "Observations on Mackinder's Eagle Owl Bubo Capensis Mackinderi Sharpe on a Kenya farm." *Journal of East African Natural History* 138 (1972): 1–20.

Somerville, Keith. "Violence, Hate Speech and Inflammatory Broadcasting in Kenya: The Problems of Definition and Identification." *Ecquid Novi: African Journalism Studies* 32.1 (2011): 82–101.

Strum, S. C. *Almost Human: A Journey Into the World of Baboons.* Chicago: University of Chicago Press, 1987.

Stynoski, J. L., L. M. Schulte, and B. Rojas. "Poison Frogs." *Current Biology* 25.21 (2015) R1026–R1028.

Tongco, M. D. C. Purposive Sampling as a Tool for Informant Selection, 2007.

Wa Njoroge, M. *Gikuu kia Nugu.* 13 October 2014. https://www.youtube.com/watch?v=qHoKvbNEQU8.

Wagner, J. E., ed. *The Biology of the Guinea Pig.* New York: Academic Press, 2014.

Wallace, G. E., and C. M. Hill. "Crop Damage by Primates: Quantifying the Key Parameters of Crop-Raiding Events." *PloS One* 7.10 (2012): e46636.

Young, O. P. "Predation on Dung Beetles (Coleoptera: Scarabaeidae): A Literature Review." *Transactions of the American Entomological Society* 141 (2015): 111–155.

Zhang, L. The Effect of Etymological Elaboration on L2 Idiom Acquisition and Retention in an Online Environment (WebCT), 2009.

19 Reading Kalenjin Popular Music as a Gem of Ethnic Violence

Kiprotich E. Sang

Introduction

This chapter interrogates the possible role of Kalenjin popular music in the construction, performance, and dissemination of violence. It proceeds from the supposition that popular music has been harnessed by composers not only to fan ethnic hatred, but also as a means of memorizing perceived transgressions against the Kalenjin community. The chapter examines how the supposed transgressions against the Kalenjin nation are structured by popular musicians to arouse and direct primitive violent energies towards perceived aggressors, whom they see as the 'other'. Primary emphasis is laid on how music texts are constructed to prime their potential listeners towards violence. The chapter locates the specific musicians within the physical Kalenjin territory in an effort to determine if the sentiments expressed are localized or widespread throughout the Kalenjin terrain. It contends that vernacular radio stations play a role in popularizing and disseminating lyrics with potential violent content implicitly legitimizing violence.

In most societies, music provides a background for the placement of symbols which express a structural perception of the feelings of the members of the society towards their cultural identity. In most instances, musicians involve themselves in (re)structuring the identity of the members of society through the manipulation of social symbols, images, histories, and myths. The implication is that every society has discernible structures which the musicians seize upon and foreground in order to create a structured conception of the nation. The musicians are involved in a process of re-fashioning society and influencing its perception of the same. However, musicians being members of a particular society are subject to influences from it, in as much as they may wish to influence perspectives of the society. In such a situation, the musicians involve themselves not only with highlighting those structures extant in the society, but also creating and promoting new structures which at times may run counter to the existing values. The result is an overall change in the ways the nation is perceived.

Christopher Waterman asserts that "every artist is involved in an interpretive project conditioned by his or her personal experience and socio-historical position" (252). It, therefore, means that the artist is constantly manipulating historical forces existing in society in an attempt to capture the history behind the society's actions which contribute towards the explanation of mental motivations of their actions. This approach at times inevitably colours the artist's interpretation of events. The end product is, sometimes, the promotion and escalation of ethnic nationalism which has at times led to violence.

In a fragmented society that aspires for unity like the Kenyan state, the role and influence of the musicians in promoting violence cannot be ignored. The special role which the musicians and their music play, become an integral part of the move towards the consolidation of the disparate groups. The restructuring of the societal vision is done through the employment of artistic strategies which make the message clear and appealing to the consumers. John McLeod asserts, "A sense of mutual national belonging is always manufactured by the performance of various narratives, rituals and symbols which stimulate an individual's sense of being a member of a selected group" (69). Musicians therefore capture and manipulate available social signifiers such as history and mythology to promote a unified perception of not only society, but also the worldview of members of a given social group.

This chapter interrogates various means through which musicians employ literary techniques to foreground Kalenjin self-consciousness among the disparate sub-ethnic groups towards the formation of a unified perception and identification with the Kalenjin construct. This is guided by Ralph Premdas' observation that "ethnic boundaries are socially constructed and reproduced in relation to the symbolic and instrumental needs of the group" (4) wherein, the individual behaviour and opinions are rooted in and shaped by structures that people operate from. In that case, the concern is the means by which musicians harness and manipulate aspects such as social symbols, allegories, images, and metaphors as vehicles and spaces in which issues of identity formation are generated and restructured to give shape to the Kalenjin aspiration for a common self-perception.

The thrust of discussions in this chapter is on the artistic strategies employed as a representation and expressions of latent nationalist sentiments and societal aspirations. The literary devices are perceived as codes through which musicians represent societal values and aspirations. The discussions arising are considered a practice in deciphering the codes. This can be attributed to the fact that 'the production of symbols is important to the construction of the myth of the nation, the function of which is to unite many individuals into one people' (McLeod 72). Consideration is placed on the notion that the issue of the nation is a psychological one and in the words of Yewah, "...not so much a physical entity but rather as a construct of the mind, a mental structure in the process of mapping and remapping itself" (48). Consequently, its perception and interpretation are best captured by recourse to symbolic (re)presentations.

The Symbolic Structures of Kalenjin National Construction

In order to ensure national unity, a national cultural identity is required to give the citizens of the nation a sense of belonging. Since solidarity and the wish for identification with a group is an emotionally charged phenomenon, the employment of powerful symbols to represent the feelings and aspirations is inevitable. Therefore, any assertion of a national identity calls for a deliberate attempt at generating and representing symbols that touch on the emotional core of the target members of the society. The use of the symbols serves as the means employed in the process of the achievement of a perfect expressiveness.

According to Mcleod "...the production of symbols is important to the construction of the myth of the nations, the function of which is to unite many individuals into one people" (72). Kalenjin musicians, therefore, have capitalized on the availability of symbols that are interpreted by various sub-ethnicities in similar ways to act as the basis for the construction of a unified Kalenjin identity. The import of this appropriation of readily available symbols is considered significant in that "ethnic identity is represented by a collection of symbols or signifiers that include such things as physical attributes, as well as behaviors, family relations, group rituals and even clothing" (De Andrade 272). In that case, members of a nation are constantly reading and interpreting symbols in the course of their daily interactions. The presentation, reading, and interpretation of symbols result in a form of social negotiation where individual members attempt to secure a position within a defined expansive social space.

Musicians have therefore harnessed various symbols and magnified their importance in an effort to foreground structural similarities inherent in the various Kalenjin sub-ethnicities. Identified symbols are then projected as a means through which a unified Kalenjin perspective is built. The symbols take on a variety of forms reflecting the varied ways in which the Kalenjin nation is conceptualized. In certain instances, they take on the structures of personalities, physical features like mountains, rivers, and even valleys. At other times, these symbols take on the shape of cultural practices in terms of the social, political, and economic occupations of a people. Certain cultural artefacts are held in high esteem to the point that they generate a life of their own and, as a result, acquire powerful symbolic significance to the extent that they influence the thoughts and actions of the members of the nation. At other times, certain institutions acquire symbolic significance. These institutions are read and interpreted as representing certain values that society holds as being central to its survival and which provide an opportunity for a structured social perception which is based on various elements offered by different structures in place that give society its shape. Alain Degenne and Michel Forse have observed the connection between structures and action in any society and assert that "structure exerts all powerful control over action" (5).

One of the most outstanding institutions that Kalenjin musicians have identified as a physical representation of Kalenjin aspiration is the radio station, Kass FM. Almost all Kalenjin musicians analysed in this chapter have a song commenting on the centrality of the radio station in developing and expressing Kalenjin consciousness. Apart from the station providing a focal point around which various Kalenjin sub-nationalities congregate, it also acts as a mouthpiece of their aspirations and fears. Consequently, the radio is brought out as something that is to be valued and defended. The Kalenjin musicians have placed the radio station at a position that demands it being considered a significant structural element in the construction of ethnic identity and consolidation. This idea is confirmed by Tirop Simatei who observes that the radio station "was not just 'imagining' its community of listeners ... it was in effect, giving form and meaning to a resurgent cultural formation..." (3). It is for this reason that the listeners of the station consider it as a mandatory component in processes of imagining the nation.

The symbolic position played by the radio station is captured vividly in the lyrics of a track entitled "Kongoi Kass FM" (Thank you Kass FM) by Kipchamba arap Tapotuk who sings:

Kongoi Kass FM nekiyomyo Kalenjin   Kass FM which has united Kalenjin.

Kongoi Kass FM koinyo gotab lolei mat.   Kass FM, our house, our fertile house.

The symbolic presentation of Kass FM as a fertile mother alludes to its potential for creating and nurturing a Kalenjin identity. Its ability to bring various sub-ethnicities under its protective wings is also given prominence, which foregrounds it as an important component in the overall perception of the Kalenjin construct.

Jane Kotut of Keiyo stars in a track entitled *Hallow Kakiptai* (Hello Egypt) intertwines the significance of the radio station with the supposed Kalenjin myth of origin in Egypt. She plays with the usual English salutation 'Hello' and proposes that communication among the children of *Kakiptai* (Egypt) be done through the airwaves. The singer foregrounds the important role that the station plays in promoting symbolic integration among the disparate Kalenjin sub-nationalities.

The station is also perceived as the central pole that holds the Kalenjin house together and gives it shape. The use of the symbol of the central pole in reference to the radio station bespeaks of its vital role in holding the nation together. It also raises the issue of sturdiness, where the station is supposed to give a strong foundation to the Kalenjin nation. The members of the Kalenjin nation are called to come together in order to ensure the continued strength of the station and the nation. The various sub-communities are seen from the perspective of the image of pots which have to be arranged in such a way that they prop each other. The musicians state that, for as long as the pots support each other, the central pole that is collectively propped up by the various pots will become strong. The musician centralizes Kass FM as a totem of Kalenjin identity. She sings:

Hallow,. Hallow konyo Kakiptai,	Hallo our house, the house of Egypt.
Hallow, Hallow, ongikatgei eng soet.	Hallo, let us greet each other over the airwaves.
Hallow, Hallow ongikatgei eng boiboiyet	Hallo, let us greet each other with happiness.
Ongeti kei kou teren, sikokimit toloita.	Let's prop up each other like pots, so that the central pole may be strong.
Hallow Kass Washington D.C.eng olinbo	Hallo Kass in Washington D.C., in America. America.

The centrality of the station in linking members of the nation even those outside the physical location of their usual domicile is captured where she mentions Kass FM, Washington D.C. This is significant in that the station is broadcast and can be accessed through the internet. Similarly, the station has an international broadcasting house that is based in Washington D.C. It is of significant importance that the international division of the station based in Washington D.C is headed by the Egyptologist, Kipkoech arap Sambu. The musician as such, highlights the important position that the station holds in providing a symbolic link to members of the nation in distant lands with those at 'home'. Therefore, it can be argued that the station provides an avenue for performing identity, albeit remotely, and also acts as an umbilical cord to the cultural values for those in the diaspora. This argument is best captured by Gongoware who in a different context observes that "The collective identity of a social movement implies the unity of a shared sense that it is a coherent action with shared ends, means and field of action, shared relationships and shared emotional investment" (486).

Kass FM can thus be said to offer an avenue through which members of the Kalenjin nation express their collective identity, transmit the same and offer an opportunity for a coherent performance over a wide spatial and historical field. In other words, the station has provided members of the Kalenjin nation a means through which the mytho-historical destiny of the nation has been linked to its present destiny not only within the usual physical geographical situation of the nation, but also connecting remotely to those not within immediate physical reach. In this case, the nation is made to think and act in a collectively focused way wherever they may be. Kass FM therefore comes out as a central point where the community's aspirations are not only performed and transmitted, but also refines their perception as well as offering a convenient space for playing out the Kalenjin identity. The radio station can thus be perceived as a symbolic shrine around which the nation congregates to pay homage not only to its values but to their collective feelings.

In other cases, names of places acquire powerful symbolic significance to the Kalenjin construct. Musicians, in the process of consolidating the people's feelings and perceptions, reify these names to offer a symbolic point of reference for the nation. One outstanding name that portrays a strong symbolic meaning to the Kalenjin nation is the "Rift Valley". On the one hand, the rift valley symbolizes the security of home and its values, while on the other hand places an individual within a wider spectrum of historical continuity. Being a member of the Rift Valley community implies a strong connection to a rich legacy of joint historical and mythical past which can be traced back to Egypt. This assertion explains Jane Kotut's deliberate omission in her track *"Rift Valley"* to recognize other nationalities apart from Kalenjin, Maasai, and Turkana as inhabitants of the Rift Valley.

The strength of the Rift Valley as a symbolic icon can further be explained by the fact that in as much as many of the members of the Kalenjin construct are inhabitants of the administrative unit known as Rift Valley province, the inclusion of the Sabaot among the inhabitants, points towards a spiritual construction of Rift Valley. Their inclusion in her rendition of the inhabitants of the Rift Valley points more to a symbolic place rather than a physical location in contrast to their physical presence in Western Province. The symbolic connection between the Sabaot and Rift Valley is strengthened further by their physical location of habitation, the Mount Elgon, known as *Tulwop Kony* among the Kalenjin. The mountain is symbolically significant to the Kalenjin nation as the last point at which the Kalenjin nation existed as a single unit before its eventual dispersal and the generation of various sub-ethnicities. The Sabaot are considered as the guardians of the ancestral home and hence their incorporation into the symbolic Rift Valley. Mt. Elgon thus can be said to provide a platform which "generates a unifying myth of origin for the Kalenjin sub-ethnic groups" (Simatei 7), hence its symbolic centrality in the consciousness of the Kalenjin.

Jane Kotut of Keiyo stars relates the importance of *Tulwop Kony* to the overall history of the Kalenjin. She highlights the relationship between the Egyptian myth of origin and the current destiny of the nation where *Tulwop Kony* provides the all-important link. In a track entitled "*Tanjawe*", she sings:

Kiong'ete Tanjawe, Misiri Tanjawe	I originated in Egypt
A'asubu tanjawe River Nile Tanjawe.	Followed River Nile.
Omong'chi tanjawe, Tulwop kony Elgon Tanjawe	And ended up in Mt. Elgon
Olinyo Tanjawe, Rift Valley Tanjawe	Our home, Rift Valley
Kiberurwech Jehova tanjawe	Given to us by God almighty,
Kongoi bikchok tanjawe, chomi Tulwop Kony.	Thank you to our people in Mt. Elgon.

The singer asserts the mythical origin of the Kalenjin nation and offers the link between Egypt and Mt. Elgon. In introducing River Nile, the musician provides a metaphor of continuity between the two places. Of note, however, is the fact that the musician does not seem to distinguish between Rift Valley the physical land, and Mt. Elgon. She claims that from Egypt, they found themselves in Mt. Elgon, Rift Valley. This means that in the psyche of the Kalenjin, there is no distinction between Mt. Elgon and Rift Valley. The two places are perceived symbolically as one and the same. The reference to "our people in Mt. Elgon" means that in the perception of the musicians, the Kalenjin nation is one. In the mental structures of the Kalenjin, Mt. Elgon provides the central point on which their identity is built and consequently magnified and projected as Rift Valley. This explains the supernatural link that is generated to assert their claim to the land. They insist that the land was God-given, which provides a subtle divine claim to it by members of the Kalenjin nation. In the process of centralizing Mt. Elgon, the musicians are constructing a symbol which unites members of the Kalenjin construct to a common perception. This provides ground for greater integration of the members.

Whereas Mt. Elgon features strongly in recreating the mythical origin of the Kalenjin nation, Tinderet, on the other hand, provides an avenue for symbolizing the nation's security and sustenance. To members of various sub-ethnicities, Tinderet stands out in their psyche as one important, symbolic feature of their identity. Jane Kotut asserts that Tinderet is just as important as Mt. Elgon to the Kalenjin nation. She sings thus:

Bikchok chomi Tulwop kony tanjawe.	Our people in Mt. Elgon.
Kap-kuko, kotam nee Tulwop Tinderet.	Our ancestoral land, and our hill Tinderet.
Ngoliel kekool bai Tanjawe.	Whose rumbling and flashes of lightning is a sign for planting.

The Tinderet Hills therefore, are taken as a symbol of food security and sustenance. The flashes of lightning on the hills portend rain which is crucial in the production of food. As such, among the Kalenjin, even those not within the physical proximity, it serves as a sign for the production of food which ensures that society is well taken care of. Similarly, the fact that Tinderet is associated with flashes of lightning and rumbling of thunder, which in Kalenjin belief system is considered an arbiter and a source of justice for the weak (Sambu 2007), implies that justice is assured and protection is guaranteed to members who at times may find themselves in vulnerable situations.

On another front Kipchamba Tapotuk in a track entitled *Tinderet* gives prominence to the security that the hills provide to the community. He sings:

Tinderet oh tinderet, tinderet chebusia	Tinderet, beautiful Tinderet
Negoliel oh, nengoliel kekol bai	When it flashes and rumbles, we plant
Tindirenyo, Tinderet malany bunyo	Our Tinderet, no enemy can conquer
Tinderet, oh Tinderet chebusia	Beautiful Tinderet
Tinderet nengelany ke	

The musician romances Tinderet hill and compares it to a beautiful girl who for all purposes is fertile and has the ability to contribute to the continuity and security of the society by ensuring that new members of the society are produced. The connection between the beauty of the land and the rain which ensures productivity of the land affirms this. Furthermore, the hill also serves as a protective buffer against the enemies apart from serving as a vantage point for the surveillance of the territory.

In as much as Tinderet is located in the heartland of the Nandi sub-nation, musicians from the other sub-nations romance it in invariably similar terms, which strengthen its claim to being a major symbol in the imagination of the Kalenjin nation. This fact is affirmed by the fact that Kipchamba Tapotuk a Kipsigis and Jane Kotut of Keiyo who perceive of Tinderet as *our* Tinderet. The collective ownership thus gives impetus to the unitary structural perception of the hill as a symbol of the imagined Kalenjin nation.

The symbolizing of national aspirations and values are sometimes captured and (re) presented by musicians through the identification and glorification of achievements of outstanding individuals in the society. These individuals and their feats are then projected as representing the symbolic image of the nation. The continued performance and glorification of the personalities, in time, come to stand for societal achievements. The individuals are thus inadvertently placed in a central position wherein the society congregates. They thus end up becoming symbols of national identity. In the Kalenjin society, individuals like athletes, political and religious leaders, and mythical figures have gained symbolic prominence in the psychology of individual members of the Kalenjin nation. Musicians, having recognized the central role that these individuals play in the creation of the nation, have harnessed them in the process of generating and promoting symbols of national identity. Yewah agrees with this assertion and quotes Jameson who says that the story of the private individual destiny, is always an allegory of the embattled situation of the public (46).

The most outstanding individuals who have captured the imagination of the members of the Kalenjin society are the athletes. Their successes both in the national and international spaces have uplifted them to the status of national symbols. The musicians have entered into the mix by generating songs that put them at a level that highlights them as social icons. For instance, Jane Kotut has several tracks dedicated to the glorification of various athletes and their achievements. In a track entitled "*Labotindet*" she pays glowing tribute to Kipchoge Keino whom she considers as the father of athletics in Kenya:

Otieni, tieni eng sobondanyu tugul	I sing this song with all spirit and emotion
Olosu ane labotindentab Kenya.	Praising the Kenyan runner.
Nekikolabat agoi konayak Kenya.	Who has exposed Kenya to the world.
Kipchoge Keino nekikksib kolabat	Kipchoge Keino who started it all.
Ine ko kwanit ago mwalimoyandet.	He is a father (figure) and a teacher.
Ineeti ruoiik ujuzi ch	

The musician is involved in a process of iconizing the athlete and attempts to create a legend out of him. When she refers to the runner as "our athlete" she is cleverly co-opting members of the Kalenjin nation in the process of placing the runner in a critical position in the structuring of the nation. Apart from Kipchoge, the musician identifies other athletes who have brought glory and honour to the nation-state of Kenya and lists among them Paul Bitok, Sally Barsosio, Daniel Komen, Moses Kiptanui, Susan Sirma, and Richard Chelimo. In another track entitled "Paul Tergat" in honour of Paul Tergat, the musician also mentions other athletes like Wilson Boit Kipketer. In yet other tracks, titled "*Moses Tanui*" and "*Rwaik*", she lists athletes who have done the nation proud. However, she brings out the significance of their achievement to the nation by insisting that the happiness of their exploits are a pride to the nation. For Tergat she sings that his home village of Riwo in Baringo

is proud of him. On the part of *"Moses Tanui"* the pride is equally that
of his villagers of Sugoi in Uasin Gishu. The singer asserts that these
runners are symbols of the Kalenjin nation when she sings in *"Rwaik"*

Kivunjan rekod Boit kingomi Zurich.	Boit won a race in Zurich.
Kitebekei chumbek kole bunu ano eng Africa	The white folk inquired his background in Africa
Kelenji bunu Kenya, Rift Valley, Kapchorwa.	The answer was Kenya, Rift Valley, Kapchorwa village.

In this regard, little doubt is left as to his position in the construction of
the Kalenjin nation. The fact that he is identified with Rift Valley implies
that he is a symbol of their aspirations.

Geoffrey Rotich of Makiche Boys Band also gives a lot of prominence
to the runners. In a track entitled *'Matelong"*, he romances the athletes
for bringing glory to the nation. In all the songs, the runners are portrayed as the property of the Kalenjin nation and any glory they bring is
first and foremost to the Kalenjin nation. One outstanding feature in the
five songs under review is that the nation-state mention is made of about
30 runners and none of them is from outside the Kalenjin nation. The musicians through their deliberate exclusion of runners from other nationalities suggest that the athletes are representatives of Kalenjin identity.
In addition, by referring to all athletes even from diverse sub-ethnicities
as 'our runners' implies that they symbolically are imagined to represent
the Kalenjin spirit and virtues collectively.

The singers, present a picture of the athletes as representing Kenya,
but since most of them are from Rift Valley or those from Rift Valley
are given prominence, stress is therefore given to a Rift Valley identity
more than to the Kenyan state. The runners, therefore, serve as symbols
which provide a leeway to the Kalenjin nation towards the bargaining
of a position within the wide Kenyan nation by highlighting their role in
the promotion of the nation state, and at the same time drawing attention to the strong presence of the Kalenjin nation. The musicians have
therefore created symbols of the nation by manipulating their achievements to stoke the emotional sense of the members of the nation in order
to draw them towards a common identification with their achievements.
The result is a unified perception which draws the members of the society closer together. The significance of the repeated highlighting of the
athletes' performance is best captured by McLeod who while writing in
a different context says that "in many national histories, certain events
are celebrated as fundamental to the nation's past fortunes and present
identity which directly connects the narration of history with the repeated performance of those symbols" (70).

The Nation Reflected: Images and Metaphorical (Re) presentations

In an effort to reflect and transmit the aspirations and feelings of a social group, artists constantly employ structural devices that best capture and expresses those feelings. According to Lindfors, the importance of the use of these devices can be attributed to the fact that "by creating bright new images [the artists] help shape and reify concepts of groups into a cohesive political unit" (154). The Kalenjin musicians possibly aware of this fact have through their songs, captured social images and metaphors in common usage to fashion out a coherent expression of a Kalenjin identity. Chebet and Dietz focusing on the significance of metaphorical expressions in the creation of a conceptual expressive construct observe that "people use metaphors to qualify their expressions for better understanding" (62). In this case, the feeling is that the use of metaphors not only foregrounds the importance of the message, but also offers a clear understanding of the process of developing it. In addition, the use of the metaphors and images, "allows a movement to ensure that memories of the past continue to remain a part of the collective memory" (Gongoware 486). This is because the images and metaphors are fashioned from socially available features which to a large extent have a strong relationship with the past historical artefacts of the society. A connection is therefore established between past historical endeavours, successes, and artefacts which are then placed in the present circumstances to form a basis of explanation for the current worldview.

Bendix asserts that the importance of images and metaphors in the transmission of information can be attributed to the fact that they have the ability to "invite participation through visual and aural channels which appeal to the emotions that in turn incite or ignite feelings" (77). The Kalenjin musicians can be seen to be interested in igniting the emotional feelings of the members of the Kalenjin nation. Their intentions are to channel the resultant reactions towards a common perception and identification with the imagined nation. When powerful images and metaphors are used in the generation of the songs, the listeners are deliberately and unconsciously manipulated by the musicians to co-participate in the process of national creation. The listeners therefore find themselves contributing to the structural conception of the nation. In most cases, the musicians latch on to images that are readily found in the environment and which the average member of the Kalenjin can easily identify and decipher its meaning. Their success in arousing strong sentiments can be attributed to their employment of those images that touch on the economic and religious practices of the community. Some metaphors are at times abbreviations of the sociocultural practices of the Kalenjin community. This gives them a force that generates a big impact on the psychology of the members of the nation. In consideration of the fact that the main purpose of the employment of the devices is possibly aimed at generating a common perception, then, it leaves very little doubt as to why the songs are very popular and why it may be supposed that they contribute a great deal in refocusing the attention of members of the Kalenjin community.

The pivotal role that musicians play in the restructuring of national thought can be attributed to what De Andrade considers as a position of control in regard to shaping public perceptions and says that as social actors, musicians are constantly, "[d]rawing on and assembling signifiers that are available to them, and which they interpret as meaningful to the social context. In so doing, they reinforce, reshape or construct the meaning of ethnicity" (272). The signifiers are taken to include images and metaphors which are readily available and easily interpreted by members of the society. The interpretation strengthens the shape of the constructed nation.

One of the images constantly employed by musicians to highlight the unity of the Kalenjin nation is milk. The musicians make use of the importance that the members attach to milk to bring them together and generate a common perception. Milk acquires a metaphorical dimension which is then conceptualized to generate a common identity for the various members of the different sub-ethnicities. For instance, musicians refer to the Kalenjin community as *bikap chego* meaning the people who live on milk which implies that milk is used as a unifying concept. The moment milk is mentioned, it hails one to identify with the aspirations of the nation. The use of milk as a powerful image of Kalenjin unity can be traced to the symbolic position that milk plays in the community's rituals and other practices. For instance, when people fight and reconciliation is necessary, milk is used to bring them together either by sprinkling on both or partaking from the same cup. The fact that milk is supposed to restore brotherhood and peace means that when musicians refer to the Kalenjin as the people of milk, they are pointing towards a brotherhood of the various sub-ethnic groups whose symbolic link is milk which stands for the peaceful co-existence of the various sub-communities. In addition, being white, it is thus considered a universal sign of peace. This can be construed to mean that in the "brotherhood of milk" there is security and stability. This understanding draws members of the various sub-ethnicities together as they perceive the security of being members of the partakers of milk. Apart from its significance to peace, milk also provides a powerful image of satisfaction. Milk is supposed to provide nourishment to all the members of the nation just like a cow provides nourishment to its offspring in their turn; the various sub-communities would perceive of themselves as siblings of a single parentage and hence their need for solidarity.

Jane Kotut in a track entitled '*Kugo*' translated as 'Grandfather' raises the significance of milk to the community's unity and says that whoever does something good must be rewarded with milk. In the song, she laments that herder was rewarded with skimmed milk. Symbolically, the lament is an indictment to those who do not follow the expected norm and a call for the closing of rank to protect one another. In the context of the Kalenjin society, skimmed milk was considered as a reject and is given to those who did not deserve to get milk. The irony brought out in the song is that the herder who ensured that the cows had enough food was rewarded with milk that was reserved for those who do not deserve it. The import of this statement can be located at the treatment that the retired President Moi received after 'herding' the people of Kenya for many years only to be humiliated. In the context of the song, the retired president is the herder, and the lament is meant to draw the attention of members of the community to their disadvantaged position in the new political order; that is after a new president who is not a Kalenjin has come into leadership. This necessarily calls for closer integration of the various sub-communities that make up the Kalenjin for their own survival. The musician is therefore capitalizing on the peoples' understanding of milk to bring them together and, through it, restructure their perception in relation to the existing political environment.

The musician Kipchamba in his track "*Koitalel Somoei*" says that when Koitalel was killed, he was holding a bundle of green grass. This means that he had gone to the Europeans to negotiate with the British for peace and prosperity for his people:

Konyo anyun Koitalel	So koitalel came
Ibunei suswot nenyalil eut	Holding bundle of green grass

The fact that he was killed holding a powerful symbol of peace and prosperity meant that the prosperity of the people that come with peace was destroyed. To the Kalenjin society, the fact that a leader who was championing for their interests was killed, called for quick integration of the various sub-nations to protect themselves against those who do not respect their symbols. The musician is therefore using the story of the nature of Koitalel's death to highlight to the Kalenjin the notion that it is only they who understand themselves and hence need to work towards the cultivation of solidarity amongst the various sub-ethnicities who value the symbolism of the grass. After the assassination of Koitalel, the symbolic artefacts of his office were taken away by the killers. Among them was the leadership staff, a club, and a split headed staff. These artefacts collectively referred to as *samburto* signified the power of the leadership from time immemorial among the Kalenjin. According to Sambu (2007:27), these articles can be traced to the ancient religion of the Egyptians whom he claims share common descent with the Kalenjin. The artefacts also underline the concept that the leader and leadership have a strong link with the supernatural being, the source of all authority. In the minds of the members of the Kalenjin nation, the artefacts symbolized wisdom and security. Their absence therefore made them vulnerable.

It is for the above reasons that when these artefacts were brought back into the country, there was celebration across Kalenjin land and Wesildhino Laboso of the Makibe Warriors, a Kalenjin popular music band, quickly capitalized on the return of the artefacts to release a track entitled *"Ong'utyin Eut"*, translated as "prepare yourselves for celebration". In the track, he asserts that Kalenjin unity which has been elusive can be confirmed by the return of the artefacts. He claims that the time of Kalenjin unity has come because the link has been brought back. The musician thus presents to the Kalenjin, a situation where their unity is hinged on the artefacts. He sings:

Le onchu nga'lek che ngikass	Listen to these words which
Kochute muguleldo,chebo bikap Kalenjin	Arouses emotions of the Kalenjin people
Ong'utyi eut ak omass	Prepare for a celebration
Otkekass eng ole	That can be felt far away
Amu kokewekwech berurto konyo ga kora	Because our blessings have been received
Kokewekwech sharishiekap Koitalel Samoe	Koitalel Samoei's leadership artefacts have been brought back
Nandi, Kipsigis, Tugen, Keiyo,	Nandi, Kipsigis,Tugen, keiyo
Marakwert koboto Sabaot	Marakwet with the Sabaot

The interest that the return of the artefacts generated was felt throughout the Kalenjin language chain as can be attested to by his mention of the various sub-ethnicities that constitute the Kalenjin national construct. It aroused a nationalist spirit and a wish towards stronger integration. The interest and excitement were further reflected clearly in the music of the gospel musician Lilian Rotich, a strong member of the Emo Development Society; a group that prides itself as a society that fronts for the collective interests of the Kalenjin. In her track entitled *"Kenyit ne Lel"* which means "a new dawn (for the Kalenjin)", she considers the return of the artefacts as a rebirth of the Kalenjin nation, especially coming at the centenary of the assassination of Koitalel. To the musician, the return of the artefacts heralded a new beginning for the Kalenjin nation:

Kenyit ne lel, kenyitab jubilee	It is a new dawn, a jubilee
eng bikab Kalenjin, kenyintap kolosunet	For the Kalenjin nation, the year of praise
Kenyitatab bandaptai end bikap Kalenjin	The year of prosperity for the Kalenjin people

In the opinion of the musicians, the return of the artefacts marked a new beginning for prosperity and unity of the Kalenjin people.

Other common images employed by musicians in the promotion of Kalenjin unity include the pot. A pot is a fragile thing that can easily break if not taken care of. The musician uses the image of the pot to show the fragility of Pan-Kalenjin unity and the need to take good care of it. When musicians Kipchamba Tapotuk and Jane Kotut sing that the Kalenjin should prop up each other like pots, they are raising the issue of the vulnerability of individual sub-ethnic group and asserting that their strength lies in unity. At other times, there is the use of the image of an upright house. A house with a strong central pole is considered as strong and the protruding piece on the roof will express its stability if it is upright. The musicians constantly refer to the Kalenjin nation as a house with a firm central pole and the extending protrusion *(kimonjokut)* serving as a sign of balanced unity. In most cases, other symbolic representations of the Kalenjin nation are reinforced by incorporating the image of the central pole.

Sometimes the images employed by the musicians end up generating strong metaphors of the nation. For instance, a relationship between the pot and the grandmother in a Kalenjin's mind evokes a feeling of security and satisfaction. It also points to a strong connection to historical links of the individual to past generations. The grandmother is also considered as the guardian of positive values of the community as well as being its symbolic representation. The musicians' creation of songs which promote the pot of the grandmother which is sometimes conceptualized as the grandmother's garden can be read as a metaphor of cultural values. The presentation of the pot as the best for cooking implies that African values are better than western values. The musician Kirwa Sojali in the track entitled, "*Kabungutab Kogo*", meaning Grandmother's pot, says:

Bikab oldokinye kokikosyindos eng kabatisiet	People in olden days worked in cooperation
Kingobat nebo goi ra, ko mutai kobat nebo goin	They helped each other in turns

Rani betusieju kokikoit rubet	These days hunger is everywhere.
Makomi kabungutab kogo	Because we no longer use grandmother's pot.

The metaphor of the garden is used to illustrate the importance of co-operation. The musician is lamenting about the destructive nature of modern ways which undermines the unity of the people. He thus subtly calls on the Kalenjin nation to fall back on the traditional values which promote unity and brotherhood. The new ways are projected as being destructive to Kalenjin unity and the safest thing is to make a detour to the traditional social values which have the ability to neutralize the modern values. The result is the achievement of unity that modern ways cannot provide in the opinion of the musician. This assertion is not however tenable in the current state of cultural mix and the influence of globalization.

On their part, Mr. 'D' and Magaret Chemeli in the track *"Kibakenge"* insist that the Kalenjin nation must consolidate their unity, and uses the metaphor of a hen sitting on its eggs. Apart from providing security to the eggs, the hen provides the warmth that generates a new life in the eggs. The musician thus insists that the members of the Kalenjin must protect the values that give shape to the society:

Oimeke ku ngekiet ne siebei maaik	Come together like a hen lying on eggs
Simakiaamak we bichu	So that you are not destroyed

The survival of the society therefore depends on their unity, just like the survival of the egg to generate life depends on the hen to provide heat. The metaphor can also be seen from the perspective of the sun. Geoffrey Rotich of Makiche Boys replaces the hen with the sun. Since the sun provides the ingredients to the substances of life, the musician creates a metaphor of unity and tactical manoeuvres for members of the Kalenjin nation. In the track *"Kutinyon"* meaning 'Our common tongue', he says:

Kikole chebo keny bikyok	An adage of old says,
Yong'any kulkul asis ochut sumat	When the sun is too hot, look for safety
Sikae osobche arechu	So that you may survive.

The musicians suggest that the survival of the nation does not depend on confrontation but on wise actions. In other words, the musician proposes that for the nation to be created, wise decisions and choices are better than confrontation. In sum, the musicians reviewed here employ images, metaphors, and symbols in an attempt to arouse and sustain the endeavour of generating sentiments of Kalenjin nationalism.

Mythical and allegorical Representation
of the Kalenjin nation

In an effort to create and promote nationalist fervour, the musicians have at times resorted to falling back on society's myths and employment of allegories which draw a parallel between the circumstance of the society at a particular time in history and their mythical past. The use of myths and allegories also provides the musicians with opportunities of looking at the society from diverse angles. In addition, it provides a link to history and in the process creates an avenue for a coherent interpretation of current circumstances.

The society at any historical point tends to find itself in circumstances which do not allow for a proper understanding of its situation. Myths and allegories are therefore used to provide a perspective through which the world can be comprehended. Yewah (2001: 46) has observed that "allegory arises from a culture in which the real world has become meaningless devoid of intrinsic value, fragmented yet mysterious". Resorting to allegories therefore affords the musicians the opportunity to offer moral instructions to the society. The moral lessons offer the members of the society an opportunity to interrogate their situations by subjecting the allegories to different interpretations which provide them with proper perspectives to understand their circumstances. The allegories also offer members of the society an opportunity to detach themselves from their circumstances and interpret the allegories as structures distinct from their circumstances. The result is an objective assessment of the impact of certain actions of a character in the allegory that fundamentally influences their lives.

In consideration of the fragility of the constructed Kalenjin nation in which various forces are constantly in conflict, the use of allegories by Kalenjin musicians to comment on the issue of nationalism provides a safe avenue through which they can critique the nation without upsetting the delicate unity. At other times, the musicians employ appropriate allegories to reinforce the positive attributes and values that the nation aspires to promote. It does not, however, mean that the musician set out to deliberately manipulate the events in the nation, but chooses to provide available alternatives from which the nation can choose and use to structure itself. This is the point that Yewah emphasizes:

> That allegorist merely arranges the fragments of this world, its images, to produce a meaning the fragments could not produce by themselves - a meaning not identical to the intention of the allegorist but reflecting his or her relation to the given history context. (47)

The Kalenjin musicians can thus be considered as allegorists collecting fragments of the nation's history, mythologies, symbols, and images which he then uses to fashion out a perception that is put forward as the generally accepted perception of the entire nation or to an extent the expected perception worthy of a member of the Kalenjin nation.

The effective use of allegories by musicians to capture the importance of Kalenjin unity is best expressed through a track by Kipchamba Tapotuk entitled "*Ngosamis muriat ko bo got nebo*". This song is, in effect, a narrative based on a popular Kalenjin proverb which can loosely be translated as "when a dead rat begins to stink it is the owners of the house where the rat died that experience the smell". The song can therefore be read as a narrative allegory of the fragile Kalenjin nation. The musician has used the allegory to inform members of the nation that petty squabbles do not help the nation. It also raises the issue of mutual responsibility of the sub-ethnic groups for each other. The musician dismisses the idea that non-members of the nation will offer support in times of difficulties except members of the nation. Furthermore, the members of the nation are under obligation to assist each other whatever the circumstances as the song points out through the allegory of the brothers. The brothers are used by the musician as a metaphor of the Kalenjin construct which though made up of distinct entities, nevertheless, consider themselves as related in many ways. The musician asserts that at critical times, it is only those with whom you share a critical bond who can come to your aid. The fact that the brother comes to the aid of his sibling, even in the face of hostilities can be translated to the latent intra-ethnic hostilities within the Kalenjin nation which in the opinion of the musician should not be a barrier to Kalenjin unity and identity.

The allegory of the brothers also raises the issue that regular squabbles among the sub-nations are in reality elements that provide ground for a strong unity. The feeling is that the greatest bonding is achieved in times of adversity. Therefore, the little misunderstandings between the Kalenjin sub-nations actually provide a ground for stronger bonding, just as Rennan states "suffering in common unifies more than joy does [and] where national memories are concerned, griefs are of more value than triumphs, for they impose duties and require a common effort" (19). The brother's obligation in the face of grief brought them closer than their estrangement during the times of joy.

The song also brings to the fore the narrative form which is an outstanding feature of Kalenjin music. The musician has rendered a popular Kalenjin proverb in the form of a narrative and presented it in the form of a song. Most of the songs in the study take on this form. The musician takes a narrative or an idea and presents it as a song. This strategy serves two functions. First, it means that the narrative is presented in a memorable form that can be performed by an individual when he is on his own, unlike a narrative which requires a second party for its actualization and appreciation. Secondly, it avails to the musician an opportunity to employ the techniques of music making and music presentation to emphasize the significant elements in the narrative, for instance through repetition which might become monotonous in a conventional narrative.

The allegorical representation of national bonding in the face of adversity for the Kalenjin nation is further exemplified by a gospel song by Bureti-Superstars entitled "Kilondoi", translated as, "We shall overcome". This song is always played on Kass FM radio station whenever there is a general perception that the Kalenjin nation is under collective threat or grief. For example, in 2005 when the government of Kenya ordered Kass FM off the airwaves owing to its perceived partisan approach in the campaign for the referendum (which was meant to lead to the adoption of a new constitution), the station played the song repeatedly for more than two hours. The immediate result was a drawing together and identification of members of the Kalenjin nation with the tribulations of the station. The interpretation was that closing the station amounted to silencing the voice of the Kalenjin. The order for stopping the broadcast was therefore seen as an affront on the Kalenjin nation's democratic rights and by extension an attempt by the ruling representatives of 'the other' to muzzle them.

In addition, the song was played over and over again when two cabinet ministers, members of the Kalenjin nation, perished in an air crash in 2008. The song with its theme of hope and will to overcome adversities provides a psychological cushion in time of serious uncertainties. The musician draws parallels with the Israelites suffering under Pharaoh and Moses' attempt at liberating them. The song thus compares the supposed persecution of members of the Kalenjin nation by agents of the 'other" which forces them to coalesce around the Kalenjin identity in order for them to overcome. The song is therefore a performed metaphor of the Kalenjin nation in suffering.

Kilondoi wee kilondoi wee kilondoi kite	We will cross, we will cross the river.
Kilondoi we tupchosiek, kilondoi we	We will cross the river brothers
Yon kokitepte kalya.	If we live in harmony.
Yon kimite ak kayanet	If we have hope and the will.
Kikorom Pharao mochomchi Musa komut	Pharaoh was cruel and denied Moses *to bik* right free them
Kikutuny Musa ak kokur Jehova.	Musa knelt and prayed to God.
Kisa Musa ago kilanda iman	Moses prayed and they crossed the river

The musicians suggest to members of the nation that people can overcome persecution and suffering through unity which is achieved through living in harmony and peace. Harmony points towards co-existence through the projection of a common identity. The appropriation of the Biblical story creates a powerful allegory that emotionally captivates members of the nation so much so that, through the regular playing of the song on the radio during times of political tensions in Kenya, the Kalenjin national identity solidifies for a common purpose.

In other instances, the musicians employ social myths to consolidate the notion of a Kalenjin identity. The commonest myth that is used to structure a pan-Kalenjin identity is the myth of origin. The myth has gained prominence as a means of consolidating Kalenjin identity through the efforts of Kipkoech Sambu, through his book *Kalenjin Peoples Egypt Origin: Was Isis Asis, a Study in Comparative Religion* (2007). The concerns of the book have been abridged and are presented by the author on the programme "Kakiptai" broadcast every Saturday evening on Kass FM. The thesis of the book is an attempt at tracing and connecting the relationship extant between ancient Egyptians and the Kalenjin nation. The writer is cleverly trying to provide the construction of the Kalenjin ethnicity with a basis of history that arises out of a commonly available and accepted myth.

The musicians on their part have appropriated the Egyptian myth of origin in an effort to justify the Kalenjin nation by appealing to their supposed common ancestry. For instance, Jane Kotut of the Keiyo stars in a track entitled *"Tanjawe"* asserts the Egyptian origin and uses the myth to promote the Kalenjin claim to common ancestry and by extension a present common identity. In addition, the myth is also used to lay claim to the symbolic land of the Rift Valley which the musician strongly connects with the myth as shown earlier. The musicians promote the myth of a common parentage to rally members of the nation together. The myth of a common father figure in Mt. Elgon and the story that the different sub-ethnic groups are brothers born of the same father reinforces the need for the projection of a common identity.

The myth is best captured and employed by Mr. 'D' and Margaret Chemeli in the track *"Kibagenge"* (Unity) when calling on members of the Kalenjin nation to unite. They sing that:

Okwe oh Lagokab kapchii   You are children of one family
Kioyopu boiyot agenge oh   You are children of one father,
  Kalenjin   Kalenjin.

The paternity myth is then employed to bring the members together, especially in issues affecting the entire nation. Just as each family has its own projects and ideas, they are expected to come together when the need arises for the protection of the integrity of the family name. Consequently, the Kalenjin sub-ethnicities can be seen from this light, basically as different independent families which need to constantly come together to protect the identity of the Kalenjin nation.

Conclusion

From the discussion mentioned above, it is clear that the Kalenjin musician consciously captures and makes use of artistic elements to generate and (re)structure the perception of the Kalenjin nation both in outlook and performance. These elements are not, however, generated for their sake. The artist aims at shaping the attitudes of the people towards certain issues and more significantly people and other cultures. In the long run, the consolidated perspectives lead to an eruption of violence directed at those who they feel threaten their way of life and their access to certain resources.

Works Cited

Bendix, Regina. "National Enactment and Discourse of Swiss Political Discourse." *American Ethnologist* 19.4 (1992): 768–790.

Chebet, Susan., and Ton. Dietz. *Climbing the Cliff: A History of the Keiyo.* Eldoret: Moi University Press, 2000.

De Andrade, Lelia Lomba. "Negotiating from the Inside: Constructing Racial and Ethnic Identity in Qualitative Literature Research." *Journal of Contemporary Ethnography* 29.3 (2000): 268–290.

Degenne, Alain, and Michel Forsé. *Introducing Social Networks.* London: Sage, 1994.

Gongoware, Timothy B. "Collective Memories and Collective Identities: Maintaining Unity in Native American Educational Social Movements." *Journal of Contemporary Ethnography* 32.5 (October, 2003): 483–520.

Lindfors, Bernth. African Textualities: Texts, Pre-Texts and Contexts of African Literatures. Trenton, NJ: Africa World Press, 1997.

McLeod, John. *Beginning Post-Colonialism.* Manchester: Manchester University Press, 2000.

Premdas, Ralph R. Ethnic Conflict and Development: The Case of Guyana. Aldershot: Avebury, 1995.

Renan, Ernest. "What Is a Nation?" In *Nation and Narration.* Ed. H. Bhabha. London and New York: Routledge, 1990. 8–22.

Sambu, Kipkoeech Araap. *The Kalenjiin People's Egypt Origin Legend Revisited: Was Isis Asiis?- A study In Comparative Religion.* Nairobi: Longhorn, 2007.

Simatei, P.T. "Kalenjin Popular Music and the Contestation of the National Space in Kenya." A Paper Read at the 12th General Assembly of CODESRIA, Younde, Cameroun, 7th–11th December, 2008.

Waterman, Christopher A. "Our Tradition Is a Very Modern Tradition: Popular Music and the Construction of Pan-Yoruba Identity." In *Readings in African Popular Culture.* Ed. Karin Barber. London: James Currey, 1997. 48–53.

Yewah, Emmanuel. "The Nation as a Contested Construct." *Research in African Literatures* 32.3 (2001): 45–56.

Part 4

Representations of
Atrocity in Kenyan Poetry

20 Repression in the Poetry of Jared Angira

Bwocha Nyangemi

Introduction

This chapter focuses on the portrayal of repression in Jared Angira's poetry anthologies; *Tides of Time: Selected Poems* and *Lament of the Silence & Other Poems*. It argues that Angira's poetry mirrors Kenya's history of repression from the 1960s to the present. Economic exploitations of the people (read the silenced voices) by the ruling elite forms the basis of this chapter, perhaps resonating well with the fact that Angira himself, as an economist, captures the people's economic woes with point-blank accuracy. The chapter establishes how silenced voices of the nation, memories of sons and daughters of the nation who are ordinarily voiceless, help unveil atrocities meted out to the silent masses. Unfortunately, the voice of the masses is drowned in the state apparatuses which are armed with both the means of violence and lucre, the two most powerful elements oppressors use to silence their subjects.

Pat Caplan (2009) aptly observes, "The processes of constituting cultures and identities are part of the making of meaning, a process in which, as will be seen, there are important continuities, ruptures and contradictions" (1). Cognizant of the nature of any given society, Caplan is of the opinion that people have multiple identities. The same is true to the Kenyan society, whether it is the question of the ethnic formation which has often been abused by the state to 'divide and rule' the people; or the culture of tokenism that has often resulted in the profound betrayal of citizens by state operatives; or it is the question of gender, disability, jobs, education, and health.

Sally Blundell (2008) contends that in the face of atrocity, humans know no other language other than silence. Their voices are thus muted by atrocious acts of fellow humans. Blundell, further, lists the Holocaust, inhuman suffering of victims of war, traumatic horrors of war genocide, and chilling indifference toward bodily (and psychological) suffering as atrocities. To this list, this chapter adds economic crimes perpetrated by dictatorial regimes, discriminatory practices such as racism, tribalism, nepotism, and sexism, to mention but a few. Embedded in Angira's words is that inner voice crying to be heard.

In her analysis of silence as a literary device, Afruza Khanom avers that non-expression in itself becomes highly expressive. Central to her interpretation is the ability of silence to intensify the atmosphere. She argues that silence "emphasizes the unspeakable nature of the cruelty of war, and deception, questions the idealism justifying death and destruction in war and disguises intense suffering within the human psyche and which seeks consolation in the images of happiness in the direst of times" (52). Silence may thus be part of a deliberate strategy aimed at distancing oneself from painful subjects (Guignery 2009). Being socially constructed concepts, both silence and voice can be negotiated, imposed, contested, and provided (Fivush 2010). By listening to or reading silence, society can obtain a collective understanding of a situation in order to design viable tools that can adequately help fight those who impose silence on the collective will of the people.

There are Kenyan writers on whom silence has been imposed, at different times, by the apparatuses of the state just like the characters who populate these writers' works. Subsequently, some of the literary works which portray repression, betrayal, and exploitation in Kenya include, Ngugi wa Thiong'o's *Petals of Blood*, and *Detained: A Writer's Prison Diary*; Ngugi Wa Thiong'o and Ngugi Wa Mirii's *I Will Marry When I Want*, Wahome Mutahi's *Three Days on the Cross*, and Francis Imbuga's *Betrayal in the City*, to name but a few. These works symbolize various forms of atrocity that the Kenyan masses have been subjected to at different times by the state apparatus. Through these works, writers attempt to educate readers about social injustices. The only difference between Angira and Ngugi, for instance, is that while the former uses verse, the latter employs prose. Thus, their works portray what the masses grapple with not only in the Horn of Africa region, but also in the third world.

Angira's poetry is anchored on the tragedy of silenced voices struggling to be heard. Maritim Cheserem observes that one of the issues Angira deals with in his poetry are socio-economic in nature. He says:

> The larger bulk of the poetry in *Juices* addresses itself to the social issues, which could be categorized into three interrelated fields: the social-economic realities, the political issues, and the cultural issues. Angira uses description in *Juices* while one notices extensive use of images in *Silent Voices* and symbolic language in *Soft Corals,* which are largely absent in *Juices*. There is pessimism in Angira's three anthologies: *Juices, Silent Voices* and *Soft Corals*. (Cheserem 1979: 30)

The three anthologies Maritim mentions here are part of *Tides of Time*, containing four of his earlier works and three new ones. The pessimism Maritim reads in Angira's poems is a product of the prevalent mood in the works; the personas there (mostly silenced voices) are grappling with injustices, the reason an atmosphere of gloom prevails throughout the poetry.

Textualization of Kenya's Economic Woes in
Angira's Poetry

Perhaps no poet best exemplifies the economic woes that the Kenyan masses have had to endure for decades than Jared Angira. These economic woes include, but are not limited to, unemployment, exploitation, bribery, artificial manipulation of prices for agricultural produce, making farmers lose heavily, lack of incentives for pastoralists, and skewed remuneration of employees in the public sector. The worst exploitation is done when meetings are held to find solutions to the people's problems only to realize that such meetings are not worth their name. The poor people are hunger-stricken, desperate, and endure sleepless nights (Angira 2004, 81). Angira (1996) interprets this economic exploitation of the people as a way used by those in power to lull the citizenry to transient sleep, their sound hushed, silenced (42–43). This opinion forms the cornerstone of the argument in this chapter, that once people are subdued economically, every other aspect of their lives stagnates! A people drenched in poverty are susceptible to ignorance and disease, for they do not understand the world thus incapable of protesting against repression, oppression, and exploitation.

In an interview with Ciugu Mwagiru (2016), Angira reveals how he had been unjustly sacked from both the Kenya Ports Authority and the Agricultural Finance Corporation for his alleged participation in the 1982 coup attempt against the Moi administration. He says that in 1986, he was unceremoniously thrown out of his job at the port (read the Port of Mombasa) for being 'anti-nyayo'. Angira's sacking here confirms the economic woes of those who dared to speak out against the ills the dictatorial establishment had subjected them to. Other such woes included not only being denied an opportunity for self-employment but also being barred from seeking employment outside the country, in both cases through forced detention and incarceration. This echoes what writers such as Ngugi wa Thiong'o went through as narrated in *Detained: A writer's Prison Diary* as well as Wahome Mutahi's woes as illustrated by the brutalities of the police state system symbolized in *Three Days on the Cross*.

Angira (1996) writes in "EXPECTATION" (21) about the ironical twist of the lives of the silenced voices where "every train arrival/and craft landing/each ship's anchor/womb a child/long in expectation/yet on each delivery/it is a girl and not a son" (21–22). The delivery of a girl here alludes to the abortive attempts by the downtrodden to stand up against the forces of reaction. It alludes to Jomo Kenyatta's sacking and detention of freedom fighters Jaramogi Oginga Odinga, Bildad Kaggia, Achieng Oneko, Paul Ngei, to name but a few, for standing up against the government's refusal to implement the nascent land policy which would have ensured fair distribution of land to the freedom heroes and other landless compatriots. Kenyatta's land policy went contrary to the expectations of the independent nation, causing what is, to this day, known as a major historical injustice:

> clouds form
> and nearer the hope comes
> only to be marred
> by the rainbow
> the wind
> in heavily moisted overcoat
> blows a whistle
> but the coconut palms
> grab the water
> before the fall. (Angira 1996, 21)

The comparison, especially in the area of diminished hope, emanates from mega economic scams associated with past regimes such as Goldenberg in which over $ 769.2 million were siphoned out of Central Bank (Warutere 2005) and Anglo Leasing (2004) where approximately $1 billion taxpayers' money was lost (The Kenya National Assembly Hanzard). The masses looked forward to benefiting from the country's economic growth only to end up with broken dreams because 'the water' that Angira talks about did not reach them because of graft. Angira portrays these economic plunders as an absurdity because the plunderers display lifestyles akin to "The attires the chicken wear/The beautiful feathers" which, according to Angira, "Only matter before their death" (Angira 1996, 126). Their death, here, implies either the time when they have lost their ill-acquired wealth or natural death, becoming 'inconsequential' like the people they had robbed. Angira calls this living in the deep freezer where "Black and red leghorns are the same" (126). When one steals what they actually do not want, their malady is kleptomania. Their lives are (re)presented by Angira as history "Made to the tutor's measure" (1996, 117).

The skewed representation of despots populates historical schoolbooks lavishing brutal dictators with praise in a bid to immortalize them. Angira cautions his readers though to take this history with a pinch of salt when he writes: "Who can blame them anyway/Everyone wants a history/For the season's end/Little slabs/When they fall from heaven" (1996, 117). The silent voices are thus given a voice this way, via means of silence. Angira (1996) philosophizes these silent voices in his poem "The Silent Voices" where he wishes to understand its voice, appreciate its beauty, and unmask the seat of its fathomless power. He regards the silent voice as having the power to shake houses apart, cripple trees, and scrap vessels in seas and oceans (read his usage of 'blues' in the last line of the first stanza). Angira then compares this silent voice to exploited populations when he writes: "You who brings rains/and yet so slim" (13). This analogy contradicts the description in the first stanza where the silent voice has "giant power"! By writing about this silent voice (representative of huge populations), Angira not only recognizes the power the masses have to overturn their way of life but also their unexploited potential. He, thus, deconstructs the ruling elite's narrative that is anti-silenced voices. Similarly, this blatant plunder of public resources is vividly captured by Angira (1996) in "A Solo for Duet":

> They weaned the heifer
>> And fed her well
> She got a calf
>> And they guarded the homestead
> Milked the cow
>> And took the seats
> To drink the milk
>> And told the shepherdsboy
> Canaan is far, lad
>> Canaan is far. (125)

The silenced voices in this poem, both past and present, are symbolized by the 'shepherdsboy' whose exploiters, in gloating smugness, dismiss his quest 'to drink the milk' (to reap what he had sowed). The title itself is telling. The lone boy (solo) works but a second operator (duet) benefits! This form of exploitation is tantamount to murder. By occupying a very healthy position as far as leadership in corruption is concerned, Kenya becomes the natural context of Angira's lad who is told that "Canaan is far" implying not yet near the Promised Land. This lad symbolizes millions of young people in Kenya who find themselves in this sorry state of affairs in which their taxes are looted in broad daylight, told that they are the leaders of tomorrow, and yet cannot do anything meaningful about it because of their failure to muster both financial muscle and popular support amongst themselves in order to overturn the status quo at the ballot. This poem thus speaks against exploitative state power. Angira (re)presents this repression by way of silence (the written word) but the damning indictment in this silence becomes an instrument he uses to galvanize support for the exploited masses in the war against such monstrosity.

How do the silenced masses respond to runaway plunder of public resources by privileged state operatives? Angira aptly responds to this in the second stanza of the poem "Moments In Sometimes":

> At times I wish
>> Mountains would bow
> And lie prostrate

                    To bring down politicians
           Whose only creed
                    Is ascending
           Into the realms
                    Of royal household (Angira 2004, 19)

The subjunctive in this stanza, that mountains would tumble and fall
taking down politicians whose only agenda is gain power and its attendant financial privileges, symbolizes unexpected occurrence: a peaceful
or violent revolution that overhauls the current order of things! Why
does Angira tend to make such a suggestion? In "Art And Multiparty"
(69), the perception of the political climate prevalent in the country is
unequivocally expressed:

           What art will wait
           For the photosynthesis
           To get a glimmer
           Of the green
           In this robbers garden
           Of the multiparty confusiocracy? (Angira 2004, 69)

This chapter argues at this point that Angira is essentially dismissive of
the narrative of multiparty democracy as practiced in Kenya. He sees the
politicians on either side of the political spectrum as being self-seeking
and gluttonous. He contrasts it with the robust socio-economic plans
that normally characterize the nation's rich intellectual resources, the
ones he refers to as great symphony from "the sane philharmonic team"
(69). Equally, Angira contrasts the noise of the bees with the taste of
honey toward the end of the poem. The bees here symbolize the masses
of workers whose relentless efforts at producing what will help change
their condition reaches a dead end when their 'honey' (L.22) is fleeced by
the political class who constitute the 'robbers garden' (L.5). Finally, Angira shows that politicians put up as 'vegetable decoration' (L.23) which
implies something that is short-lived meant to hoodwink the public. He
writes that this is not the 'touch of beauty' (L.24) thus his attempt at
giving the silenced voices a vehicle through which they could be heard.
Angira compares contemporary Kenya to a situation in which a brother
has descended upon the neck of his brother and "Fathers snatching the
little/The children try to gather" (24). Implied here is not only the moral
degeneracy inherent in this society but also the indifference and lack
of compassion exhibited by those in power. Silence is thus used here in
a bid to break the silence of the masses. Being a metaphysical revolutionary whose silent lament would nudge his readers to concretize his
call for revolt, Angira portrays the Machiavellian irrationality of the-
end-justifies-the-means practiced by the exploitative oligarchy in Kenya's
political scene.

Discriminatory Fiscal Practices

Functioning as a metaphor for the masses who are discriminated against for their political persuasions in this analysis are the silenced voices. Right from the dawn of independence, the Kenyan political oligarchy has consistently adopted this policy. Angira's (2004) poem "Victoria Nyanza" (77) paints the effects of estrangement and neglect of the fishermen in Nyanza by the government. The government's refusal to help rid the lake of the menacing hyacinth is what Angira has historicized in his text:

> Victoria Nyanza, this new carpet
> Swallowed the siren
> Of Port Bell steamers
> Consumed the beauty
> Woke up the hippos
> To a new beginning
> Floating on the floatation final. (77)

The lake is not the lake anymore. The hideous picture of the 'floating carpet' on the fresh waters of Kisumu and Homa Bay, for instance, means that fishermen have lost their trade. Angira further portrays this calamity in the form of an elegy in 'The Green Carpet Elegy' (78–79):

> They have been blessed
> > Awarded green carpet
> To extinction
>
> The last fisherman
> > Lost his net
> Consumed in the greens
> > Lost his hook, line and sinker
> Stuck in the roots
> > Lost his lifeline for tomorrow's rays (78)

Angira's use of 'carpet' reeks of irony tinged with sarcasm. The carpet does not punctuate life with grandeur but heralds its extinction. What they had invested as their lives' insurance (hook, line. and sinker being the tools of trade here) have been rendered sterile. The children are hungry because the parents are penniless:

> Hungry children
> > Longing for defilleted heads
> Long forgotten
> > Now stare at the sky
> Grassless and blue
> > Even the vultures
> Who used to harass the planes (79)

The poet has also thrown in the towel, wondering whether God will ever sympathize with these **motherless** (read victims of a punitive state which abandons those who do not toe the line) children:

> Will God ever pity
> These children
> These descamisados
> Abandoned to an existence
> Void of any tiny crumbs? (79)

This discriminatory fiscal practice that denies the people of Victoria Nyanza national government assistance to get rid of the hyacinth on the lake is captured by Friedrich Ebert Stiftung who writes that among other reasons for this discrimination:

> The fourth explanation of ethno-regional disparities, marginalisation and other inequalities in Kenya are related to the state, the struggles to control the state and other institutions of the state as well as the state's discriminatory and exclusionary policies that were meant to either provide advantages to certain communities and regions or to discriminate against others. This has taken a number of forms: First, political patronage and other policies pursued by successive governments in Kenya (including the colonial state) tended to provide state resources in such a skewed manner that they benefited mostly those that controlled the state and/ or certain regions. (17)

These discriminatory and exclusionary policies disadvantage the people of Victoria Nyanza for the simple reason that they are opposition-leaning. Victoria Nyanza here not only represents the area surrounding Lake Victoria but also marginalized areas such as Baringo, Turkana, Mandera, Wajir, and the coastal area of Kenya. Okoth Ogendo has succinctly captured this in "The Gambler" where he writes that "gunmen freely execute/ insane commands" Cook and Rubadiri (1971, 133)! Ogendo's words do not only imply the barbarous act of soldiers firing on a crowd in Kisumu during the funeral of slain charismatic minister Tom Mboya in 1969, but also suggest that soldiers should be able to disobey unjust orders! Angira's textualized history thus tends to be congruent with Stiftung's historicized text. The skewed distribution of national resources has always benefited those who control state power.

Citizens are not only silently repressed but also left at crossroads by the discriminatory fiscal practices. Angira captures this oxymoronic crux of hope and despair in the poem the "Lines In Midstream" (Angira 1996, 121), where the people are subjected to despair – "to an endless journey/ Undoing/Penelope's web" (LL.4–6) – their attempt at "Reducing pain/ To a wanted pleasure/Lighting a bonfire each day/To burn out despair"

(LL. 12–15) in order "To live in a world full of hope" notwithstanding (L.28) and also in "Knots In Visions":

> Man walks the lanes
>> Under the shadows
> Of the unknown travelers
>> Each with well woven baskets
> Tailor made for the harvest
>> Each steps down the boulevard
> A return steps to the alleys
>> A few grains of hope
> Food for the birds of the air
>> Hope disappears down the gullet
> Stored in the crop of time
>> Steadily trudging down the vale
> Searching for the key
>> To open the spectrum
> They are flowers too
>> Opening their petals anew
> There are voices
>> Rehearsing the coming Pentecost
> But they too, locked in the gourd
>> They too, struggling against darkness
> Late moon caught in daylight
>> Now confessing hypocrisy
> Parasite on the sun's light
>> For where the moons' lantern
> To lead her into her ken? (85)

The journey presented here, just like the one discussed before it, is punctuated with uncertainty. While the travellers are driven by the desire to reap what would better their lives, the means to achieve this kind of life appears as elusive as what the poet calls "Late moon caught in daylight" (L.21). The "voices/ rehearsing the coming Pentecost" (LL.17–18) connote the travellers' wish for divine intervention in their journey. This is sharply contrasted in the next line: "But they too, locked in the gourd/They too, struggling against darkness" (LL.19–20). The silenced voices [read the actual usage of the word 'voices' (L.17) in the poem] are thus struggling to be heard, but wonder aloud when their efforts are met with barren promises by those who seem to be naturally powerful (read the symbolic significance of the sun and the moon). The poem thus places the silenced voices at the junction between hope and despair vindicating Angira's use of Penelope's web, something akin to Jim Reeve's (1961) ships that never come in!

Angira's use of 'holy' for silence is ironic. This is true to his use of 'harvest of peace' as well. The ceremony that is 'disrupted' implies the

violent end of a tyrant's reign. The long period of silence the people assumed as tyranny reigned thus becomes atrocious. Similar the criminals'
season's end is echoed in Angira's (1996) "Rosary At Dust" where he
suggests that though the masses (read fighters referred to in "we have
fought wars") have struggled against tyranny, injustice, exploitation,
and murders (read his use of the word, wars), the real perpetrators of
these heinous crimes remain unpunished for "We have left untouched/
The steel gates/Of the castle/Harbouring the devils" (135). Unlike the
so-called common mwananchi who lives in ordinary houses, the un-
touched ruling clique (oligarchy) reside in castles whose main creed is
to conceal all manner of opacity and culpability. While the common
mwananchi's ordinary house symbolizes modesty, the oligarch's castle
stands for the rot in the establishment, something the oppressors must
hide from public glare. Angira's writing, a silent mode of protest, thus
becomes a silent means of breaking the long-standing silence in the face
of repression.

A Glimpse at the Future: Light at the End of the Tunnel?

Despite the pessimism that Angira depicts in his poetry, he still suggests
ways of liberating the exploited, repressed, and silenced voices. A number of poems in the two anthologies show a sense of hope and optimism among the common masses. Among them, "FREEDOM TRAIN"
(1996, 133) asserts that there is hope/life in a season "For those who
roam/The pastures/With hope/For those whose eyes/Have shed off/The
vegetable paintings". The use of hope and life, each twice, illuminates
the darkness that has been characteristic of the life of the repressed,
and gives voice in their struggle for human dignity. Shedding off the
vegetable paintings symbolizes the end to all hindrances paving the way
to progress, giving the repressed a chance to reclaim their voice. This is
echoed in "Dialogue" (1996, 90) where the persona (I) and a lady identified as She are engaged in a debate about the realities of life. Throughout
this debate, the lady wonders why the persona has not achieved several
milestones in life. The persona responds in a manner that portrays him
as being in a better or worse position in life because of either his will
to be free or his incapacity to meet certain conditionalities imposed on
him. A few illustrations will suffice here: "I looked at the Sun, it shone
at will." This implies the speaker's freedom of choice just like the sun's
freedom to shine or not to; "The balance of payment rocked in a whirlwind mess" connoting lack of financial wherewithal; " I recalled the
cripples who'd never stood upright" implying that the persona is better
off than most people in life; "I looked down the west and saw the sun
sink slowly down" connoting diminishing vitality due to ageing; and
"I recalled the many tombs in the deserted vale" implying that despite
the challenges he is facing, the persona is far better facing them than

those buried in the aforementioned tombs because they no longer have a chance to better their condition. The lines quoted here are responses to questions from the woman in the conversation, whose answers render life hopeful. This perhaps informs the repressed masses that as long as they have a chance to fight for a better tomorrow, they should not give up, but instead soldier on.

Similarly, in "A Freedom Train" (2004, 24–27), Angira introspectively comes to the conclusion that Africans will not attain their true independence by employing foreign methodologies, according to the "Gospel edited in Europe" (26) but instead, the people must love the plough and the sickle, not the contrary. This is juxtaposed with "Flamelights From Legends, Viii" (148) where Angira emphasizes that "Every soul struggles/ To pluck the leaves of success…Success is what you make/Of life…Success, dear love, is that which/ You win with feelings and hope." This means, as indicated earlier (26) that one who hates the plough and abhors the sickle (one who cannot struggle) cannot succeed. Perhaps Angira is admonishing his audience that burning ambition and constant desire for success, coupled with undying effort, are the only paths to success. This challenge squarely puts the people's destiny in their own hands. By extension, Angira is unequivocally stating that nobody else can set the repressed masses of repressed free save for themselves. Their voice is thus borne not only in their desire to succeed but their expenditure of energy and resources in order to gain their freedom.

In the poem 'The Fire Tomorrow", Angira (2004) prophesies a violent uprising in the event that the people have completely run out of peaceful mechanisms to change the status quo:

There is a fire
    Burns so low
At moments of grief
    From police brutality
The taming of emotions
    Collective fear
Of death and decay

We've stock piled for tomorrow
    Bullets and grenades
Extinction of enemies perceived
    For a bloomer tomorrow
Where actors on stage
    Are the selected ducks
Of Lorenzian axis

But the coal in the store
    Is so black; deadly black

No one knows of a chemical property
    That works it up
Red to the flame
    Torn into crimson defiant
Boils the water for the engine
    Turns the turbines
To anger at the falls
    And burns Sodom
And Gomora to ashes. (71)

Angira's words here echo Peter Barry's (1995), whose analysis of Michel Foucault's 'discursive practices' ultimately implies the birth of a revolution (122). Foucault theorizes that power is always in motion, revolving, never anyone's possession and always rotating. In this case, Angira speculates that this police brutality that the silenced voices are subjected to is a fire burning "so low" (L.2). He sees this fire, which symbolizes the growing anger and discontent among the masses, as a stockpile of "Bullets and grenades" (L.9), the weapons that will make the revolution possible. The mention of the black coals in the store whose chemical elements no one knows, points to the deadly hate that has been building up among the silenced masses. The burgeoning hate will reach a tipping point resulting in a deadly explosion that will tear the walls of hell apart thus bringing down the foundations of the evil oligarchy that has subjugated the masses for over half a century now! This is echoed in Nyagemi's (2017) "Before We Knew Better" where the persona 'I' who later becomes 'we' warns that in order to overthrow dictators on the African continent, "Goodwill, courage and arms" (3) are needed. This is within the realms of possibility. A similar message resonates in Nyagemi's (2017) "Enough" where the population is urged to rise up and reclaim their country for they would "Better valiantly stride into purgatory/Than cowardly live in the lavatory! (44)" In OBBLIGATO FROM THE PUBLIC GALLERY (1996, 81), the majority of the masses (the overwhelming poverty-stricken citizenry) has evidently lost hope in party politics, lost belief in democracy, lost confidence in the nation, and has no more patience (Angira 1996, 81). He asserts that all the public wants is bread, rice, a belief that they will not be dead tomorrow, thus hope! When the population is hemmed in to the wall with surviving one extra day being their top priority, the nation becomes a huge powder keg waiting to explode. Thus, the silent voices will not be silent anymore for doing so will make silence triumph over voice.

Conclusion

This chapter concludes that Angira is perhaps Kenya's one and only poet to have devoted his life to writing revolutionary poetry aimed at not only creating awareness in society but also nudging the population to stand up against ruthlessness and exploitation. His poetry as discussed in this chapter highlights the plight of silenced voices. The regimes are designated in this chapter as ruthless for the simple reason that they have plundered and mismanaged public resources at the expense of development. Similarly, this chapter concludes that economic enslavement of the population is the major portal through which the repressive apparatuses of the state silence the citizenry and that once a people are economically suppressed their voice in every other aspect of life is hushed. As demonstrated in this analysis, skewed distribution of development programs and resources by oppressive governments, looting of public resources, denying critics state jobs, and opportunities for self-employment through arbitrary detentions and incarcerations to name but a few, ensure that the citizenry are hemmed in to the wall and consigned to perpetual indigence, a situation that ensures they are Angira's "silent voices"! Besides, distortion of facts by presenting official narratives which whitewash the ills perpetrated by state operatives and the strongmen they support adds to the conclusions this chapter arrived at. therefore, continued repression of the population will only leave them with no other way than rising up in violent militancy with the sole aim of reclaiming their human dignity and self-determination!

Works Cited

Aduda, David. "2015 KCSE Leakage Was the Worst in History of Exam". *The Daily Nation* 25 March 2016. Web. 13 Nov. 2016.

Ahad, A.M. "Corruption Perceptions Index 2015". *Transparency International.* Web. 18 Nov. 2016.

Alighieri, Dante. *Divine Comedy – Inferno.* Henry Wadsworth Longfellow English Translation and Notes. Web. 30 Nov. 2016.

Al Jazeera. "Kenyans Rally against MP Pay Hike". *Al Jazeera.* Web. 21 Nov. 2016.

Amateshe, A. D. *An Anthology of East African Poetry.* Harlow: Longman, 1988. Print.

Angira, Jared. *Cascades.* London: Longman, 1979. Print.

———. *Juices.* Nairobi: East African Publishing House, 1970. Print.

———. *Lament of the Silent & Other Poems.* Nairobi: East African Educational Publishers, 2004. Print.

———. *Silent Voices.* London: Heinemann, 1972. Print.

———. *Soft Corals.* Nairobi: East African Publishing House, 1973. Print.

———. *The years Go By.* Nairobi: Bookwise, 1980. Print.

———. *Tides of Time: Selected Poems.* Nairobi: East African Educational Publishers, 1990. Print.

Asego, Nicholus. "Silence Given a Loud Voice": A Review of *Lament of the Silent & Other Poems. The East African Standard* 13 Apr. 2007. Web. 25 Oct. 2016.

Barry, Peter. *Beginning Theory: An Introduction to Literary and Cultural Theory.* Aberystwyth: University Press, UCW, 1995. Print.

BBC. "Kenya"'s NAIROBI CITY HIT by Pig Protest Over MPs Pay". *BBC*. Web. 21 Nov. 2016.

Blundell, Sally. "Unspoken Stories: Silence in the Literature of Atrocity". A Journal Paper published in *Double Dialogues, Art & Lies II Literature; Aesthetics and Visual Arts*: Issue 9, Autumn 2008. Print.

Brustein, Robert. *Theatre of Revolt: An Approach to the Modern Drama.* Chicago: Ivan R., 1991. Print.

Calder, Angus. (1979: 37). 'Jared Angira: A Committed Experimental Poet'. In *Individual and Community in Commonwealth Literature.* Ed. Daniel Massa. Malta: University of Malta Press, 1979. 37. Print.

Caplan, Pat. "Cultural Dynamics of Pre-Colonial and Colonial Swahili Society." A paper originally given as a keynote lecture for the conference '*Cultural Dynamics of Pre- colonial and Colonial Swahili society*' held at Hankuk University of Foreign Studies, Seoul, Korea, 14–15th May 2009. Print.

Cheserem, Maritim. '*Modern East African Poetry: The Case of Jared Angira.*' B.A. Dissertation. University of Nairobi, 1979. Print.

CNBCAFRICA. "Kenya Ranked 6th Most Corrupt Nation Globally". CNBCAFRICA 5th April 2017. Web. 8 Apr. 2017.

Cook, David, and David Rubadiri, eds. *Poems from East Africa.* Nairobi: Heinemann, 1971. Print.

Dickinson, Margaret, ed. *When Bullets Begin to Flower.* Nairobi: E.A.E.P., 1989. Print.

Dowden, Richard. "Export Scam Robs Kenya of Millions: Richard Dowden Reports that Government Officials Approved Bonuses for Bogus Sales of Gold and Jewellery". *The Independent Online* 8 June 1993. Web. 30 Nov. 2016.

Fivush, Robyn. "Speaking Silence: The social Construction of Silence in Autobiographical and Cultural Narratives" Under the Chapter Memory 18.2 (2010) in *Psychology Press Taylor & Francis Group*: Emory, Georgia, 2010. Print.

"Fulgencio Batista Y Zaldivar." *Microsoft®Encarta®2007* [DVD]. Redmond, WA: Microsoft Corporation, 2006. DVD.

Guignery, Vanessa. *Voices and Silence in the Contemporary Novel in English.* Cambridge Scholars Publishing, 2009. Print.

Herbling, David. "Kenyan Legislators Emerge Second in Global Pay Ranking". *Business Daily.* Web. 21 Nov 2016.

Hope Sr, Kempe Ronald. "Kenya's Corruption Problem: Causes and Consequences". *The Journal of Commonwealth & Comparative Politics* 52.4 (2014). Web. 10 Nov. 2016.

Hornsby, Charles. Kenya: "A History since Independence." *Narratives on Repression in Kenya* Google Books, 2013. Web. 11 Oct. 2016.

Imbuga, Francis. *Betrayal in the City.* Nairobi: East African Educational Publishers, 1986. Print.

"Jerry John Rawlings." *Microsoft®Encarta®2007* [DVD]. Redmond, WA: Microsoft Corporation, 2006. DVD.

Kariara, J., and E. Kitonga. *An Introduction to East African Poetry.* Nairobi: Oxford University Press, 1982. Print.

Kemoli, Arthur. *Pulsations: An East African Anthology of Poetry.* Nairobi: East African Literature Bureau, 1973. Print.

Khanom, Afruza. "Silence as Literary Device in Ambrose Bierce's 'The Occurrence at Owl Creek Bridge'" in Teaching American Literature: *A Journal of*

Theory and Practice, University of Dhaka, Bangladesh. Spring 2013 (6:1). Print.

Kiarie, Lilian. "Sh500b State Funds Cannot Be Accounted for, says Auditor General Edward Ouko". *The Standard Media* 24 March 2014. Web. 5 Nov. 2016.

Knoema. "GDP Per Capita Ranking 2016|Data and Charts" *Knoema* 2016. Web. 21 Nov. 2016.

Luvai, Arthur, I. *Boundless Voices*. Nairobi: East African Educational Publishers, 2000. Print.

Machel, Samora. "A Luta Continua (One of the Most Powerful Speeches by an African President!)". *YouTube*. YouTube. 17 April 2016. Web. 28 Nov. 2016.

Maosa, Horia. "Relationships between Voice, Silence and Identity Formation in Organizations". *Bulletin of the Transilvania University of Braşov* 5.54 No. 1–2012 Series VII: *Social Sciences Law*. Web. 28 Sep. 2016.

Munene, Ishmael. "'Ethnic Tensions at Kenya's Universities Are Becoming More Violent'. The Conversation Africa"'. *The Huffington Post* 12 Jan. 2016. Web. 13 Nov. 2016.

Musau, Nzau. "Uhuru Omits Jaramogi, Raila from First and Second Liberation Heroes List". *The Standard Media* 21 Oct. 2016. Web.

Mutahi, Wahome. *Three Days on the Cross*. Nairobi: East African Publishers, 1991. Print.

Mwagiru, Ciugu. "Jared Angira: How I Became an Economic Refugee in America." *The Daily Nation* 1 January 2016. Web. 8 Nov. 2016.

Ndegwa, Alex. "Secrets of Members of Parliament Pay Deal". *The Standard Media* 15 June 2013. Web. 21 Nov. 2016.

Nganga, Gilbert. "Kenya: Call for 'Tribal' Vice-Chancellors to Be Moved". *University World News* 22 Aug. 2010. Web. 13 Nov. 2016.

Ntiru, Richard Carl. *Tensions*. Nairobi: East African Publishing House, 1971. Print.

Nyagemi, Bwocha. 2016. *Cynics and Skeptics*. Tabora: TMP, 2016. Print.

———. 2017. *The Hard Trek*. Tabora: TMP, 2017. Print.

Opiyo, Peter. "Shock of Tribalism in Public Universities". *The Standard Media*. 7 Mar. 2012. Web. 13 Nov. 2016.

Rée, Jonathan. *I See a Voice. A Philosophical History of Language, Deafness and the Senses*. London: Flamingo, 1999. Print.

Reeves, Jim. (1961). "I'm Waiting for Ships that Never Come In". Web. 6 Sep. 2015.

Roscoe, Adrian. *Uhuru's Fire: African Literature East to South*. London: Cambridge University Press, 1977. Print.

Selden, Raman, Peter Widdowson, and Peter Brooker. *A Reader's Guide to Contemporary Literary Theory, 4th edition*. London: Prentice Hall, 1997. Print.

Stiftung, Friedrich Elbert. *Regional Disparities and Marginalisation in Kenya*. Nairobi: Elite PrePress, 2012. Print.

Tejani, B. 'Jared Angira.' In *African Literature Today*. Ed. Eldred Durosimi Jones, No. 6. Nairobi: East African Publishing House, 1970: 158–159. Print.

©The Star 2015. "Kenya: The Scandals That Have Hit Jubilee". *The Star* 9 November 2015. Web. 30 Nov. 2016.

The Kenya National Assembly Official Record (Hanzard), 2 Nov. 2004. Print.

Thiong'o, Ngugi. *Detained: A Writer's Prison Diary.* Oxford: Heinemann Educational Books, 1981. Print.

———. *Petals of Blood.* Oxford: Heinemann Educational Book, 1977. Print.

Thiong'o, Ngugi and Ngugi wa Mirii. *I Will Marry When I Want.* London: Heinemann, 1982. Print.

Wainaina, Kaara. "How Corruption Kills Investment and Jobs in Kenya". *The Standard Media* 11 June 2015. Web. 13 Nov. 2016.

Wanjala, Chris, and Angus Calder. *Faces at Crossroads.* Nairobi: East African Literature Bureau, 1977. Print.

Warutere, Peter. *The Goldenberg Conspiracy: The Game of Paper Gold, Money and Power.* Pretoria: Institute for Security Studies, 2005. Print.

21 Swahili Poetry and Atrocity in Postcolonial Kenya

Accounts of Three Kiswahili Poets

Nahashon O. Nyangeri

Introduction

Kenya has experienced unspeakable and horrific gross violations of human rights characterized by ethnic conflicts. Such violence includes massacres, torture, and ill-treatment and various other forms of violence. In the light of this fact, various artists have contributed as much on the subject, poets included. Poetry is one of the most important Kiswahili literary genres with a long history serving different purposes, where the poet warns, incites, chronicles, or foretells. This chapter, therefore, explores how atrocity and protest are expressed in a poetic and disquieting fashion in three Swahili anthologies of poetry: *Chembe cha Moyo* (Mazrui 1988), *Bara Jingine* (Mberia 2001), and *Sauti ya Dhiki* (Abdalla 1973). Often brutality meted out on innocent victims precipitate action, a reassurance of an obvious end with retribution. Swahili Poetry is seen as a tool to reflect on various social and political violations and as a means of expressing personal reactions to violence. It is read as an avenue to revolt against oppressive situations and regimes, convey the "unconveyable", and provides an alternative voice for articulating issues bedevilling society.

Kenya's history is full of horrific accounts of massacres committed by state security agencies in the guise of security operations. Various regimes have presided over a government that was responsible for numerous gross violations of human rights that include the wars,[1] Massacres,[2] (extra-judicial) killings,[3] torture,[4] collective punishment, denial of basic needs (food, water, and health care); political assassinations[5]; systematic and arbitrary detention, torture, and ill-treatment of political opponents and human rights activists. With this long and diverse list, such atrocities are bound to attract a poet's attention to address them. This chapter analyses selected works of three postcolonial Kenyan poets – Abdilatif Abdalla, Alamin Mazrui, and Kithaka wa Mberia. The chapter analyses postcolonial atrocities as represented by these poets by exposing the ideas and values voiced by each of them, their drive, their style and attempts at comparing and contrasting them.

A study of Kiswahili literature demonstrates that the Swahili people used their art to demand political and economic freedom. Swahili poetry, therefore, became an avenue through which the artist gave a "voice to suffering" (Dawes 2007). Thus, poetry is a huge store of African history where various atrocities are recorded. Kiswahili stands out as one of the languages of resistance since pre-colonial times. Its literature developed as a form of language with double meaning: one for the oppressors, who could understand only the surface meaning; and the deep meaning being for the oppressed. The deep meaning was vague and new to the oppressor. This ambivalence is what clothed verse to survive banishment and censorship. Poetry is used as a technical instrument of verbal craftsmanship (Njozi 1998) to express and expose views and opinions. Ambiguity, incompleteness, and strength of the poetic language make it possible to comment on subtle social issues (Samson 1996). In the subsequent sections, we analyse how Kiswahili poets have used these attributes to convey the message of atrocity in the Kenyan situation.

Who has the Right to Speak? A Victim's Biography

Abdilatif Abdalla wrote *Sauti ya Dhiki* (1973) while he was serving a jail term. This anthology painfully exposes atrocities of his prison experience. *Sauti ya Dhiki* begs the question "Who has the right to speak, and how far does that right extend? as asked by Dawes (2007) in *That the World may Know*. The written word has served as a candle in the dark to bear witness to these atrocities. These witnesses offer their answers to the question of "what does it mean to be a Kenyan?" by giving their personal experiences of being treated as less than human. *Sauti ya Dhiki* recounts Abdilatif Abdalla's personal story of life behind bars at Shimo la Tewa, and later Kamiti prisons. This work serves as a chilling reminder of one of the darkest moments in human history and his resolve to seek justice and be a surrogate voice for the oppressed in society.

Persistence is what will bring an end to atrocities. In "N'shishiyelo ni Lilo" [That is my word] (*Sauti ya Dhiki* 1–4) the poet avows that he will never stop speaking of the inhumane acts that are meted out to those who oppose the government. He is aware that those who oppose will be met by various inhumane acts as demonstrated in "Kamliwaze" [soothe him/ her] (*Sauti ya Dhiki* 5). In order to emphasize the message of Kamliwaze, a month later he pens down "Tuza Moyo" [Comfort your soul] (6), which is a monostanzaic poem laden with a weighty message of encouragement. He says that patience and prayer are what is required to ensure that all comes to pass. This is an overriding theme that qualifies Kiswahili poets as messengers of hope as seen in his poem "Yatakoma" [They will end] (*Sauti ya Dhiki* 28), where he reiterates that what is important during times of suffering is patience for all, including himself where he implores his "self" to exercise endurance. This conversation with the self occurs in "Moyo iwa na Subira" [Have Patience my Soul] (*Sauti ya Dhiki* 48–50). He informs his soul that naturally the world is full of atrocities and therefore mourning about the situation will be worthless. It is instructive to mention that whatever the moment, those are not the last painful experiences; more are on the way and one should be prepared to meet them. All that is required is patience because change is inevitable. Therefore, the poet challenges everybody to converse with their "self" in readiness to conquer any eventuality as soldiers combat all kinds of atrocities (See Nyaigotti-Chacha 1992). This makes him an "advocate of reason and toleration" like Voltaire (*Treasure* 156). These prophetic lines came to pass with the various wars, assassinations, police tortures culminating in the 2007/2008 post-election violence. Thus, unlike historians and poets, literary writers do not just "relate what has happened, but what may happen" (Aristotle quoted in Bressler 23).

Atrocities in Kenya have a long history, dating as far back as the pre-colonial period.[6] Using the metaphor of a boil, Abdalla in *Jipu* [Boil] (*Sauti ya Dhiki* 7–8) narrates how atrocities begin in a minor and unsuspecting form only to metamorphose into full-blown abuse of all forms of human rights. He regrets having not realized this in time in order to take necessary measures to prevent it. Now that he is late, time is his only hope of refuge. But for this to happen in the meantime, he has to join the war, (verse 9) to dress the "boil" and offer his poetic medicine for him to regain his health back, that is, peace (verse 11). This is when the oppressor will be subdued. His motivic call for patience and standing to claim rights, instead of lamenting the present state recurs in *Mamba* [Crocodile] (*Sauti ya Dhiki* 10). Because of its viciousness and destructive power, the crocodile signifies fury and evil (Cirlot 2001) and human hypocrisy (Ferber 2007). These are attributes of state agencies that commit inhumane acts on innocent Kenyans, like Abdilatif Abdalla who was jailed for questioning the state in his famous publication of *Kenya Twendapi?*

While in prison, Abdalla wrote the dialogical poem "Mnazi: Vuta N'kuvute" [the Coconut: Push and pull] (*Sauti ya Dhiki* 17–22]. In verses 4–7 of this poem, he mentions that personalization or privatization of public resources is the cause of strife. When Alii demands that Badi comes down from the tree so that he may also have a share, he is insulted and is later deprived of his shares of the cooperate ownership of the coconut. This was the state of affairs in post-independent Kenya in the 1960s when there was a tug of war between the then vice president, Jaramogi Oginga Odinga, and the president, Jomo Kenyatta, with whom he had fallen out. The push and pull that ensued between the two leaders, led to violent protests which in turn led to the Kisumu massacre of 1969 at the opening of the Russia Hospital. It is a pity to note that at the time of independence, KADU, a minority party, had joined KANU, the same way Badi and Alii had come together, only to realize that their friendship was cosmetic and union short-lived. In the dialogue, the poet mentions that the only antidote is honest dialogue as opposed to the strong stand taken by Badi. Arrogance and pride brew further chaos and Alii swore to demand his share. This culminates in the atrocities we have mentioned. The long debate between Alii and Badi attests to the claim made by TJRC that "massacres are usually the product of long-running and deeply felt social and economic antagonisms" (Vol. 2A, 155).

From the Bhakhtinian dialogic thought of heteroglossia and hybridization (see Bressler 45), Alii and Badi represent one's inner conversations with the "self" where a variety of "voices" are significant. This implies as Treasure puts it, that there is "a civil war in every soul" (156), a fact recognized by UNESCO in the preamble to its constitution, "Since wars begin in the minds of men, it is in the minds of men that the defenses of peace must be constructed" (7). In this type of civil war the voice that wins the dialogue defines our consciousness. In this way the poet gives the reader the responsibility of choosing whether or not to end acts that injure fellow human beings, for it is how man chooses to hear and respond to this multitude of competing and conflicting "voices", each vying for prominence, that develops who they are and shapes who they become individually and collectively. Each participant in this poem "tests the ideas and lives of the other participant, creating a seriocomic environment" in the process (Bressler 2007, 46). This is Abdalla's philosophy of ending atrocities – that a conversation with one's self is important.

Rain has numerous symbolic aspects; it is a fertilizing agent and it signifies purification, a symbol of suffering or bad luck (Cirlot 2001; Ferber 2007). Rain often stands as a synecdoche for all bad weather and thus a symbol of life's unhappy moments. In "Telezi" [Luge] (*Sauti ya Dhiki* 24–5) the author uses imagery to discuss the excessive use of force by the police at the 1969 official opening of the Nyanza General Hospital in Kisumu which the TJRC regards as a form of extra-judicial killing (TJRC 2013). In the course of opening of the Russia Hospital, (now New Nyanza General Hospital) there was an unexpected outbreak of chaos. It is said that the police literally shot their way through to the waiting motorcade. During this incident TJRC vol. IIA records:

> Odinga was not invited, but he and his supporters came in force shouting Dume ... In the ensuing commotion, a full-scale riot erupted, the presidential escort and the dreaded crack paramilitary General Service Unit (GSU) surrounded the president, shot their way through the threatening crowd and continued shooting 25 kilometers outside the town. [In] the 'Kisumu Massacre' ... many [were] shot dead, including school pupils, by the presidential security. (23)

It is this shooting that is alluded to as rain in the poem. The rain, according to Abdilatif fell accompanied by thunderbolt and lightning.

In "Mamaetu Afrika" [Mother Africa] (*Sauti ya Dhiki* 36–41) the poet goes beyond chronicling and shows the causes and consequences and suggests solutions to the unending dispute that caused chaos in Kenya and by extension Africa. The poet therefore is no longer the preserver of events but "a man speaking to men" (William Wordsworth quoted in Bressler 2007, 36). Mother symbolizes the collective unconscious (Ferber 2007). In employing this symbol, the poet calls for citizens' unity to realize who their real enemy is as a solution to stop the perennial wars that are witnessed. The animosity amongst the people was introduced by the colonial masters who after realizing that they have been defeated changed their tack. Postcolonial atrocities, therefore, are a progeny of the colonial era. According to Kituo Cha Sheria, during the colonial period, the military screened and interrogated people to extract information from them concerning Mau Mau. It is from these processes that widespread and institutionalized torture has emerged. The military would continue to use similar brutal tactics way into the post-independence era and as recently as March 2008 during *Operation Okoa Maisha* (Operation to save lives) in Mt. Elgon (2013). The poet describes this sorry state in "Mamaetu Afrika" and opines that unity is key to ending brutalities in society. In verse 13, the poet alludes to the atrocities committed during the Mau Mau war leading to several deaths as indicated in verses 18–21. In verse 21 the poet says:

> Nyingi mno damu yetu, ikabidi kumwagika
> Baadhi ya ndugu zetu, roho zao zikatoka
> Na kila kilicho chetu, kwa wingi kikatumika
> Kwa kutaka kuiweka, hadhi yetu nawe Mama. (39)
> [It behooved the gore, we had to spill
> Some of our comrades, to lose their lives
> And every possession, copiously used
> That we may uphold, our dignity Mama].

The poet refers to the blood that was shed in the fight for independence during the Mau Mau war. According to the TJRC's 2013 report, both the locals and the colonialists committed atrocities. In effect the Mau Mau assaulted the aged, women, and children perceived as local beneficiaries of colonial power (TJRC vol. 4, 12 and vol. IIc, 93). During the war, many were subjected to traumatic experiences and atrocious crimes committed. During this war, Lari and Hola Massacres happened. It is said that in the Lari massacre, the Mau Mau hanged 71 collaborators. At the Hola camp, 11 political detainees were executed.[7]

The Importance of Combat: Atrocity Symbolized

It can be argued that Swahili poetry vaccinates atrocity, heals the deep-rooted causes of historical injustices and violations given that it is an art that reaches and appeals to the soul. Kithaka wa Mberia philosophically treats atrocities as a social or individual inner problem often touching

334 *Nahashon O. Nyangeri*

on broader political or social issues. Bertoncini (2010) thematically classifies Kithaka wa Mberia's poems in *Bara jingine* [Another continent],
into two broad categories: socio-political poems and poems on environment and nature. In the first category are poems commenting on
events of topical interest like *Kikaoni Addis Ababa, Jumapili ya damu*,
as well as those that denounce various shades of gender-based violence
and the rape of schoolgirls that completely ruin their lives (*Giza mbele,
Pamela, Flora na wenzake*), or prostitution instigated by poverty (*Mimi
Monika*), and others that focus on hope for the future and social justice
(*Nakumbuka ulivyokuwa, Ni sumu kwa watoto, Hatutaaga ndoto* and
Bara jingine). Accordingly, Dawes (2007) says, "genocide and war, after
all, are all about our power over other people's bodies". This means
that rape is used as a weapon of war and therefore we do not subscribe
to Bertoncini's categorization. The poems could be seen as addressing
the subject of atrocity as well. However, as indicated earlier, ambiguity
is one of the characteristics that adds color to art hence Bertoncini's
logocentric classification, though narrow, holds. The environmental
category for Bertoncini highlights the author's concern with his surroundings. In this group Bertoncini includes *Ngao, Jinamizi, Bwawa
la Ithanje, Mimi mto Nairobi, Matone ya Mvua, Kamba na jabali*, and
Nieleze. We contend this classification too, especially poems *Mimi mto
Nairobi* and *Kamba na Jabali*. Their inclusion in the second category is
purely on the semantic basis, whereas on a pragmatic plane, the symbols therein have a totally different connotation that will move them
to the first category, a fact that contradicts her assertion that "symbols and allegory are recurrent tropes in Kithaka's poetry" (2010: 94).
Mimi, mto Nairobi, [I, the Nairobi River] (63) on the degradation of
the Nairobi River, which makes the author an environmental conserva-
tionist of sorts, it is rich with symbolism and metonyms making it have
dual meanings. The river may refer to the local populations who have
welcomed foreigners into their land where the visitor does not seem to
reciprocate the feeling but ends up harming the host, hence the regret
we see in stanza four:

Majuto	regrets
Yanitafuna moyo	masticate my heart

History has it that during the Garissa and Bulla Karatasi Massacres, in an
effort to cover up the massacre, security agents involved in the operation
disposed of the bodies of those killed into the Tana River.[8] Against this
historical fact, this poem could be addressing these atrocious acts where
litter thrown into the Nairobi River, refer to the unwanted population
thrown into the Tana. This only comes out when analysed from a deconstruction perspective where the deep-seated contradictions in the poem
are brought to the fore. Hence showing that there is more meaning that

lies below its surface meaning. On the other hand, the persona regrets allowing the foreigner to become their neighbor who now unleashes terror to them instead of appreciating the welcome accorded him/her. This can be interpreted to mean the "outside communities" that went and settled in the Rift Valley but later on underestimated the welcome (TJRC 2013) which led to the ethnic cleansing of 1992 and 1997.

Kithaka wa Mberia benefits from ambivalence too like Abdilatif Abdalla. Ambiguity is a safe haven in which an otherwise delicate and subtle message survives censure. In the poem *Mimi, mto Nairobi* [I, the Nairobi River] (*Bara Jingine* 63), besides the pro-environmental protection, there is a protest message that is well-garbed in the river lamentation. The persona (river) laments of the atrocities of the urbanites meted out to it that range from "simple" acts of wringing the neck to actually killing by all means. This is through various types of weaponry like *mafuta, makopo, tairi, and tarimbo*. The atrocities reached the peak and to such an extent that the river cannot bear them any longer but protest. The river regrets welcoming them, suggesting that combating atrocities is an inside-out process rather than outside-in. As such, a conversation with "self" is an important step. Politically instigated atrocities are due to us giving them the position that they have used to torment us. It is required of us to clean our voting behavior first before we can move out to clean others.

The river has been pressed into many metaphorical uses. It marks territorial boundaries (see, Ferber 2007). The Nairobi river therefore marks a boundary of sorts, marking territorial boundaries, the urbanites cross the boundary and encroach into the river. This becomes a precipice for the chaos that erupted in each Kenyan electoral cycle in the 1990s. Especially in the Rift Valley province "forigners" crossed the boundary and entered the Rift Valley to live with the natives. In this election-triggered wars, the locals are said to target the forigner whom they referred to as *madoadoa* [spots] (TJRC 2013).

Rivers also mark changes in symbolic states as Ferber (2007) explains. In this vein, the Kiswahili aphorism goes, *bahari iliko ndiko mito iendako* [a river flows towards where there is a sea]. This means that it is the wealthy that are fortunate and have everything going their way. In this dictum therefore, rivers represent the less fortunate that have to flow towards the sea (read the fortunate). The sea represents the alien and dangerous place (see Ferber 2007), showing where the river may take you if you rattle it. Littering the river therefore is symbolic of the atrocities that the visitor subjects the host to. The colonialists committed several crimes on Kenyans. Conversely, complaints made by the river in this poem are in line with the saying *mto huzamisha mwogeleaji shupavu* [a river can drown a dexterous swimmer]. The complaints are a warning of the ability of the river. This came to pass in the 2007/2008 post-election violence that almost plunged the country into civil war. In this way, the poet warns that the injured are part of the problem as they kept disturbing the peace of the river, hence the significance of self-retrospection in alleviating atrocities.

Another poem on politically instigated violence is *Jumapili ya Damu* [Bloody Sunday] (*Bara Jingine* 6–9). Violence is the norm in every five-year electoral cycle. Before elections, there is merrymaking courtesy of voter bribery. When the campaign period reaches fever pitch, violence ensues. Gunshots are heard all over and many deaths witnessed. The mood turns from happy to sombre. The government employs state machinery to ensure it retains power. This attests to the fact that politicians vow to use politics to ensure they retain power, suffocate democracy and alternative opinions (See Commission of Inquiry Into Post Election Violence 2008, 78). The poet suggests that it is the leadership's clinging to power which precipitates election-related atrocities referring to Id Amin of Uganda and Mobutu of Zaire. These leaders bear full responsibility of what befell their countries by refusing to relinquish their seats having lost in the elections. However, Mberia mentions Obasanjo as an example to be emulated for his bold step of surrendering after losing. His act averted a possible crisis in Nigeria. The poet lauds Obasanjo in the poem to appreciate him (*Bara Jingine* 17–18) unlike the others mentioned earlier who cannot leave office unless by the bullet. Obasanjo therefore is an allusion which does not necessarily refer to the former leader of Nigeria but "conjures up some extra meaning, embodying some quality or characteristic" that he actually exhibited (Delahunty, Dignen, & Stock 2010). This offers a shorthand language to describe the qualities of leaders who avow their aversion for atrocity. This allusion evokes a complex experience of atrocities that have been seen not only in Kenya but the whole continent by the mention of prominent figures that succinctly create the aura of violence and its consequences. Here the poet offers a solution. The number of those mentioned against Obansanjo's name is instructive of the volume that it should worry every one of the directions being taken.

In *Kikaoni Addis Ababa* [Addis Ababa Summit] (*Bara Jingine* 2), the poet reads hypocrisy in African leaders who met in Addis Ababa and branded P.W Botha a tyrant for incarcerating and detaining freedom fighters. In Kenya many are suffering whereas those who ought to defend them turn a deaf ear, blind eye, and shut their mouth, so as to ensure that the ruling party, KANU, remain in power. The veracity of politically instigated atrocities is mentioned in the final stanza:

Maghala na familia
Zinatafunwa na miako
Kusudi kusaidia jogoo
Kuendelea kuwika. (2)

[Stores and families
Crushed by fires
To assist the cock
To continue crowing]

The stores and families crushed by fire refer to the destroying of pos-
sessions by the attackers so as impoverish them further. A strategy that
was used by the security forces during the Shifta war of 1964–1967. The
TJRC reports that the "government agents strategically killed livestock
to hasten the misery of the locals" (vol. 2A, 121). Therefore all the atrocities had only one goal – to ensure that the part retains power against the
raging opposition.

Despite the numerous atrocities, the poet believes time will bring all
suffering to an end. In *Hatima ya Mbu* [Mosquito's Fate] (19) he warns
any future oppressors who will try to emulate the fallen oppressor of dire
consequences. The fallen oppressor he alludes to is the KANU regime.
The use of an insect is one way to understand the greater aggressiveness
of man than of other animals as Dutton (2007) has rightly put it:

Katika vitabu vya historia
Huu mwisho wa karaha yako
Utakuwa funzo azizi
Kwa mbu wengine
Au ukoo wenu
Ni sikio la kufa? (19)
[In annals of history
Are records of the end of your baneful acts
A fitting example you are
To other mosquitoes
And your progenies
Is it a deaf ear?]

Dutton says that "humans exhibit a greater capacity for cruelty than do
other animals, leading some to think that a certain level of brain development … is essential for cruelty" (x). In this regard, the analogy of the
mosquito here being a lesser oppressor than human beings mocks the
"rational" human being who claims to be higher than the tiny mosquito.
The desire to kill is driven by a societal awareness of power and destiny.
The mosquito regarded as the savage in this poem, alludes to the human
savages. The poet uses the mosquito metaphor, a savage that human
beings disdain.

War, whatever we may think about it, is an object of fascination. It
seems to have an illuminating effect: it allows people to show the worst
of which they are capable, as well as the best. According to Bostock, it is

"legitimised atrocity" (2002). For every version of the terrors of the battlefield, there is another about the extraordinary fraternity that prevails
within a fighting unit. Frésard says, "For every act of cruelty recorded
there is an act of bravery or heroism ... and [it] is not unusual to find
texts relating how the protagonists of war, after living through inde-
scribable suffering and surviving countless dangers, look back nostalgi-
cally once peace has been restored to the time when their lives seemed
to have meaning," (2004: 18). In "Kamba na Jabali" [The Rope and the
Rock] (3) Mberia paints a picture of hope for the oppressed and a warning to the oppressor:

> *Kamba ya wadhulumiwa*
> *Hukata jabali gumu*
> *Ambalo miungu-wa-kinamo*
> *Hutumia kuziba njia*
> *Ya binadamu*
> [The rope of the oppressed
> Breaks a hard rock
> That the ductile gods
> Use to block avenues
> For humankind]

When the political leadership assumes office for the first time they are
deemed good people by the electorate. But as time goes on they change,
which is why they are branded as ductile gods by the poet. They are
easily swayed, influenced, and manipulated and soon fall into the same
game of playing political cards of unleashing terror on the same people
who assisted them into office. This is the case with each regime in Kenya
since colonial times as shown in the TJRC report (2013). In as much as
the poet seems to blame the electorate for their predicament, he gives
them hope that there will come a time that this will change and warns
the oppressor to be wary of the unity of the oppressed as it will push
him/her into the abyss of regret.

The rope in this poem, according to Cirlot (2001) is a general symbol
for binding and connexion. The poet brings together the idea of unity
of the oppressed and the power of that unity. It is their unity that will
liberate them from the suffering that they find themselves in, which is
represented by the rock, a symbol of permanence, solidity, and integrity.
There is hope for the oppressed that suffering is never permanent and
that soon the solidity of the oppressor will be liquidated.

In *Machozi ya Damu* [Bloody Tears] (*Bara Jingine* 1) the poet warns
of the repercussions of the elastic (unending) game[9] played in the workshop of politics. Little did they know that the puppets will change into
tyrant demigods and demi-goddesses who will unleash terror on the

innocent civilians, as the title suggests. To this end, the poet points at the politics of violence and thirst for power as the twin causes of tension that ends up in violence.

Atrocities are rampant because of poverty, disease, and ignorance. This is the basis of the poem *Hatutaaga Ndoto* [Won't relent our dream] (*Bara Jingine* 4–5). The leaders find themselves in a difficult position when donor countries freeze their support. The local population suffers. Their leadership has no choice but to cage this poor population in the fashion of the *villagisation*, a form of forced confinement used during the Shifta war (see TJRC report, vol. 2). The poet says:

> Nao mazimwi wajeuri
> Waliokatalia kwenye enzi
> Wametunzungushia seng'eng'e
> Kama mateka wa vita (4)
> [And the tyrant ogres
> Who stuck to the throne
> Enclosing us with barbs fence
> Like war captives]

This paints a picture that the government continued using colonial tactics. These were used to compel the victims to renege on their demands. However, as it turns out such treatments fuel the violence all the more.

Cataloguing Atrocity through Poetry: Why Do You Say It?

Mazrui's concern for the unending atrocities in Africa in general, and Kenya, in particular, is a subject that cannot be overemphasized. His quest to find why they occur ceaselessly is clearly depicted in his 1988 anthology written in free verse *Chembe cha Moyo* [Heart's trepidation]. He asks the philosophical question "why" in the poem "Jinamizi" [Monster] (*Chembe cha Moyo* 39). A question which he goes ahead to answer in most of the poems therein as this section will elucidate: "What difference do they make?" He talks about our collective moral future. It is however expedient to say here that, in "Jinamizi", the poet identifies the elephant in the room. According to Cirlot (2001) monsters symbolize the interstellar forces at a stage that is one step removed from chaos—from the 'non-formal potentialities'. From a psychological perspective, they allude to the base powers which form the deepest strata of spiritual geology, seething as in a volcano until they erupt in the shape of some monstrous apparition or activity. Monsters suggest an unbalanced mental function: the affective scourging up of desire, seizures of the indulged imagination, or indecorous intentions. Socially, they are symbolic of the ill-fated rule of a wicked, tyrannical, oppressive, or impotent emperor. Fighting a monster suggests a struggle to free consciousness from the grip of the unconscious. Mazrui in this poem feels that the worst monster that bedevils society is one's own consciousness and therefore seeks to liberate this first in order to fully address the subject of atrocity. It is clear that the poet is aware of "poetry's emotional quality" (Bressler 2007). He directly implores the reader's mind to search within itself where the problem could be situated so as to free itself. This enables him to reach into what lies at the base of consciousness, to retrieve it, and turn it into words, painfully difficult to endure. The effect is "to excite and stimulate the quiet and thinking people" and while arousing and exciting to ready their intellect for "action" (Kidder 2). Mazrui in the poem says, "Kwa nini mpaka sasa jinamizi kutufuata," [Why till now does the monster trail us]. This is to directly ask everyone to ask himself/herself on how he/she has contributed to the "unsolutionlessness" that has been with them for far too long. This is strategically to use an in-out problem-solving approach. Unless we start with ourselves, the mission to find a solution is a mirage. Probably failure to implement the recommendations of many commissions of inquiry that have investigated past injustices is what is being addressed here (see TJRC Report 2013) and the silence of society in asking this important question. Somehow he feels that society suffers a "spectator" and/ or a "global bystander" silence (Dawes 2007) and is not ready to intervene at all in an effort to extinguish the rising tensions. It is this "imperturbable bystander passivity" (as well as international timidity) that the poet says that is the major hindrance. His sense of duty as an artist drives him to "overcome the powerful urge of silence" (Dougherty n.d) to save the people.

Mazrui relying on the "why" question shows that exile is one of the consequences of atrocity, as it can be seen in "Kwa n'nini?" [Why] (Chembe cha Moyo 58). He incites the reader to become proactive. The poet asks the locals to challenge the minds to ask if it is right to throw dissents into an abyss of possible oblivion. This was a common phenomenon in the 1970s to the 1980s when many were detained without trial, tortured in the Nyayo and Nyati house chambers, or assassinated (TJRC 2013). It is the duty of the poet to unearth all the atrocities that people go through in the society they live in. Mazrui wants to find answers to why atrocities have not abated, if not ended. This is clearly put across in the poem "Risala" [Communiqué] (Chembe cha Moyo 24). He requests all and sundry to bring their painful experiences to him so that he may construct an atrocity library.

Mazrui believes that documenting atrocity will go a long way in saving many in the future. According to him the collection, that he purposes to build once completed, he will invite God to read and probably act. By invoking help from heaven, the poet is privy to the fact that many commissions have collected and documented all past atrocities whose recommendations were never implemented. He, therefore, assumes the position of those commissioners, but unlike them, he will not present the findings to the state but to a different body (probably our consciousness) that may see fit to act on it. It is along this line that we agree with the statement he makes in "Barua ya Mpenzi" [Letter to my Darling] (*Chembe cha Moyo* 49), that (his) poetry is a letter trying to persuade the reader who is a dear friend to him to bring forth all that he/she is enduring wherever he/she is incarcerated. By stating "humo kifungoni mwako" [in your prison], he alludes to "personal prisons" that have to do with psychic power or will which he aims to enter through his poetry to unshackle the "inmate". Mazrui is aware that this is the hardest prison cell to break into. This is evident in "Kushinda" [Conquering] that "kushinda hii nafusi, si jambo lilo sahali" [conquering this psyche, is no easy mission] (61). However he doubts if God knows how to read. And probably, if He knows, then He does not allow poets to speak as indicated in "Ulimi" [Tongue] (51). A fear that runs through his other poem "Sauti" [Voice] (22). These verses indicate the absurd ideology of Mazrui. In Sauti, he gives his opinion on how the government systematically eliminates the dissenting voices, without fear of riots and protests from the population because they are forgetful people.

Mazrui, however, warns that one day all the killings, murders, executions that are done in the "safe" hiding of the bushes or forests will be brought to the fore. There is no hidden secret that time won't bring to the fore. When the leaves that are watching the horrific acts finally dry they will drop to the ground, and anybody who steps on them will be told what was done there in the past. This is the only hope left for the poet since he sees that God, who has been witnessing all this has not taken any action, a thesis he draws from his analysis that they have tried all that can help uplift their country but in vain. They have tried to achieve the benchmark set by the other states but it has not worked as he indicates in "Ni ipi njia yetu?" [Which is our path?] (*Chembe cha Moyo* 32). The irony of it all, as he indicates is that all his efforts have been thwarted by those who see that all he does comes to nothing. Instead of receiving praise, he is mocked and punished, an action that breeds war.

Mazrui longs for a government of inclusivity that will give equal chances to all, including the youth as a sure way of solving the unending animosity and atrocity that is within (see "Nayayusha Pingu" [I melt the manacles], *Chembe cha Moyo* 33). In this poem, Mazrui states that atrocity is caused by the class differences between the rich and the poor. Those who live in abject poverty have reached a state where they can't persevere anymore. His advice therefore is clear; the poor should be given their rightful share as well as a chance to participate in nation-building. The only remedy being time, a motif characterizing his works, and he keeps on asking when this time will come as, for example, in the poem

342 Nahashon O. Nyangeri

"Lini" [When] (*Chembe cha Moyo* 43). This demonstrates the poet's anxiety. To satisfy his curiosity and probably give others a taste of this time he goes ahead to define as to when it will come.

Ovid in Ferber (2007) refers to time as being "gluttonous of things", an analogy that is reiterated by Shakespeare as a "bloody tyrant", "eater of youth" and "cormorant devouring Time". Time has been a metaphor that may be traced back to Kronos. In this vein, Mazrui believes time will consume the atrocities created by itself. In "Mkulima" [the Crofter] (*Chembe cha Moyo* 41) he defines this time. This is when the poor man's anger will have reached the brim and he will have to react in the process of demanding his dignity as shown in the poem. Here, the poet warns of the simmering tensions and the repercussions thereof. This indicates that he is a keen observer of the goings-on in his society and gives a prior warning. This makes him a soothsayer who suggests that the oppressor should treat all equally. It is also a message of hope to the oppressed as to when their pain will finally cease.

In "Mtabiri" [The Prescient] (*Chembe cha Moyo* 52–53) he asserts that he is the one who links times past, present, and future. With such a high office, he is under obligation to inform the society of the impending calamity that will befall them. He says that he saw in a dream wars all over. Hatred among its people of unimaginable magnitude. True to this word, Kenya has experienced numerous tribal clashes, skirmishes, ethnic cleansing, post-election violence after the publication of *Chembe cha Moyo*. These were not a phenomena that just erupted but a volcano of unattended injustices that finally culminated in war. It is an expression of dissatisfaction and alienation. This must have been the leads that enabled the poet to prophesy thus, "vita na vita vikazaana" [wars begat wars] (52). As Bressler (2007) avers "the poet is the greatest because the poet alone can see the future in the present". Hence poets are no ordinary people, but teachers and prophets. Mazrui however admits that he does not know the solution that time has put in place for him:

> *Ni jawabu gani alowekewa na wakati*
> *Kuipoza ghadhabu ya kiu ingawa katiti*
> *Kuiliwaza hamaki ya njaa hii ya dhati*
> *Njaa ya maisha itokayo kushibishwa.* (24)
> [What solution has time put for you
> To at least quench your rage
> To soothe this serious angry hunger
> Life's hunger that needs to be satisfied.]

The only virtue of time that allows Mazrui to depend on it as the sure cure to atrocity is that it heals wounds and truth being its daughter, as recorded by Lucrece in Ferber (2007). It is said time can "unmask falsehood and bring truth to light and has the power to redress wrongs and reward diligence". Time, therefore, has the ultimate rights of being the only savior.

While other poets enable us to explore tensions of an oppressive past, Mazrui's *Chembe cha Moyo* invites us to see the future in remembering, reflecting, and inscribing the past atrocities with a deliberate consciousness and in the realms of present and future we can move forward. Indeed, while other poets have looked at some past historical injustices as a general survey, he injects persuasion into the heart of the oppressed that's beyond remembering. It is high time we reflected and take a step to invert the status quo. In this way, Mazrui engages the audience in a discourse to awaken the desire for a future by inviting the reader to participate in the process of bringing about that necessary change. He gives accounts of the infamous Nyayo and Nyati house torture chambers in "Kizuizini" (Detention, 27) without necessarily being told of their offence. This was a time when detention without trial was in place. The detained were dehumanized, tortured, and abused. Mazrui says the inmates could not sleep, a fact confirmed by TJRC Report (2013) where it is recorded that torture and ill-treatment in these included "detention in water-logged cells; being sprayed with hot and cold water; denial of food, water, and medical attention; beatings; humiliation; and the use of insects to terrorize and attack detainees" (Vol. 4, 30).

Mazrui delves into finding the reasons for war and ethnic clashes in his country. He lists land as a major source of violence in his poem "MwapiEDITgania kitu gani?" [What are you fighting over?] (*Chembe cha Moyo* 62–63). He reveals that it does a society no good to swim in a "sea of blood" at the expense of having a section of its members enjoy expansive tracts of land. He is bitter and therefore makes an inquiry into who is actually responsible for the war. According to TJRC (2013), the land was the major cause of tensions. Regardless of all the effort, the poet advises the warring parties that they kill and maim each other yet none is the beneficiary. Instead, it will help them better if they used that energy to fight their true enemy. What is clear is that those who fight, rarely understand the reasons for their action. Mazrui, therefore, uses his poetry to educate them to use reason to liberate themselves. Accordingly, a recollection of the past and of the dead will significantly inform, and possibly entrust, the living with some forms of knowledge. Eventually, being inured to the lessons of both the past and present and dead and living may expedite new forms of wisdom which will be the most essential of all wisdom.

Despite all this, Mazrui stands out as a poet of hope. In *Vitaturudia* [We will be Recompensed] (*Chembe cha Moyo* 6–7) he indicates that whatever the people are going through will soon pass. The land, which has been the main issue that drives the violence will be returned and all other resources. He defines the beneficiary as the injured who are patient, long-suffering, and eager. His message of patience is reiterated in the poems *Nitangojea* [I will wait] (*Chembe cha Moyo* 8) and *Nilivuka* [I crossed over] (*Chembe cha Moyo* 10). In "Nilivuka" despite having crossed over, he realizes that he is not out of the woods yet, therefore, he is disgusted. He finds out the peace is quite elusive and never to be found. Atrocities abound and never come to an end. Mazrui equates Africa to a whirlwind that is full of war with no end in sight. This is symbolized by the long night without a morning. He is however optimistic. He looks forward to the day when all this will come to an end for he believes "nothing is going to remain the way it is" since "change is imperative" (Boal 2008, ix, xxiii).

Mazrui speaks of prison atrocities. He mentions the oppression of prisoners in *Kizuizini* [Detention] (*Chembe cha Moyo* 27). Hunger, lack of proper clothing, being flogged and abused often, and unending punishment, as well as lack of proper sleep or rest, are mentioned. These are made more explicit in the poem *Damu ya harara* [Feverish blood] (*Chembe cha Moyo* 16) where he talks of torture chambers in the cells:

> *Roho yaja ya kiyama*
> *Kusaka na kuzichoma*
> *Ngome za dhuluma*
> *Na dharau kuzitema*
> [The judgment spirit fast approaches
> To seek and to burn
> Cages of tyranny
> And spew contempt]

Here the poet is able to present the unpresentable to those who are born after the atrocities and know about them only through representations which enables them to comprehend the incomprehensible. Like the other two poets, Mazrui blends symbolism with truth to appeal to the readers' emotions in a fashion advocated by Philip Sydney, to delight "every sense and faculty and the whole being" (Bressler 2007, 31). This is what is demanded of artists – to allow readers "to comprehend it, to grasp the experiences, to imagine the suffering, through identifying with those who suffered" (Robert Eaglestone 2004 quoted in Boswell 2008). In the words of Ziauddin Sardar, the reader can feel a soul in turmoil, hear a voice that speaks directly to him/her, and see the prison cell injustices described taking place in front of him/ her (forward in Fanon 2008). Here the poet directly lets "his stream of consciousness wash on to the chapter" (Fanon, xi), a directness of simmering anger, makes us uncomfortable because "civilized society" does not like uncomfortable truths and naked honesty.

Mazrui therefore aims to "to warm man's [the reader's] body and leave him" (Fanon 2) to fill in the gaps in the text and conjecture about the characters' actions, personality traits and motives (Bressler 84). This happens by the fact that texts do not tell the readers everything that needs to be known about the characters, situations, or relationships. The reader fills the gaps given that the author "cannot tell us everything in a story" (Robinson 2010). In this way Mazrui widens what Wolfgang Iser calls "horizons of expectation" about what will, may, or should be done about the atrocities (op. cit.). This is in line with what Voltaire says in Treasure (1985) that "the most useful books are those which the readers themselves contribute half; they develop the idea of which the author has presented the seed" (157). This implies that a poet makes causes out of cases. "If theatre [read poetry] is an efficient weapon for liberation" as Boal claims in *Theatre of the Oppressed* (2008, xxiii), then the three poets under the present discussion took the requisite step to liberate the masses. As Treasure says, "they find it easier to criticise than to change society and its laws" (1985, 156).

Conclusion

There have been more atrocities in Kenya's history than can be discussed in a single chapter as this. For the poet, these numerous inhumane acts make the task of leveraging language to describe such horrors nearly impossible. Finding words can confront the unspeakable which is a problematic task. In this chapter, however, attempts have been made to examine how the selected poets depict the horror of atrocity using painful but brilliant imagery, metaphor, and language. The discussion reveals that war, a precipice for atrocities, was a prominent phenomenon in the long history of Kenya's search for freedom and liberty. This truth did not escape the attention of the three poets. The poets considered this to be amongst the worst evils, and its eradication required the input of all. It was from this understanding that they sought to persuade the reader's mind, by probing their intellect to fill the knowledge gaps spawned by the wording of the verses. This task of filling the gaps that the poet assigns the reader is the fuel that drives the wheel of protest aimed at eliminating the torture in society and give them the opportunity to understand it. Poetry therefore becomes an ideal vehicle to liberate the oppressed. To a poet, life is a mission to ensure that the reader hears the cry of the victims in the process of filling the gaps when the language prompts is used. The poets invoke gruesome scenes of torture so specific that the reader imagines the physical realities behind the descriptions. This vivifies the atrocity of torture in detailed clarity that is enriched by the reader filling the gaps. This creates a thirst on the part of the reader who will therefore be required to fill the missing parts. This promotes the immediacy to action that is sought by engaging and stirring the readers.

Poetry has served as an important documentary that has survived to tell the untold tale. The survival is courtesy of the poets who avoid a direct description of the ghastly scenes that may turn the art into horror. Poetry has formed an important part as a social commentary that survives longer than other genres, a practice that has survived to contemporary times. We can use language to alter the operations of violence with more far-reaching ramifications than the bullet. These writers' literary legacy contains dozens of verses devoted to or which directly bear upon the painful subject of atrocity. In them we see the causes and consequences of inhumane acts as well as a solution to the problem.

Poetry is used as a documentary to compel us to witness atrocity. The imagery used is combined with understated emotion to give the sense that whatever is recorded goes beyond what we are able to comprehend. In other words, poetry lies wholly outside our normal experience, even as the reader is invited to witness what it describes. This encourages us to read and fill the gaps. Under such a scenario, the poet is able to distance himself/herself from the poem, and feels that he/she is not implicated in the situation described. This pulling of the reader into the poem and giving them the chance to participate in its composition indicates that the audience is part of the telling. In this way the reader psychologically participates in the horrid scene of horror.

The three poets examined herein have shown that the ballad can achieve more than the bullet. This is clear as poetry seeks to eliminate physical suffering by using words as they enable poets to perform certain types of speech acts. In this way, poetry touches on a very arguable issue in conveying the solution rationally rather than the mechanical bullet language: the artistic construct as opposed to its combative counterpart. We see all the poets striving to reach the readers' soul through their figurative use of language. This aims at propelling readers to take some form of action. Poetry exploits the allusive aspects of language to convey what could otherwise not be conveyed. This makes their message survive censorship and scrutiny. It may appear that Kiswahili works are not what we may term as "extremist poetry" in the strict sense. But this is not the case since the language is diabolical in its love for aphorisms.

Notes

1 An example is the Mau Mau war in Kenya.
2 These include Kedong Massacre, Giriama Rebellion, Kollowa Massacre, Lari Massacre, Hola Massacre, Turbi and Bubisa Massacres (2005), Murkutwa Massacre (2001), Loteleteit Massacre (1988), Bulla Karatasi Massacre (1980), Wagalla Massacre, (1984), Lotirir Massacre (1984); and Malka Mari Massacre(1981), Garissa Massacre (1980).
3 These include the official opening of the Nyanza General Hospital in Kisumu in 1969; Saba Saba riots in 1991; and 2007/2008 Post-election Violence.
4 Especially in Nyayo House and Nyati House torture chambers.
5 Those assassinated include Pio Gama Pinto, Tom Mboya, J.M. Kariuki, Dr. Robert Ouko, Bishop Alexander Muge Crispine Odhiambo Mbai, Father John Kaiser.

6 See The Truth Justice and Reconciliation Commission Report of 2013.
7 See TJRC and Kituo cha Sheria Report on TJRC Reports.
8 See The Truth Justice and Reconciliation Commission Report of 2013 Volumes 2 and 4.
9 Echoing his earlier poem *Mchezo wa Karata* [Game of Cards].

Works Cited

Abdalla, Abdilatif. *Sauti ya Dhiki.* Nairobi: OUP, 1973.

Boal, Augusto. *Theatre of the Oppressed.* Translated by C. A., M.O. L. McBride and E. Fryer. London: Pluto Press, 2008.

Bostock, W. W. "Atrocity, Mundanity and Mental State." *Journal of Mundane Behavior* 3.3 (2002): 351–364.

Boswell, Matthew. *The Holocaust Poetry of John Berryman, Sylvia Plath and W.D. Snodgrass.* PhD thesis, Submitted to the University of Sheffield, September 2008.

Bressler, Charles E. *Literary Criticism: An Introduction to Theory and Practice.* London: Pearson Prentice Hall, 2007.

Cirlot, Juan Edwardo. *Dictionary of Symbols.* 2nd ed. Routledge: London, 2001.

Commission of Inquiry Into Post Election Violence. *Report of the Commission of Inquiry Into Post Election Violence.* Nairobi: Government Printer, 2008.

Dawes, James. *That the World May Know.* Cambridge: Havard University Press, 2007.

Delahunty, Andrew, Sheila Dignen, and Penny Stock. *The Oxford Dictionary of Allusions.* Oxford: Oxford University Press, 2010.

Dougherty, E. A. "War, Literature & the Arts." *An International Journal of the Humanities,* n.d.

Dutton, D. G. *The Psychology of Genocide, Massacres, and Extreme Violence Why "Normal" People Come to Commit Atrocities.* Westport, CT: Praeger Security International, 2007.

Fanon, Frantz. *Black Skins White Masks.* New ed. Translated by C. L. Markmann. London: Pluto Press, 28 July 2008.

Ferber, Michael. *A Dictionary of Literary Symbols.* Cambridge: Cambridge University Press, 2007.

Frésard, J.-J. *The Roots of Behaviour in War: A Survey of the Literature.* Geneva: International Committee of the Red Cross, 2004.

Kidder, Frederic. *History of the Boston Massacre.* New York: Joel Munsell, 1870.

Kituo Cha Sheria. *Summary of the Truth, Justice and Reconciliation Commission (TJRC) Report.* Nairobi: Kituo cha Sheria, 2013.

Maitaria, Joseph Nyehita. "Sauti ya kiharakati katika ushairi wa Abdilatifu Abdalla." In *Kiswahili na Maendeleo ya Jamii,* Ed. M. Mukuthuria, J. O. Ontieri, M. Kandagor, and L. Sanja. Dar es Salaam: TATAKI (CHAKAMA), 2015. 193–210.

Mazrui, Ali. *Chembe cha Moyo.* Nairobi: EAEP, 1988.

Mberia, Kitaka. W. *Bara Jingine.* Nairobi: Marimba Publications, 2001.

Njozi, Hamza Mustafa. Critical Artistry in Utenzi wa Shufaka. *AAP* 55 (1998): 41–51.

Nyaigotti-Chacha, Chacha. (1992). *Ushairi wa Abdilatif Sauti wa Utetezi*. Dar es Salaam: Dar es Salaam University Press.

Povey, John F. "English-Language Fiction from South Africa." In *A History of Twentieth Century African Literatures*. Ed. O. Owomoyela. Nebraska: University of Nebraska Press, 1993. 84–104.

Robinson, Jenefer. "Emotion and the Understanding of Narrative." In *A Companion to the Philosophy of Literature*. Ed. G. L. Hagberg and W. Jost. Chichester: Blackwell Publishing, 2010. 71–92.

Samson, Ridder. "Tungo za kujibizana: 'Kuambizana ni sifa na kupendana'." *AAP*, 47 (1996) 1–10.

TJRC. *Report of the Truth, Justice and Reconciliation Commission Vols 1–4*. Nairobi: Truth Justice and Reconciliation Commission (TJRC), Kenya, 2013.

Treasure, Geoffrey. *The Making of Modern Europe (1648–1780)*. London: Routledge, 1985.

UNESCO. *Manual of the General Conference*. Paris: United Nations Educational, Scientific and Cultural Organization, 2002.

Wamitila, Kyallo Wadi. *Misingi ya Uchanganuzi wa Fasihi*. Nairobi: Vide~Muwa, 2008.

Zúbková-Bertoncini, E. "Some Remarks on Kithaka wa Mberia's Poetry." *Swahili Forum* 17 (2010): 91–103.

Index